Weimarer Schriften zur Republik

Herausgegeben von
Michael Dreyer und Andreas Braune

Band 15

German Politics and the 'Jewish Question', 1914–1919

Lucia J. Linares

Franz Steiner Verlag

Umschlagabbildung: Propagandaplakat mit Aufruf Kaiser Wilhelms II. an das deutsche Volk.
Berlin, 1914, Lithographie, Inv.-Nr.: P 96/1975
© bpk / Deutsches Historisches Museum

Bibliografische Information der Deutschen Nationalbibliothek:
Die Deutsche Nationalbibliothek verzeichnet diese Publikation in der Deutschen
Nationalbibliografie; detaillierte bibliografische Daten sind im Internet über
<http://dnb.d-nb.de> abrufbar.

© Franz Steiner Verlag, Stuttgart 2021
Layout und Herstellung durch den Verlag
Druck: Memminger MedienCentrum, Memmingen
Gedruckt auf säurefreiem, alterungsbeständigem Papier.
Printed in Germany.
ISBN 978-3-515-13069-1 (Print)
ISBN 978-3-515-13074-5 (E-Book)

Acknowledgements

I wish to start by thanking the Weimar Republic Research Centre, and the anonymous reviewers, for seeing promise in my dissertation and supporting its publication.

None of this would have been possible, however, without the unwavering support I received throughout these past years from my supervisor, Martin A. Ruehl. I am forever grateful for his guidance and insights, and how he was able to skilfully balance criticism and encouragement in careful measure.

This book would also not have come about without the generous funding of several institutions. For their faith in me and this project, I would like to thank the Government of Gibraltar, the *Studienstiftung des deutschen Volkes,* the Kusuma Trust, the British Federation of Women Graduates, the German History Society, the Cambridge History Faculty and the Simon-Dubnow Institute.

Looking back on my postgraduate experience, I will always remember my time as a Leo Baeck Fellow fondly. The guidance I received from Daniel Wildmann, Sharon Gillerman, Raphael Gross and Peter Pulzer helped shape this book. The warm and welcoming staff of the Oxford Centre for Hebrew and Jewish Studies and the Leopold Müller Library made my stay as a visiting student in Oxford a delight. I am especially grateful to David Rechter for his mentorship. Thanks are also due to my examiners Duncan Kelly and Michael Dreyer for their insightful comments and encouraging words during my viva.

Wolfson College Oxford, like Darwin in Cambridge, became a home away from home. I greatly value all the friends I made over these past few years who turned trying moments into joyful ones. Lastly, I could not have finished this book without my family and Jonas. It is to them that it is dedicated.

Lucia J. Linares
March 2021

Abbreviations

AA   *Auswärtiges Amt*, Political Archives of the Foreign Office, Berlin, Germany
CV   *Centralverein deutscher Staatsbürger jüdischen Glaubens*, Central Association of Germans of the Jewish Faith
CZA   Central Zionist Archive, Jerusalem, Israel
HASt *Hauptstaatsarchiv Stuttgart*, State Archive Stuttgart, Germany
KfdO *Komitee für den Osten*, Committee for the East
VdJ   *Verband der deutschen Juden*, Alliance of German Jews
ZVfD *Zionistische Vereinigung für Deutschland*, Zionist Federation for Germany
WZO   World Zionist Organisation

Table of Contents

Introduction

> Everybody is talking about the "Jewish Question". But if you ask what the Jewish question really is, then out of a hundred respondents fifty will awkwardly remain silent or stammer something insufficient, and from the other fifty you will hear different answers.[1]

With this remark Sigbert Feuchtwanger[2], the lawyer and Vice President of the Jewish Cultural Community of Munich, captured a quintessential problem of the so-called 'Jewish Question' (*Judenfrage*)[3] as it was debated in Germany in the early twentieth century. His comments suggested the multitude of issues at stake. What seems most revealing about Feuchtwanger's statement, published in July 1917, is that in an Empire faced with famine, the burden of total war and a government in crisis, the Jewish Question was on the public agenda at all. In this thesis, I examine how the Jewish Question functioned in German political discourse and German politics. Focusing on the years of the First World War, I explore the ways in which the Jewish Question sheds light on Germany's liminal period between its autocratic-militaristic past and parliamentary-republican future. Jewish questions revealed the paradoxes of German state-building and the difficulties of breaking down older forms of corporate identity for the sake of national-cultural homogeneity. Using the Jewish Question, I aim to reassess the difficult birth of the Weimar Republic.

In what follows, I will begin by outlining the origins of the Jewish Question in German states in order to argue that the term was not, as is commonly assumed, solely

---

1 'Die "Judenfrage" führt jeder im Munde. Aber fragst du, was eigentlich die Judenfrage ist, so werden von hundert Befragten fünfzig verlegen schweigen oder Unzulängliches stammeln, von den anderen fünfzig wirst du verschiedene Antworten hören'. Sigbert Feuchtwanger, 'Grundsätzliches zur deutschen Judenfrage', *Neue jüdische Monatshefte* 1, no. 19 (10 Juli 1917): 543.

2 Sigbert Feuchtwanger (1886–1956) lawyer in Munich, editor of *Jüdischen Echo* and Vice President of the Jewish Cultural Community of Munich (*Israelitische Kultusgemeinde München*, IKG), emigrated to Palestine in 1937. For Feuchtwanger's profile see *Deutsche Biographie* [https://bit.ly/2LVUgXx, accessed 18/05/18].

3 In order to demonstrate the complexity of the term, its associated meanings and how it was used by various agents, the Jewish Question and Jewish questions will be used interchangeably throughout the thesis. When denoting the plural form, the q will not be capitalised.

an antisemitic trope imposed on the Jews. Rather, I contend, it was a multivalent and contingent term, which was also invoked frequently by Jews. The intractability of the Jewish Question, I argue is reflected in the modern scholarly literature where different interpretations of the Jewish Question abound. More often, it is referenced in connection with the rise of Nazism, or in the debate on the German-Jewish symbiosis without a detailed analysis of what the term meant, or how it functioned. Addressing this omission by analysing the function of the Jewish Question in German politics, I focus on political ideas and practices in their cultural context. Lastly, I explain the scope selected for this thesis from the outbreak of the First World War in August 1914 to the ratification of the Weimar constitution in August 1919. In these seminal years the Jewish Question was no longer confined to public intellectual debates (see chapter one) but became a practical concern in German domestic and foreign policy (see chapters two to five). These discussions on practical Jewish questions in the Foreign Ministry and Reichstag, I argue, became *de facto* debates about the future of the German state. They revealed the hopes, fears and preoccupations in Germany's path from Empire to Republic.

In principle, the Jewish Question should have ended with Jewish emancipation, that is, when the civil and political rights of German Jews were enshrined within the 1871 constitution, which founded the German Empire.[4] Whilst Jewish emancipation began even earlier in German states, it was a long and gradual process. Westphalia was the first German state to issue a royal decree to abolish taxes imposed on Jews in 1808. In 1811, a Jewish emancipation edict was issued in the Grand Duchy of Frankfurt. The following year, Prussian Jews were granted civil and (limited) political rights. After 1848, however, the suppression of the revolutions brought a series of reactionary measures which included revoking or limiting Jewish rights.[5] When the Jewish Question (*Judenfrage*) first appeared in print in 1838 and reached prominence as a popular catchword in 1842, it concerned the question of the legal equality of Jews in the Prussian state.[6] By 1871, after years of advances and set-backs in the struggle for emancipation, the Jewish Question in Germany, had effectively been resolved. The term should have lost its momentum and eventually faded from public discourse entirely. Yet quite the opposite occurred. Following Jewish emancipation, the term was no longer used to discuss Jewish political and civic rights *de jure*, however it was frequently tied into debates about *de facto* Jewish equality.

---

4 The emancipation of the Jews in the 1871 constitution was a principle adopted from the 1869 North German Confederation constitution. On the 22 April 1871 Jews in all of Germany were emancipated when the constitution was extended to Bavaria.

5 For a list of these emancipation edicts and which German states later rescinded these rights see Raphael Mahler, *Jewish Emancipation: A Selection of Documents*, Pamphlet Series Jews and the Post-War World 1 (New York: American Jewish Committee, 1942).

6 Jacob Toury, '"The Jewish Question" A Semantic Approach', *The Leo Baeck Institute Year Book* 11, no. 1 (1 January 1966): 92.

After ceasing to be a political-constitutional question about emancipation, the Jewish Question moved into what Peter Pulzer has termed the 'unofficial sphere'.[7] Institutional discrimination continued against Jews in spite of legal equality. They were barred from entering the officer corps in the military, professions in politics, the civil service and public universities.[8] Where the Jewish Question no longer focused on the legal equality of the civil and political rights of Jews, it became about their place and social equality within German society. Antisemites picked up on the Jewish Question, framing it in cultural language and as a question of race.[9] The suggestion that Jews were of a different race undermined the Enlightenment model according to which Jews had become members of the state on the basis of religious equality.[10] Moreover, it challenged the trend amongst the majority of German Jews towards conversion and mixed marriages.[11] Around the same time, Zionists also began to invoke the Jewish Question as a catchword. Zionists turned an externally imposed question into an internal one and used it to question the Jewish diaspora and advocate for a Jewish state.[12] By the turn of the century, the term was re-defined within Zionist circles as the quest for a Jewish homeland and the revival of a Jewish national and cultural identity.[13]

Lacking any concrete practical political meaning since emancipation, the Jewish Question became a multivalent term appropriated by a multitude of agents for different purposes. With the outbreak of the First World War, the term altered as the singular *Judenfrage* was often replaced by its plural form, *Judenfragen*. 'Does a Jewish Question exist? Strange question! We see it everywhere! One almost wants to say: there are just so many Jewish questions' wrote Arthur Cohen, Professor of Economics and Finance at the Technical University of Munich.[14] The prominence of Jewish questions after the outbreak of the war was further illustrated by the publication of a three-

---

7 Peter Pulzer, *Jews and the German State: The Political History of a Minority, 1848–1933* (Detroit, Michigan: Wayne State University Press, 2003), 19.

8 Ibid.

9 See for example Dühring Eugen, *Die Judenfrage als Racen-, Sitten- und Culturfrage. Mit einer weltgeschichtlichen Antwort*, 1st ed. (Karlsruhe und Leipzig: Verlag von H. Reuther, 1881).

10 For a useful transnational analysis of Jewish emancipation and its relationship with Enlightenment values see Pierre Birnbaum and Ira Katznelson, *Paths of Emancipation: Jews, States, and Citizenship* (Princeton, New Jersey: Princeton University Press, 2014).

11 Donald L. Niewyk, *The Jews in Weimar Germany* (Manchester: Manchester University Press, 1980), 98.

12 Leon Pinsker was the first to suggest that the 'Jewish Question' could only be resolved through the founding of a Jewish homeland in *Autoemancipation! Mahnruf an seine Stammesgenossen von einem russischen Juden* (1882). However, his pamphlet forms one of three seminal works in the development of the Jewish national homeland movement. Moses Hess's *Rom and Jerusalem* (1862) proposed that Jews should sacrifice emancipation over nationality and return to Palestine. In 1896, Theodor Herzl's *Judenstaat* more fully developed a plan for the founding of a Jewish homeland as a solution to the Jewish Question.

13 Buber was a seminal figure in the Zionist movement who advocated for a cultural, national, Jewish revival. See Martin Buber, *Drei Reden über das Judentum* (Frankfurt am Main: Rütten & Loening, 1911).

14 Arthur Cohen, 'Die Judenfrage – Eine Minoritätenfrage', *Neue jüdische Monatshefte* 3, no. 7/8 (19 Januar 1919): 164.

part series in July 1919 on the theme of the Jewish Question in the future Europe in the German-Jewish magazine, *Ost und West*.[15]

Rather than speaking to Jewish particularity, the Jewish Question began to be recognised as an expression of larger contemporary political issues, tied into questions pertaining to minority rights, national autonomy and homogeneity. Arthur Cohen argued that the Jewish Question was not unique to the Jews but present in other social and national groups. He equated it with the 'minority question':

> The Jewish Question is only an example of the heterogeneity of the masses. The antagonism between Jews and non-Jews is not special: everywhere, where two diverse groups co-exist, the same phenomenon of antagonism appears.[16]

Written at the end of the war, Cohen invoked the Jewish Question to expose the limits of the modern state and the increasing desire for greater homogeneity. In another article, Helene Hanna Cohen, a journalist based in Munich and close friend of Julius Berger,[17] opined that the Jewish Question related more broadly to the concept of the nationality principle, defined as groups without states.[18] Ludwig Quessel, a representative of the Social Democratic Party (*Sozialdemokratische Partei Deutschlands*, SPD) in the Reichstag, considered how the encounter with the masses of Eastern European Jews during the war revealed that the Jewish Question had 'always' been 'not only a social, but also a national problem'.[19] He re-framed the term as a question of the emancipation of Eastern European Jews and the rights of Jews to Palestine. The work of Quessel and his contemporaries illustrated the multivalence of the Jewish Question in Germany.

The First World War marked a pivotal moment in German history, raising vital new questions in the spheres of domestic as well as foreign policy. As the fortunes of war shifted, so did borders, populations and national allegiances. In a period of acute and almost constant political crisis, the German government faced issues concerning citizenship, minority rights and religious as well as national identity. I will analyse these concerns through the lens of the Jewish Question, that is, on-going debates about the status of the German-Jewish population in German politics and society. From a term

---

15 Leo Winz, 'Die Judenfrage im künftigen Europa, I: Anschwellen die judenfeindlichen Strömungen', *Ost und West: Illustrierte Monatsschrift für das gesamte Judentum* XIX, no. 7/8 (Juli 1919): 162–66.
16 Cohen, 'Die Judenfrage – Eine Minoritätenfrage', 165.
17 Julius Berger founded a successful construction firm, Julius Berger Tiefbau AG. In the 1970s it merged with Bilfinger, one of the largest construction companies in Germany. Berger also participated in the Paris Peace Conference as an Industrial representative. Less is known about Helene Hanna Cohen. Evidence of their relationship can be found in Seymour Drescher and Allan Sharlin, eds., *Political Symbolism in Modern Europe: Essays in Honor of George L. Mosse* (New Brunswick, London: Transaction Books, 1982), 94.
18 Helene Hanna Cohen, 'Die Judenfrage in Der Internationale', *Neue jüdische Monatshefte* 2, no. 6 (25 December 1917): 136.
19 Ludwig Quessel, 'Die Judenfrage als nationales Problem', *Neue jüdische Monatshefte* 2, no. 13 (10 April 1918): 299.

on the margins of public discourse, the Jewish Question in the course of World War One re-entered the realm of mainstream parliamentary politics shaping domestic and foreign political theory and praxis.

The Jewish Question, I contend, casts important new light on Germany's difficult path towards a new democratic and pluralistic constitution in 1919. One of my principal aims in this book is to offer a novel interpretation of the role that the much discussed 'problem' of German Jewry played in the political debates and decisions that paved the way for the Weimar Republic. The significance of the Jewish Question, as one of many questions that arose in the formation of the modern state in Germany, is that it provides an understanding of the complex political processes that developed throughout the First World War. The Jewish minority was a unique group that grappled with its place in the German polity. They were members of a community that transcended national boundaries whilst being, at the same time, citizens of Germany. The Jewish Question provides unique insights into German political debates about the fraught relationship between the nation and the state.

The core of the book focuses on three distinct moments, between 1914 and 1919, when the Jewish Question catalysed a debate on the German nation-state. These moments are: the involvement of Zionists in German foreign policy, the 'Jew census' (*Judenzählung*) and the debate on minority rights in the Weimar constitution and at the Paris Peace Conference. Taken as a whole, they reveal the struggles and preoccupations of Germany in its transition towards a pluralistic, democratic Republic. Whilst events tend to be recorded and remembered based upon the final outcome, often to the detriment of history, this book shifts away from the final outcome and turns to hidden processes. These distinctive moments may not have fundamentally altered the *status quo*, nor did they lead to any specific legislative changes. However, they shed light on three possible roads which Germany could have taken in its political development. From the potential of Imperial Germany as a greater colonial power in Eastern Europe and the Middle East, to a country institutionalising antisemitic[20] policies to, alternatively, a multi-ethnic Republic recognising the rights of national minorities.

German states have had an enduring presence of Jewish communities since the fourth century.[21] This language, but also cultural, affinity of (Ashkenazi) Jews to Germany, in spite of their mass emigration east in the tenth century, arose time again binding the Jewish Question intimately to the German Question. It explains why in a country where the Jewish minority represented approximately 1% of the German population, at the time of unification in 1871, Jewish questions became a part of the

---

20 I spell antisemitism without a hyphen to denote a modern form of Jew-hatred. See Shmuel Almog, 'What's in a Hyphen?', SICSA Report: Newsletter of the Vidal Sassoon International Center for the Study of Antisemitism 2 (1989): 1 2 [https://bit.ly/2SjROvf, accessed 16/07/19].
21 David Levinson, *Jewish Germany: An Enduring Presence from the Fourth to the Twenty-First Century* (Portland, Oregon: Valentine Mitchell, 2018).

political agenda. The Jewish Question can provide an insight into the distinctive anxieties, expectations and concerns shaping German politics. As Peter Gay noted, 'the so-called Jewish Question had no reality in isolation. It was part of, and a clue to, the larger question: the German Question'.[22]

The Jewish Question was certainly not the only issue framed as a question within Germany. Others included the *soziale Frage, Bauernfrage, Frauenfrage, Arbeiterfrage, Polenfrage*.[23] The Jewish community was not the only minority group to receive attention in parliamentary debates. Poles were in fact the largest national minority group in Germany.[24] In addition, there were Alsatians, Danes, Wends, Sorbs. As the largest religious minority, the Catholics also featured prominently in these discussions. The period of the *Kulturkampf* against the Catholic, and by association the Polish minority under Bismarck, testifies to the centrality of other minority concerns in German politics as does the Zabern Affair in 1913 in Alsace-Lorraine.[25]

What made the Jewish Question unique, however, was that the identity of the Jewish population was far more complex than these other groups. Not always mutually exclusively, Jews saw themselves as a religious community, a community of kinship (*Stamm*), an ethnic community and national community, which spanned across geographic boundaries. Unlike the Polish,[26] Danish and Alsatian minorities in Germany, Jews identified as Germans, as 'insiders' and whenever permitted, acted as such.[27]

The insider status of Jews was also reflected in their engagement with German politics. Unlike the other religious and national minorities such as the Catholics, the Danes, Poles and Alsatians, the Jewish community was not represented by a single

---

22 Peter Gay, *Freud, Jews and Other Germans. Masters and Victims in Modernist Culture* (New York: Oxford University Press, 1978), 19.
23 On the shift towards thinking in questions in the nineteenth century see Holly Case *The Age of Questions* (Princeton: Princeton University Press, 2018); Holly Case, 'The "Social Question," 1820–1920', *Modern Intellectual History* 13, no. 3 (2016): 747–75. For a contemporary account on the difference between these questions and the Jewish Question see Winz, 'Die Judenfrage im künftigen Europa', 164.
24 The Polish minority numbered just over three million, meaning in 1871 they represented approximately 8 % of the total German population. See Volker R. Berghahn, *Imperial Germany, 1871–1914: Economy, Society, Culture and Politics* (Providence, RI and Oxford: Berghahn Books, 1994), 111.
25 On Bismarck's Kulturkampf and the role it played in German unification see Eley Geoff, 'Bismarckian Germany' in *Modern Germany Reconsidered, 1870–1945*, ed. Gordon Mantel (London: Routledge, 1992), 1–32, especially 20–25. On the Zabern Affair and the political outcry see David Schoenbaum, *Zabern 1913: Consensus Politics in Imperial Germany*, 1st ed. (London: Harper Collins, 1982).
26 The Polish minority sat in between the Jewish and Danish minority. They were neither stateless nor did they have a nation. Polish labourers and landowners, like Jews attempted a 'cultural synthesis' in Germany. This however was different for Polish aristocrats who maintained a strong Polish national identity. See Berghahn, *Imperial Germany*, 110–118.
27 Anthony McElligot writes, 'The Jews of Weimar, then [...] felt German, which is all we need to know'. Anthony McElligott, *Rethinking the Weimar Republic: Authority and Authoritarianism, 1916–1936* (London: Bloomsbury, 2014), 238. See also Peter Gay, *Weimar Culture: The Outsider as Insider*, 1st ed. (New York: Harper & Row, 1968), i–viii.

political party.[28] Since unification, the Danes in Schleswig-Holstein were represented by the Danish Party and consistently held one seat in the Reichstag. Poles living to the east of Germany, despite being a Catholic majority, were represented by a separate party, the Polish Party, which never held less than thirteen seats in the Reichstag. To the west, the French-speaking minority in Alsace-Lorraine had political representation in the Reichstag, numbering never less than ten seats. Germany's largest religious minority, Catholics, were represented by the Catholic Centre Party, which continued even after the war to consistently and successfully secure representation in the Reichstag.[29] At the end of the war, as German territory in the north, east and west was ceded to Denmark, Poland and France respectively these parties disbanded, no longer deemed necessary. In contrast, the Jewish community, due to a lack of consensus, was unable to form a united political party despite several attempts.[30]

Unlike other minority groups, the Jewish minority did not have a distinct representation in parliament. Politicians of Jewish descent did not act more generally on behalf of Jewish sectional interests. However, as most were representatives in the Liberal parties (the National Liberal Party and the Progressive Party), Jews tended to vote for these parties.[31] Following a nadir in Jewish politics (starting around 1880) marked by the end of the dominance by Liberal parties,[32] Bismarck's shift in political alliances towards the Catholic Centre Party and the growth of organised political antisemitism, a number of Jewish politicians began to alter their focus. Jewish politicians engaged in Jewish affairs and held political positions alongside acting as representatives of newly founded Jewish defence organisations such as the Central Association for German

----

28 On the attempts by the Jewish community to form a political party see Jacob Toury, 'Organizational Problems of German Jewry: Steps towards the Establishment of a Central Organization (1893–1920)', *The Leo Baeck Institute Year Book* 13, no. 1 (1968): 57–90. For Zionists efforts at political representation in German politics see Yehuda Eloni, 'The Zionist Movement and the German Social Democratic Party, 1897–1918', *Studies in Zionism* 5, no. 2 (1984): 181–199.

29 On pre-1945 political parties in Germany see Vincent E. McHale, ed., *Political Parties of Europe*, vol. 1 (Westport, Connecticut: Greenwood Press, 1983), 400–438.

30 In December 1900 the attempt to form a 'general Jewish Diet' failed miserably due to a lack of consensus. See Toury, 'Organizational Problems of German Jewry', 64. See also Marjorie Lamberti, 'The Attempt to Form a Jewish Bloc: Jewish Notables and Politics in Wilhelmian Germany', *Central European History* 3, no. 1–2 (1970): 73–93.

31 On Jewish voting behaviour and political participation in Germany see Pulzer, *Jews and the German State*; Ernest Hamburger, *Juden im öffentlichen Leben Deutschlands: Regierungsmitglieder, Beamte und Parlamentarier in der monarchischen Zeit, 1848–1918*, Schriftenreihe wissenschaftlicher Abhandlungen des Leo Baeck Instituts 19 (Tübingen: JCB Mohr Paul Siebeck, 1968); Jacob Toury, *Die politischen Orientierungen der Juden in Deutschland: von Jena bis Weimar*, Schriftenreihe wissenschaftlicher Abhandlungen des Leo Baeck Instituts 15 (Tübingen: Mohr Siebeck, 1966). On how Jews in the latter years of the Weimar Republic used their votes strategically in an effort to save the Republic see Anthony D. Kauders, 'Weimar Jewry', in *Weimar Germany*, ed. Anthony McElligott, Short Oxford History of Germany (Oxford: Oxford University Press, 2009), 234–59.

32 In 1880 the National Liberal Party split. The left-wing fraction of the party joined the Progressive Party to form the German Free-minded Party.

citizens of the Jewish faith, (*Centralverein deutscher Staatsbürger jüdischen Glaubens,* CV) founded in 1893.[33]

Compared to their relative size in the population, Jewish politicians were well-represented in the Reichstag during the Wilhelmine period.[34] Between 1867 to 1916 approximately 1.73 % of all delegates in the Reichstag were of Jewish descent, this included Jews that were baptised.[35] Deputies of Jewish descent sat in political parties from the right to the left of the political spectrum.[36] However, the majority sat in the Liberal parties.[37] This changed in the Reichstag in 1893 when the Social Democratic Party held the highest membership figures of Jewish deputies.[38] The concentration of Jews within these left-leaning parties was largely due to the willingness of these parties to allow Jews to stand as candidates. This, however, varied considerably in each state where the system of franchise differed.[39] Throughout the Wilhelmine period Jewish representation in the Reichstag and State Diet gradually increased. As this book traces Germany's transition towards a parliamentary democracy, it also reflects on the participation of German Jews in politics. It illustrates the influence they were able to exert over domestic and foreign policy during the war culminating with the birth of the Weimar Republic which heralded a new era for German Jewish political participation as they took a dynamic role in the life of the Republic.

Historiography

The five years that this book covers have attracted much scholarly attention, not least in the past few years. With the recent centenaries of the beginning and end of the First

---

33 Other organisations included the Kartell-Convent of German Students of the Jewish Faith (*Der Kartell-Convent der Verbindungen deutscher Studenten jüdischen Glaubens,* KC) founded in 1896 and the Alliance of German Jews (*Verband der deutschen Juden,* VdJ) founded in 1904. On other forms of Jewish defence see Ann Goldberg, *Honor, Politics and the Law in Imperial Germany, 1871–1914* (Cambridge: Cambridge University Press, 2010).

34 In 1871, the Jewish share in the total population was 1.25 %. It declined to 0.95 % by 1914. Berghahn, *Imperial Germany,* 102.

35 Out of 3000 deputies, 52 were of Jewish descent. On the distribution of these deputies in political parties see Hamburger, *Juden im öffentlichen Leben Deutschlands,* 250–54.

36 These parties included the Conservatives (*Konservative*), German Imperial Party (*Reichspartei/Freikonservative*), National Liberals (*Nationalliberale*), German Progress Party (*Fortschrittspartei/Freisinnige*) and the German People's Party (*Süddeutsche Volkspartei / Deutsche Volkspartei*). See ibid, 252–53.

37 These Liberal parties included the National Liberals and the Free-minded Union (*Freisinnige Vereinigung*) and the Free-minded People's Party (*Freisinnige Volkspartei*), which having split, reunified in 1910.

38 Whilst this figure applies to the overall majority, most baptised Jews sat in the National Liberal Party. Amongst professing Jews, most were Social Democrats. See ibid, 254.

39 Pulzer, *Jews and the German State,* 106–48.

World War, research on this period has been given renewed significance.[40] Moreover, with the global rise of populist movements and, in particular, the support for right-wing parties, there has also been a recent international interest in German history, especially the years of the Weimar Republic.[41] Both of these topics – the First World War and the Weimar Republic – have their own historiographical debates. Recent scholarship on the First World War, for example, continues to engage with the causes of the outbreak of the war and the parties responsible.[42] Research on the Weimar Republic is often guided by its weaknesses that led to the rise of Nazism.[43] These are not, however, the questions asked within this book. I instead investigate how practical Jewish questions shaped Germany's geopolitical aims during the First World War. And rather than studying the Weimar constitution with an aim to assessing why the Republic failed, I examine what Jewish questions in the constitutional debates revealed about Germany's political development.

Each individual chapter engages with distinct moments that have their separate historiographical debates including the involvement of Zionists in German foreign policy,[44] the 'Jew census' (*Judenzählung*)[45] and the debate on minority rights in the Weimar constitution and at the Paris Peace Conference,[46] respectively. I, however,

---

40 Christopher M. Clark, *The Sleepwalkers: How Europe Went to War in 1914*, 1st ed. (New York: Harper, 2013); Margaret MacMillan, *The War That Ended Peace: The Road to 1914* (New York: Random House Trade Paperbacks, 2014); Margaret MacMillan, Anand Menon, and Patrick Quinton-Brown, 'Introduction: World Politics 100 years after the Paris Peace Conference', *International Affairs* 95, no. 1 (2019): 1–5.

41 Martin Kettle, 'The Political Landscapes of Brexit Britain and Weimar Germany Are Scarily Similar', *The Guardian*, 16 May 2019 [https://bit.ly/2JmvrDT, accessed 15/07/19]; Dominik Peters, 'Was Weimar für den umgang mit der AfD lehrt', *Spiegel*, 6 February 2019 [https://bit.ly/2JxwPm2, accessed 15/07/19].

42 Andreas Gestrich and H. Pogge von Strandmann, *Bid for World Power? New research on the outbreak of the First World War*, Studies of the German Historical Institute London (Oxford: Oxford University Press, 2017).

43 For a comprehensive review of this scholarship see Peter C. Weber, 'The Paradoxical Modernity of Civil Society: The Weimar Republic, Democracy and Social Homogeneity', *Voluntas* 26 (2015): 629–648.

44 Isaiah Friedman, *Germany, Turkey, and Zionism 1897–1918* (Oxford: Oxford University Press, 1977); Zosa Szajkowski, 'The Komitee für den Osten and Zionism', in *Herzl Year Book*, ed. Raphael Patai (New York: Herzl Press, 1971), 199–240.

45 Michael Geheran, 'Rethinking Jewish Front Experiences', in *Beyond Inclusion and Exclusion: Jewish Experiences of the First World War in Central Europe*, ed. Jason Crouthamel, Tim Grady, and Julia Barbara Köhne (New York and Oxford: Berghahn Books, 2019), 111–43; Timothy L. Grady, *A Deadly Legacy: German Jews and the Great War* (New Haven and London: Yale University Press, 2017); Peter Appelbaum, *Loyal Sons: Jews in the German Army in the Great War* (London and Portland: Valentine Mitchell, 2015); David J. Fine, 'Jewish Integration in the German Army in the First World War' (Berlin and Boston: Walter de Gruyter, 2012); Derek Penslar, 'The German-Jewish Soldier: From Participant to Victim', *German History* 29, no. 3 (2011): 423–44; Jacob Rosenthal, *Die Ehre des jüdischen Soldaten: Die Judenzählung im Ersten Weltkrieg und ihre Folgen* (Frankfurt am Main: Campus, 2007); Werner T. Angress, 'The German Army's "Judenzählung" of 1916: Genesis – Consequences – Significance', *The Leo Baeck Institute Year Book* 23, no. 1 (1978): 117–38.

46 Karen Schönwälder, 'The Constitutional Protection of Minorities in Germany: Weimar Revisited', *The Slavonic and East European Review* 74, no. 1 (1996): 38–65; Carole Fink, *Defending the Rights of Others: The Great Powers, the Jews, and International Minority Protection, 1878–1938* (Cambridge: Cambridge University Press, 2004); David Engel, 'Perceptions of Power – Poland and World Jewry', in *Simon Dubnow Institute*

bring these distinct moments together through the perspective of the Jewish Question to analyse Germany's political development in a period of momentous change.

Although the period of 1914 to 1919 in German history features several mature historiographical debates, they have all contributed to one of the most controversial and significant scholarly debates of the twentieth century, the *Sonderweg* thesis. The historiographical debate, which is nearing its sixtieth anniversary, is based on the notion that Germany followed a peculiar (*Sonder*) path (*weg*) towards modernity. Starting in the 1960s, Fritz Fischer argued that the aggressive war-aims of German decision-makers testified to Germany's responsibility for the outbreak of the First World War. Contributing to this debate, historians of the 'Bielefeld School' began to assess when Germany's peculiar development began. They studied the failure of the 1848 revolution and the delayed modernisation of Germany's political structures.[47] British historians David Blackbourn, Geoff Eley and Richard Evans subsequently criticised the *Sonderweg* thesis for being ahistorical. They found evidence that a 'silent bourgeois revolution' had taken place in Germany and argued that the country was not unique in experiencing dynamic capitalism, materialism and cultural despair.[48]

Against the determinism of Fischer and Wehler that Germany was on a special path (*Sonderweg*) towards authoritarian governance and following the work of Eley and Blackbourn, my work refutes the argument of German exceptionalism. By illustrating the multivalence of the Jewish Question, especially its invocation by Jews, I contend that one cannot trace a linear development of the Jewish Question in Germany that culminates in the Holocaust. The antisemitic strain of the German right in Wilhelmine Germany was not more visceral than in the Russian Empire or the Habsburg lands. Moreover, the Dreyfus Affair (1984–1906) and the Leo Franks Affair (1913–1915) illustrate that antisemitism was rife and could have vicious consequences in the democratic Republics of France and America.[49]

Yearbook, 1st ed. (Stuttgart und München: Deutsche Verlags-Anstalt, 2002), 17–29; Erwin Viefhaus, *Die Minderheitenfrage und die Entstehung der Minderheitenschutzverträge auf der Pariser Friedenskonferenz 1919* (Würzburg: Holzner Verlag, 1960).

47 Robert Moeller, 'The Kaiserreich Recast? Continuity and Change in Modern German Historiography', *Journal of Social History* 17, no. 4 (1984): 655; Hans-Ulrich Wehler, *Das deutsche Kaiserreich, 1871–1918* (Göttingen: Vandenhoeck & Ruprecht, 1973); Jurgen Kocka, 'German History before Hitler: The Debate about the German Sonderweg', *Journal of Contemporary History* 23, no. 1 (1988): 3–16.

48 David Blackbourn and Geoff Eley, *The Peculiarities of German History: Bourgeois Society and Politics in Nineteenth-Century Germany* (Oxford: Oxford University Press, 1984); Richard J. Evans, *Society and Politics in Wilhelmine Germany* (London and New York: Croom Helm; Barnes and Noble, 1978).

49 Both affairs divided their respective publics. During the Dreyfuss Affair in France, a Jewish Alsatian Officer was accused of treason and falsely convicted. In America, Leo Franks, a Jewish factory worker, was sentenced to death for a murder he did not commit. When his sentence was overturned, despite his innocence, he was lynched. See Ruth Harris, *The Man on Devil's Island* (London: Allen Lane, 2010); Leonard Dinnerstein, *The Leo Franks case*, revised ed. (Athens, Georgia: University of Georgia Press, 2008).

More often, however, the Jewish Question in Germany is viewed in hindsight, through this lens of the Holocaust. This obscures the contingency of the term, the manifold agents that appropriated it, its various meanings and how it functioned. I argue that Jewish questions reveal the silent, or what I term, hidden processes of Germany's democratic, and progressive, development. By using the Jewish Question to investigate the changing character of German political discourse and practice, I offer the first sustained examination of the ways in which questions about German-Jewish citizenship, minority rights and religious, national identity shaped the politics of the last Imperial government and influenced the processes of parliamentarisation and democratisation in the final years of the war.

In recent years there has been a growing interest in silent parliamentarisation and German exceptionalism amongst scholars of Wilhelmine Germany.[50] The debate centres on where power and authority were concentrated, in either the democratically elected Reichstag or unilaterally in the hands of the Kaiser and the chancellor. Pace the narrative that the German Empire was an 'autocratic-democratic' state with a static political development advanced by Hans-Ulrich Wehler and Volker Berghahn, scholars such as Manfred Rauh, Thomas Nipperdey and Wolfgang Böckenförde have suggested that starting in around 1890, parliament began gaining increasing influence in shaping political decisions.[51] As a consequence of this, they date Germany's transformation into a 'full democracy' earlier than 1919 when the Weimar Republic was established.[52]

Although in formal constitutional clauses parliament had little control or influence over government formation and legislative power, Nipperdey, Böckenförde, Frauendienst have studied the informal ways in which the Reichstag wielded power.[53] Following scholars such as Rauh, Schönberger, Nipperdey, I illustrate the informal, normative powers of parliament. Jewish questions, I argue, punctuated attempts to enforce constitutional checks and balances. They exposed the inconsistencies within the Empire

---

[50] This discussion began in the 1970s see Manfred Rauh, *Föderalismus und Parlamentarismus im Wilhelminischen Reich*, Beiträge zur Geschichte des Parlamentarismus und der politischen Parteien; Band 47 (Düsseldorf: Droste, 1973); Manfred Rauh, *Die Parlamentarisierung des Deutschen Reiches*, Beiträge zur Geschichte des Parlamentarismus und der politischen Parteien; Band 60 (Düsseldorf: Droste, 1977). For a recent book which engages with this scholarship see Mark Hewitson, *Germany and the Modern World, 1880–1914* (Cambridge: Cambridge University Press, 2018).

[51] Wehler, *Das deutsche Kaiserreich*; Berghahn, *Imperial Germany*; Rauh, *Föderalismus und Parlamentarismus im Wilhelminischen Reich*; Thomas Nipperdey, *Deutsche Geschichte 1866–1918*, vol. II, Machtstaat vor der Demokratie (Munich: Verlag C. H. Beck, 1992); Wolfgang Ernst Böckenförde, 'Der deutsche Typ der konstitutionellen Monarchie im 19. Jahrhundert', in *Recht, Staat, Freiheit* (Frankfurt am Main: Suhrkamp, 1986), 112–45.

[52] For a useful overview of this debate see Marcus Kreuzer, 'Parliamentarization and the Question of German Exceptionalism: 1867–1918', *Central European History* 36, no. 3 (2003): 327–57.

[53] Nipperdey, *Deutsche Geschichte*; Werner Frauendienst, 'Demokratisierung des deutschen konstitutionalismus in der Zeit Wilhelms II', *Zeitschrift für die gesamte Staatswissenschaft* 113, no. 4 (1957): 721–24; Böckenförde, 'Der deutsche Typ der konstitutionellen Monarchie'; Kreuzer, 'Parliamentarization and the Question of German Exceptionalism', 335–48.

between *de jure* and *de facto* Jewish civil and political equality. Ministers recognised the importance of their platform in the Reichstag and used it to highlight the injustices of constitutional transgressions. They petitioned not for legislative changes but for the principles of the 1871 constitution to be upheld and respected. Resolving these constitutional transgressions was instrumental to Germany's development towards a secular, tolerant, inclusive and pluralist democracy. Jewish questions exposed problems in the accountability of the government and its ministries for its (unconstitutional) actions which parliament ensured were redressed.

The historiography on the Jewish Question can be divided into two bodies of scholarship. In the first category are works that, I suggest, make implicit references to the Jewish Question. The second category consists of authors that explicitly analyse the character and dynamics of the Jewish Question. In the case of the former, I identify two sub-genres that fall into this category, the scholarship on the Third Reich, in particular the rise of Nazism and the Holocaust, and German-Jewish relations, specifically the literature on the German-Jewish negative symbiosis. In viewing the Jewish Question ahistorically, that is, in light of the Holocaust, I argue that these two literatures reinforce a teleological and anachronistic reading of the Jewish Question. Of the scholarship that falls into the latter category, what I term the explicit historiography on the Jewish Question, I contend that its overarching feature is that it is a reflection of the multivalence of the Jewish Question in the primary sources. As a result, these works have little in common, beyond a consideration of the Jewish Question, as they each establish different temporal and geospatial parameters to the study of the Jewish Question.

A common feature in the scholarly literature on German-Jewish history is the casual reference to the Jewish Question, without any detailed consideration of the author's intention in using the term and what, in the given context, it meant. I call this the implicit historiography on the Jewish Question. Historians writing about either the rise of Nazism or German-Jewish relations often show this tendency. The vast amount of literature on the Jewish Question and antisemitism as it played out in modern Germany still tends to treat the phenomenon anachronistically with hindsight, that is, from the vantage point of the Holocaust and from a largely social or cultural historical perspective.[54] As the Jewish Question was appropriated by antisemites and tied into several myths that became relevant during the Weimar Republic, but which emerged

---

54 Philip Spencer and Robert Fine, *Antisemitism and the Left: On the Return of the Jewish Question* (Manchester: Manchester University Press, 2017); Élisabeth Roudinesco, *Revisiting the Jewish Question*, trans. Andrew Brown (Cambridge: Polity, 2013); David Nirenberg, *Anti-Judaism: The Western Tradition*, 1st ed. (New York: W. W. Norton & Co., 2013); Helmut W. Smith, *The Continuities of German History: Nation, Religion, and Race across the Long Nineteenth Century* (Cambridge: Cambridge University Press, 2008); Michael Mack, *German Idealism and the Jew: The Inner Anti-Semitism of Philosophy and German Jewish Responses* (Chicago: University of Chicago Press, 2003); Marvin Perry and Frederick M. Schweitzer, *Antisemitism: Myth and Hate from Antiquity to the Present* (New York: Palgrave, 2002); Paul Lawrence Rose, *German Ques-*

in the First World War, the term features frequently in the scholarship on the völkisch movement, the rise of Nazism and the Holocaust.[55] While it does not ignore the short- and long-term effects the Jewish Question had on the rise of German antisemitism, I stress the contingency and ambivalence of the term. Moreover, I am neither interested in social or cultural aspects to the Jewish Question but rather political aspects. This I define as the relationship between Jews and the modern nation-state, including questions of citizenship rights, secularism and nationhood.

A consequence of the association between the Jewish Question and antisemitism is that outside of academic circles the term has become almost synonymous with antisemitism.[56] Not only has this connection obscured the manifold meanings of the term historically, overlooking its contingency, it has also perpetuated a narrative of Jewish victimhood, removing Jewish agency from German history. This book extracts the Jewish Question from antisemitism by emphasising the engagement by Jews in German politics as active subjects and not passive objects, which I will explain in more detail below.[57]

Alongside the literature on Nazism, the Jewish Question is also frequently referenced in the scholarship on German-Jewish relations, including before and after the period of the Third Reich (1933–1945). The central question of this scholarship, which was asked by Gershom Scholem in his 1962 essay, was whether or not a German-Jewish dialogue ever existed.[58] He argued it had not and sparked an extended discussion that was termed the 'German-Jewish negative symbiosis', a phrase coined by Hannah Arendt.[59]

In line with Scholem, historians including Dan Diner and Jack Zipes argued that a two-sided German-Jewish dialogue did not exist prior to 1933 and that from this date forth, it could only be described in negative terms.[60] George Mosse and Amos Elon subsequently looked back to the German Enlightenment and argued that Jews embraced the notion of *Bildung*, acculturating not because they were expected to, but

---

tion / *Jewish Question: Revolutionary Antisemitism in Germany from Kant to Wagner* (Princeton: Princeton University Press, 1990).

55　See, for example, Guy Tourlamain, *Völkisch Writers and National Socialism: A Study of Right-Wing Political Culture in Germany, 1890–1960*, Cultural History and Literary Imagination (Oxford and Bern: Peter Lang, 2014), 25–34.

56　The Alt-Right movement continues to use the term to promote antisemitism, abbreviating it to 'JQ'. See Emma Green, 'Paul Nehlen's Fringe Anti-Semitism', *The Atlantic*, 24 January 2018 [https://bit.ly/2DxbFPx, accessed 31/07/19].

57　Peter Pulzer stresses the importance of drawing a distinction between the Jewish Question and antisemitism. Pulzer, *Jews and the German State*, 14.

58　Gershom Scholem, 'Wider den Mythos vom deutsch-judischen Gespräch', in *Auf Gespaltenem Pfad: Für Margarete Susman*, ed. Manfred Schlösser (Darmstadt: Erato-Presse Verlag, 1964), 229–33.

59　Dan Diner, 'Negative Symbiose: Deutsche und Juden nach Auschwitz', *Babylon* 1 (1986): 11.

60　Diner, 'Negative Symbiose'; Jack Zipes, 'The Negative German-Jewish Symbiosis', in *Insiders and Outsider: Jewish and Gentile Culture in Germany and Austria*, ed. Lorenz Dagmar and Gabriele Weinberger (New York: Palgrave, 2002), 31–45.

because they wanted to integrate into German culture and society.[61] This scholarship is predominantly concerned with cultural and social questions: Jewish communal identity, acculturation, the Jewish experience of *Bildung*, their engagement in popular culture and the everyday dynamics of German-Jewish life.[62] Lars Fischer has considered the wealth of literature on this subject to amount to a historiography on the Jewish Question.[63]

This book contributes to this scholarly debate to the extent that I argue that Jews both engaged with and exerted an influence on German domestic and foreign policy. They were not passive bystanders but influenced political decision-making. Beyond this claim, I do not situate my work within this literature. Not only because I do not focus on the social or cultural dynamics of German-Jewish relations but also, because the scholarship on the 'German-Jewish negative symbiosis', I argue, examines only one of the facets of the Jewish Question, the societal relations between Jews and Gentiles, but not the term in its entirety. I suggest this also involves examining the relationship between the Jews and the nation-state on a national as well as international level.

Alongside the body of indirect scholarly work on the Jewish Question there exists a more specific historiography on the Jewish Question. This literature attempts to understand the temporal and spatial limits of the term, and the agents that employed it. Two distinctive characteristics of this literature stand out. Firstly, there are far fewer works that analyse the Jewish Question. Secondly, beyond a focus on the term, they often share little else in common. This is a consequence of the primary sources on the Jewish Question, which vary considerably and featured in the economic, cultural, social and political sphere.[64] Alex Bein, who wrote the first book dedicated to the Jewish Question, recognised this issue writing, 'the Jewish Question is a problem that encompasses all areas of life and transcends the boundaries of specialised fields'.[65]

As a term without a fixed meaning, and chronology, scholars have tended to devise their own temporal and spatial parameters to the Jewish Question. Whilst Jacob Toury's often cited article on the semantics of the Jewish Question dated its first us-

61 George Mosse, *German Jews beyond Judaism* (Illinois: Hebrew Union College Press, 1985); George L. Mosse and Klaus L. Berghahn, *The German-Jewish Dialogue Reconsidered: A Symposium in Honor of George L. Mosse*, vol. 20, German Life and Civilization, (New York: Peter Lang, 1996); Amos Elon, *The Pity of It All: A Portrait of Jews in Germany 1743–1933* (New York: Picador, 2002).

62 Steven E. Aschheim and Vivian Liska, eds., *The German-Jewish Experience Revisited*, Perspectives on Jewish Texts and Contexts (Berlin and Boston: De Gruyter, 2015).

63 Lars Fischer, 'The Non-Jewish Question and Other "Jewish Questions" in Modern Germany (and Austria)', *The Journal of Modern History* 82, no. 4 (2010): 876–901.

64 Different approaches to the Jewish Question in the secondary literature abound. For a Marxist perspective see Enzo Traverso, *The Jewish Question: History of a Marxist Debate*, trans. Bernard Gibbons, Historical Materialism Book Series; 178 (Leiden and Boston: Brill, 2019). For a sociological and anthropological approach to the Jewish Question see Spencer and Fine, *Antisemitism and the Left*.

65 Alex Bein, *The Jewish Question: Biography of a World Problem*, trans. Harry Zohn (Rutherford, N.J.: Fairleigh Dickinson University Press, 1990), 57.

age in Europe to the eighteenth century, both Élisabeth Roudinesco and Alex Bein trace the antecedents of the Jewish Question back to medieval Christian-European anti-Judaism.[66] They also widen the temporal parameters of the Jewish Question to the establishment of the State of Israel. Roudinesco even suggests that the Jewish Question remains part of the challenge faced by Israelis to either 'turn their state into an even more secular and more egalitarian democracy' or to 'affirm the Jewish character of their state, thereby accepting that it will cease to be Israeli and democratic, becoming instead religious and racist'.[67] These works differ, however, in their geographical parameters to the Jewish Question. Roudinesco, for example, concentrates on French intellectual and political history whilst Bein examines the Jewish Question from a global perspective. Given the presence of the Jewish diaspora scattered around the globe, this is a common feature of research on the Jewish Question which extends beyond national histories.[68]

Historians such as Reinhard Rürup and Peter Pulzer have taken the opposite approach to the Jewish Question by focusing on the term in a specific time period (c. 1850–1870) and country (Germany) to make inferences about what it meant and how it functioned. Both authors contributed to the debate on the Jewish Question by clearly separating it into two principle aspects: emancipation and modern antisemitism.[69] Moreover, they both argue that the Jewish Question was a result of political structures and the development of German society. Rürup suggests that the slow and difficult development of modern bourgeois society, enabled the Jewish Question to remain a constant feature of political life in Germany.[70] Similarly, Pulzer argues that the Jewish Question persisted in Germany owing to the incomplete transition from a feudal absolutist to bourgeois-capitalist order as well as the continued governance by member-states, not the Reich, even after unification.[71] By examining the Jewish Question in relation to Germany's political development, the work of Reinhard Rürup and Peter Pulzer more closely aligns with my thesis. I, however, extend the temporal parameters of analysis beyond those of Rürup and Pulzer whose studies end in 1871 when, they contend, the constitutional Jewish Question disappeared. Moreover, rather than concentrating on what changes in German society shaped the Jewish Question, I shift

---

66 Roudinesco, *Revisiting the Jewish Question*; Bein, *The Jewish Question*.

67 Roudinesco, *Revisiting the Jewish Question*, 185.

68 See Lawrence D. Kritzman, ed., *Auschwitz and After: Race, Culture and 'the Jewish Question' in France* (Oxford, New York: Routledge, 1995); John Doyle Klier, *Russia Gathers Her Jews: The Origins of the 'Jewish Question' in Russia, 1772–1825* (Illinois: Northern Illinois University Press, 1986).

69 Reinhard Rürup, 'Emancipation and Crisis: The "Jewish Question" in Germany, 1850–1890', *Leo Baeck Institute Year Book* 20 (1975): 13–25; Pulzer, *Jews and the German State*, 28–43.

70 Reinhard Rürup, *Emanzipation und Antisemitismus: Studien zur 'Judenfrage' der bürgerlichen Gesellschaft* (Göttingen: Vandenhoeck & Ruprecht, 1975).

71 Pulzer, *Jews and the German State*, 34–37.

the focus to instead asking what the Jewish Question reveals about the dynamics of German politics.

In order to study how the Jewish Question functioned in German politics, I examine two levels of political discourse: one at the level of government and the other at the political cultural level. With regard to the former, I rely on an array of printed and manuscript sources, from the minutes of parliamentary sessions and committees to internal correspondence from the Foreign Ministry, War Ministry and Ministry of the Interior, which I collected through archival visits to the Federal, Foreign Ministry and War Ministry archives.

Although this work concerns the Reichstag, Supreme Army Command, Foreign Ministry and War Ministry it does not follow the traditional study of political or military history.[72] Extending beyond the traditional objects of analysis in political history, I situate political events and ideas within their cultural context in line with the method of 'new political history'.[73] I examine the influence of lesser-known individuals such as lawyers and journalists in German politics through their engagement with German diplomats, the submission of memorandums and the publication of political commentaries in popular newspapers. Rather than studying political structures, I investigate Germany's political culture by looking at the role of ideas in politics as well as the informal behaviours that lead to political action.[74] The lesser-known individuals of this book, though not involved in the inner circles of political decision-making, wielded significant influence in domestic and foreign affairs. They include Max Bodenheimer, Franz Oppenheimer, Oskar Cohn, Richard Lichtheim, Oskar Cassel and Hugo Preuss. Their political actions testify to the different manifestations of power in Wilhelmine Germany.

Whilst the focus of this book is on political theory and praxis, I do not intend to provide an exhaustive examination of the Jewish Question as a political term. Rather I use the Jewish Question as an analytical tool to investigate German politics. Exploring a series of moments when Jewish questions catalysed debates about the German nation-state, I study these ideas on rights, religion and nationhood in their particularised and changing forms, not as abstract or perennial concepts.[75]

The Jewish Question distils otherwise overwhelming and complicated political ideas and practices in the German state and nationalism. The term itself speaks to the relationship between society and the individual, minority groups and the state. As a

---

72 See Geoffrey R. Elton, *Political History: Principles and Practice* (London: Allen Lane, 1970).
73 See David M. Craig, '"High Politics" and the "New Political History"', *The Historical Journal* 53, no. 2 (2010): 453–75.
74 See Ronald P. Formisano, 'The Concept of Political Culture', *The Journal of Interdisciplinary History* 31, no. 3 (2001): 393–426.
75 McCormick and Gordon stress the importance of not conflating 'continuity with teleology'. Peter Eli Gordon and John P. McCormick, *Weimar Thought: A Contested Legacy* (Princeton: University Press, 2013), 4.

minority group living within a relatively homogenous nation, German Jews both had to confront and were frequently confronted by questions relating to the extent of their acculturation, (legal) integration and identity formation.

Alex Bein writes that 'three factors combined in the consciousness of the Jews from the beginning: the one God as the God of Israel, the people of Israel and the land of Israel'.[76] This eternal covenant with its inseparable parts became the basis of Jewish consciousness, a people, linked by a monolithic religion to the land of Israel. This union of people, religion and territory, offers an insight into the complex interrelationship between political and communal structures in the modern nation-state. Examining how politicians and political commentators approached the discussion on the place of the Jews in German society enables an assessment not only of the unique attributes associated with German Jewry, but more importantly what it meant to belong to the German Empire.

In as much as German Jews had to decide on the extent of their acculturation into German society, in line with the nineteenth century Self-Other dialectic the Jews became a subject against which to define the parameters of German nationhood and statehood. The Jewish Question exposed the hypocrisies and disparities within the nation-state model whereby Jews held the rights of German citizens but were often denied their status as fellow nationals.

Given that from its genesis the Jewish Question was riddled with contradictions, using it as a prism is not without its difficulties. Whilst broadly speaking, the term was used in the context of judgments on the place of Jews in the modern European polity it could concern questions of the law, society, culture, politics such that any discussion of the Jewish Question could at once refer to all or one of these aspects. As a result, the Jewish Question was used to discuss, sometimes simultaneously, race, religion, identity, demographics, citizenship and sovereignty.

The purpose behind using the term also varied considerably. On the whole, the Jewish Question was invoked to problematise Jewish existence in German society, and thus was often associated with antisemitism. And yet, the Jewish Question was also instrumentalised as a means to a strategic end. For example, the German Foreign Office used it during the Paris Peace Conference to juxtapose the barbarity of the Poles to the civility of the Germans and, on this basis, demand minority protections in the peace treaty with Poland.[77]

The existence of so many appropriations of the term had to do with the phrase itself. Often, whilst worded in the singular, the Jewish Question was used to describe a host of issues. In turn, related Jewish questions were frequently discussed without the explicit invocation of the term itself. In 1981 Robert Weltsch, Editor-in-Chief of

---

76 Bein, *The Jewish Question*, 52.
77 'Document 57: German Counterproposals of May 29, 1919' in Alma Luckau, *The German Delegation at the Paris Peace Conference*, 2nd ed. (New York: Howard Fertig, 1971), 306–405, especially, 338.

the *Jüdische Rundschau*, reflected on the German Jewish Question in his book of the same name. Having lived in the Austro-Hungarian Empire, the Weimar Republic, and the National Socialist Dictatorship, Weltsch described the ubiquity of the term and its flexibility according to the context and agent. He wrote,

> it should be evident that throughout the stormy history of the Jewish people in recent centuries hardly any domain has been left untouched, directly or indirectly, by the crucial concept of the Jewish Question.[78]

Scope

The years of the First World War and its immediate aftermath offer a convenient timespan to investigate the dynamics of political processes including constitutional transgressions within Germany. Jewish questions as they arose in 1914, 1916 and 1919 exposed the Empire at crucial transitional periods on the path towards the Republic. They provide an insight into a country caught between its past and future. 1919 marks the end of this book as following the ratification of a pluralistic democratic constitution, the replacement of an Empire with a Republic and as Germany negotiated its new place in the world, a different set of problems, questions and debates emerged.

Examining the shifts in the frequency of the use of the term *Judenfrage* in German publications illustrates that in the years proceeding, and during the First World War there was a steady increase in German publications referencing the Jewish Question.[79] From the first German Reich to the Third Reich, the use of the term *Judenfrage* increased in frequency in three periods, between 1876–1884 and 1912–1919 and again after 1926.

The first period coincides with the infamous 'Antisemitism Dispute' in Berlin (starting in 1879), which saw the publication of over four hundred pamphlets relating to Jewish questions.[80] The 1870s were overshadowed by the gradual rise of political antisemitism, which found institutional manifestation in the 1887 Reichstag elections when, for the first time ever, an openly antisemitic party won a seat.[81] And yet despite this rising

---

78 Quoted in Otto Kulka, 'Introduction' in Rena R. Auerbach, *The "Jewish Question" in German-speaking Countries, 1848–1914: A bibliography*, Vidal Sassoon International Centre for the Study of Antisemitism (New York; London: Garland, 1994), x. Within the parameters of a German Jewish Question from 1848 to 1914, Auerbach lists over 2,000 documents (articles, essays, books, pamphlets) dealing with the subject.
79 This information was collected using the digital tool, Google N-gram. This tool searches all German publications from 1871 to 1933 which feature the term *Judenfrage*.
80 Smith, *The Continuities of German History*, 173. See also chapter one for the *Antisemitismusstreit*.
81 Several parties campaigned on antisemitic platforms including the Christian-Socialist Party *(Christlich-Soziale Partei)*, German Reform Party *(Deutsche Reformpartei)*, German-Socialist Reform Party *(Deutsch-Soziale Reformpartei)*, German-Socialist Party *(Deutsch-Soziale Partei)* and as of 1907, the Economic Union

political antisemitism the number of publications concerning the *Judenfrage* did not increase, suggesting that the term did not only feature in antisemitic pamphlets.

The frequency increased once again from 1912 to 1919, coinciding with the 1912 Reichstag elections, when for the first time ever, the Social Democratic Party won the highest number of seats, the First World War and the Paris Peace Conference. Waning in the period of the early Weimar Republic, the term became popular once again in the latter half of the 1920s when the National Socialist Party was beginning its political ascent. Notably, there are several limitations to using digital tools to assess the frequency of the term, Jewish Question, in German publications. The data is compiled only from digitised publications and therefore excludes any manuscripts that have not yet been digitised. Moreover, the data does not reveal the details of each publication whether they are fiction or non-fiction, literary or academic. It is also not possible to infer if only documents with *Judenfrage* in the title have been included or also those referencing the word in the text.

Tracing the occurrences of the phrase *Judenfrage* in the stenographic reports of parliamentary sessions,[82] reveals that the phrase was used a total of ninety-nine times over this seventy-year period. There was a notable absence of the term in the parliamentary debates of the Third Reich suggesting that either separate meetings on the Jewish Question were held (such as the Wannsee Conference) or, more generally, the period saw the gradual erosion of all parliamentary authority.

The term appeared frequently throughout this seventy-year period in reference to antisemitism. Either it was invoked by antisemites wishing to rescind Jewish emancipation or by individuals countering these demands. The term was also used frequently to condemn the immigration of foreign, mostly Russian, Jews into Germany, often following violent pogroms. This accounts for the increased use of the term in the 1890s (the Pale Settlement pogroms), 1905 (Kiev and Odessa pogrom), and, in part, from 1917 to 1925 (collapse of the Russian Empire). Germany was not often the final destination but rather an important transit zone for Eastern European Jews escaping violence in the Russian Empire. This did not stop the fear that *Ostjuden* (as they were often referred to) would settle in Germany.

The second discussion in which the Jewish Question featured prominently was in reference to the exclusivity of promotions in the (Prussian) army. These discussions were mostly raised by Jewish politicians in left-wing parties (Social Democratic Party, Progressive Party) and Catholic Centre Party politicians who argued against denomi-

---

(Wirtschaftliche Vereinigung). See Gerhard A. Ritter and Merith Niehuss, *Wahlgeschichtliches Arbeitsbuch. Materialien zur Statistik des Kaiserreichs 1871–1918* (München: C. H. Beck, 1980), 38–43. For a translated table of these results see [https://bit.ly/2Jba9cW, accessed 13/03/19].

82 I traced the term using the database of the *Verhandlung des deutschen Reichstags.* The files end in 1941 and thus I could not trace the term any further than this. Whilst the database brought up all files containing the term (e. g. indexes, biographical reports on ministers who might have written on the 'Jewish Question'), I focused my research specifically on the use of the term in parliamentary sessions.

national discrimination in the Officer Corps in the years leading up to the outbreak of war in 1914. The re-emergence of these debates in the aftermath of a census authorised to count Jews serving on the front lines, is the subject of chapter three. The link between the Jewish Question and discussions on secularism within the German state can also be located in parliamentary sittings concerning primary and secondary education. These discussions, however, are not the focus of chapter three as they were not overtly political but also delved into the social sphere. Moreover, education was regulated at the state level, whereas I am interested in federal, high-level political debates on the Jewish Question.

Nearing the end of the war and into the first years of the Weimar Republic, the frequency of the *Judenfrage* increased again. It mostly was used in reference to (Jewish) minority rights, both within Germany and Romania where guarantees, enshrined in the Treaty of Berlin in 1878, had been violated and as aforementioned, with regard to the immigration of Eastern European Jews into Germany. Chapter four focuses on the discussion of (Jewish) minority rights in Germany specifically with regard to the Weimar constitution. However, as a result of the scarcity of discussions on Jewish rights in Romania these are not the focus of the chapter. Neither is the subject of Eastern European immigration into Germany as this became an issue in the first years of the Weimar Republic (c. 1921), which is beyond the scope of this book.

I focus on the years 1914 to 1919 in order to analyse this crucial period of transition in Germany history where I argue Jewish questions had practical implications. Whilst the Jewish Question was invoked more frequently in parliament in the period preceding the war (eighty-six times) it was often either in the context of antisemitism or protesting discrimination against Jews. During the First World War, when discriminations against Jews were removed, these protests took on a new meaning. They concerned preserving legal and social equality and not reverting back to former discriminations. During the Weimar Republic the Jewish Question was only raised four times, the last time in 1923. This testifies to the distinctive political change that took place in Germany whereby the Jewish Question was not invoked in parliamentary sessions to make antisemitic comments or raised in order to protest continued discriminations against Jews. The four times it was used, once concerned the debate on minority rights – see chapter four – whilst the other three times was in reference to the immigration of Eastern European Jews into Germany.

Chapter outline

Chapter one offers a genealogy of the Jewish Question tracing the intellectual antecedents of the term prior to World War One. In historicising the Jewish Question, chapter one provides clarification on who utilised the term and what it meant for individual agents. Rather than following a linear trajectory, chapter one reveals that at particular moments in time between 1842 (when the term took hold as a popular catchword) and 1914, a discussion on the Jewish Question sparked a larger debate on the modern state and the place of Jews within it. Several themes pertaining to the Jewish Question emerged out of these debates and resurfaced during the First World War. These included the role of religion in the state, the relationship between nationality, patriotism, citizenship and the divided Eastern-Western Jewish experience.

Chapter two examines the first years of World War One when the Axis powers (Germany and the Austro-Hungarian Empire) occupied West Russian territory (an area which came to be known as *Ober-Ost*) and were confronted with governing a population of approximately six million Jews. Responding to the politically opportune moment, representatives of the Committee for the East (Max Bodenheimer and Richard Lichtheim) submitted memoranda outlining the benefits of collaboration between the German government and Jews who, they argued, spoke a dialect of German, Yiddish. In return for protection, Russian Jews were offered as mediators of German interests in Eastern Europe and Palestine which would help secure Germany's colonial and Great Power ambitions. Whilst neither of these plans came to fruition – both petered out in the winter of 1916 due to several developments in the war – the discussions demonstrated how the German army was confronted with a practical Jewish Question in its foreign policy objectives. The important legacy of this relationship was evidenced when after the war a Jewish Affairs department was established in the German Foreign Ministry.

Chapter three focuses on the year 1916, specifically on an event in domestic politics, the authorisation by the War Ministry of a decree to count the number of Jews serving on the front lines. The 'Jew census' (*Judenzählung*), as it was termed, revealed the fault lines in the Empire as it was trapped in its past prejudices and future as a modern state. Whilst in principle the constitution and Kaiser Wilhelm II advocated religious tolerance and unity, the disconnect between law and reality exposed the Empire as a state wishing to exert control and single out one of its minority groups. Paying lip service to the civic truce (*Burgfrieden*) declared by the Kaiser, the Minister of War's announcement of the census sparked a debate in parliament and in public on the place of religion within Germany and the possibility of a post-war *de facto* modern secular state. Whilst the decree was rescinded after a few months and Germany did not descend down the path of government sanctioned antisemitism the event had a lasting legacy within far-right circles as it was instrumentalised to blame Germany's defeat in the war on the Jews.

Chapter four turns to the end of the war when Hugo Preuss was authorised to draft a constitution for the new Republic. As the wording of the constitution was being finalised, a Jewish Question emerged out of a discussion on the wording of Article 113, the policy on minority rights. Ultimately, the wording of the article saw only minor changes from the initial draft and yet focusing on the end result would ignore the process. In the course of events a series of discussions unfolded in parliament and subcommittees on how to categorise minority rights. It invoked a discussion on how to define the majority and exposed the complex understandings of rights, citizenship and the concept of nationality within Germany.

Chapter five builds on chapter four by contextualising constitutional debates within Germany in light of emerging international principles on minority rights as discussed at the Paris Peace Conference in 1919. It focuses on the preparations for peace by the German delegation who organised a meeting on the Jewish Question in the Office for the Peace Negotiations. Despite these provisions, the German delegation was not invited into negotiations with the Allies and had little influence over minority rights. During the Paris Peace Conference, minority rights in the Treaty of Versailles became a German, not Jewish, Question. The discussion concerned Germany's future borders and the rights of German minorities living abroad.

In the conclusion I summarise how Jewish questions exposed a series of critical junctures in the political development of the German Empire. Turning to Jewish questions during the inter-war years, I trace both its positive bifurcation in the Weimar constitution as well as its negative bifurcation in the antisemitic tropes of Judeo-Bolshevism and the *Dolchstoßlegende,* suggesting further avenues of research. Finally, I reflect on my findings against the backdrop of political developments in the Federal Republic. I analyse the pertinence of Jewish questions in Germany's process of coming to terms with its past and show how the discussions which Jewish questions catalysed on the German state in Wilhelmine Germany continue to resonate in the Berlin Republic today.

I   A genealogy of the Jewish Question

'What once again has been called the Jewish Question is merely a German Question'[1] declared Moritz Lazarus, Professor of Philosophy at the University of Berlin, to an auditorium of students at the Academy for the Science of Judaism (*Hochschule für die Wissenschaft des Judenthums*) in December 1879. In his lecture entitled *Was heißt natio-nal?* Lazarus was responding to a wave of renewed anti-Jewish agitation in Germany. Disputing the claims of a separate Jewish and German nationality; Lazarus argued that the German nation was heterogeneous. The idea of the 'will', he suggested, enabled distinct and formally hostile tribes (*Stämme*) to unite to form the German Reich and it was this concept of the will (the willingness to form a community of national spirit) that defined the nation. Lazarus explored the Jewish Question in order to expose the fault lines of the German Question, namely upon what criteria the German nation-state was based: language, descent, religion, geography or culture?

Lazarus identified a relationship between the Jewish Question and the German state. He suggested that it had not been recognised despite existing for years prior to 1879. Lazarus's lecture reveals that the Jewish Question did not emerge in 1914 but had intellectual antecedents. In what follows, I trace a series of episodes from 1842 to 1912 when the Jewish Question was debated and revealed the hopes and fears of the German state and its Jewish minority. I investigate why the Jewish Question became a ubiquitous term, who employed it, what vocabulary they used, and how it was under-stood. Examining the pre-history of the Jewish Question is crucial to understanding the ideas and discourse concurrent with the term, including investigating which con-cepts changed, which remained constant, and why. The Jewish questions which arose in parliamentary debates during and after the First World War, which became practi-cally relevant for German domestic and foreign policy, did not operate in a vacuum.

---

[1] Moritz Lazarus, *Was heißt national? Ein Vortrag von Moritz Lazarus* (Berlin: Dümmlers Verlag, 1880), 5 [https://bit.ly/2VqUbRV, accessed 19/03/19]. For a translated English version see Moritz Lazarus, 'What Does National Mean? A Lecture', [2 December 1879] in *The State, the Nation, and the Jews: Liberalism and the Antisemitism Dispute in Bismarck's Germany*, trans. Marcel Stoetzler (Lincoln, Nebraska: University of Nebraska Press, 2008), 317–359.

They invoked concepts that had a longer legacy associated with the Jewish Question, tracing back to earlier debates on religious equality, cultural homogeneity, nationhood and citizenship.

From 1842 until 1912, several publications concerning the so-called Jewish Question written by Gentile and Jewish authors sparked heated debates on secularism in the German state, the *Kulturnation* versus the *Staatsnation*, the relationship between nation and state, nationality and citizenship, and the divide between the lived experience of Western and Eastern Jews. These authors and their works were characterised by a shared vocabulary and semantic consideration of the Jewish Question and betrayed a similar approach to Jewish questions by considering them not in isolation but as a window into political questions.

Bruno Bauer (1809–1882), Heinrich von Treitschke (1834–1896), Franz Oppenheimer (1864–1943) and Werner Sombart (1863–1941), were all prominent public intellectuals who made crucial contributions to the discussion on the Jewish Question. Of the various notable publications by the aforementioned authors, the following section will focus in-depth on publications which triggered debates on the Jewish Question including, Bruno Bauer's, *Die Judenfrage* (1843), *Unsere Aussichten* (1879) by Heinrich von Treitschke, Franz Oppenheimer's *Stammesbewusstsein und Volksbewusstsein* (1910) and *Die Zukunft der Juden* (1911) by Werner Sombart. Alongside these more well-known publications and debates, there existed lesser-known ones that also sparked heated debates on the Jewish Question. This chapter will focus on two pamphlets written by Zionists that crucially presented different answers to similar questions. The first was published anonymously, entitled *Der Nationaljude als Staatsbürger* (1897), the second by Moritz Goldstein (1880–1977) who made his name publicly known through his article *Der deutsch-jüdische Parnass* (1912). Focusing on these six publications and the debates they generated on the Jewish Question I will examine the concepts, ideas, and frames of references that emerged in order to demonstrate their later relevance to practical Jewish questions during the First World War.

These publications indicate that the cultural sphere was the site where political ideas were rehearsed and refined before they were deployed in institutional settings. This, however, is not to say that the Jewish Question was not discussed in parliament before 1914. Several historians have shown how the Jewish Question was a feature of parliamentary debates preceding unification, embedded within discussions about the constitution.[2] Notably, however, a political-constitutional Jewish Question was thought to have ended when unification brought the emancipation of Jews in all German states. Taking this as my departure point, I demonstrate that the Jewish Question continued as a prominent feature of German politics. Firstly, however, this chapter will survey the intellectual precedents of the debates considered in chapters two to four.

───────

2 See, for example, Rürup, *Emanzipation und Antisemitismus*; Pulzer, *Jews and the German State*.

Reform in the Prussian state: Bruno Bauer's *Die Judenfrage* (1842)

In 1842 Bruno Bauer, the left Hegelian philosopher, published a pamphlet entitled, *Die Judenfrage*, in which he famously developed his critique of the concept of emancipation and religion in the state.[3] Bauer was responding to a draft law which began circulating in 1841 which proposed standardising the legal status of Jews in Prussia. Those of the 'Jewish faith' in Prussia had first been granted civil rights and limited political rights in March 1812. They were declared 'natives' (*Einländer*) and Prussian citizens.[4] Under Section 9, on the admission of Jews into public service and government office, the edict intimated the future promise of regulation by law, although this was not granted until the constitutional charter of Prussia in 1848.[5] Thus, in 1842, the subject of full Jewish emancipation had not yet been concluded.

In the 1841 draft law, rather than granting Prussian Jews the rights which they had been afforded under Napoleonic occupation, the law proposed the reinstatement of medieval laws, recognising the Jews as a corporation, which were still being applied to Jewish communities in eastern Prussia. Facing strong opposition, the draft law, also known as the *Judengesetz* never came to fruition.[6] Nonetheless, its circulation triggered an animated debate on 'the meaning of Jewish history, the meaning of Jewish law, and the relationship of Jews to the state'.[7]

The subject of Bauer's pamphlet had a longer legacy than the 1841 draft law and earlier debates informed Bauer's thinking. Specifically, in the 1780s the archivist of the Prussian War Office, Christian Wilhelm von Dohm, and the Enlightenment philosopher, Moses Mendelssohn had debated Jewish emancipation. Dohm was the first Prussian official to advocate for the immediate unconditional granting of almost full equality to the Jews.[8] To be worthy of these rights Dohm demanded Jewish regeneration and rehabilitation, a position that though one of the first of its kind, would become a common trait of German liberals.[9] Responding to Dohm, Mendelssohn argued that the

---

3 Bruno Bauer developed this critique over two articles, *Die Judenfrage* (Braunschweig: Verlag von Friedrich Otto, 1843) [https://bit.ly/2H1qMn2, accessed 08/05/19] and 'Die Fähigkeit der heutigen Juden und Christen, frei zu werden' in *Einundzwanzig Bogen aus der Schweiz*, ed. Georg Herwegh (Zürich und Winterthur, 1843), 56–71.

4 Mahler, *Jewish Emancipation*, 32–35.

5 Ibid.

6 Toury, '"The Jewish Question" A Semantic Approach', 93.

7 Julius Carlebach, *Karl Marx and the Radical Critique of Judaism* (London, 1978), 68. Quoted in Yoav Peled, 'From Theology to Sociology: Bruno Bauer and Karl Marx on the Question of Jewish Emancipation', *History of Political Thought* 13, no. 3 (1992): 466.

8 Ismar Schorsch, *Jewish Reactions to German Anti-Semitism, 1870–1914*, (New York and London: Columbia University Press, 1972), 2.

9 Wilhelm von Humboldt also supported emancipation in the hope that it would precipitate the dissolution of organised Jewry. This view was similarly expressed by Heinrich von Treitschke as well as Theodor Mommsen. Most advocates of this view desired that Jews abandoned all Jewish particularities and take to the baptismal front.

improvement of the civil status of the Jews was dependent on the modernisation of the Prussian Monarchy.[10] The question of Jewish emancipation according to Mendelssohn had exposed the limits of state reform. Influenced by the work of Mendelssohn,[11] Bauer framed his response to the subject of the 1841 *Judengesetz* as a response to the *Judenfrage*.[12] Bauer's article prompted a number of responses and helped propel the term *Judenfrage* into mainstream discourse, initially in Germany, and subsequently abroad.[13]

Bauer criticised the allegiance to religion by the state and Jewry. For Bauer only once all religious privileges were abolished could Jews and Christians be 'emancipated' in the state. Rather than equality, Bauer saw power and privilege as the principle governing the Prussian Christian Monarchy. Religion was merely instrumentalised to uphold subordination. Thus, only with state reform, specifically the abolition of religion, could Jews be integrated into the national community, according to Bauer. Elevating the importance of the secular state to international proportions Bauer created the dichotomy of the 'chimera' nation (governed by religious adherence) to the 'real' nation (based on universal human rights). 'Not the Jews only, we, too, are no longer content with the chimera. We want to be real nations', wrote Bauer.[14] He elevated the Jewish Question from a particular concern about the status of Jews, to advocating more generally for religious and political reform.

Following the publication of several articles on the *Judengesetz* in 1842, including Bauer's radical thesis on the emancipation of the state from religion, a public debate about the Jewish Question unfolded. The debate primarily concerned Jewish legal equality in Prussia. However, it also opened up the question of the possibilities and constraints of political reform in Prussia. Bauer's publication elicited several responses, most famously by his own pupil and fellow young left Hegelian, Karl Marx who published his reply in 1844, *Zur Judenfrage*.[15] Marx criticised Bauer's definition of emancipation distinguishing between emancipation in the state, the granting of citizenship rights ('political emancipation'), and emancipation from the state, from 'commerce and money' ('human emancipation'), the latter of which Marx associated with Juda-

---

10 Christian Wilhelm von Dohm, *Über die bürgerliche Verbesserung der Juden*, (Berlin, Stettin: Friedrich Nicolai, 1781). Moses Mendelssohn *Jerusalem oder über religiöse Macht und Judentum* (Berlin: Friedrich Maurer, 1783).

11 On Mendelssohn's influence on Bauer see Peled, 'From Theology to Sociology', 467–68.

12 Bruno Bauer is associated with first using the term the Jewish Question in the German context. See Anne Purschwitz, 'Von der "bürgerlichen Verbesserung" zur "Judenfrage": die Formierung eines Begriffs zwischen 1781 und 1843', in *Die 'Judenfrage': ein Europäisches Phänomen?* (Berlin: Metropol Verlag, 2013), 23–53. Although a series of articles, employing the latter term were published in 1842, Bauer's article was one of two articles that was re-edited and issued as a booklet the following year. For a list of these pamphlets, see, Toury, '"The Jewish Question" A Semantic Approach', 93.

13 Toury, '"The Jewish Question" A Semantic Approach', 93.

14 Bauer, *Die Judenfrage*, 61.

15 Marx also criticised Bauer's argument on emancipation in *Die heilige Familie* (1845) written with Friedrich Engels. On the so-called 'Marx-Bauer debate' see Peled, 'From Theology to Sociology'.

ism.[16] Thus emancipation could only occur for Marx once Christians and Jews were liberated from the 'empirical nature of Judaism', that was 'commerce and its presuppositions'.[17] Whilst Marx would retrospectively come to be known as Bauer's most famous respondent,[18] Bauer's article elicited numerous responses from well-known figures including the socialist Karl Grün, the theologian Friedrich Wilhelm Ghillany and several responses from Jewish authors such as Gabriel Reisser, Sammuel Hirsch, Abraham Geiger.[19]

The Jewish respondents to Bauer refuted his explanation of the economic activities of Jews as well as his ahistorical analysis of Judaism. They also condemned Bauer for claiming that Jews were not a legitimate part of the modern state.[20] Of the two most famous Gentile contemporaries to reply to Bauer, Ghillany utilised Bauer's position to provide further support for his own view on emancipation, namely that Judaism needed to reform.[21] Grün, on the other hand, took issue with Bauer's position on the modern era. For Grün in the modern state religion could continue to exist in the private sphere as in the United States of America where Judaism had already reformed. It was society that was at fault for separating the Jews, according to Grün. He argued that equality must come through a single constitution for all religious denominations.[22]

Bauer's article and the subsequent public debate embedded the Jewish Question within the discussion of reform in the Prussian state. Moreover, the term, *Judenfrage*, which had previously been used sparingly, caught on as a political catchword in reference to the subject of Jewish legal equality. The Jews were described as a religion and it was on this basis that proponents argued for their equality within the state. They sought to uphold the rights that had been granted to Jews in Prussia under Napoleonic rule. Opponents, however, restricting liberal and constitutional reforms in neighbour-

---

16 Karl Marx, 'Zur Judenfrage', vol. 1 (Paris: Deutsch-Französische Jahrbücher, 1844) in Karl Marx / Friedrich Engels Werke, Band 1 (Berlin: Dietz Verlag, 1976), 347.

17 It is in this latter point that one can see the origins of Marx's critique on capitalism Karl Marx, 'On the Jewish Problem (1844)', in *The Jew in the Modern World, A Documentary History*, ed. Paul Mendes-Flohr and Jehuda Reinharz, 2nd ed., (Oxford and New York: Oxford University Press, 1995), 327.

18 For recent accounts which place prominence on Marx's essay see Robert Fine and Philip Spencer, 'Marx's Defence of Jewish Emancipation and Critique of the Jewish Question', in *Antisemitism and the Left* (Manchester: Manchester University Press, 2018), 30–43; Roland Boer, 'Friends, Radical and Estranged: Bruno Bauer and Karl Marx', *Religion and Theology* 17, no. 3–4 (2010): 358–401; Peled, 'From Theology to Sociology'.

19 For a detailed analysis of the responses to Bauer see Nathan Rotenstreich, 'For and against Emancipation: The Bruno Bauer Controversy', *The Leo Baeck Institute Year Book* 4, no. 1 (1959): 3–36; Toury, '"The Jewish Question" A Semantic Approach', 102–5. Leopold acknowledges Bauer's numerous respondents but does not dedicate any space to discussing their views on his article, David Leopold, 'The Hegelian Antisemitism of Bruno Bauer', *History of European Ideas* 25, no. 4 (July 1999): 180.

20 Rotenstreich, 'For and against Emancipation', 12–18.

21 For Ghillany the historical conditions that Judaism needed to overcome included praying for the resumption of sacrifices, the abasement of women and circumcision. Ibid, 18–21.

22 Ibid, 21–23.

ing European countries, held onto the medieval system of assigning Jews limited rights as a corporation and upheld Prussia as a Christian state, thus making the argument for granting emancipation based on individual rights futile.

The 1842 debate revealed that the Jewish Question not only concerned Jewish emancipation, but also the modernising potential of the Prussian state. For Bauer, the Jewish Question was merely the symptom of a greater underlying cause: the freeing of humanity from religious prejudice. And yet, with the failure to establish a constitutional state in the 1848 revolutions, and the disbanding of the Young Hegelians, the hopes for the establishment of a modern secular nation-state dissipated and with it erstwhile, the Jewish Question.

Race and the nation: Heinrich von Treitschke's *Unsere Aussichten* (1879)

When in 1842 the Jewish Question emerged as a popular catchword it concerned the practical question of Jewish emancipation in Prussia. Whilst equal rights for all religions was enshrined in the 1849 St Paul's Church constitution and constitutional charter of Prussia, with the repression of the revolutionary wave, it was only in 1869 when this provision was preserved within the constitution of the North German Confederation. On this basis, Jews as members of a community of faith, were granted full rights in North German Confederation and by 1871 in all German states acceding to the German Empire.[23]

Eight years after Jews had been granted full legal rights in the German Empire, a flurry of publications deploying the term, *Judenfrage* appeared in print. Although the term remained the same, its subject had changed. Under scrutiny was not the topic of Jewish emancipation but the necessity of Jewish assimilation for the unity of the German Empire. At the time of unification 1.25 % of the German population was Jewish (512, 153).[24] Jews were one of the smallest minority groups in Imperial Germany compared to the Catholics (36 %), Poles (8 %), Alsatians (3.6 %) and Danes (0.97 %).[25] Conversions to Christianity were gaining in popularity and between 1871 to 1909 around 3 % of the Jewish population had been baptised.[26] Mixed marriages were also on the rise and some contemporaries began to predict the disappearance of the Jewish minority within a few generations.[27]

---

23 Mahler, *Jewish Emancipation*, 57–58.
24 Berghahn, *Imperial Germany*, 102.
25 Otto Pflanze, *Bismarck and the Development of Germany, Volume II: The Period of Consolidation, 1871–1880* (Princeton, New Jersey: Princeton University Press, 2014), 114–17; Berghahn, *Imperial Germany*, 96–123.
26 Berghahn, *Imperial Germany*, 102.
27 Niewyk, *The Jews in Weimar Germany*, 98.

In spite of these 'assimilationist' trends amongst the German Jewish minority, when the Jewish Question arose once again in public debate, unlike in 1842 it did not concern religion in Prussian state, but rather cultural homogeneity in the German nation. The article which sparked this discussion was written by the National Liberal political commentator and Professor of History at the University of Berlin, Heinrich von Treitschke. Published in November 1879 in the popular journal the Prussian Yearbook, his article was entitled *Unsere Aussichten*, 'Our Prospects'.

The 'German Jewish Question' for Heinrich von Treitschke was how to amalgamate the Jewish people into the German nation and avoid a German-Jewish mixed culture. According to Treitschke, a homogeneous, unified culture (*Einheitskultur*) was imperative for the unity of the German nation, which was still at an embryonic stage. The necessity of this question was precipitated for Treitschke by the mass immigration of an 'alien people' (Eastern European Jews) into Germany.[28] The answer he offered was simple. Treitschke implored Jews to become German 'without qualification'. By suggesting the answer to the Jewish Question was assimilation, Treitschke engaged with a traditionally liberal argument.[29] The paradox in Treitschke's argument was that whilst promoting assimilation, he described Jews using racialised language, affording them peculiar ethnic, national, traits. In doing so, Treitschke distanced himself from the liberal premise that Judaism was a religion and undermined his own argument.

Over three articles Treitschke refined his position on the Jewish Question. These were collectively published as a brochure entitled *Ein Wort über unser Judenthum*. The brochure reached a wide audience, and as a result of its popularity was printed in four editions. Between the winter of 1879 to the summer of 1881 a heated public debate on the Jewish Question, producing at times violent outbreaks, erupted.[30] This debate sparked by Treitschke's article and which over the years has received extensive scholarly attention came to be known as the 'Berlin Antisemitism Dispute' (*Berliner Antisemitismusstreit*).[31]

---

28 In 1880, 10,000 Eastern European Jews were expelled from Germany. Marion A. Kaplan, *The Making of the Jewish Middle Class: Women, Family, and Identity in Imperial Germany* (Oxford University Press, 1991), 14.
29 Liberals favoured assimilation as they perceived Jewish particularities to be based on Jewish tradition rather than biological differences. By emphasising blood differences antisemites removed any 'hope of assimilation through the adoption of German customs and the Christian religion'. Tourlamain, *Völkisch Writers and National Socialism*, 26.
30 The most comprehensive sourcebook on the 'Berlin Antisemitism Dispute' is a two volume publication by the Centre for Antisemitism Research, Karsten Krieger, *Der 'Berliner Antisemitismusstreit,' 1879–1881: eine Kontroverse um die Zugehörigkeit der deutschen Juden zur Nation*, Kommentierte Quellenedition, 2 vols (München: K. G. Saur, 2003).
31 See Walter Boehlich, *Der Berliner Antisemitismusstreit*, Sammlung Insel; 6 (Frankfurt am Main: Insel-Verlag, 1965); Michael Meyer, 'Great Debate on Antisemitism – Jewish Reaction to New Hostility in Germany 1879–1881', *Leo Baeck Institute Year Book* 11, no. 1 (1966): 137–70; Marcel Stoetzler, *The State, the Nation, and the Jews: Liberalism and the Antisemitism Dispute in Bismarck's Germany* (Lincoln, Nebraska: University of Nebraska Press, 2008).

Treitschke's *Unsere Aussichten* began as a review of the eleventh volume of Heinrich Graetz's *Geschichte der Juden* (1870). Heinrich Graetz was one of the first historians to write on the history of the Jewish people from a Jewish perspective. Graetz dedicated over half of his eleventh volume to the history of Jews in Germany, despite German Jews representing less than a tenth of the world Jewish population.[32] Departing from the traditional theological narrative on Judaism, Graetz described a people with national characteristics including a unique history and politics and used the words *Stamm*, *Volk* and *Rasse* interchangeably to describe the Jews.[33] Treitschke who had begun engaging with Graetz's eleventh volume to write his own multi-volume, *Deutsche Geschichte im Neunzehnten Jahrhundert* (1878–1894) was infuriated by Graetz's historiography. Graetz had praised Jews who sought to integrate modernity into Judaism, paving the way for Jewish revival and rejuvenation, over Jews that assimilated.[34] For Treitschke, Graetz's narrative evidenced that some Jews were not upholding their side of the emancipation contract, the elimination of all national elements. It was against this backdrop that Treitschke framed his understanding of the Jewish Question.

Treitschke recognised that whilst the 'influence of Jewry on our national life [...] created much good in earlier times, nowadays [it] shows itself in many ways harmful', terming it a 'serious danger' and 'critical defect [*Schaden*] in the new German life'.[35] Treitschke's answer to this German Jewish Question was simple, assimilation. 'They should become Germans. They should feel themselves, modestly and properly, Germans – and this without prejudicing their faith and their ancient, holy memories, which we all hold in reverence' wrote Treitschke.[36] For Treitschke these 'ancient and holy memories' stemmed from the religion of Judaism. In accordance with the 1871 constitution, Treitschke suggested that Jews could continue to practice their faith as long as this did not infringe on their public life and participation within the German nation-state. He described any discussion of the revocation of Jewish emancipation an 'open injustice', distancing himself from this common antisemitic argument.[37]

The contradiction in Treitschke's article was that in making a liberal argument in favour of assimilation, he used language describing the Jews as a 'race', 'civilisation', 'Israelites', 'Semitic', 'people of such pure blood' to suggest that they exhibited distinct and collective differences to other Germans. Despite despising Graetz's recognition of the unique attributes of Jews as a nation and not a religion, Treitschke employed

---

32 Michael A. Meyer, 'Heinrich Graetz and Heinrich von Treitschke: A Comparison of Their Historical Images of the Modern Jew', *Modern Judaism* 6, no. 1 (1986): 1.
33 On Graetz's work see Stephen L. Sniderman, 'Bibliography of Works about Heinrich Graetz', *Studies in Bibliography and Booklore* 14 (1982): 41–49.
34 For a detailed account on how Graetz's historiography angered Treitschke see Meyer, 'Heinrich Graetz and Heinrich von Treitschke'.
35 Heinrich von Treitschke, 'Unsere Aussichten', *Preußische Jahrbücher* 44 (15 November 1879): 572.
36 Ibid, 573.
37 Ibid, 575.

similar language. In doing so, he undermined his own answer to the German Jewish Question. The significance of Treitschke's article was that he used the language of race in the context of a liberal response to the Jewish Question, providing this discourse with an unprecedented credibility.

Underpinning Treitschke's article was the necessity he saw in an *Einheitskultur*. It was on this basis that he voiced his fear of an 'era of a German-Jewish mixed culture' (*deutsch-jüdische Mischcultur*).[38] The root cause of the German Jewish Question for Treitschke was Germany's struggle for national unity. Given that German culture 'lack[ed] a national style, an instinctive pride, a thoroughly imprinted character' Treitschke opined that it had 'stood defenceless against alien essences' (*fremdes Wesen*).[39] For Treitschke, resolving the German Jewish Question was bound to the 'rise of the German state'. He praised Jews 'who understand that their racial brothers must adapt to the morality and ideas of their Christian fellow citizens'.[40]

Treitschke's article embodied liberal ambivalence. Whilst he suggested that there was a place for Jews in the German nation-state and offered them a path to become 'German without qualification', he left no room for an alternative route. Although Treitschke advocated a liberal pro-assimilation argument, which stemmed from the position that Jewish characteristics were not biological but lay in Jewish tradition he employed language to suggest the contrary. As Meyer writes, 'for Treitschke this was a liberal, and certainly a non-racist position. But, of course, it left no room for dialogue'.[41] Liberal ambivalence was demonstrated throughout Treitschke's article which was riddled with incompatible dualisms that suggested the impossibility of assimilation.[42]

The significance of Treitschke's article was that it shifted the parameters of the discussion on the Jewish Question. In 1842, the public debate on the Jewish Question considered Jews to be a confessional group and concentrated on their legal equality within the state. In 1879, Treitschke introduced the language of race into the Jewish Question and offered an answer on how to integrate the Jews into the German nation in order to create a singularly German *Einheitskultur*. The importance of Treitschke's article for the Jewish Question was that it revealed the ambivalence of term, evidenced by the inconsistencies in Treitschke's argument. This inconsistency in the Jewish Question only became apparent after 1871 when emancipation had effectively resolved the Jewish Question and yet the term re-surfaced in public discourse. It was further sub-

---

38 Ibid, 573.
39 Ibid, 575.
40 Ibid.
41 Meyer, 'Heinrich Graetz and Heinrich von Treitschke', 4.
42 Some of these dualisms included Treitschke's praise of Jews who embodied the 'good traits of the German spirit' including Mendelssohn, Veit, Riesser, whilst stressing that numerous other Jews lacked the 'goodwill' to become thoroughly German. He also outlined that most German cities have respectable Jewish firms, but that Jews 'share [the] guilt for [...] fraudulent business practices, and that base materialism of our day'. Ibid, 572–74.

stantiated in how the discussants approached the term, including Treitschke, whereby it was possible to advance a liberal argument whilst employing illiberal language.

Of the many respondents to Treitschke, one in particular stood out, the Jewish Professor of Philosophy at the University of Berlin, Moritz Lazarus. Lazarus argued that the German Empire was heterogenous and that the concept of the nation in Germany was based on the willingness to be part of the nation, an idea associated with the *Staatsnation* promulgated by the French academic Ernest Renan.[43] Lazarus's response deserves particular attention as both the ideas he formulated, and the language utilised continuously resurfaced in subsequent debates on the Jewish Question.

Moritz Lazarus criticised the importance of homogeneity in the nation in a lecture to the Academy for the Science of Judaism[44] held three weeks after the publication of Treitschke's article.[45] Attempting to answer the question posed by the title of his lecture, 'What does it mean to be national?', Lazarus concluded that the nation rested on subjective conditions, the self-understanding of a communal equality and belonging together (*Gleichheit*) and the individual will to be part of it.[46]

Lazarus began his lecture by surveying the work of his colleague Richard Boeckh[47] who dismissed all common 'misconceptions' on the foundations of nationality to conclude that language was the defining characteristic.[48] Lazarus expanded on the relevance of language and irrelevance of descent distinguishing between the objective (language) elements of national unity which alone cannot define the nation without its subjective (spirit) counterpart. Setting out his definition Lazarus outlined that

---

43 Ernest Renan, 'What is a nation?' [*Qu'est-ce qu'une Nation?* Paris: Sorbonne, 11 March 1882], in *Becoming National: A Reader*, ed. trans. Geoff Eley and Ronald Grigor Suny (Oxford; New York: Oxford University Press, 1996), 41–55.

44 Founded in 1819, the *Wissenschaft des Judentums* recognised Jews as a *Volk* but disputed the idea that nations needed an ethnic core.

45 Unlike Lazarus, Hermann Cohen agreed with Treitschke on the importance of a homogenous population. He saw religious unity as pivotal for German unity and the development of a modern *Kulturvolk*. Cohen's criticism of Treitschke was that he saw no glaring religious differences between Jews and Christians. Instead, Cohen argued that the Jewish religion had already begun to merge with Protestantism in historical and cultural terms. See Herman Cohen, 'Ein Bekenntniß in der Judenfrage' (1880), in Krieger, *Der 'Berliner Antisemitismusstreit'*, 337–60.

46 Lazarus, *Was heißt national?* 13.

47 Richard Boeckh (1894–1907) was a well-known demographer who worked for the Prussian Statistical Office. He developed a statistical method termed the 'B. method' which was later employed in all statistical offices of the Empire. Boeckh also published on the statistical significance of the language as a signifier of nationality.

48 For Boeckh, as for Lazarus, morals, customs, religion could not define the nation as differences in these could be found both within and across nations. Neither could territorial unity or state citizenship given the shifting of borders, the expansion of territory into colonies, leaving people of the same nationality distributed across different territories and states. Making a subtle stab at the 'facilely taken as synonymous' connection between nationality and descent, Lazarus pointed to the absence of any nationality of 'pure unmixed descent'. Left, like Boeckh, with language as a central component of national identity, Lazarus concluded it was the 'most essential category after all others have been refuted'. Ibid.

the concept of the nation arises out of the interventions by spiritual and historical conditions into naturally given differences; and a nation becomes a nation not according to
objective criteria such as descent, language, etc. but rather the subjective view of all those
who together consider themselves a nation.[49]

Distinguishing between 'the people' and 'the nation' Lazarus argued that 'the nation' was created by individuals coming together to overcome their isolation. This awareness of the 'spiritual creation' of a 'national spirit' in turn was expressed by the 'notion of the people'.[50]

Lazarus recognised that each nation would have a different self-consciousness based on objective elements such as 'descent, language, political life and so on' but that these attributes were only experienced through the 'subjective free act of self-realisation as a whole and as a people'.[51] He stressed that 'common destiny' united a nation more than language.[52] 'It has been proven that will alone has formed unity within the German Empire among those who, less than a decade ago, had fought each other as blood enemies'.[53]

Appreciating the 'still somewhat problematic conception of the pure subjectivity of the national spirit', Lazarus dedicated a section of his lecture to disputing Treitschke's definition of nationality by illustrating the irrelevance of descent and rejecting the language of blood as materialist. Moreover, given that nationality was based on language, Lazarus declared that this made Jews, German. Deploying language utilised in descriptions of the German cultural nation, Lazarus professed that 'mother tongue and Fatherland are German, the two sources of our inner life'.[54]

On the subject of descent Lazarus acknowledged that German Jews were Semitic but dismissed that all Germans were necessarily Germanic by descent, arguing that Germany was heterogenous. Just as a Swiss or American could descend from Germanic lines but not belong to the German nation, Lazarus illustrated how similarly Slavs from the Elbe region, or Prussians had become Germans.[55] 'Blood-and-race theory' for Lazarus was simply a 'product of a general coarsely sensualist-materialist worldview',

---

49 'Auf diesem Eingriff nun der geistigen, geschitchtlichen Verhältnisse in die natürlich gegebenen Unterschiede beruht der Begriff Volk; und das, was ein Volk zu eben diesem macht, liegt wesentlich nicht sowohl in gewissen objektiven Verhältnissen wie Abstammung, Sprache u. s. w. an sich als solchen, als vielmehr bloß in der subjektiven Ansicht der Glieder des Volks, welche sich alle zusammen als ein Volk ansehen'. Ibid, 12–13.
50 Ibid, 13–14.
51 Ibid, 14.
52 Ibid.
53 Ibid, 15.
54 Ibid, 19. On the use of paternal language and the perpetuation of Germany as a cultural nation see Arndt Kremer, 'Transitions of a Myth? The Idea of a Language-Defined Kulturnation in Germany', *New German Review: A Journal of Germanic Studies* 27, no. 1 (2016): 53–75.
55 Lazarus, *Was heißt national?* 19.

and in polemical flourish declared that 'blood means bloody little to me' (*das Blut bedeutet mir blutwenig*).[56]

The significance of Lazarus' lecture was that even before Ernest Renan's famous lecture 'What is a nation?' in 1881, Lazarus had already linked the idea of the will, a shared history and fate to his definition of the nation. Whilst employing the language and ideas of the *Kulturnation* revealing his understanding of traditions of German nationalism, Lazarus offered a different narrative on the German nation, one that was pluralistic, consisting of people from varying lines of descent, different religions, with different morals and customs that could be united through the will to belong to the German nation and over generations participate in its objective elements, the German language, a shared education, art, service to the state, and a common fate. In contrast to Treitschke, Lazarus envisioned a national principle where difference was accepted and existed alongside a shared German national unity.

Although Lazarus was the first, he was not the only thinker to believe in a pluralistic German nation. Gabriel Riesser and Ludwig Bamberger similarly envisioned this possibility.[57] Similarly, Lazarus was not the only respondent to recognise that at the core of the debate was the misunderstanding of the principle of nationality. Ludwig Philippson and Harry Breslau similarly identified this as a problem in their responses to Treitschke. Yet, Lazarus was unique for not only recognising this problem, but setting out an alternative definition of the concept of German nationality. The theoretical statements Lazarus made about the nation that challenged concepts related to the *Kulturnation* in favour of ideas associated with the *Staatsnation* (without employing these terms) resurfaced in later parliamentary debates.

While the majority of critics were of Jewish descent,[58] Treitschke's article received a wave of support from anti-Jewish sympathisers. The first newspaper to come out in public support was the semi-official organ of the Catholic Centre Party, *Germania*.[59] The article expressed that finally a 'hyper-Prussian-historian' had both recognised the 'existence of the Jewish Question' and expressed views on it that *Germania* had been

---

56 Ibid, 22.

57 For an account of this vein of thought amongst Jewish intellectuals see Mathias Berek, 'Neglected German-Jewish Visions for a Pluralistic Society: Moritz Lazarus', *The Leo Baeck Institute Year Book* 60 (2015): 45–59.

58 These included, in order of their replies, Moritz Lazarus (December 1879), Seligmann Meyer (December 1879), Heinrich Graetz (December 1879), Ludwig Philippson (December 1879), Harry Breßlau (January 1880), Ludwig Bamberger (January 1879) and Hermann Cohen (March 1880). See Krieger, *Der 'Berliner Antisemitismusstreit'*.

59 The leading Catholic newspaper in Germany was the *Kölnische Volkszeitung*, founded in 1860 by Josef Bachem. *Germania* was founded around the same time as the Catholic Centre Party (1871) and was referred to as the semi-official organ of the party, despite the fact that it often was in conflict with more moderate Catholic leaders of the party. It was known for its militant attacks on liberals, Jews and Bismarck. See Barnet P. Hartston, *Sensationalizing the Jewish Question: Anti-Semitic Trials and the Press in the Early German Empire*, Studies in Central European Histories; vol. 39 (Leiden: Brill, 2005), 289–90.

discussing for years.[60] Hopefully the debate would demonstrate the need for 'serious measures to protect the Germans against the taking-over of the Jewish nationality', the article concluded.[61] The short article at once encapsulated the support that Treitschke's position on the Jewish Question gave to those holding anti-Jewish views. It illustrated how Treitschke moved the Jewish Question from a taboo subject, into one that could, in the eyes of the public, credibly be discussed using the language of race.

Treitschke published his article in the midst of a wave of antisemitism in Berlin.[62] The League of Antisemites (*Antisemiten Liga*) was founded in September 1879, Adolf Stöcker founder of the Christian conservative, openly antisemitic, Christian Social Worker's Party (*Christlich-soziale Partei,* CSP) managed to secure a seat in the Reichstag, and the following year the first ever large-scale antisemitic student demonstrations took place in Berlin.[63] The significance of Treitschke's article was that his reputation, as one of the most prominent contemporary historians in Germany, lent his work an unprecedented credibility and his pronouncements struck a chord with the student fraternities (*Burschenschaften*) and antisemites.[64] As such Treitschke's article was seized upon by antisemites who extracted sections of his article using it to confirm their fears that Germany was becoming *verjudet* and that Jewish rights needed to be rescinded (which Treitschke had explicitly dismissed).[65]

In August 1880 an 'Antisemitic Petition', addressed to Reich Chancellor Bismarck began to circulate. It outlined four measures to guarantee the safety of the nation including the prohibition or limitation of Jewish immigration to Germany, a census of

---

60 Anonymous, 'Heinrich von Treitschke über die Judenfrage', *Germania,* Nr. 275, (28.11.1879) in Krieger, *Der 'Berliner Antisemitismusstreit,'* 1879–1881, 20. The Catholic Centre Party traditionally adopted the position that the Jews had supported the *Kulturkampf,* which helped legitimise antisemitic utterances. For more on the Catholic Centre Party's position on the Jewish Question see Uwe Mazura, *Zentrumspartei und Judenfrage, 1870/1933: Verfassungsstaat und Minderheitenschutz* (Mainz: Mathias Grünewald Verlag, 1994).
61 Anon., 'Heinrich von Treitschke über die Judenfrage', 20.
62 In the same year before Treitschke's pamphlet, Wilhelm Marr published the twelfth edition of *Der Sieg des Judenthums über das Germanenthum* in which he argued that the social structure of Germany was 'Judaised'. Wilhelm Marr, *Der Sieg des Judenthums über das Germanenthum. Vom nicht confessionellen Standpunkt aus betrachtet* (Bern: Rudolph Costenoble, 1879).
63 The first antisemitic student demonstrations took place in Berlin in early September, coinciding with lectures by Eugen Dühring. The second demonstration followed in mid-November when 600 students showed their support for Treitschke after the publication of the manifesto against antisemitism see Krieger, *Der 'Berliner Antisemitismusstreit',* 875.
64 Student fraternities became a hotbed of antisemitism. Herzl's rejection from fraternities became one factor that awoke him to the reality that he would never be fully accepted in society as a Jew. See Theodor Herzl, *The Complete Diaries of Theodor Herzl,* ed. Raphael Patai, trans. Harry Zohn, I–V vols (New York and London: Herzl Press and Thomas Yoseloff, 1960).
65 Antisemites argued that emancipation was a contract that the Jews had failed to comply to. Rather than assimilating, Jews had retained their particular cultural and religious differences. As emancipation had not been realised, they concluded it should be revoked. For an example of this argument written by the former private secretary of Bismarck see Anon. [Moritz Busch], 'Die deutschen Juden in der Gegenwart, und was nun?', *Die Grenzboten,* 39, (1880), 177–194, in Krieger, *Der 'Berliner Antisemitismusstreit',* 458–85.

Jews living in Germany, and the exclusion of Jews from positions of government authority and from teaching positions in public schools.[66] The significance of the petition
was that it became one of the first steps towards the development of political antisemitism. Conceived by a school teacher Bernhard Förster, the petition was intended as a
'plebiscite of the German people on the Jewish Question' and by October had amassed
265,000 signatures.[67] Inspired by the popularity of the petition, another school teacher
Ernst Henrici, disillusioned by the policies of the German Progress Party (*Deutsche
Fortschrittspartei*, DFP) where he began his political career, founded the first openly
antisemitic party, the Social Imperial Party (*Soziale Reichspartei*).[68]

The support that the petition was able to garner was evidenced when on the 13 November an inquiry was submitted by a representative of the Progressive Party Albert
Hänel to the Prussian Chamber of Deputies requesting the government take an official
position on the 'Antisemitic Petition'.[69] The aim of the inquiry was to try and force the
government to oppose the petition, and discredit public assertions that it had the full
support of the Reich Chancellor. In what came to be known as the *Judendebatte*[70] over
the course of two sessions on the 20 November and 23 November, the petition was
debated by ministers across the political spectrum.[71] For opponents of the petition, the
debate was a pyrrhic victory. On the one hand, the Prussian government asserted that
it had no intention to change the equal treatment of citizens along religious lines, and
yet, reassurances extended no further. Although individual ministers condemned the
recent antisemitic activities in Berlin, voicing support for Kantorowitcz,[72] the official
government representative at the session did not comment on anti-Jewish agitation, or

---

66 The full text of the petition can be found in *Schmeitzner Internationale Monatsschrift: Zeitung für die Allegemeine Vereinigung zur Bekämpfung des Judentums* (Chemnitz und Dresden, 1883), 314–16.

67 Of these signatures, over half came from Prussia, and just under 5 % from Berlin. Quoted in Richard
S. Levy, *The Downfall of the Anti-Semitic Political Parties in Imperial Germany* (New Haven and London: Yale
University Press, 1975), 21.

68 Henrici wanted to challenge Stöcker's hold over the antisemitism movement. The party was short-lived
as in the parliamentary elections of 1881 it was unable to win electoral support beyond Berlin. See Christian
Davis, *Colonialism, Antisemitism, and Germans of Jewish Descent in Imperial Germany* (Michigan: University of Michigan Press, 2012), 32. At the first of several meetings held by Henrici outlining the party's new
programme, the event at the Berliner Reichshallen drew 3,000 attendees. Krieger, *Der 'Berliner Antisemitismusstreit'*, 874.

69 'Interpellation des Abgeordneten Dr Hänel im preußischen Abgeordnetenhause betreffend die Agitation gegen die jüdischen Staatsbürger', in ibid, 555–68.

70 Hartston, *Sensationalizing the Jewish Question*, 43.

71 The debate was reported in the *Allegemeine Zeitung des Judentums* on the 7 December. See Anon., 'Die
Verhandlung des preußischen Abgeordnetenhauses', *Allegemeine Zeitung des Judentums*, 49 (7 Dezember
1880), 769–776, in Krieger, *Der 'Berliner Antisemitismusstreit'*, 676–94.

72 The 'Kantorowitcz Affair' erupted on the 8 November when a Jewish businessman, Ernst Kantorowitcz
slapped a school teacher Carl Jungfer when he and his colleague, Bernhard Förster, made antisemitic remarks. The event took place in the midst of the Antisemitism Dispute, and, as with Treitschke's article,
polarised the public. For an account of the affair see Hartston, *Sensationalizing the Jewish Question*, 37–51.

single out instigators of antisemitic acts. 'On a higher social and political level, [...] a "Jewish Question" once again existed in Germany'.[73]

The turning point in the Antisemitism Dispute came in November 1880 when a number of prominent Berlin Notables in politics, industry, and academia signed a manifesto concerning the 'Jewish Question',[74] in which they protested against the wave of antisemitism.[75] The denial of the equal rights and duties of all Germans was equated to breaking the rule of law and honour. The only liberal Gentile[76] to publicly condemn Treitschke's article, was the famous scholar of classical antiquity, Theodor Mommsen who published his response a month later, in December 1880.[77] Unlike Lazarus, Mommsen did not take issue with Treitschke's premises but rather with the consequences of his article.[78] Mommsen thought Treitschke's publications had incited a civil war of the majority against the minority endangering not only the Jews, but also the German nation.[79] He defended Jews as citizens of the state, but like Treitschke, offered no suggestion as to how they could viably become members of the nation, given the 'sentiment of strangeness and difference still held today by the Christian German against the Jewish German'.[80] Of Treitschke's critics, Lazarus stood alone in suggesting how to reform ways of thinking about the German nation rather than demanding Jews to change.

---

73 Norbert Kampe, *Studenten und 'Judenfrage' im Deutschen Kaiserreich* (Göttingen: Vandenhoeck & Ruprecht, 1988), 28. Quoted in Krieger, *Der 'Berliner Antisemitismusstreit,' 1879–1881*, 555.

74 In his letter to the Notables, Theodor Mommsen described the situation as *die Judenfrage*. See Theodor Mommsen an Emil du Bois-Reymond, [Sonntag, dem 14.11.1880] in ibid, 569.

75 It featured in the Sunday supplement of several liberal Berlin newspapers. For the manifesto and list of signatories see 'Manifest der Berliner Notablen gegen den Antisemitismus', (12 November 1880) in ibid, 151–154.

76 Other Gentiles that publicly criticised Treitschke were lesser-known antisemites who thought the article too liberal. These included Wilhelm Endner's *Zur Judenfrage*, which responded to Harry Breßlau's (a historian and Professor in Berlin) pamphlet by the same name, and Johannes Nordmann under the pseudonym H. Naudh who criticised Treitschke for his liberalism which clouded his understanding of the present. See Stoetzler, *The State, the Nation, and the Jews*, 21, 42.

77 Prior to his article, Mommsen had criticised Treitschke indirectly in a lecture given to the Prussian Academy of Sciences in March 1880 without mentioning him by name. Mommsen's endorsement of the 'Declaration against Antisemitism', marked the start of a tense exchange between the colleagues, which played out in various private letters and newspaper articles. This came to a head when Mommsen published his article entitled *Auch ein Wort über unser Judentum*. For the text of the article see Krieger, *Der 'Berliner Antisemitismusstreit'*, 695–709.

78 Like Treitschke, Mommsen defended legal emancipation and demanded that the Jews, not the state, resolve the Jewish Question by 'becoming German'. Mommsen was not concerned with Treitschke's article but its effect stating, 'in issues like this one, everything depends on how one says something, not what one says'. See Stoetzler, *The State, the Nation, and the Jews*, 25.

79 Theodor Mommsen, *Auch ein Wort über unser Judentum*, (Berlin, 1880) in Krieger, *Der 'Berliner Antisemitismusstreit'*, 695–715.

80 Ibid. Mommsen was the subject of antisemitic attacks in newspaper articles, brochures and the speeches of Henrici. Mommsen once again became the Gentile face of the fight against antisemitism by helping to establish the *Verein zur Abwehr des Antisemitismus* in 1890. Although defending antisemitism, the league supported the 'full amalgamation' of Jews, which was not supported by many Jews.

When in 1879 a Jewish Question arose once again in public discourse the parameters had shifted significantly from 1842. As Jewish emancipation had been granted in 1871, the debate focused not on the law, but on culture. Not on the Prussian state, but on the German nation. Where in 1842 the answer to the Jewish Question demanded state reform, in 1879 the onus lay on the Jews to assimilate into German Christian culture. Most importantly, however, where the German constitution granted Jews political and civic rights on the basis of full religious equality for all individuals, in 1879 Treitschke recognised Jews once again as a collective group, bound not only by faith but by their race, an immutable characteristic.

Whilst Treitschke suggested Jews could become part of the German nation through assimilation, he identified a Jewish characteristic that could never be renounced, not even through baptism. For the majority of German Jews who conceived of their identity in religious terms, Treitschke's argument was perceived as purposefully exclusionary. However, for a small but vocal minority of Jews, Treitschke brought to a public audience their own understanding of their community identity as a nation. And rather than seeing this as incompatible with the German nation-state, they revised the concept of nationality, separating their national loyalty towards Judaism from their patriotic loyalty towards Germany.

Nationalism and patriotism: *Nationaljude als Staatsbürger* (1897)

Contrary to the common misconception which views the Jewish Question as a purely antisemitic construct, as a result of reading German Jewish history in hindsight, the Jewish Question was employed extensively by Jews who began using the term in parallel to its appropriation by antisemites. When the Zionist Federation for Germany (*Zionistische Vereinigung für Deutschland*, ZVfD) was founded in 1897, its genesis was framed not as a reaction to antisemitism but rather as a response to the Jewish Question, specifically the failure of emancipation.[81] Whilst for the majority of German Jews, the Jewish Question was rarely employed as a term, existing often only in their 'imagination,'[82] Zionists transformed this state of affairs as they took control of the phrase. In the first Zionist publication to employ the term in 1882, Leon Pinsker wrote 'only [...] when the equality of the Jews with the other nations becomes a fact, can the

---

81 *Erstes Propaganda-Flugblatt der ZVfD* [Anfang 1898], CZA, Z 1/433 in Jehuda Reinharz, ed., *Dokumente zur Geschichte des deutschen Zionismus 1882–1933*, Schriftenreihe wissenschaftlicher Abhandlungen des Leo Baeck Instituts; 37 (Tübingen: JCB Mohr Siebeck, 1981), 51–53. See also Alan Levenson who argues that Zionism developed not in response to antisemitism but radical assimilation. Alan Levenson, 'German Zionism and Radical Assimilation before 1914', *Studies in Zionism* 13, no. 1 (1992): 21–41.
82 Bein, *The Jewish Question*, 20.

problem presented by the Jewish Question be considered solved'.[83] Zionists presented the Jewish Question as a political question concerning not only the acknowledgment of a national Jewish identity but also changes in the international sphere.

In 1842 and 1879 the Jewish Question was posed as an external question about the Jews, their legal equality in the state and cultural assimilation into the nation. Conversely, in 1879 the Jewish Question concerned whether or not it was possible to retain a Jewish national identity within the German nation-state. For Zionists, the language of race was not the greatest danger. Rather it was assimilation, leading to the erosion of a Jewish identity.[84]

The debate pitted the Zionist Federation against the Central Association of German Citizens of the Jewish Faith. Building on the premise of Treitschke's argument that the Jews were a nation, the Zionists criticised assimilation and offered an alternative vision of German-Jewish nationhood. Decoupling the concept of nation and state, the Zionists demonstrated how it was possible to be loyal to the Jewish nation whilst remaining a German patriot and abiding German citizen.[85] Investigating these German Zionist debates illustrates how these political concepts were conflicted, continuously rehearsed and had lasting political effect. In the First World War these questions and concepts came to the fore with practical relevance as the Russian, Ottoman, German and Austro-Hungarian Empires were replaced by the new 'ideal' polity of homogenous nation-states.

The first resistance towards the Zionist Federation in Germany by the German-Jewish community came in response to the announcement that the First Zionist Congress would be held in Munich. The protest movement succeeded in halting the congress, which instead was held in Basel.[86] The objection to the Zionist Congress was on two grounds. Firstly, the Jewish community was German in nationality and only separate in religion. Secondly, by demanding a Jewish nation-state, the Zionist movement undermined the fight for equal rights within Germany. 'What perturbed [the liberal Jewish community] were the disconcerting similarities between the anti-Semitic position on the "Jewish Question" and the Zionist ideology of national separatism.'[87]

---

83 Leon Pinsker, *Auto-Emancipation: An Appeal to His People by a Russian Jew* (1882) trans. (Masada: Youth Zionist Organisation of America, 1935), 5.

84 Between 1889 and 1910, there were approximately 12,000 Jewish conversions to Protestant Christianity, which did not include those who had converted before this date. This meant around 2% of the Jewish population in Germany converted. Tourlamain, *Völkisch Writers and National Socialism*, 26.

85 Theodor Herzl did not share this sentiment. He was not concerned with dual loyalty and said life in the diaspora was meaningless. On these issues he was opposed by his contemporaries including Bodenheimer and other first-generation German Zionists.

86 This movement was led by Rabbi Sigmund Maybaum and Rabbi Heinemann Vogelstein. The initial choice of Munich was because the headquarters of the WZO were in Germany. In addition, many of the individuals involved in the movement were from German-speaking countries or spoke German.

87 Marjorie Lamberti, 'From Coexistence to Conflict – Zionism and the Jewish Community in Germany, 1897–1914', *Leo Baeck Institute Year Book* 27 (1982): 55.

Liberal Jews were anxious that Zionism would undermine the political status of Jews and give government officials an excuse for excluding Jews from positions in public office on the basis of their separate national identity. Certainly, these views were not without historical basis in the German Empire where 'social pluralism and toleration of diversity were not widely-respected principles'.[88] According to critics of Zionism, even the struggle for equal rights in practice did not warrant the Zionist call for mass emigration. A gulf was emerging within the German-Jewish community, between those who could turn a blind eye towards liberalism's failure to eradicate prejudice and those who believed full emancipation could never be achieved.

In response to this public outcry in the Jewish community, the Zionist Federation published the anonymous pamphlet, *Der Nationaljude als Staatsbürger*.[89] The pamphlet began by juxtaposing nationality and religion as defining principles of German Jewry. The Zionists argued that where one's faith could change, nationality was given at birth, a matter of chance, and could not be renounced. Attacking the liberal Jewish organisation, the Central Association, the pamphlet argued that Jews could not be de-nationalised as they embodied particular characteristics unique to Jews, a 'Jewish type', a shared kinship (*Stamm*) identity. Elevating the subject to international proportions, the pamphlet claimed that refusing the existence of a Jewish nationality meant denationalising all nations. Unpicking the assimilationist argument, the author questioned if by denying Jewish nationality did Jews 'become a Pole, Russian, Czech or Croat?' The reality the author maintained was that 'I remain what I am'.[90]

Not only on the basis of unique Jewish attributes but also based on the external perception of Jews, the author exposed the limits of assimilation. The pamphlet acknowledged daily antisemitism and the obsession with the physiognomic characteristics of Jews, and Jewish particularities. Judaism 'must be a strange denomination if it can be singled out in a nose or face' stated the pamphlet. Yet rather than succumbing to antisemitic tropes, the author of the pamphlet flipped these encounters into a message of empowerment of Jewish difference. Playing on the different meaning of *Glauben* (using it as a noun and adjective), the author emphasised that 'faith' cannot be singled out as a defining principle of German Jews as few have 'faith' in it.[91]

Whilst advocating immigration to a Jewish state, the pamphlet outlined how Jews could remain members of the German state. Separating patriotism from nationality, the author argued that Jewish nationalism did not negate loyalty, patriotism, to the German state. This position was typical of German statist Zionists (including Max Bo-

---

88 Ibid.

89 *Jüdischer Nationalismus und Deutscher Patriotismus*, [Juli/August 1897], CZA W 147/1, in Reinharz, *Dokumente zur Geschichte des deutschen Zionismus*, 45–47.

90 *Jüdischer Nationalismus und Deutscher Patriotismus*, in Reinharz, *Dokumente zur Geschichte des deutschen Zionismus*, 46.

91 Ibid.

denheimer, Franz Oppenheimer) who unlike their Eastern European counterparts felt loyalty towards the state in which they resided. Framing nationalism in the language of emotions, specifically love, the pamphlet suggested that a historical nationalism based on 'an intimate relationship to the Holy Land, the memory of its past, and the hope for its future' did not diminish a contemporary nationalism to 'their present home' in Germany.[92]

Statist Zionists appreciated that the Jewish people required a place of refuge beyond Germany, and yet they believed this did not require immediate immigration. Moreover, a commitment to the Jewish state project did not reduce an emotional commitment or present patriotism to the German Fatherland. The more Jewish rights were contested within Germany, the more precious they became, the pamphlet declared. For statist Zionists their mission to establish a Jewish state was seen only as a reality that future generations could achieve. They intended for the Jewish diaspora to continue, and thrive, but wanted to avoid an overwhelming and unsustainable numbers of Jews in the German diaspora. The Jewish state project, as conceived by German statist Zionists, was intended for Eastern European Jews to avoid their mass immigration and settlement in Germany.[93] On these grounds, the statist Zionists shared similar concerns to Heinrich von Treitschke, but they offered a different model for solving the issue. Foregrounding emotions, the Zionists circumvented the complex terrain of dual nationalism within a traditional model of German nationhood. This involved recognising that whilst birth (one's nation) was chance, patriotism was a conscious choice. A national loyalty towards Judaism did not negate civic consciousness towards the German state.

The most vocal criticism of the pamphlet, unsurprisingly, came from the Central Association, which the anonymous author had subtly attacked.[94] Whilst the debate unfolded between two Jewish organisations on the subject of Jewish nationalism, it opened a discussion about the principles of the German state. Moreover, the debate also illustrated the intellectual legacy and the practical consequences of the *Antisemitismusstreit*, specifically the ideas of Treitschke and Lazarus, which were referenced, either directly or indirectly, in subsequent debates on the Jewish Question.

---

92 Ibid.

93 It was this mindset that underpinned Bodenheimer's memorandum and guided Sobernheim's strategy in the Jewish Affairs section towards *Ostjuden*. Nicosia writes that 'Sobernheim's strategy was quietly to direct the energies of his office to halting Jewish immigration into Germany, to promoting the emigration of as many East European Jewish refugees from Germany as possible, and to the effective integration of those who were to remain in Germany into the Jewish community'. See Francis Nicosia, 'Jewish Affairs and German Foreign Policy during the Weimar Republic: Moritz Sobernheim and the Referat für jüdische Angelegenheiten', *The Leo Baeck Institute Year Book* 33, no. 1 (1988): 273.

94 Wanting to represent the whole of the German Jewish community, the CV had to play its cards carefully. It opposed the Zionist movement and the mass emigration it advertised but did not want to ostracise Zionists. The CV desired a united German-Jewish front and, for this reason, held off from denouncing the pamphlet until after the Basel Congress. See Lamberti, 'From Coexistence to Conflict', 56.

One of the first and the most revealing responses to the Zionist pamphlet came from Ludwig Fuld, a Bavarian lawyer, who argued that the Zionists had misunderstood the role of religion and nationality in the modern state[95] Fuld began by disentangling the concept of nationality, differentiating between 'national Jews' (*Nationaljuden)* and 'Jewish citizens' (*jüdische Staatsbürger)*. Referencing Moritz Lazarus, Fuld similarly argued that whilst there was no such thing as a 'German religion', neither could nationality be determined by religion as 'today, every nationality includes multiple religions, as every religion includes multiple nationalities'.[96] Building on Lazarus, Fuld argued that whilst Jews shared a common descent (*Abstammung*), this had 'no significance for nationality'.[97] According to Fuld, Jews no longer have their own nationality.[98] They draw on 'the people's spirit' of the nation of which they have become part. Whoever denied this, Fuld concluded, knew nothing about the 'essence of the modern state'.[99] What Fuld feared most was that 'non-scientific' Zionist assertions on nationality were confirming views expressed by intellectual antisemites. 'Now the antisemites have received confirmation from Treitschke to Ahlwardt and Lueger that German Jews do indeed feel like a particular nationality'.[100] In a situation of 'teritus gaudens', Fuld expressed his fear that antisemites were revelling in the conflict between the Zionist Federation and the Central Association.[101]

Although critical of the Zionist position on Jewish nationality, the official policy that the Central Association adopted towards the establishment of the Zionist Federation was conciliatory. Under the Presidency of Max Bodenheimer, the Zionist Federation did not intend to jeopardise the political status of Jews in Germany and heeding the concern of the Central Association, removed *nationaljüdisch* from its title, replacing it with Zionist to avoid the term appearing as an 'antithesis to *nationaldeutsch*'.[102] In conjunction with the name change, the programme of the ZVfD was also revised and, mirroring the language of the Central Association, declared that 'German citizens of Jewish descent' were a people united by historic ties which did not undermine their loyalty as German citizens. This satisfied Eugen Fuchs, one of the founders and President of the Central Association, who believed that German Zionists would soon realise that social integration and a sense of 'Jewish pride' could be achieved without

---

95 Fuld, Ludwig, 'Der Nationaljude als Staatsbürger', *Im deutschen Reich*, III (11 November 1897): 531.
96 Ibid, 532.
97 Ibid, 533. The author did not employ the terminology of *Stamm* in the article, presumably as this would have conceded to an ethnic identity. Just over a decade later, however, members of the Central Association began to use the terminology of *Stamm*.
98 Ibid, 532.
99 Ibid, 533.
100 Ibid, 530.
101 Ibid, 529. *Teritus gaudens* refers to a situation where one party benefits from conflict between two others. The phrase is often attributed to the work of the sociologist Georg Simmel.
102 CZA, A142/59/2, Arthur Hantke to Alfred Klee, Berlin 25 October 1987. Cited in Lamberti, 'From Coexistence to Conflict', 57.

renouncing Judaism as a religion or loyalty to the German Fatherland.[103] Responding to the moderate non-doctrinaire Zionist tone set by Bodenheimer, the Central Association agreed the following year to institute a policy of neutrality and withheld from criticising Zionism in its official organ.[104]

The 1897 debate on the Jewish Question reveals the primacy of Jewish voices on the Jewish Question and the diverse contexts where these questions were discussed and challenged. The debate built on some of the ideas and discourse from the 1879 Anti-semitism Dispute and applied them to a different context: a German Jewish response to the Jewish Question. Like Treitschke, the Zionist Federation similarly argued that Jews were united by peculiar national traits. Notably, however, whilst both Treitschke and the ZVfD described the Jews as a *Stamm*, Treitschke also used the language of race (*Rasse*) to describe the Jews which, in this pamphlet, the ZVfD did not employ, but rather termed them a nationality (*Nationalität*).

Building on the 1879 debate, the Zionist Federation started from the same premise as Treitschke but reached a different conclusion to Jewish assimilation. For the Zionists, assimilation was futile. Instead, they proposed two alternative responses to the German Jewish Question. Firstly, they negotiated a space within Germany for Jewish nationality by separating between the nation and the state. As long as Jews remained patriotic to the German state, their civic consciousness could not be undermined by a Jewish nationality. Secondly, they advocated for the creation of a Jewish state, which would help mitigate the immigration of Eastern European Jews into Germany. In 1897, the leaders of the Zionist Federation faced criticism only from the Central Association, which continued to maintain that Jews were German nationals and citizens of the Jewish faith. Only a few years later, however, several German Zionists began to question their allegiance to the German nation-state and offered a more radical response to the German Jewish Question: immigration to Palestine.

The question of national consciousness in Franz Oppenheimer's *Stammesbewusstsein und Volksbewusstsein* (1910)

Published in February 1910, Franz Oppenheimer's *Stammesbewusstsein und Volksbewusstsein* created a stir by publicly acknowledging an emerging division within the Zionist Federation on the Jewish Question.[105] The split was between an older generation of Zionists who continued to affirm their loyalty to Germany and a younger gen-

---

103 See Eugen Fuchs, *Um Deutschtum und Judentum, Gesammelte Reden und Aufsätze (1894–1919)* (Frankfurt am Main: Verlag von J. Kaufmann, 1919).
104 Lamberti, 'From Coexistence to Conflict', 57.
105 Franz Oppenheimer, 'Stammesbewusstsein und Volksbewusstsein', *Die Welt*, XIV, no. 7 (18 Februar 1910): 139–143.

eration of Zionists who rejected this in favour of settlement in Palestine. Oppenheimer interrogated the concept of nationality by distinguishing between types of national consciousness assigning these to an East-West divide in the Jewish community. The latter theme was central to the Jewish Question and pertinent not only to debates within the Zionist community but also within German politics, before, during and after the war.[106] Given the language affinity of Yiddish to German, the presence of this group within Germany raised several questions about the principles of the cultural nation, which became practically relevant in the First World War when the Germany army occupied West Russia. These debates provided the conceptual foundations that influenced Max Bodenheimer and his interactions with the German Foreign Office during the First World War when the German army confronted a practical Jewish Question on the Eastern Front.[107]

Oppenheimer's article was published at a moment when tensions within the Zionist Federation of Germany had reached their zenith. The same year, Arthur Hanke replaced Max Bodenheimer as President of the Zionist Federation and began restructuring the organisation, based on a new ideological programme crafted by Kurt Blumenfeld, Party Secretary since 1909.[108] A policy of 'Palestine-centrism' (*Palästino-zentrismus*), settlement in Palestine, was encouraged. The policy was in line with the new approach of the World Zionist Organisation, which had begun promoting practical, cultural work in Palestine. It was opposed to the tactics of Herzl and statist Zionists who had pursued diplomatic channels with the Great Powers in an attempt to garner support for a Jewish state.[109]

Led by Kurt Blumenfeld and Arthur Hanke this younger generation of Zionists appealed to the existential crisis of German Jewish youth, who as victims of political

---

106 Germany was a country of transit for many Jews fleeing the Russian Empire, both in the aftermath of the 1881 pogroms but also after First World War. In the nineteenth century two-thirds of Russian Jews fleeing the pogroms emigrated to America. On this basis, the Jewish Question was closely connected to the Eastern European Jewish Question (*Ostjudenfrage*) in parliamentary debates.

107 On this subject, see chapter two.

108 These changes correlated with the need to increase the membership of the ZVfD. From 1904 to 1908, membership had only increased by 239 from 6,000. In comparison, the CV numbered 100,000 members in 1903, which had doubled by 1916. As a result of changes in the ZVfD, in 1913, in one year alone, membership increased by 9,000 thereby almost doubling the overall representation of Zionists within the German Jewish community. Hagit Lavsky, *Before Catastrophe: The Distinctive Path of German Zionism* (Detroit, Jerusalem: Wayne State University Press, Magnes Press, 1996), 29. See also Schorsch, *Jewish Reactions to German Anti-Semitism, 1870–1914*, 119.

109 Many of the second-generation Zionists (including Kurt Blumenfeld, Julius Berger, Martin Rosenblüth) had close professional links to the WZO having previously worked there. These links had been strengthened since 1904 when the headquarters of the ZVfD moved from Cologne to Berlin, where the WZO was located. After the war, a third generation of Zionists took over, known as the Pioneer Zionists. They continued prioritising settlement in Palestine as the mission of the ZVfD. On the different generations of Zionists and their programmes see Stefan Vogt, *Subalterne Positionierungen: Der deutsche Zionismus im Feld des Nationalismus in Deutschland, 1890–1933*, 1st ed. (Göttingen: Wallstein Verlag, 2016).

antisemitism, and dissatisfied with the denial of Jewish nationality, often by their parents, began to look for their 'home in the *Volkstum*'.[110] In contrast to the political-statist Zionists, for the national-cultural Zionists the focal point of Palestine was not about demanding territorial integrity and sovereignty. Settlement would be encouraged on the basis of rekindling a Jewish national-cultural, spiritual existence. Life in the diaspora was perceived as the root cause of Jewish persecution and discrimination and thus was not considered to be an existence worth engaging in or fighting for. As such, all participation in the diaspora, including any engagement in German public or political life, and the fight against antisemitism, was halted. The Jewish Question was no longer perceived as one externally imposed and externally answered.

Motivated by external in as much as internal affairs, these young Zionists responded to larger social transformations affecting middle-class Central European youth in the pre-war era. Many disillusioned with the capitalist industrial society, framed within the confines of liberal individual freedom, looked for comradery and a return to nature and simplicity. Although asserting a national-cultural, non-statist consciousness, politics was not wholly devoid from this movement. Rather, the young Zionists drew terminology from German political thinkers such as Fichte and Herder for their apolitical end betraying their background despite seeking to reject it.[111] Whilst insisting on an independent, unique Jewish cultural-nationalism they drew on the language of German Romantic thinkers (Herder, Schiller and Novalis), much like völkisch groups, to frame their existence.[112] By 1912 the takeover of the Federation was complete and as a result, a number of older (political-statist) Zionists, including Franz Oppenheimer, temporarily stopped engaging in Zionist activities.[113]

In his article which made explicit this divide within the Federation, Oppenheimer drew on the vocabulary of the 1897 debate, when he observed that Zionists employing the term *Nationaljude*, had misunderstood the concept of the nation. Nation, Oppenheimer explained, had etymological roots denoting descent. Often *Stammesbewusstsein* was correlated with national consciousness when temporally the two categories differed. *Stamm* stemmed from historical roots, whilst national from contemporary, or present, circumstances. Central to Oppenheimer's argument was that these categories

---

110 *Der Jüdische Student*, 28 Februar 1913, 373. Cited in Lamberti, 'From Coexistence to Conflict', 70.

111 On the influence of Fichte on German Zionism see Stefan Vogt, 'The First World War, German Nationalism, and the Transformation of German Zionism', *Leo Baeck Institute Year Book* 57 (11 July 2012): 271.

112 Buber emerged as one of the leading intellectuals of this movement and drew on the language of 'blood, descent and roots'. See Buber, *Drei Reden über das Judentum*. On the influence of Romantic thinkers on cultural Zionist thought see Vogt, 'The First World War, German Nationalism, and the Transformation of German Zionism', 271.

113 At the Zionist convention in Posen, the Palestine centric proposals were unanimously accepted. On the relevance of the Posen declaration, see Lavsky, *Before Catastrophe*, 30–31. See also Jehuda Reinharz, *Fatherland or Promised Land: The Dilemma of the German Jew, 1893–1914* (Ann Arbor: University of Michigan Press, 1975), 144–70. In 1914, at the Zionist convention in Leipzig, this Palestine centric policy was re-confirmed.

emerged from the different experiences of Eastern and Western Jews. 'Western Jews' he wrote have a 'Jewish kinship consciousness' (*Stammesbewusstsein*) whereas Eastern Jews (*Ostjuden*) had a 'Jewish national consciousness' (*Volksbewusstsein*).[114]

Stammesbewusstsein was described as the awareness of coming from 'a shared lineage (*Abstammung*), a shared blood, or at the least a former shared nationhood (*Volkstum*), [and] a shared history'.[115] Although writing for a Zionist audience, Oppenheimer by using the language of *Stamm* invoked a longer legacy of conceptualising Jewish identity. Adolf Jellinek, a Rabbi from Vienna, was the first to frame Jews as one of many *Stämme* in the Austro-Hungarian Empire.[116] In Germany, Moritz Lazarus ventured that Jews formed one of the many religions and *Stämme* of Germany.[117] Moreover, during the Antisemitism Dispute, Theodor Mommsen also used the language of *Stamm* to describe German Jews.[118]

For Oppenheimer, national consciousness, in contrast to kinship consciousness, was a product of external circumstances, more specifically the historical development of countries in which Jews resided. These differences meant that within the concept of *Volksbewußtsein* (national consciousness) which Oppenheimer defined as sharing similarities in 'language, customs, economic and legal relationships and spiritual [*geistige*] culture',[119] two further forms of consciousness emerged, *Nationalbewußtsein* (national consciousness) and *Kulturbewußtsein* (cultural consciousness). Whereas Western Jews belonged to their respective cultural communities, for Oppenheimer, the barbarity faced by Eastern Jews meant that becoming cultural 'Russians, Romanians or Galicians' was impossible forcing Eastern Jews to develop a unique Jewish culture, becoming *Kulturjuden*.[120] Yet rather than disparaging the Western Jewish experience, Oppenheimer advised Eastern European Jews to acknowledge and forgive Western Jews for having followed a path which internalised the culture of their respective countries.

For Oppenheimer, the concept of *Nationalbewußtsein* entailed an inseparable formalised political status and cultural belonging. Western Jews belonged to their respective cultures (German, American or English) and on this basis were nationals and citizens. Similarly, culturally united Eastern Jews had a separate 'national' understanding rooted in Jewishness. Eastern Jews were National Jews because they were and saw

---

114 Oppenheimer, 'Stammesbewusstsein und Volksbewusstsein', 139.
115 Ibid.
116 Till van Rahden, 'Germans of the Jewish Stamm: Visions of Community between Nationalism and Particularism, 1850 to 1933', in *German History from the Margins*, ed. Neil Gregor, Nils H. Roemer, and Mark Roseman (Bloomington: Indiana University Press, 2006), 31.
117 Lazarus, *Was heißt national?*. On the history of the language of *Stamm* in Germany and its use by German Jews see van Rahden, 'Germans of the Jewish Stamm', 27–48.
118 Yfaat Weiss, '"Wir Westjuden haben jüdisches Stammesbewußtsein, die Ostjuden jüdisches Volksbewußtsein". Der deutsch-jüdische Blick auf das polnische Judentum in den beiden ersten Jahrzehnten des 20. Jahrhunderts', *Archiv für Socialgeschichte* 37 (1997): 159.
119 Oppenheimer, 'Stammesbewusstsein und Volksbewusstsein', 139.
120 Ibid, 140.

themselves as 'belonging to a foreign people [*Fremdvolk*] that lives, without a home [*Heimat*] under foreigners [*Fremden*]'.[121] Only in the Zionist state could a Western Jew derive a Jewish *Volksbewußtsein* and be a 'National Jew' and retain instead, a German *Stammesbewusstsein*. Eastern Jews too frequently used the term to denote their status within non-Jewish states because they felt compelled to fill the gap in their national consciousness (which denied them a culture or state administration they could feel any patriotism towards) with their kinship consciousness, according to Oppenheimer.

Referencing the 1897 debate once again, Oppenheimer clarified his understanding of loyalty to the state and patriotism. Where Romanian and Russian Zionists had to describe themselves as 'loyal citizens', in the West, outlined Oppenheimer, 'we are patriots.'[122] Oppenheimer re-iterated the dual loyalty of statist Zionists who retained the 'national consciousness of the tradition [*Volkstum*] which we were born into'. Alluding to one of the points of tension within the Zionist Federation, Oppenheimer clearly distinguished between the practical Zionist objective (emigration to Palestine), supported by cultural Zionists, and the political Zionist objective (establishing a Jewish state), advocated by statist Zionists. A disciple of the latter, Oppenheimer suggested that although supportive of the Jewish state, this did not necessitate abandoning life in Germany. 'We are not guests that want to move on tomorrow, we are citizens in the long run' clarified Oppenheimer.[123] Crucial to the statist Zionist position was the decoupling of nationhood from statehood, enabling Zionists to be Jewish nationals and German citizens.

In words that would have sounded alien to a Jew living in the Russian Empire, Oppenheimer professed, 'we love our fatherland and its people, its culture and its territory' and are committed to 'serve its future that should also be our future'.[124] For Oppenheimer, and for statist Zionists more generally, the Zionist project focused on freeing Eastern European Jews from the shackles of their unequal and restricted existence under the Tsar. Revealing his liberal, assimilated, bourgeois upbringing, Oppenheimer had no intention of renouncing life in Germany. Statist Zionists envisioned that they were building the Jewish state for generations to come. Herzl had even conjectured in *Der Judenstaat* that those who initiated the project of a Jewish state would 'scarcely live to see its glorious completion.'[125] As such, the statist Zionists believed that their actions did not undermine their standing as patriotic Germans. However, an increasing number of younger Zionists saw these pronouncements as naive, dangerous, and in complete opposition to what they understood Zionism, nationhood and statehood to mean.

---

121 Ibid, 141.
122 Ibid, 142.
123 Ibid.
124 Ibid.
125 Theodor Herzl, *The Jewish State* (London: Penguin Books, 2010), 3.

Whilst Oppenheimer framed his argument around the concept of identity (states of consciousness), central to his argument was understanding the political environment within which Jewish communities resided. Oppenheimer saw the state based on the rule of law (*Rechtsstaat*) as the ideal polity. Those that 'can live as a citizen in a *Rechtsstaat* deserve all hate if they do not show gratitude'.[126] The different political environments of Western and Eastern Jews were central to their community identity formation. Unlike Eastern Jews, Western Jews historically lived in countries that 'in most cases' had offered Jews full equality and thus there was no reason to 'feel as guests in a country where our ancestors have lived for forty generations'.[127] Oppenheimer's diagnosis of the two states of (national) consciousness explained the internal splintering of Zionist Federation. For him, it was simple. Zionist objectives differed substantially because Western Jews were able to derive a national consciousness from their surroundings, whilst Eastern Jews were dependent on their Jewishness. For the latter, violence and oppression presented an urgency, which could only be satisfied by 'practical' solutions, mass emigration and settlement in Palestine. A plan that Oppenheimer and other statist Zionists saw as 'idealistic'.

Oppenheimer's article unleashed a heated and lengthy debate.[128] Responses were predominately limited to the pages of the organ of the World Zionist Organisation, *Die Welt* and featured in issues for several months after the article first appeared.[129] Neither the organ of the Central Association (*Im deutschen Reich*) nor the mainstream media commented on the controversial article.[130] However, the memory of the Oppenheimer debate remained in the German-Jewish community and the premise that European Jewry had a divided national consciousness had a lasting legacy.[131]

---

126 Oppenheimer, 'Stammesbewusstsein und Volksbewusstsein', 142.

127 Ibid.

128 Reinharz suggests that most German Zionists and the leadership of the Zionist Federation supported Oppenheimer's point of view. See Reinharz, *Fatherland or Promised Land*, 133. Accounts of the Oppenheimer debate have tended to focus on its consequences for the Zionist Federation rather than on the language of the debate and its responses. See van Rahden, 'Germans of the Jewish Stamm', 34; Weiss, '"Wir Westjuden haben jüdisches Stammesbewußtsein, die Ostjuden jüdisches Volksbewußtsein"', 158–61; Steven E. Aschheim, *Brothers and Strangers: The East European Jew in German and German Jewish Consciousness, 1800–1923* (Madison, Wisconsin: University of Wisconsin Press, 1982), 97–98; Reinharz, *Fatherland or Promised Land*, 128–35.

129 It appears that Oppenheimer, unlike Moritz Goldstein, did not reflect on the controversy caused by his article. Perhaps because those that criticised him were a small minority of Zionists. See Franz Oppenheimer, *Erlebtes, Erstrebtes, Erreichtes: Lebenserinnerungen* (Düsseldorf: Joseph Melzer Verlag, 1964).

130 This is the conclusion of research conducted in *Im deutschen Reich* and in the morning and evening papers of the *Berliner Tageblatt* in the weeks, and months following the publication of Oppenheimer's article. I was able to find only one early response to Oppenheimer's article in a non-Zionist Jewish paper. See, Dr R., 'Zionismus ohne Volksbewußtsein', *Frankfurter Israelitischen Familienblattes* 8, no. 10 (11 März 1910): 5.

131 On the 30 March 1913 the Central Association adopted a policy of *modus vivendi* towards the Zionists. The issue was framed as a 'Jewish Question' as Fuchs and Holländer, noted that they did not want to 'solve the German Jewish Question internationally', in other words, through the establishment of a Jewish homeland in Palestine. Fuchs also mentioned Sombart, Oppenheimer and Goldstein's article, evidencing

The writer and artist Richard Huldschiner (1872–1931) was the first to reply to Oppenheimer. He distinguished between culture and civilisation to argue that culture was not learnt or acquired but inherited at birth.[132] 'Culture is the sum of all spiritual aspirations [*geistige Strebungen*] of a people [*Volk*] that is held together through objective kinship qualities and language'.[133] In turn, 'civilisation' is external, not tied to personality, and allows for co-habitation. Americans, for example, originated from different European cultures but as a whole formed an American civilisation. For Huldschiner German Jews participated in German civilisation but not culture. This *Stammeskultur* they shared instead with Eastern Jews. Speaking candidly, the author highlighted the disconnect in Germany whereby a Jew could hold German citizenship but not be fully German. They remained members of an uprooted people.[134] Employing a two-fold understanding of national identity, the author suggested that being a Zionist meant belonging to the Jewish *Stamm* but also the 'will' to be Zionist invoking the language utilised by Lazarus but applying it in a Zionist context.[135]

The first session of the Free Zionist Discussion Club was dedicated to Oppenheimer's article. In the discussion Oppenheimer's conceptual definitions were heavily criticised as historically oriented and not relevant to the present. Martin Buber declared that Oppenheimer was simply providing a historical account of present circumstances and was confusing the true purpose of Zionism. He rejected the distinction of an Eastern and Western Jewish experience, asserting that assimilation also occurred amongst Eastern Jews. Buber juxtaposed assimilation with Zionism maintaining that Oppenheimer misrepresented that Zionism was not a practical concern, like assimilation. Rather, Zionism was an idealistic goal that gave Jews the power to shape their existence.[136]

Oppenheimer had struck a chord within the Zionist Federation, such that four years later, at the fourteenth Zionist Delegation Day, his article was once again debated.[137] However, rather than only being confined to Zionist circles, the debate on a Jewish *Volksbewußtsein* or *Stammesbewußtsein* resonated within wider Jewish circles.[138] When

---

the legacy and consequences of these articles for the Jewish community see Eugen Fuchs, *Um Deutschtum und Judentum*, 242.

132 Richard Huldschiner, 'Stammesbewusstsein – Volksbewusstsein', *Die Welt* XIV, no. 9 (4 März 1910): 179.

133 Ibid.

134 Ibid, 180.

135 This distinction was also made by Oskar Cohn in his argument on changing the wording of Article 113 and is discussed at greater length in chapter three.

136 Anon., 'Deutschland: Zur Oppeneheimer-Debatte', *Die Welt* XIV, no. 13 (1 April 1910): 287.

137 Anon., 'Die Woche, Berlin, 24 Juni 1914', *Allegemeine Zeitung des Judentums* 28, no. 26 (26 Juni 1914): 304.

138 Not only German Zionists, but also German Jews began to increasingly employ the language of *Stamm*. See Egmont Zechlin, *Die deutsche Politik und die Juden im Ersten Weltkrieg* (Göttingen: Vandenhoeck & Ruprecht, 1969), 70.

in 1913 the Central Association announced their official position on Zionism, Oppenheimer's argument was used to clearly delineate an opposition towards national Jewish
sentiments rather than feelings of kinship (*Stamm*).[139] A few years later, in 1917, the
Director of the Central Association, Eugen Fuchs, described himself as a 'Jew on account of religion and kin' (*Stamm*). For Fuchs, the concept of the nation was 'not a
question of being' but reflected 'an act of volition'. German Jews were like German
Christians, 'just like a Friesian peasant's tribal [*Stamm*] heritage does not separate
him from a Rheinish industrial worker or a Berlin proletarian'.[140] Walther Rathenau
similarly described himself as a 'German of the Jewish kin' (*Stamm*).[141] In a distinct
shift in discourse, more liberal German Jews began to frame their identity by appealing
to the vocabulary of the German cultural nation (*Stamm, Abstammung*) to espouse an
alternative model of statehood. This was based on volition to the state; a tradition associated with French, not German, models of political belonging.

Oppenheimer crucially interrogated the idea of community consciousness. He distinguished between being part of a shared history and descent, and engaging with the
present condition, a shared language, customs, culture. This debate was a Petri dish for
ideas that would become practically relevant in the First World War when vast swathes
of territory with different ethnic populations came under the jurisdiction of the Central Powers. As the dormant Polish Question resurfaced, the German army also faced
the so-called *Ostjudenfrage;* what to do with the population of six million Jews? In an
unprecedented situation, 'instead of the ghetto coming to Germany, Germany came
to the ghetto [as] Prussian soldiers, impoverished inhabitants of countless shtetls, and
middle-class German Jews were flung together'.[142] Countless German Jews through the
encounter with Eastern European Jews, for the first time, had to confront their self-
understanding of *Nationalbewußtsein* and *Volksbewußtsein*. Jews, however, were not the
only soldiers to be challenged by their ethnic and national understandings. Instances
abounded of Prussian soldiers being accused of dual loyalty as some began to openly
identify with the culture of Baltic ethnic groups on the Eastern Front.[143]

When the Russian Empire, and its Entente allies (Britain and France), were declared
enemies of Germany, many German Zionists saw the war as an auspicious moment,
even the last hope, for the liberation of Jews from the yoke of Tsarist Russia, thus in-

---

139 'Referat über die Stellung des Centralvereins zum Zionimus in der Delegierten-Versammlung vom
30. März 1913' in Fuchs, *Um Deutschtum und Judentum*, 241.
140 The article was originally published in *Neue jüdische Montashefte* 1, no. 22, (1917): 629–641. Quoted in
van Rahden, 'Germans of the Jewish Stamm', 35.
141 Walter Rathenau, *An Deutschlands Jugend* (Berlin: 1918), 9. Quoted in Walther Rathenau, *Walther Rathenau, Industrialist, Banker, Intellectual, and Politician: Notes and Diaries, 1907–1922*, ed. Hilary Pogge von
Strandmann and Caroline Pinder-Cracraft (Oxford: Clarendon Press, 1985), 6.
142 Aschheim, *Brothers and Strangers*, 139.
143 Vejas Gabriel Liulevicius, *War Land on the Eastern Front: Culture, National Identity, and German Occupation in World War I* (Cambridge, UK: Cambridge University Press, 2000), 192.

fusing lingering debates over Jewish questions with a renewed practical urgency.[144] For statist Zionists such as Bodenheimer and Oppenheimer, the war actualised their understanding of dual nationality. They embodied this dual loyalty as they lobbied for Jewish nationalist aspirations through negotiations with German Foreign Office officials where they offered Jews as guarantors and promoters of German colonial interests in Eastern Europe and Palestine. The importance of Bodenheimer was that his ideas indebted to those espoused by Oppenheimer, as will be shown in chapter two, had a legacy.

The Oppenheimer debate built on earlier discussions on the Jewish Question by re-affirming the national characteristics of the Jews. However, where previous debates in 1879 and 1897 alluded to an East-West divide in the Jewish community, Oppenheimer made this the focal point of the Jewish Question. He suggested that, unlike Western Jews, Eastern Jews, as a consequence of the violence and inequalities they faced in their respective countries were forced to derive their national consciousness from their Jewish culture. Western Jews, instead, could claim a historical connection to Jewish nationhood through their *Stammesbewusstsein,* without this undermining their German nationality.

Following the position of the Zionist Federation as outlined in their 1897 pamphlet, Oppenheimer had decoupled nationhood from statehood. However, the ensuing debate revealed another facet to the Jewish Question. A younger generation of Zionists argued against the older generation that Jewish nationality and German citizenship were incompatible. They suggested that the Jewish Question concerned the national-cultural revival of the Jewish people in Palestine. Similar to Treitschke, they insisted on cultural homogeneity, their focus however was not on the German but rather the Jewish people. This project of promoting an exclusive nationalism based on an incorporated Jewish nationality and statehood became formally institutionalised in the Zionist Federation in 1912. The same year, however, the prominent sociologist, Werner Sombart, offered a new solution to the Jewish Question. He advocated for the toleration of national groups, including Jews, and outlined a model for a culturally pluralist Germany.

Nations in the German state:
Werner Sombart's *Die Zukunft der Juden* (1911)

Only a year following Oppenheimer's article, in the autumn of 1911 to 1912 a series of publications triggered a public discourse on the Jewish Question most of which were contributed to or commissioned by the eminent sociologist Werner Sombart.[145] The

---

144   This was a majority view held in the German Jewish community. See Jehuda Reinharz, 'Ideology and Structure in German Zionism, 1882–1933', *Jewish Social Studies*, 42, no. 2 (1980): 130.

145   Aside from this lecture series, these publications included an edited book by Sombart, *Judentaufen* published in 1912 and an anthology on the Jewish Question which Sombart contributed to, published the

focus of this section, however, will be on Sombart's lesser-known lecture series which was published as a brochure entitled, *Die Zukunft der Juden*.[146] Employing similar language to both Treitschke and the ZVfD, Sombart offered yet another answer to the Jewish Question. Similar to the Zionist position, Sombart also rejected Treitschke's demand for the full assimilation of Jews into German culture arguing that it was not only impossible, but also not desirable. Although starting from the same premise as Treitschke, by recognising the separate (racial and national) characteristics of Jews, Sombart reached a different conclusion. Sombart urged Jews to embrace their separate cultural identity and national characteristics, framing these, in contrast to Treitschke, as a positive attribute. Rather than demanding change of the Jews, Sombart advocated in favour of a pluralist model, the co-existence of separate nations within Germany.

In Berlin in the closing months of 1911 Werner Sombart was feeling compelled, as an expert on capitalism and the Jews, to respond to the 'problem of practical Jewish politics'.[147] He organised a series of lectures on the subject of, 'the future of the Jews', which was published as an edited pamphlet the following year. It was in this two-part lecture series that Sombart explicitly outlined his view on the Jewish Question. Concerning himself with this subject, Sombart was, in his view, responding to the *Zeitgeist*. 'Once again Israel is on everyone's lips,' he wrote, 'once again wider circles of the population

---

same year entitled, *Die Judenfrage: Ein Sammelband*. Although the surveys had been published in various newspapers over the years, the anthology offered the first comprehensive collection on public responses to the 'Jewish Question'. For a comprehensive analysis of the anthology see Thomas Gräfe, 'Der Hegemonie-verlust des Liberalismus. Die "Judenfrage" im Spiegel der Intellektuellenbefragungen 1885–1912', in *Jahrbuch für Antisemitismusforschung 25*, ed. Stefanie Schüler-Springorum (Berlin: Metropol Verlag, 2016), 74–100. The former brochure (*Judentaufen*) invited contributions from prominent figures including Matthias Erzberger, Friedrich Naumann, Richard Dehmel, Franz Oppenheimer, Ferdinand Tönnies, Alfred Weber. The brochure contributed to a debate on Jewish conversion which began with an article published by the *Deutsche Montags-Zeitung* suggesting the only way for Jews to fully assimilate was through conversion to Christianity. Walter Rathenau responded with a series of articles which were collectively re-printed as *Staat und Judentum* in 1911. For Rathenau, conversion was opportunistic more often not based on faith, thus an act he could not endorse. Moreover, it meant supporting an unjust policy of discrimination by the Prussian state, a 'pseudo-Germanic exclusiveness', which Rathenau claimed he would fight against. See Rathenau, *Walther Rathenau, Industrialist, Banker, Intellectual, and Politician*, 98–99. Shulamit Volkov, *Walther Rathenau: Weimar's Fallen Statesman* (New Haven: Yale University Press, 2012), 105–106. Sven Brömsel, Patrick Küppers, and Clemens Reichhold, *Walther Rathenau im Netzwerk der Moderne* (Oldenbourg: Walter de Gruyter GmbH & Co KG, 2014), 269.

146 Werner Sombart, *Die Zukunft der Juden* (Leipzig: Verlag von Dunckert & Humblot, 1912).

147 In 1911, Werner Sombart's *Die Juden und das Wirtschaftleben* was declared the book of the year. Sombart built on Max Weber's *Die protestantische Ethik und der Geist des Kapitalismus* (1904), in which, as the title suggests, Weber argued that the protestant work ethic was a driver of capitalism. Sombart accepted the premise of Weber's study, that the origins of modern capitalism stemmed from religious roots but turned his analysis to the relationship between Jews and capitalism. An important distinction, however, was that Sombart did not argue that it was the Jewish religion that was a driver of modern capitalism but rather the corporate status of Jewry, based on their supposed racial and physiological characteristics. Sombart's book opened a discussion on Jews and capitalism and whether highlighting Jewish particularities was in itself antisemitic or not. Friedrich Lenger, *Werner Sombart, 1863–1941: eine Biographie* (München: Beck, 1994), 209.

in all cultural lands (*Kulturländern*) are concerned with the question of the future of the Jews, because the present brings our awareness every day back to "the Jewish Question".[148] Between 1871 and 1910, the Jewish population in Germany had increased by 100,000 to 615,000 of which around 13 % included newly settled Eastern European Jews.[149] Despite this increase in the Jewish population, as the German population had expanded by 58 %, the Jewish share of the population dropped to 0.95 %.[150] Jews now represented an even smaller share of the population and yet the question of their status within Germany remained on the political agenda.

For Sombart, the subject of the Jews in Western Europe was no longer a topic of public discussion, partly due, in Sombart's opinion, to the decision by the liberal press to ignore the subject.[151] These circles held onto the hope that the 'time of the Jewish problem' would soon be resolved and that continuous discussions would only hinder the 'healing process of this wound'.[152] Yet for Sombart this *Totschweigepolitik* was both 'short-sighted and unwise'. Instead, he stressed that differences in opinion were only made sharper when one prevented them from appearing on a public stage.[153]

Dispelling charges that his lectures promoted antisemitism, Sombart differentiated between criticising the political status of Jews and highlighting the problems in German-Jewish cohabitation. For Sombart the charge of antisemitism belonged to those who sought to reverse emancipation and ultimately hated the Jews.[154] However, Sombart did not agree it was antisemitic to identify that there were certain 'Jewish particularities and bad habits' and that living together with Jews was a 'serious problem'.[155]

Much like Oppenheimer's article a central theme of Sombart's lecture was the East versus West divide within the Jewish community, which he brought to a much larger and more public audience than Oppenheimer had. Sombart began his lecture by highlighting the separate existential conditions (*Daseinsbedingungen*) amongst the European Jewish populations, which meant that 'their futures will be (and should be) different'.[156] 'The problem of the Eastern Jews is a problem of their accommodation, persecution and more precisely, settlement or resettlement' wrote Sombart.[157] Given that the legal and economic situation of Eastern Jews would most likely not improve, Sombart concluded that continued colonisation of Palestine offered the 'best solution'

---

148 Sombart, *Die Zukunft der Juden*, 5.
149 Berghahn, *Imperial Germany*, 102.
150 Kaplan, *The Making of the Jewish Middle Class*, 5–7.
151 Sombart, *Die Zukunft der Juden*, 6.
152 Ibid.
153 Ibid.
154 Sombart wrote that he could not comprehend this hatred for a whole people. Lenger, *Werner Sombart*, 211.
155 *Norddeutsche Allgemeine Zeitung*, (10 Februar 1912). Quoted in ibid.
156 Sombart, *Die Zukunft der Juden*, 10.
157 Ibid, 27.

for Eastern European Jews.[158] Making an argument that political-statist Zionists had been advocating since the turn of the century, Sombart stressed that a large Jewish population in Palestine would serve as a commercial 'asset' for European nations.[159]

In 'direct antithesis' to the experience of Eastern Jews, Sombart analysed the experience of Jews in Western Europe and America employing racist stereotypes of Jews to illustrate the problem of 'assimilationist politics'.[160] Charting the influence of Jews in German society, Sombart claimed that that they occupied a quarter of all managerial positions in German corporations and an eighth of all directorial posts. In economic terms, Jews tended to be three to four times wealthier than Christians and in the cultural sphere, Sombart noted that whilst Jews did not necessarily always have all cultural industries 'in their grip', still they significantly influenced 'our art, our, literature, our music, our theatre and our large press'.[161] According to Sombart, Jews were also politically influential having participated in the genesis of liberalism and socialism and dined with 'a golden spoon at the table of the Kaiser'.[162] As a result of these developments Sombart concluded that Jewish elements existed in the German population.

For Sombart, 'assimilation politics' were problematic because they eroded a unique Jewish culture and were a source of conflict with the Gentile population. Moreover, he challenged if full assimilation could ever be possible on the basis that Jews could 'step-out' (*austreten*) of their religious community, but not of their race due to differences in physiognomy.[163] Whilst starting from the same premise as Treitschke, separating Jews from Gentiles on the basis of race, Sombart reached a radically different conclusion. Jews not only exhibited differences in their 'attitude and gestures' to Gentiles but juxtaposing the difference in blood between Jews and 'Aryan tribes', Sombart concluded that this difference could never be overcome.[164] Rather than demanding Jews assimi-

---

158 Ibid, 32.

159 See chapter two for how, during the war, the German government sought to use Russian Jews as mediators of German interests in Palestine. In his lecture, Sombart credited Arthur Ruppin's *Die Juden der Gegenwart* for influencing his work. Ibid, 10.

160 Ibid, 33.

161 Ibid, 35.

162 Ibid, 36.

163 Ibid, 36, 52. Sombart's discussion of the physiological features of Jews was not novel but stemmed from a turn towards the scientific method of the classification of groups in German scholarship. In the nineteenth century scholarship moved away from the use of (ambiguous) terms such as *Volk* and towards a scientific method of classifying national peoples. By 1838, a popular periodical the *Deutsche Vierteljahrsschrift* described the Jews using physiognomic criteria, and a decade later ran an article listing the universal physiological features of the Jewish 'race'. See Pierre James, *The Murderous Paradise: German Nationalism and the Holocaust* (Westport, Connecticut: Greenwood Publishing Group, 2001), 129.

164 This notion of blood lines was disputed by Max Weber in his post humorous, *Wirtschaft und Gesellschaft*, in which he argued that ethnic groups were not based on an 'objective blood relation' but rather on subjective conditions. A belief in common descent, for Weber, stemmed from similarities of 'physical type or customs or both, or because of the memories of colonisation and migration'. Max Weber, *Economy and Society*, ed. Guenther Roth and Claus Wittich, 2 vols (California: University of California Press, 1978), 389. Weber's conception of descent mirrored that of Lazarus rather than Sombart.

late to become Germans, Sombart urged Jews to maintain the 'purity' of their type (*Art*). 'Need I say that in the Jewish people [...] we see before us one of the most valuable species that the human race has produced?'.[165] For Sombart Jews and Germans suffered in the mixing of their essences (*Wesen*) writing, 'I wish that the "Judaization" [*Verjudung*] of broad areas of our public and spiritual life comes to an end, to the salvation of German culture, but equally to the Jewish'.[166]

Sombart idealised the purity of species and praised the 'Jewish renaissance' framing it as the 'national rebirth' of the Jews.[167] Sombart encouraged the colonisation of Palestine by Eastern European Jews but not Western European Jews, a view also advocated by statist Zionists.[168] The departure of Western Jews, according to Sombart, would cause an irreconcilable crisis in the economy. Sombart used the example of the expulsion of Jews from Spain and Portugal under the Conquistadors to stress the adverse effect the same actions would have on Germany.[169] Rather than involving Western Jews in the practicalities of building the Jewish state, which would be to the detriment of the German economy and culture, Sombart held up the Jewish state, with a reference to Kantian philosophy, as a 'regulative idea'.[170] By this he advocated for an internal change, a reform in attitude (*Gesinnungsreform*) within Jewry whereby the will to be Jewish was strengthened for the preservation of Jewish culture and tradition.[171] The notion of a revival of Jewish identity sat uncomfortably with the majority of liberal bourgeois German Jewry but spoke to a younger generation of Zionists.

Having built a case against assimilation but also Jewish emigration, Sombart outlined how Jewish nationals could continue to live in Germany. 'How will, how can, how should populations [*Völker*] live together with Jewish nationals [*empfindenen Judenschaft*]?'[172] Sombart praised the addition of Jewish elements to the 'colourful mixture that represents "us Germans"'. Yet, in the following sentence he criticised (once again) the mixing of Jewish physiognomic 'dark features' with 'blond' Germans.[173] To improve the co-existence of Jews and Germans Sombart encouraged the redistribution of Jews throughout Germany to avoid their concentration in large numbers. However, concentration did not correlate with communal cohesion. Whilst in 1910, Posen had a low concentration of Jews (1.3 % of the population) it was the only part of the Empire where Jews were 'sufficiently rooted for them to act as a group', especially in munici-

---

165 Sombart, *Die Zukunft der Juden*, 56.
166 Ibid, 58.
167 Ibid, 59–60.
168 Ibid, 67.
169 Ibid, 68.
170 Ibid, 65.
171 Ibid, 69.
172 Ibid, 70.
173 Ibid, 71.

pal politics.[174] Against the charge that his thesis would lead to the erection of ghettos, Sombart declared in little else than a rhetorical flare, there will be 'no renaissance of the ghetto alongside the renaissance of the Jews'.[175]

For Sombart, the Jewish Question concerned how Jews, as a national group, and Gentiles could co-exist within Germany. In order to present a viable programme, Sombart delved into the larger challenges brought on by modernity. He envisioned a cosmopolitan and globalised existence, rooted in the idea of a homeland. 'When the modern man stands with his feet on his homeland, he can project his love into various foreign cultures and can live within them'.[176] In line with the notion espoused by statist Zionists, Sombart proposed that national consciousness and citizenship could, and should, be decoupled he wrote,

> What do national consciousness [*Volksbewusstsein*] and citizenship [*Staatsbürgertum*] have to do with one another? Can one not at the same time be a self-conscious Jew and a very good German (in citizenship terms)?[177]

Criticising the nation-state model, Sombart described the union of these ideas as a negative by-product of the era. 'Our egalitarian time and the lack of talent of our states-men have the same goal: to standardise all citizens in cultural and national terms'.[178] As for many Germans at the time, Sombart recognised that culture was inseparable from national understanding within Germany but condemned ethnically homogenous na-tions. Sombart declared that it would be a 'horrid impoverishment' for a land like Germany if all the various ethnic groups (*Stammesarten*) were extinguished only to be replaced by a singular Prussian *Stamm* and encouraged the promotion of national characteristics, especially language, in Germany's minorities including the Poles and French.[179]

Turning to the Jewish minority and the problem of professional discriminations against Jews, Sombart missed the essence of the Jewish fight for equality. He did not consider the difficulties for Jews to receive a professional appointment as a case of the 'violation of a fundamental right'.[180] Rather, in instances where Jews were excluded from the Officer Corps, Sombart professed it was of benefit for the Jews as this profes-sion should be reserved for military families.[181] In a prophetic tone, Sombart affirmed

---

174 Pulzer, *Jews and the German State*, 130.
175 Sombart, *Die Zukunft der Juden*, 73.
176 Ibid, 74.
177 Ibid, 76.
178 Ibid.
179 Ibid, 76.
180 Ibid, 77–80.
181 Ibid, 84.

that should 'Jewish elements' start entering the Officer Corps the 'antisemitic dynamite' would alight.[182]

Contrary to demanding the full realisation of *de facto* equality, Sombart postulated that the social situation of Jews in Germany was better than in other European countries and America,[183] because Jews had not 'penetrated' all areas of society, creating fewer areas of friction.[184] Similarly, denying that full equality could exist between peoples, Sombart concluded that certain relationships between people could not be equalised through legal measures, such as emancipation, but required changes in individual behaviour. For Sombart this epitomised the relationship between Jews and Gentiles in the modern state. 'States give their Jewish citizens full equality' and in return, according to Sombart, 'Jews will have the wisdom and tact to not utilise this equality to the full and in all settings.'[185]

Sombart concluded by reflecting on the *Zeitgeist*. First, he interrogated the relationship between the collective and the individual, between nationhood (*Volkstum*) and humanity (*Menschtum*) to explore how politics and culture were inextricably linked.[186] Sombart then turned to the generational divide in politics and nationalist turn. Where the older generations encouraged 'cosmopolitanism' and 'internationalism', the younger generations – described as 'we' by Sombart – renounced these ideas in favour of focusing on differences in 'blood' and 'culture'.[187] In light of this nationalist turn, Sombart stressed to not lose sight of the individual. He encouraged thinking about individuals (*Menschen*) rather than nations (*Völkern*). Sombart reminded his audience of the humanitarian values espoused in Christianity and the Enlightenment, which underscored the obligations towards the individual such as 'love, compassion and goodwill'.[188]

Sombart's emphasis on the individual and humanity directly related to the relationship between Jews and non-Jews, a subject he thought 'should not be necessary to emphasise'. Referencing the 'raw' and 'carnal' persecution of the Jews in the east (most likely the Russian Empire) Sombart challenged manifestations of antisemitism (hatred, distain, sneering, brutal treatment of Jews). He did not condemn 'apathetic

---

182 Ibid, 86.

183 Sombart thought America was one of the countries with the highest levels of antisemitism. For an analysis of the levels of antisemitism in different European countries from 1899 to 1939 see William I. Brustein and Ryan D. King, 'Anti-Semitism in Europe before the Holocaust', *International Political Science Review* 25, no. 1 (2004): 35–53. On antisemitism in America see Leonard Dinnerstein, *Antisemitism in America* (Oxford University Press, 1995).

184 Sombart, *Die Zukunft der Juden*, 85.

185 Ibid, 87.

186 Ibid, 88–91. *Volkstum* and *Menschtum* find no comparable translation in English. *Volkstum* aside from nationhood also denotes nationality, national traditions, national character, ethnicity, folklore. *Menschtum* appears to be a word coined by Sombart to represent the values bestowed by the Enlightenment and Christianity which honour the individual.

187 Ibid, 88.

188 Ibid, 89.

antisemitism' conceding that it was a product of humanity that would last for eternity, 'as long as the Earth exists'. Nonetheless he urged that 'despite differences in blood, [...] in countries with a humanity, [...] we have to recognise [Jews] as our fellow human brothers'.[189]

In a utopian vision, Sombart projected that at a certain 'height of humanity' one which separates the 'masses' from the 'citizens', group instincts and national characteristics would cease to exist and 'Germans, English and Russians, Blacks, Jews and the Chinese will find themselves in a united community bound by humanity'. Individual friendships would transcend national differences.[190] Furthermore, he saw no contradiction between *Volkstum* and *Menschtum* but rather thought together they would lead to 'the richness of our culture'.[191]

The responses to Sombart's lecture series varied considerably. Whilst Sombart's lecture series was reported on extensively in German Jewish liberal and Zionist newspapers, it received far less attention in the non-Jewish German press. According to the *Jüdische Rundschau*, the *Berliner Tageblatt* had not reported a single word on Sombart's two lectures in Berlin.[192] In his second lecture, Sombart also remarked on the absence of reports on his lectures by the 'liberal press'.[193] Thus, it is difficult to gauge the public reaction to Sombart's lecture series.[194]

One possible indicator of the significance of Sombart's lecture series was that it contributed towards a growing interest in the Zionist movement amongst Gentiles. During the First World War Zionism emerged as a 'factor on the international stage'.[195] In Germany institutional support was given to the movement when in April 1918 the German Committee for the Promotion of Jewish Settlement in Palestine (*Deutsches Komitee zur Förderung der jüdischen Palästinasiedlung*) was established.[196] The committee was founded by notable Gentiles and included prominent individuals such as Hans

---

189 Ibid.
190 There are numerous examples of individuals not perceiving any contradiction in problematising Jewish existence in Germany, whilst claiming personal friendships to Jews. See Lenger, *Werner Sombart*, 216.
191 Sombart, *Die Zukunft der Juden*, 91.
192 Anon., 'Sombart und wir', *Jüdische Rundschau* XVI, no. 50 (15 Dezember 1911): 589.
193 Anon., 'Letzter Vortrag Professor Sombarts', *Jüdische Rundschau* XVI, no. 50 (15 Dezember 1911): 591.
194 Without a record of the exact dates Sombart gave his lectures, or when his lectures were published, it is difficult to locate responses within popular newspapers. Moreover, some of the major papers in Germany, such as the *Frankfurter Allgemeine* and *Berliner Tageblatt* were published by Jewish-owned publishing houses. It would not have been in the interest of these publishers to promote Zionist views, which is why Goldstein's article was rejected. Perhaps they did not want to give a platform to Sombart's work. Most secondary sources focus on the Jewish response to Sombart's lecture series, suggesting that Gentile sources have either been difficult to locate, or that a substantial debate did not take place.
195 Friedman, *Germany, Turkey, and Zionism*, vii.
196 The *Jüdische Rundschau* reported on the 3 May 1918 on the founding of the committee. For an account on the history of the first committee see Zechlin, *Die deutsche Politik und die Juden im Ersten Weltkrieg*, 413–48.

Delbrück, Major Franz Carl Endres, Gustav Noske and Georg Gothein.[197] The extended committee of thirty-four members, included Werner Sombart, Alfred and Max Weber, Matthias Erzberger, Philip Scheidemann and Börries Freiherr von Münchhausen.[198] The 1918 committee was short-lived, ceasing all activities the following year. However, coinciding with Germany's entry into the League of Nations, the committee was revived with minor changes to the original manifesto. The renamed German Pro-Palestine Committee (*Deutsches Pro-Palästina Komitee*) publicly supported Jewish work in Palestine with the aim to expand German economic relations in the region.[199]

In contrast to the Gentile reaction to Sombart's lectures, the response from the German Jewish community was animated. Within the German Jewish community, Sombart's ideas were misread by both Zionists and liberals as promoting a Zionist agenda. Liberal Jews were shocked that Sombart supported the Zionist contention that Jews were a nation, a view held by less than 1 % of the German Jewish community and the Central Association urged its members to boycott Sombart's lectures.[200] Zionists, in turn, delighted in the platform and public attention created by Sombart.[201] As the *Jüdische Rundschau*, the German Zionist organ expressed, Sombart's lecture reached a public that otherwise would not have listened, nor responded, to the same questions asked by a Jew. Sombart had achieved the first point in Herzl's programme, to open a European public discussion on the Jewish Question.[202]

One Zionist commentator, praised Sombart's lecture for its 'objective, unemotional, free from academic antisemitism' account on the future of the Jews.[203] A highpoint in the lecture, was the discussion of the blood differences between Jews and their 'host nations' (*Wirtsvölkern*).[204] He praised Sombart for tackling a subject which, in his view, was either condemned outright, dismissed as uncomfortable, or labelled antisemitic.

---

197 Georg Gothein was the only committee member of Jewish descent who sat in the central eight-person committee. In the extended committee of thirty-four members, four were of Jewish descent. See Josef Walk, 'Das "Deutsche Komitee Pro Palästina" 1926–1933', *Bulletin des Leo Baecks Instituts* 15, no. 52 (1976): 163.

198 The fact that an avowed National Socialist was part of the committee illustrates its broad political spectrum.

199 Walk, 'Das "Deutsche Komitee Pro Palästina"', 164.

200 In 1910, the Zionist Federation had 6,200 paying members. Lavsky estimates that including their families, Zionists represented around 2–3 % of the German-Jewish population. See Lavsky, *Before Catastrophe*, 22–23.

201 Lenger, *Werner Sombart*, 213.

202 Anon., 'Sein oder Nichtsein?', 541.

203 Hans Goslar, 'Werner Sombart über die Zukunft der Juden' *Jüdische Rundschau* XVI, no 46 (17 November 1911): 543–44.

204 The appropriation of antisemitic language of race by Jews had already started at the turn of the century and was not uncommon especially amongst national and Zionist Jews. This trend was analysed by Friedrich Hertz in *Moderne Rassentheorien* (Wien: C.W. Stern, 1904) [https://bit.ly/2Ysnoib, accessed 17/06/18]. Karl Kautsky also tackled the subject in his pamphlet *Rasse und Judentum* (Berlin und Stuttgart: J.H.W. Dietz, 1914), which was disparaging of Sombart. Kautsky correlated the emergence of Zionism with antisemitism and argued that Jews were not a race. Instead he presented an alternative vision of the future of the Jews where inequalities would be overcome through the socialist productive state and Jews would

Amongst the diverse responses from the German Jewish community on Sombart's lecture series, they shared one similarity. They agreed that Sombart was not an expert on Jewish issues. One article reported that Sombart's lectures had offered 'nothing new' on the subject of the 'Jewish Question' and had made 'a few incorrect statements'. The article warned against thinking that the Zionists had a 'special reason' to appreciate Sombart's lectures, or claim him as a 'Zionist-friend'. Rather, what interested the Zionists were not the conclusions Sombart drew, but the questions he posed. The future of the Jews was a 'fateful question [*Schicksalfrage*] that only Jewry could give an answer to'. For Zionists, the importance of Sombart's lecture series, which drew 1,500 listeners, was that it evidenced that a large part of German society was interested in Jewish affairs.[205]

Liberal Jews agreed with Zionists that Sombart was not an authority on the Jewish Question. Eugen Fuchs, President of the Central Association, published a nuanced review on the lecture series, which captured the contradictions in Sombart's work. Where Treitschke said, 'the Jews are our misfortune', reported Fuchs, Sombart states that they are our 'fate willed by god'.[206] Rather than trying to categorise Sombart, Fuchs chose to challenge Sombart's method and the inconsistencies in his argument which Fuchs described as 'an attempt to vindicate the denial of equality'.[207] Fuchs illustrated how Sombart described Jews as foreigners but stressed they should remain in Germany. He termed them a 'magnificent species' but called for an end to *Verjudung*. Jews had to be given equality, according to Sombart, but they had to tactfully not exercise it to the full.[208] Fuchs was most concerned with the consequences of Sombart's lecture series for the Jewish community especially the delicate relationship between the Central Association and the Zionist Federation, which was not defined by Jewish nationhood, 'concepts such as *völkisch* [...] *staatlich*'. Rather, the organisations were united through a commitment to peaceful cultural work for the improvement of the social situation of Jews.[209]

The significance of Sombart's lecture series was bringing the recognition of Jews as a nation to a public audience from the perspective of a liberal Gentile public intellectual rather than an antisemite or Zionist. Whilst Sombart described differences in blood and spirit between Jews and Aryans, using the language of race was not antisemitic. Race was commonly used as a 'conceptual framework' by Jewish intellectuals and was regarded as objective academic scholarship. It was for this reason used by antisemites

---

no longer be viewed as a separate nationality. For the English translation, see Karl Kautsky 'Are the Jews a Race?' from the 2nd German ed. (London: Jonathon Cape, 1926).

205 Anon., 'Sein oder Nichtsein?', 541.
206 Eugen Fuchs, 'Die Zukunft der Juden', *Im deutschen Reich* 6 (June 1912): 267.
207 Ibid, 265.
208 Ibid.
209 Ibid, 274.

to add rigour and legitimacy to their work.[210] Whilst not a self-declared Zionist, Sombart did reveal his indebtedness to Zionist writings, employing vocabulary and ideas from Zionist debates on the Jewish Question in 1897 and 1910. Sombart criticised assimilation politics given that Jews could never renounce their race and proposed the decoupling of the nation from the state arguing that a Jewish nationality did not negate German civic consciousness.

Crucially, however, for Sombart the Jewish state was only a regulative idea. For statist Zionists, such as Oppenheimer, whilst immigration to Palestine was encouraged for Eastern European Jews, they nonetheless envisioned that they were contributing towards the establishment of a Jewish state for future generations. For Zionists, the Jewish state was a constitutive idea and in this way their response to the Jewish Question differed from Sombart.

In contrast to the 1879 public debate on the Jewish Question, which pivoted around assimilation and the necessity of an *Einheitskultur* in Germany, Sombart urged Jews to embrace their national and cultural differences, which he argued should be protected within Germany. Where the 1879 debate exposed Treitschke's liberal ambivalence towards the Jewish Question, Sombart exhibited the position of a diversity liberal by advocating for a culturally pluralist Germany.

Although in principle inclusive of different nations and cultures Sombart, like Treitschke, placed the onus on Jews to change to enable this coexistence to function. Specifically, he encouraged Jews to regulate their behaviour in order to not exercise their equal rights in all contexts. He also suggested that Jews relocate across Germany to avoid their concentration in large numbers. Discrimination against Jews in public professions, for Sombart, was not a matter of the violation of a fundamental right. Rather, it had helped avoid additional areas of friction in society. Although Sombart promoted an inclusive nationhood, peaceful co-existence would be ensured not by the state but by Jews regulating their behaviour. The respondents to Sombart's lecture series were predominately Jewish and for this reason, it is difficult to gauge Gentile responses to the proposal of multiculturalism in Germany. The same year, however, a relatively unknown journalist Moritz Goldstein published an article on the existence of a separate Jewish culture in Germany. His article triggered a public debate eliciting numerous responses and provides a unique insight into both liberal Jewish and Gentile reactions to the idea of a separate national cultural community of Jews within Germany.

---

210 For Jewish intellectuals writing on race see Mitchell Bryan Hart, *Jews and Race: Writings on Identity and Difference, 1880–1940*, The Brandeis Library of Modern Jewish Thought (Waltham, Massachusetts: Brandeis University Press, 2011).

Jewish questions, European questions:
Moritz Goldstein's *Deutsch-Jüdischer Parnaß* (1912)

Published shortly after Sombart's lecture series, Moritz Goldstein's article *Deutsch-Jüdischer Parnaß*, featured in the popular cultural magazine (*Der Kunstwart*) edited by Ferdinand Avenarius, similarly addressed the question of the future of Jews in Germany. Whilst it is difficult to gauge the extent to which Goldstein was influenced by Sombart, Goldstein was living in Berlin at the time of Sombart's lectures. He was a student at Berlin University, active in the Zionist student movement and might have attended Sombart's lectures.[211] Certainly, the editor, Avenarius, was aware of Sombart's lecture series and timed the publication of Goldstein's article. In his introduction to Goldstein's article, Avenarius, quoting Sombart, agreed with him that the 'Jewish problem' was the 'biggest problem for humanity' which should be recognised by 'those who think that everything in Germany is comfortable'.[212]

Der Kunstwart was known to publish works reflecting *Ausdruckskultur*,[213] the 'genuine expression of the characteristics of a nation, and especially of the German nation'.[214] It was on this basis that having faced rejection from three publishers, including the *Berliner Tagesblatt*, Goldstein submitted his article to the prestigious cultural journal.[215] Like Sombart, Goldstein, from the outset, had intended to stimulate an open and honest discussion on the characteristics of the German nation, and the place of Jews within this, which he argued either often descended into allegations of antisemitism when raised by Christian Gentiles or alternatively was outright denied as an issue by liberal Jews.[216] Equating 'Jewish questions' with 'European questions', Goldstein thought it appropriate to have the 'non-Jewish general public' act as witness to the debate. To all intents and purposes, Goldstein's article generated a public discussion on the Jewish Question, although it was only six months after it was published, in the August issue of *Der Kunstwart* where the debate was framed as such.[217]

---

211 Mortiz Goldstein, 'German Jewry's Dilemma', *The Leo Baeck Institute Year Book* 2, no. 1 (1957): 246.
212 Ferdinand Avenarius, 'Aussprachen Mit Juden', *Der Kunstwart* 25, no. 22 (August 1912): 226 [https://bit.ly/2VrJfmN, accessed 03/07/2019].
213 This thematic leaning was also included in the sub-title of the journal for the editions published between 1907 to 1915. *Der Kunstwart. Halbmonatsschau für Ausdruckskultur auf allen Lebensgebieten (1907–1912); Der Kunstwart und Kulturwart. Halbmonatsschau für Ausdruckskultur auf allen Lebensgebieten (1912–1915)*.
214 Goldstein, 'German Jewry's Dilemma', 245.
215 For a recent short account on this debate see Thomas Gräfe, 'Deutsch-Jüdischer Parnaß (Artikel von Moritz Goldstein, 1912)', in *Handbuch des Antisemitismus. Judenfeindschaft in Geschichte und Gegenwart*, ed. Wolfgang Benz, vol. 7 (Berlin: De Gruyter, 2015), 68–70.
216 Mortiz Goldstein, 'Deutsch-Jüdischer Parnaß', *Der Kunstwart* 25, no. 11 (März 1912): 281–82 [https://bit.ly/2H8YZ4i, accessed 03/07/2019].
217 Ferdinand Avenarius, 'Aussprachen mit Juden', 225–236; Anon., 'Sprechsaal: Aussprache zur Judenfrage', *Der Kunstwart* 25, no. 22 (August 1912), 236–261 [https://bit.ly/2Wx2tnC, accessed 03/07/2019].

The problem summarised by Goldstein was that 'Jews administer the spiritual possession (*geistigen Besitz*) of a peoples (*Volkes*)' that denies Jews 'both the right and the ability to do so'.[218] Whilst addressing the specific topic of Jews in German culture, Goldstein opened a much larger debate which challenged the premise of whether Jews could ever fully integrate, and be fully accepted, into German society. His thesis conceded that there was an interconnection between *Judentum* and *Deutschtum* but simultaneously singled out the Jews as not really 'German' in all their characteristics and tendencies. 'Just as Sombart had asserted that the Jews dominated the economic and political, so Goldstein asserted they monopolised the intellectual and cultural life of Germany'.[219]

Tracing the predominance of Jews in the theatre and music scene, in the press and as German thinkers, Goldstein questioned their continued foreign status in Germany but in doing so, used language separating Jews from Germans.

> Are we, as you want it to be, still the strangers [*Fremden*], the foreigners, that speak the German language "as foreigners" as a "learnt language not a mother tongue"? We still have one thing in common with you, service to culture, service to humanity.[220]

Goldstein spoke to the essence of the identity crisis sweeping the secular Jewish youth who were witness to a rising tide of antisemitism, especially in higher education, and no longer accepted the assimilationist narrative of their parents but sought an alternative vision of Jewish life in Germany.

Goldstein stressed the 'barbarian injustice' shown towards Jews in Europe in order to highlight the hypocrisy that Europe could possibly be termed the 'paradise of fairness'. On the subject of the Jews, Goldstein asserted, even intelligent, well-educated people misrepresented the facts to justify hatred of the Jews.[221] Where Sombart had outlined a plan for the separate co-existence of Western Jews and Germans, so did Goldstein. This vision, however, left no room for an integrated German-Jewish *Volk*, a fear the Central Association had voiced about the Zionist movement as early as 1897.[222] Concluding his article Goldstein presented an answer to the problem of the Jewish Question that was similar to Sombart. Further assimilation was self-denial, he argued, Jews needed to create a separate and specifically 'Jewish' culture in Germany.

Ferdinand Avenarius, a poet and member of the cultural reform movement, who founded and edited *Der Kunstwart* described himself as feeling 'German-national "to his bones" but … not antisemitic'.[223] The journal had a conservative leaning and was

---

218 Goldstein, 'Deutsch-Jüdischer Parnaß', 283.
219 Jay Geller, *The Other Jewish Question: Identifying the Jew and Making Sense of Modernity* (Fordham University Press, 2011), 260.
220 Goldstein, 'Deutsch-Jüdischer Parnaß', 284.
221 Ibid, 284.
222 Lamberti, 'From Coexistence to Conflict', 54.
223 Avenarius, 'Aussprachen Mit Juden', 225.

well-regarded. Yet whilst Avenarius officially distanced himself from the antisemites, the journal's literary critic, Adolf Bartels had a reputation as a 'notorious antisemite'.[224] In the debates which unfolded in the wake of Goldstein's article, *Der Kunstwart* became a platform for several burgeoning antisemitic arguments.

When the March 1912 issue was published with Goldstein's piece featuring as the first in the volume, in the words of the author himself, 'the effect was sensational'.[225] For some time, Avenarius had wanted to orchestrate a public discussion on the Jewish Question and in his reply to Goldstein's submission had written that he thought it 'convenient that a Jew should open [this discussion]'.[226] To facilitate it, Avenarius increased the visibility of the journal and opened its opinion columns to readers' responses. The proceeding discussion developed in multiple issues in the form of special sections called *Sprechsaal*, which were dedicated to responses and opinion pieces on Goldstein's article. The first was published a month later in the first April issue under the title *Deutschtum und Judentum*. It was followed by another *Sprechsaal* in August in the second issue entitled, *Aussprache zur Judenfrage*.

In the introduction to the opinion column (*Sprechsaal*) of the August 1912 issue, Avenarius included a lengthy editorial essay which made explicit the subject under discussion, namely the Jewish Question.[227] Avenarius was careful to outline that his use of the plural pronoun referred to individuals that felt as 'national Germans' like himself and not 'antisemites'. However, the last, and lengthiest, commentary on the debate, penned by a 'Ph. Stauff', made a series of questionable claims. While even Avenarius thought 'Ph. Stauff' an antisemite, he published the essay, leaving the reader to form an opinion on the view expressed.[228] The Central Association lamented that Stauff misused the goodwill of Avenarius to write antisemitic comments that would otherwise have been unacceptable.[229] Avenarius also engaged in language that designated Jews as a separate group. He referred to them as a 'people' (*Volk*), 'racial community' (*Rassengemeinschaft*) and 'foreign tribe' (*fremde Stamm*). As well as suggesting Jews would be able to sympathise with the 'members of the host nation' (*Angehörigen eines Wirtsvolkes*) implying Jews were guests in Germany rather than full members of the nation-state. The delicate balance between censorship, freedom of speech and libel in the German Empire and how the debate on the Jewish Question wavered between

---

224 Goldstein, 'German Jewry's Dilemma', 246.
225 Ibid.
226 Ibid, 247.
227 The *Sprechsaal* for the April issue did not include a lengthy introduction but rather two short paragraphs outlining that the article had triggered a lively discussion in the so-called 'antisemitic' press and silence in the liberal so called 'Jewish' press.
228 Goldstein, 'German Jewry's Dilemma', 249.
229 Felix Goldmann-Oppeln, 'Der Ausklang der "Kunstwartdebatte"!', *Im deutschen Reich* 12 (Dezember 1912): 533–540.

these extremes was illustrated by the decision of *Der Kunstwart* to offer a platform for antisemitic views whilst the *Berliner Tageblatt* rejected the article.

The reception of the debate in *Der Kunstwart* offers an insight into the initial public that engaged with the Jewish Question; it was split between antisemites, conservative Gentiles, liberal Jews and Zionists.[230] What emerged was an ambivalence towards exclusionary, verging on antisemitic language, and the engagement with it by Jewish liberals. Even amongst the latter there was an acceptance of a 'hypostatised conception of [Jewish] essences' that were either visible or invisible.[231] Ernst Lissauer, the famous Jewish poet, and first respondent to Goldstein, conceded that Jewry exhibited characteristics (both physical and mental) that had been acquired through the experience of the ghetto. Whilst he claimed that these could be eradicated he acknowledged this would take time.[232] The idea of a 'Jewish spirit' (which had been written about by antisemites in the nineteenth century) was more openly discussed, also amongst Zionists, some of whom constructed a 'German spirit' that Jews could not rid themselves of.[233] This debate marked the beginning of a turning point in the Jewish Question whereby Judaism was not only a religion, a race but also a psychological condition affecting every Jew on an intimate, personal level.

With his article Goldstein sought to illustrate a shared German-Jewish history and culture. He did not intend to place in doubt the capacity or the right of Jews to engage in German cultural activities. He never meant for his article to be a Zionist call to action, or to suggest that Jews could not continue living in Germany as Germans. Rather he had written it, to be 'free of a tormenting trouble by ventilating it'.[234] Treitschke and Sombart had similarly given this as their motivation for writing on the subject. Like Sombart, Goldstein had brought to a wider public a statist Zionist perspective on the Jewish Question, namely that the Jews exhibited separate cultural characteristics. Similar to the 1897 policy of the Zionist Federation, Goldstein did not advocate the immigration of Jews to Palestine but rather the recognition of these unique characteristics. Fatally, however, Goldstein merely stated the problem without suggesting, like

---

230 Goldstein wrote that eventually 'the German-speaking press was full of discussion of my essay'. Similarly, Ascheim remarks that the debate moved outside of the realm of *Kunstwart*. Goldstein, 'German Jewry's Dilemma', 246; Steven E. Aschheim, '1912 The Publication of Mortiz Goldstein's "The German-Jewish Parnassus"', in *Yale Companion to Jewish Writing and Thought in German Culture, 1096–1996* (New Haven; London: Yale University Press, 1997), 300.

231 Aschheim, '1912 The Publication of Mortiz Goldstein's "The German-Jewish Parnassus"', 301.

232 Ernst Lissauer's view echoed that of Christian Wilhelm von Dohm who similarly suggested that Jews were a product of their environment, namely that their character had been shaped by their historical treatment, Lissauer, 'Sprechsaal: Deutschtum und Judentum', 6–12.

233 Aschheim, '1912 The Publication of Mortiz Goldstein's "The German-Jewish Parnassus"', 300.

234 Goldstein, 'German Jewry's Dilemma', 250.

Sombart, a future for Jews as a national, not religious, community in Germany. He thus left his article open to appropriation by antisemites.[235]

Significantly, the debate triggered by Goldstein's article revealed an eagerness in certain sections of German society to discuss the Jewish Question. Goldstein successfully brought the issue from a private conversation into a public forum. However, the lack of nuance in his argument merely stating a problem, as he retrospectively recognised, meant it descended into either rejecting the national characteristics of Jews in favour of religious traits or acknowledging them, to argue that German culture had been *verjudet*. Compared to prior debates on the Jewish Question, there was a greater recognition of the peculiar traits of Jews in cultural, physiological but also psychological terms. The debate was dominated by discussions on the (in)compatibility of Jews in the German cultural nation. The exclusiveness of this political model for national minorities within Germany was not challenged.

The Jewish Question: emancipation, assimilation, cultural homogeneity

It is made apparent throughout the course of these debates that the Jewish Question was caught in a balancing act between contingency and continuity. Whilst the meaning of the term was contingent on the context and agent, its continuity was that it became a litmus test for the health of the German nation. Both Gentiles and Jews contributed in equal part to the terms of the debate. They used similar vocabulary on the Jewish Question but brought different political and ideological agendas to their writings. Examining the place of the Jewish minority in Germany enabled discussants to decouple the nation from the state. Where some insisted on the importance of a unified, homogenous culture in the German state, others advocated for a pluralist, multicultural Germany.

The Jewish Question first caught on as a political catchword in 1842 during the public debate on the legal rights of Jews in Prussia. Whilst focused on the Jewish minority, the debate opened up a discussion on the role of religion in the modern state. The debate took place against the backdrop of revolutions and a wave of liberal reforms whereby Jewish populations in several countries (including America, France, the Netherlands, Belgium, and Canada) were granted political and civil rights on the basis of full religious equality. Jewish emancipation became closely associated with

---

235 In 1935 the 'Institute for the Study of the Jewish Question' published an anonymous book entitled 'The Jews in Germany' which attempted to legitimise and justify the treatment of the Jews by the National Socialists. The book dedicated the seventh chapter to the subject of the Jews as 'administrators of German culture' and all the credit for the coining of this phrase was given to the 'Jewish cultural writer Moritz Goldstein'. Ibid, 236–37.

modernising tendencies, progressive politics and the standard of democratisation in society. Thus, the 1842 debate established the parameters of the Jewish Question. It concerned Jewish emancipation and the necessity of state reform in Prussia. Crucially, Jews were described as a confessional group and their equal rights were demanded on the basis of religious equality. A few years later, in the year of the 1848 revolutions, Jews were granted full rights under the freedom of religion in the constitutional charter of Prussia.

Alongside the unification of Germany in 1871, the equality of all confessions was enshrined in the constitution signalling an end to the debate on the Jewish Question. As such, when in 1879 a public debate erupted on the subject of the Jewish Question, the parameters had shifted significantly. The context had moved from a focus on Prussia to the German Empire, and away from the state as it turned to the nation. All subsequent debates on the Jewish Question hereafter concentrated on the German nation and the compatibility of the German Jewish minority within this model. The only commentators to challenge Jewish legal rights were antisemites, all other discussants on the Jewish Question did not question the state as a neutral arbiter on the Jewish Question. Instead, discussions pivoted around the nation, specifically the possibilities of Jewish assimilation, the necessity of an *Einheitskultur*, the difference between national and cultural consciousness, and whether or not nationality had to be compatible with citizenship.

Significantly, the debates revealed that Jews and Gentiles inhabited the same discursive and conceptual world on the Jewish Question. Notably, the language of culture featured prominently as the debates and revealed the centrality of conceptions of Germany as a cultural nation (*Kulturnation*). Moritz Lazarus, one of the few discussants to suggest an alternative model of national belonging based on the principles of the political nation (*Staatsnation*), by invoking the vocabulary of *Stamm* and foregrounding the importance of language, conceded his indebtedness to the traditional discourse of the German cultural nation. Accompanying a discourse of culture in the Jewish Question was a shift towards conceiving of the Jews as more than just a religious community but also a race (*Rasse*), a kinship (*Stamm*) as well as a nation (*Volk*). In the constitution, Jews had been afforded rights as one of several confessional groups and had not been singled out as a distinct group or corporation within the Empire. However, unofficially, in the discussion on the Jewish Question, beginning with Heinrich von Treitschke's article published in 1879, they were publicly conceived of in group terms as a race and nation.

The identification of a Jewish national identity was not, however, only external. A small but growing number of German Jews began to identify as Jewish nationals, founding in 1897 the Zionist Federation of Germany. In the organisations' first pamphlet the Zionist stance on the Jewish Question was outlined. Unlike Treitschke, Zionists rejected assimilation, disregarded cultural homogeneity and focused instead on decoupling the nation from the state by interrogating the relationship between nationality and citizenship. Whilst liberal Jews denied a Jewish nationality, Zionists separated the concept into national and patriotic loyalty. They argued that Jewish nationality was compatible with German patriotism as they remained loyal German citizens. The appropriation of the Jewish Question by Zionists marked a significant shift in agency whereby the object became both the subject and object of analysis. Moreover, debates on the Jewish Question by the German-Jewish community forces us to reorient how we think about the normative Jewish past as one, more often, of victimhood rather than agency.

Over a decade later from 1910 to 1912, the subject of nationality and the necessity of a homogeneous culture in the German nation-state arose, once again, in debates on the Jewish Question. During these debates there was a greater public awareness about Jewish nationality. Discussants described the potential of a pluralist, multicultural Germany, whilst a growing number of Zionists declared that Jewish nationalism was incompatible with the German nation-state.

Throughout the debates, with every discussion of the Jewish Question certain factors remained constant. For Bauer, Treitschke and Sombart, the purpose of their publications remained the same: to offer an answer on how to resolve what they observed as the problem of Jewish life in German society. The answers also all remained the same: a demand for Jewry to change. For Bauer, Jews had to renounce their religion, Treitschke demanded they assimilate, and Sombart urged Jews to adapt their behaviour to ensure peaceful co-existence.

The most significant common thread throughout the debates was that the Jewish Question was symptomatic of an underlying issue in Germany: the need for political and national-cultural reform. A homogenous national culture was not necessarily the issue at stake but rather how it was being conceived of in Christian terms, excluding both Jewish contributions to German culture and hindering their integration. Until this was addressed, as the subsequent debates will demonstrate, the Jewish Question remained a feature in German public political discourse.

Significantly, as the First World War propelled the nation-state ideal into the forefront of international affairs, neither could the Jewish Question fully disappear from German politics. The malleability of the term testifies to its enduring legacy. This chapter has demonstrated how the Jewish Question erupted at particular moments and prompted discussions which concerned the nation-state and its confrontation with the processes of modernisation. The following chapters will investigate a series of moments when the Jewish Question took a central position in shaping debates on the fears and preoccupations in the German state during its transition from Empire to Republic.

II The Jewish Question in war time: Germany's eastern policy, 1914–1916

Zionism is the 'necessary and only possible solution of the Jewish Question' wrote Max Bodenheimer in a memorandum to the German Foreign Office in February 1902.[1] President of the Zionist Federation for Germany, Bodenheimer outlined a mutually advantageous agreement involving the promotion of German foreign policy through collaboration with Russian Jews, which, he stressed, would also resolve the problem of East European Jewish immigration to Germany. The Germans would help liberate Russian Jews from violent persecution under Tsar Alexander III and aid their resettlement in either Syria or Palestine. In return, Russian Jews would help secure German influence and colonial ambitions in the region by acting as mediators and promotors of German economic and cultural interests. Receiving no guarantee from the Foreign Minister Oswald von Richthofen, Bodenheimer shelved his 1902 memorandum. Twelve years later, with the outbreak of the First World War, Bodenheimer seized the opportunity to return to the ideas of his 1902 memorandum, modifying it slightly. With Germany's declaration of war on Russia, Bodenheimer suggested collaborating with Russian Jews to secure German dominance over the lands of Western Russia. Once secured, as a buffer against future Russian aggression, Bodenheimer proposed the establishment of an East European Federation (*ein osteuropäischer Staatenbund*) of autonomous national communities, loyal to Germany.[2] As war on the Eastern Front erupted and the forces of the Central Powers encountered a population of six million

---

1 Max Bodenheimer, 'Denkschrift über die gegenwärtig in der deutschen Judenheit herrschenden Zustände und die durch den Zionismus angebahnte Lösung der damit im Zusammenhang stehenden Frage, Cöln, Februar 1902', in Theodor Herzl and Max Bodenheimer, *Im Anfang der zionistischen Bewegung: Eine Dokumentation auf der Grundlage des Briefwechsels zwischen Theodor Herzl und Max Bodeheimer von 1896 bis 1905*, ed. Henriette Hannah Bodenheimer (Frankfurt am Main: Europäische Verlagsanstalt, 1965), 219–27.
2 The original memorandum has been difficult to locate, however, Bodenheimer published a version of it in 1916. See M. I. Bodmer, 'Ein neuer Staatenbund und das Ostjudenproblem' in *Der Deutsche Krieg: Politische Flugschriften*, ed. Ernst Jäckh, Heft 73 (Stuttgart und Berlin: Deutsche Verlags-Anstalt, 1916), 5–36.

East European Jews, unlike in 1902, in the autumn of 1914, Bodenheimer's memorandum piqued the attention of the German leadership.

Bodenheimer's memorandum prompted several meetings in the Foreign Office in Berlin and eventually a meeting in the occupied territory of West Russia (*Ober-Ost*) with the Generals of the High Command, Ludendorff and Hindenburg, who voiced their support for Bodenheimer.[3] Before the outbreak of war, the Chancellery had devised plans for an expansion eastwards in order to establish a 'Frontier Strip' with ethnic-national groups, loyal to Germany.[4] This strip was to act as a barrier against Russian aggression, similar in concept to the East European Federation proposed by Bodenheimer in his memorandum. Moreover, as war on the Eastern Front unfolded, news filtered back from the front lines that Eastern European Jews, exhausted by Russian anti-Jewish violence welcomed the Central Powers' forces with enthusiasm, as Bodenheimer had predicted.[5] However, in 1916, as the German army faced staggering losses, the Central Powers adopted a new strategy: promising the creation of a Polish nation[6] to garner support from Polish volunteer soldiers.[7] With this, the plans for an East European Federation supported by a German-Jewish alliance, faded into oblivion.

The sequence of events, and the exchange of ideas during the first two years of World War I nonetheless provide a unique insight into the practical manifestation of a Jewish Question in German wartime policy. At a time of upheaval and political change, when a number of debates crystallised about the understandings of nationhood and statehood, Bodenheimer's vision of an East European Federation offers a different perspective on the perception of European Jewry. Moreover, given the language affinity of Russian and Polish (Yiddish-speaking) Jews to German, this encounter also raised questions pertaining to the future of the German polity. This was both in terms of the structure of Germany's external borders as well as the categorisation of German nationality, based historically on its development as a *Kulturnation*.

As shown in the previous chapter, the divergent lived experience of Russian Jews and German Jews was not new to many German Zionists. Nor were discussions on the concept of nationality and the idea of dual national loyalty. By the time these debates

---

3 Henriette Hannah Bodenheimer, *Max Bodenheimer 1865–1940: Political Genius for Zionism*, trans. David Bourke, (Edinburgh: The Pentland Press, 1990), 75.

4 Fritz Fischer, *Germany's Aims in the First World War*, 113–17.

5 Tracey Hayes Norrell, *For the Honor of Our Fatherland: German Jews on the Eastern Front during the Great War* (Landham, Maryland: Lexington Books, 2017), 10. See also Alexander Victor Prusin, *Nationalizing a Borderland: War, Ethnicity, and Anti-Jewish Violence in East Galicia, 1914–1920* (Tuscaloosa, Alabama: University of Alabama Press, 2005), 68.

6 This nation would consist of a Polish state, Polish army and self-government. However, this declaration breached international law, as the Kingdom of Poland was still legally part of Russia signalling that the manifesto was more a signifier of a gesture rather than a fully-fledged programme. For the aforementioned reasons, the manifesto elevated the question of the future of Poland to an international issue.

7 Jan Karski, *The Great Powers and Poland: From Versailles to Yalta* (Landham, Maryland: Rowman & Littlefield, 2014), 12–13.

were catapulted into mainstream German foreign policy discussions during the First World War, they had already reached maturity within German Zionist circles. These debates, which grew out of the political Zionist movement, where Bodenheimer was a central figure, reveal an internal dynamic to the Jewish Question; one with Jewish agency and a political answer that with the outbreak of world war, was deemed achievable.

It is crucial to understand these internal Zionist debates as they provided a vocabulary for Bodenheimer and formed the basis for the ideas behind his memorandum. More significantly, however, the discussions within the German-Jewish community on the understanding of concepts related to the modern state became an arena where ideas about nationality, statehood, citizenship, secularism were being rehearsed. The debates were unique precisely because of the conflicted conceptions between Zionists and liberal Jews on notions of dual loyalty, nationalism and patriotism. Whilst these debates were internal to the Zionist circles, with the outbreak of world war, they became practically relevant not only for the German army, but also globally as the war witnessed the reawakening of historic nations demanding self-determination and sovereignty.

Where chapter one traced the internal debates in the Jewish community on the Jewish Question, as a necessary precursor to understanding the foundational ideas of Bodenheimer's memorandum, this chapter focuses on a practical Jewish Question in German war time policy. To this end, it turns to the years of 1914 to 1916 tracing Bodenheimer's ideas in the Central Powers' eastern policy, to highlight the close relationship between theory and praxis and demonstrate the practical relevance of otherwise theoretical Jewish questions.

In particular, the chapter will emphasise the role of the prominent political Zionist, Max Isidor Bodenheimer, First President of the Zionist Federation and one of the founders of the Committee for the East (*Komitee für den Osten*, KfdO), in proposing a blueprint for German foreign policy in West Russian territory. Whilst Bodenheimer appears on the cast list of several historians' work, the persistence with which he has been denied the role of the protagonist is surprising.[8] More often, in the history of Zionism, Bodenheimer has been overshadowed by Theodor Herzl. In this chapter I aim to rescue Bodenheimer from obscurity. However, rather than concentrating on his work in the Committee for the East, I will emphasise the ideas he espoused in his memorandums to the German leadership, tracing their intellectual indebtedness to

---

8 Jay Ticker's research on Bodenheimer's pro-German Zionism advocacy in the First World War is one of the few exceptions. To date, the only biography I have been able to locate on Max Bodenheimer remains the one written by his daughter Henriette Hannah, relying on his personal documents, published in 1986. Bodenheimer also wrote his memoirs, published eighteen years after his death in 1958. Jay Ticker, 'Max I. Bodenheimer: Advocate of Pro-German Zionism at the Beginning of World War I', *Jewish Social Studies* 43, no. 1 (1981): 11–30; Bodenheimer, *Max Bodenheimer*; Henriette Hannah Bodenheimer, ed., *Prelude to Israel: The Memoirs of M. I. Bodenheimer*, trans. Israel Cohen (New York; London: Thomas Yoseloff, 1963).

Karl Renner, later Chancellor of the Republic of Austria, in his work, *Staat und Nation* written in 1899.

Bodenheimer's memorandum serves as an ideal case to explore the progression of ideas into practice and the development of practical Jewish questions. Briefly sketching the founding of the Committee for the East, the organisation through which Bodenheimer sought to enact his plan, I subsequently examine the German army's co-operation with Russian Jews who became mediators in the occupied territories. Investigating the shifting battle lines on the Eastern Front, and the German army's change in tactics to promising a Polish nation, reveals that whilst the blueprint for an extended area of German influence using Jews as mediators remained unused, ultimately the fight for securing the cultural autonomy of Jews continued. Thus, ensuring Bodenheimer's and the KfdO's enduring legacy.[9]

Bodenheimer was not alone in lobbying the Foreign Office to use Russian Jews as mediators of German interests in their place of settlement. Richard Lichtheim, a member of the KfdO and the Zionist Organisation (later the World Zionist Organisation, WZO),[10] worked tirelessly in Constantinople in the hope of securing a Jewish homeland in Palestine under German protection. Unofficially he secured support from the German Ambassador to Constantinople, Hans Freiherr von Wangenheim, and prominent figures in *Mitteleuropa*[11] circles encouraged cooperation with the Zionist movement in Palestine. Zionists were certainly not the only ones to build relationships with the German leadership. Notably, the liberal Jewish aid organisation, Aid Association of German Jews (*Hilfsverein der deutschen Juden*), founded by Paul Nathan and James Simon, established several education initiatives in Palestine, supported by the German government. However, these were driven by philanthropy, whilst the activities of the Zionists were also motivated by a political objective, and for this reason will be the focus of the section. Moreover, the Foreign Office was more inclined to work with the Zionists because of the influence they were able to exert on Jews abroad, particularly those in the United States of America.

In 1916 relations deteriorated with Bodenheimer and Oppenheimer on the Eastern Front. In the same year, Lichtheim was expelled from Constantinople on suspicion of

---

9 This is not to say that Jews were no longer significant in promoting German interests. Bodemann argues that in post-war Germany the Jewish population became important mediators in Germany's democratic transition, a term he calls performing 'ideological labour'. See, Y. Michal Bodemann, 'The State in the Construction of Ethnicity and Ideological Labor: The Case of German Jewry', *Critical Sociology* 17, no. 3 (1 October 1990): 35–46.

10 The Zionist Organisation was founded at the First Zionist Congress in Basel, Switzerland in 1897. It was renamed the World Zionist Organisation in 1960.

11 *Mitteleuropa* was a term that was used in a diverse range of contexts and had varying meanings. In this specific case it denoted an economic and cultural union in Central Europe under German dominion. It was also used to refer to a larger area of German cooperation in the Middle East. One of the first accounts to explore this contested concept was, Henry Cord Meyer, *Mitteleuropa in German Thought and Action, 1815–1945* (The Hague: Martinus Nijhoff, 1955).

espionage. The British Balfour Declaration recognising a Jewish homeland in Palestine was a further blow to decades of German Zionist diplomacy. Despite the breakdown of relations and the limited practical influence Bodenheimer, Oppenheimer and Lichtheim's diplomatic efforts had on official German policy and the outcome of the war, the unofficial assurances and support they received from the Foreign Ministry throughout the war illustrates the political force of German Zionism. Moreover, German Jews, especially Zionists, achieved success in another form: institutional. They gained unprecedented political representation in 1918 when the German Foreign Ministry established a Jewish Affairs section headed by another member of the KfdO, Moritz Sobernheim. This section became especially important for German foreign policy during the Weimar Republic as 'World Jewry [was recognised] as an important protagonist in international relations'.[12]

From Stuttgart to Berlin: the diplomatic work of Max Bodenheimer

(Max) Isidor Bodenheimer[13] was born in Stuttgart on the 21 March 1865.[14] As was typical for many German Jews, the Bodenheimer family defined their Judaism in religious not national terms.[15] Despite his acculturated upbringing, and six years before Theodor Herzl's famous pamphlet on the necessity of a Jewish state, Bodenheimer reached the same conclusion.[16] Bodenheimer was asked frequently, how as an assimilated German Jew he could arrive at the concept of Zionism. Yet, rather than one event, a series of instances marked gradual discord in the 'strong patriotic feelings'[17] of his youth, not least antisemitism at university,[18] and the arrival, in Stuttgart, of Russian Jews fleeing from pogroms. In 1891, at the age of twenty-six, a year after he completed his training as a lawyer and moved to Cologne to practice law, Bodenheimer wrote his first Zionist article, *Sind die russischen Juden eine Nation?*

This paper was the first of a series of articles where Bodenheimer outlined his views on the future of the Jewish diaspora and the organisation of international Jewry. It was through common interests that Bodenheimer became acquainted with David Wolff-

---

12 Nicosia, 'Jewish Affairs and German Foreign Policy During the Weimar Republic', 261.
13 Isidor was Bodenheimer's given name after his maternal grandfather Isaac. The name caused him much annoyance and as his friends called him Max, he came to use this name. Bodenheimer, *Prelude to Israel*, 36.
14 It appears that the birth date of Max I. Bodenheimer is often confused with the 12 March, as listed on the website of the 'Society for the Commemoration of Max I. Bodenheimer and Hannah Henriette Bodenheimer', [https://bit.ly/2Y6B7J4, accessed 8/10/2018]. This date differs from that given by Bodenheimer in his memoirs, see Bodenheimer, *Prelude to Israel*, 29.
15 Ibid, 39.
16 Ibid, 12.
17 Ibid, 33. For a description of the impression the Franco-German war had on Bodenheimer see also, 29–35.
18 Ibid, 35–36.

sohn, and together they founded the National-Jewish Federation (*National-Juedische Vereinigung*) in Cologne in 1894. Only three years later, the National-Jewish Federation for Germany (*National-Juedische Vereinigung für Deutschland*) was established, renamed the Zionist Federation for Germany, which was presided over by Bodenheimer as Chairman until 1910. Bodenheimer also held a number of other positions in organisations supporting Jewish national aspirations including the Zionist General Council (1897–1921) and the Jewish Colonial Trust (1899–1940). In 1907, he was appointed the first Chairman of the Jewish National Fund (JNF). Of interest for this paper, however, was Bodenheimer's diplomatic work alongside that of Theodor Herzl, the man generally viewed as the founder of Zionism.

Bodenheimer's diplomatic work began in the autumn of 1898 as part of the Zionist Delegation to Jerusalem led by Herzl.[19] Two years earlier, when Herzl published *Der Judenstaat*, he had outlined how Zionism could benefit colonial aspirations in the Middle East. In return for Palestine, Herzl offered the Jews as financiers of Turkey for His Majesty the Sultan.[20] As European allies, Jews in Palestine would become 'an outpost of civilisation' against barbarism, gatekeepers to Asia, and guardians of the holy places of Christendom.[21] Before any large-scale immigration and colonisation of Palestine, however, Herzl wanted to secure the minimum guarantee of protection from a sovereign power, ideally from not just one, but several.[22]

Lobbying for the support of Germany under Kaiser Wilhelm II was not only practical, but also tactical.[23] The German Empire had entered the race for colonies significantly later than its European rivals and was strongly in favour of securing influence in the politically unstable Ottoman Empire. In addition, the German Empire had already begun to exert its authority in the region through the construction of the Berlin-Baghdad Express.[24]

In 1897, just following the first Zionist Congress, Herzl secured a meeting with a close relative of the Kaiser, the Grand Duke Friedrich von Baden, whom he was able to convince of the Zionist cause. Herzl received assurances from the Duke that the

----

19 Other members of the delegation included Theodor Herzl, with whom Bodenheimer had established correspondence in 1896, David Wolffsohn, Joseph Seidener and Moses T. Schnirer.

20 Herzl, *The Jewish State*, 30.

21 From the outset Herzl framed the Jewish connection to Palestine in historical terms rather than religious. Ibid, 30.

22 Friedman, *Germany, Turkey, and Zionism*, 122.

23 Appealing to Germany was practical due to the communication opportunities offered. In addition, Herzl's first followers were from the German-speaking world and many saw themselves as leaders of the Zionist movement. Many American upper-class Jews also originated from Germany and thus could easily rally behind support for an alliance with Germany. See Klaus Polkehn, 'Zionism and Kaiser Wilhelm', *Journal of Palestine Studies* 4, no. 2 (1975): 77.

24 Sean McMeekin, *The Berlin-Baghdad Express* (Cambridge, Massachusetts: Harvard University Press, 2010).

Kaiser was prepared to supervise the protectorate of the Jewish state.[25] Several other meetings with the Chancellor Prince Hohenlohe-Schillingsfürst and Under-Secretary of the Foreign Office, Bernard von Bülow, convinced Herzl that the establishment of a Jewish state in Palestine under a German protectorate was within reach.[26] When the Kaiser announced his expedition to the Middle East, Herzl swiftly began making arrangements for a Zionist Delegation to travel to Jerusalem to coincide with the Kaiser's visit.

The enthusiasm of the Zionist Delegation was swiftly dampened in the course of the excursion.[27] During the first short encounter with the Kaiser in Constantinople, Herzl received only a general assurance that the Kaiser would consult the Sultan on the Zionist proposition. The second meeting in Palestine, some days later resulted similarly. The Kaiser declared that he had no intention of announcing an open alliance with the Zionists, which could upset German Christians as well as relations with the Sultan.[28] The practice of Zionism was recognised, namely Jewish settlement activity (which the Sultan had not opposed[29]) but the Kaiser would not support its politics: a Jewish state.

In spite of any tangible success Herzl, Wolffsohn[30] and Bodenheimer clung on to the hope of securing international, Great Power, support for the Zionist movement and did not concede to the growing demand within Zionist circles to prioritise practical settlement initiatives in Palestine. On returning from Constantinople, Bodenheimer met with Under Secretary of State Oswald von Richthofen with whom he discussed Jewish colonial work and its advantages for Germany. It was in this meeting that Bodenheimer first voiced an idea, which would later form the basis of his wartime memorandum. Bodenheimer suggested a means by which to divert East European Jewish migration away from Germany and, at the same time, aid the Empire's colonial ambitions. He presented East European Jews as mediators of German interests in the Middle East, given that this group was not only sympathetic towards Germany but also spoke a language similar to German. Richthofen, however, displayed little interest in the proposal.

---

25 Max Bodenheimer, 'Ein Erinnerungsblatt', in Herzl and Bodenheimer, *Im Anfang der zionistischen Bewegung*, 109. See also Bodenheimer, *Prelude to Israel*, 115.

26 The Duke had informed Herzl that the Kaiser was enthusiastic, but Herzl confessed to Bodenheimer that Bülow and Hohenlohe gave less 'gratifying impressions'. See Bodenheimer, *Prelude to Israel*, 116.

27 The excursion took the delegation to Constantinople, Smyrna and Palestine (Jerusalem, Motza, Jaffa).

28 In a meeting with the Grand Duke of Baden which took place sometime later, Max Bodenheimer wrote in his memoirs that the Duke recounted that the Kaiser had approached the Sultan twice concerning Zionist ambitions. As the Sultan was not wholly aware of this movement he offered no clear reply, which the Kaiser took as a dismissal of the proposal. Bodenheimer, *Prelude to Israel*, 148.

29 In meeting with the Turkish Ambassador to Germany, Bodenheimer noted that the Turkish did not oppose scattered Jewish settlements but rather an autonomous state. Ibid, 143.

30 Wolffsohn travelled twice more to Constantinople to no avail. On the 25 October 1907, after correspondence with Turkish officials, Wolffsohn travelled to Constantinople to present his plan for the establishment of a Zionist agency in Constantinople, under the guise of a bank. Nothing came of the negotiations. He was also active in meeting government ministers in Austro-Hungary and Russia where he promoted Zionist aims.

In one of the last attempts at colonial diplomacy with the German Empire, in 1902 Herzl requested that Bodenheimer write a memorandum to the Foreign Office outlining the aims of the Zionist movement. In this memorandum Bodenheimer built on his conversation with Richthofen years prior, sculpting his thoughts into a detailed plan of action. The memorandum began by stressing that Zionism was the 'only possible solution of the Jewish Question' and offered a way to resolve the problem of East European Jewish immigration to Germany.[31] The 'significant advantages' for Germany lay in the sphere of economic and trade policy. Describing Yiddish as a 'German *Volksdialekt'*, Bodenheimer stressed the kinship in language. With the relationship to the 'Occident' and tribal affinity with the 'Orient', Bodenheimer described the 'Jewish element' as a 'living bridge', between Germany and the Middle East, thus ensuring that the German language and culture would dominate in the region. Bodenheimer contrasted German Zionist work with that of the *Hilfsverein der deutschen Juden,* a liberal Jewish aid organisation, to argue that it was more advantageous to cooperate with Zionism. The *Hilfsverein* actively pursued 'Germanness', which might incite opposition from those with anti-German sentiments. Whereas Zionism was influenced by German culture and language as a result of the background of its founders (the First Zionist Congress was held in German). Importantly, however, Bodenheimer stressed that Zionism was 'not a German state project'.[32] Thus, the German leadership could capitalise on this fortunate German bias without any political consequences.[33] 'Never have German political interests been offered such a fine opportunity' boasted Bodenheimer.[34]

The proposal submitted by Bodenheimer was well-received and even read by the Kaiser.[35] However, what Herzl described as a *Meisterwerk*[36] did not precipitate any immediate political consequences in his lifetime. Herzl died only two years later. It would take the outbreak of world war for Bodenheimer's ideas to garner support in the German High Command and to see their, albeit partial and brief, practical manifestation.

---

31 'Denkschrift über die gegenwärtig in der deutschen Judenheit herrschenden Zustände und die durch den Zionismus angebahnte Lösung der damit im Zusammenhang stehenden Frage' in Herzl and Bodenheimer, *Im Anfang der zionistischen Bewegung,* 221.

32 Ibid, 225–26.

33 Elias Auerbach (1882–1971) writing in 1903 explored the relationship between Zionism and Germanness to conclude that one does not negate the other. This was a frequent topic of discussion within Zionist circles. See Elias Auerbach, 'Deutsche Kultur in Zionismus', *Jüdische Rundschau* VIII, no. 7 (13 Februar 1903): 49–51 in Reinharz, *Dokumente zur Geschichte des deutschen Zionismus 1882–1933,* 68–69.

34 Herzl and Bodenheimer, *Im Anfang der zionistischen Bewegung,* 223.

35 In his memoirs Bodenheimer wrote that he was informed a few years later (after Herzl's death) by Hermann von Lucanus, Head of the Kaiser's Cabinet, that the Kaiser had been aware of the memorandum and that the Kaiser continued to look on the Zionist movement with great favour. Bodenheimer, *Prelude to Israel,* 147.

36 Herzl and Bodenheimer, *Im Anfang der zionistischen Bewegung,* 218.

Planning the *Zwischenreich*: Bodenheimer's memorandum

Bodenheimer resolutely believed that only a victory by the Central Powers could ensure a political renewal for Russian Jews. Unlike Jews living in America, Western and Central Europe, on the eve of the First World War, only Jewish communities in the Kingdom of Romania and the Russian Empire had not been granted legal equality.[37] Throughout the eighteenth and nineteenth century, European countries had gradually granted emancipation.[38] In contrast, the Russian Empire – in the same period – implemented a series of increasingly restrictive laws, confining the Jewish population to an area known as the Pale Settlement. This area, to the west of the Russian Empire, extended over present-day Lithuania, Poland, Belarus, Ukraine and Moldovia. Jews in the Russian Empire numbered approximately five million at the turn of the century and around 95 % lived in this region.[39] These restrictive decrees culminated in the infamous May Laws of 1882, under Tsar Alexander III. Whilst these restrictions were implemented as temporary measures they continued until 1917.[40]

Throughout this period the laws were continually revised as Jews were subjected to increasing restrictions. These included, but were not limited to, the right to settle anew, own property, conduct business transactions on Sundays, sell alcohol, adopt a Christian name and participate in local elections. Mass deportations took place within the Empire as Jewish communities were forced to relocate to the Pale Settlement. The restrictions, combined with large-scale pogroms erupting in the summer of 1881, sparked one of the largest ever migration movements as over two million Jews left the Russian Empire.[41] Whilst the majority of Russian Jews continued their journey beyond Germany (two thirds travelled to the United States of America), with its access to the sea, it became an important transit country on the migration route.

Against this backdrop Bodenheimer wrote his article, *Ein neuer Staatenbund und das Ostjudenproblem*.[42] The title encapsulated Bodenheimer's two-fold purpose. As witness to the plight of Russian Jews escaping pogroms, and as a Zionist, Bodenheimer was committed to liberating these Jews. However, he was also aware of the mounting fear within Germany of the mass immigration of East European Jews, the so-called *Ostjudenproblem*. With Germany's declaration of war on Russia, Bodenheimer recognised an opportune moment to alleviate the concerns of both of these groups. Writing

---

37 Mahler, *Jewish Emancipation*, 62.
38 For a global history of emancipation in decrees and edicts see ibid, 9–72.
39 Richard H. Rowland, 'Geographical Patterns of the Jewish Population in the Pale of Settlement in Late Nineteenth Century Russia', *Jewish Social Studies* 48, no. 3 (1986): 207–8.
40 Hans Rogger, *Jewish Policies and Right-Wing Politics in Imperial Russia* (Berkeley Los Angeles: University of California Press, 1986), 144.
41 Ibid, 178.
42 Bodmer, 'Ein neuer Staatenbund und das Ostjudenproblem', 5–36.

to a fellow Zionist in November 1914, Bodenheimer revealed, 'I feel that in this war the interests of Russian Jews and those of the German Reich are identical'.[43]

As with many German Zionists, Bodenheimer was convinced that only a victory by the Central Powers, and an alliance between the Russian Jews and Germany, would offer a viable future for Eastern European Jewry. His plan at once aligned his views as a German citizen and Jewish national, as he expressed in the same letter to his friend Warburg, 'Although I am convinced that the Zionist Organisation has a paramount interest in this question, I undertook my task simply as a German patriot and as a Jew out of sympathy for my people and national solidarity'.[44]

The aforementioned article, *Ein neuer Staatenbund und das Ostjudenproblem*, was published by Bodenheimer under the pseudonym M. I. Bodmer in 1916 in a collection of political writings on the 'German War' edited by Ernst Jäckh.[45] In the article, Bodenheimer outlined in detail ideas that he had originally articulated in several memorandums to the Foreign Office including one sent on the 4 August 1914 entitled, 'Memorandum on Russian Jews in the case of the occupation of West Russian territory by German and Austrian forces' of which only a brief memo remains.[46] For this reason, Bodenheimer's published article offers the most detailed account of his proposed German foreign policy plan in the east.[47]

In the article Bodenheimer presented three possible outcomes in West Russia. The first proposed annexation, the second, a Polish state in union with Austria-Hungary and the third, the creation of a liberated, multi-ethnic, East European Federation. Bodenheimer dismissed the first two outcomes, annexation would produce hostility between ethnic tribes and Germans, a Polish state might cause renewed tensions between Germany and Russia and settled on the third: a multi-ethnic federation.

The federation that Bodenheimer proposed would run from the Baltic to the Black Sea. It would consist of a multi-ethnic population enjoying national autonomy. The

---

43 Bodenheimer, *Prelude to Israel*, 231.

44 Ibid, 231–33. Bodenheimer was bound to German national feeling and interests, as well as his Jewish 'kin people' (*Stammesgenossen*). He suggested a commitment to two peoples, the Germans and the Jews and described this in visual language as two circles: the first was the Zionist aspiration for a national Jewish homeland in Palestine, the other German patriotism.

45 As Professor of Turkish History at the University of Berlin, during the First World War, Jäckh was a strong advocate of the German-Turkish alliance. In the Weimar Republic he founded a liberal think tank called the *Deutsche Hochschule für Politik*. Under the Nazis, Jäckh left Germany first to Britain where he became the International Director of the New Commonwealth Society and later to America where as a Professor at Colombia he founded the Middle East Institute in 1948.

46 See CZA, A15/VIII 10/720, Max Bodenheimer, *Zur Lage der Russischen Juden* (undated).

47 Ironically at the time of publishing, the Central Powers had elected to create an independent Polish state. According to Henriette H. Bodenheimer, Max Bodenheimer published the article after his return from Lodz, Poland in the summer of 1915 where he had travelled to enter negotiations with the Polish Club. Bodenheimer, *Max Bodenheimer*, 77.

Poles would be the largest national group, numbering twelve million,[48] but their dominance would be balanced by Ukrainians, 'White Russians' (Belarussians), Lithuanians, Latvians and Estonians.[49] Overall, this constellation would weaken Russian influence, reducing its population by sixty-five million, thus ensuring a long-lasting peace.[50]

Rather than a Polish 'buffer state' Bodenheimer envisioned a multi-ethnic *Zwischenreich*.[51] Four ethnic areas (*Volksgebiete*) would make up the federal states in the new commonwealth (*Gemeinwesen*). The Baltic Sea provinces and Lithuanians would together form one of the ethnic areas. Each state would have a special governor from the Austrian or German ruling dynasty. Unlike the other ethnic communities, Jews and Germans would be spread out throughout these states, existing as separate elements. For this reason, Bodenheimer stressed, the cultural autonomy of individual peoples (*Völker*) would have to be constitutionally guaranteed. Thus, crucial for German influence in this federation would be the population (*Volkselemente*) of 'seven million' Jews.[52] If these Jews were to align with the German minority population of around two million, they would balance Polish dominance.

Russian Jews were bound to the Germans through language, observed Bodenheimer. Of the Jews in the region, 96 % spoke the national dialect (*Volksdialekt*), Yiddish.[53] If left in their Slavic environment, Bodenheimer warned that through the 'natural process of assimilation', Yiddish would cease to be a language. Framing the issue as part of the possible decline of German elements in the region, Bodenheimer argued that much of the region consisted of areas where the German language and culture thrived. This had to be protected against Slavic elements (*slawisierenden*).[54] Not only German culture, but German commerce and industry would also find a permanent home and thrive in the region. As Herzl had earlier offered the Jews as accountants for the Sultan, gatekeepers for Christians of the holy sites, in Bodenheimer's plan they could act as bastions of *Deutschtum*.[55]

---

48 Unlike Bodenheimer, Friedman lists this figure as eight million, meaning that the German-Jewish alliance would have been about equal to the number of Poles at almost eight million (six million Jews and just under two million Germans, 1.8m). He lists the other population figures as follows, Ukrainians (five million), White Russians or Belarussians (four million), Lithuanians, Latvians and Estonians (three and a half million). See Friedman, *Germany, Turkey, and Zionism*, 231.

49 Bodmer, 'Ein neuer Staatenbund und das Ostjudenproblem', 6.

50 Ibid, 24.

51 Ibid, 20.

52 Seven million is the figure given by M. Bodenheimer. This figure most likely included all Jews living in Congress Poland (two million), the Pale Settlement (four million) and in Austro-Hungary, specifically Galicia (one million). Ibid, 6.

53 Ibid, 6.

54 Ibid, 25.

55 Both Herzl and Bodenheimer clung to the view that *Ostjuden* embodied German culture, however, this was a projection of their hopes and desires rather than grounded in reality. David Goldberg writes that 'German Jewry's most persistent delusion [was] that there was a natural symbiosis between Teutonic values and

Bodenheimer blamed the lack of the cultural development of Russian Jews on the absence of civil equality and national self-administration, which, once enabled, would allow these Jews to fulfil the 'cultural duties of the developed nations'.[56] Although Bodenheimer's blueprint was intended for after the war with a victory by the Central Powers, he urged that these developments should start to take place during the war. And to an extent they did. During the German occupation the draconian, discriminatory restrictions on the Jews, imposed by the Russian Empire were removed. The Germans fully restored the civil rights of Jews and they were allowed the autonomy to continue operating their cultural, educational and political organisations.[57] Although the Jews were not granted national status by the German authorities, they were given fair representation in municipal councils. Compared to the reign of the Tsar, for many Jews, the occupation by the Central Powers was a welcome respite. One contemporary announced that they 'suddenly, as if by magic, ceased to feel like a pariah'.[58]

Bodenheimer framed the existence of national minorities as the 'fateful question' (*die schicksalsschwere Frage*) threatening Europe.[59] 'How was it possible for different tribes with different languages and cultures to live together and build peace?' wrote Bodenheimer 'Austria has tried to find a solution,' he continued, 'Switzerland has practically solved it' and he challenged Germany to be 'ground-breaking' in this regard as well. Compared to some of its neighbours, in Germany national minorities were not numerically significant. On the basis of language, of a total German population of forty-one million, over three million were non-German speaking.[60] Danes resided in the area of North Schleswig,[61] Alsatians in the South West.[62] Prussia was host to several minority groups including Poles,[63] Kashubians, Masurians,[64] Lithuanians, Wends and

---

Judaism's teachings'. David Goldberg, 'A dream world', *The Guardian*, 3 May 2008 [https://bit.ly/2R5sUBj, accessed 19/12/2018].

56 Bodmer, 'Ein neuer Staatenbund und das Ostjudenproblem', 25.

57 Prusin, *Nationalizing a Borderland*, 68.

58 W. Kaplun-Kogan, *Der Krieg: Eine Schicksalsstunde des jüdischen Volkes* (Bonn: A. Marcus & E. Webers Verlag, 1915), 19. Quoted in Prusin, 68.

59 Bodmer, 'Ein neuer Staatenbund und das Ostjudenproblem', 21.

60 In order of demography, the Poles living in Prussia were the largest minority followed by Danes, French, Lithuanians, Wends and Czechs. Pflanze, *Bismarck and the Development of Germany, Volume II*, xii.

61 In 1866 Schleswig-Holstein was annexed, which consisted of a population of 401,925 inhabitants of which 36 % (142, 940) spoke Danish. For more information on the 'Danish Question' see ibid, 114–17.

62 Alsace-Lorraine was annexed in 1871. Its population numbered 1,549,600 of which 12 % (185,000) spoke French. Many residents were, however, bilingual. Importantly, despite speaking German, the majority of the inhabitants of Alsace-Lorraine were opposed to German rule. After two centuries of French rule and the revolution, their loyalties surpassed any ethnic ties. Ibid, 117–26.

63 The Polish minority was the largest minority in Germany, consisting of three million Poles in the east, and four-hundred thousand in the Ruhr area. See Berghahn, *Imperial Germany*, 110–17.

64 The Kashubians are an ethnically Slavic group closely related to the Poles, historically stemming from Pomerania. The Masuria is a region in northern Poland where the residents speak a Masurian dialect of Polish. In the German Reich, this area was inhabited by Baltic Prussians.

Czechs.[65] The larger of these minority groups, the Poles, Danes and Alsatians, each had their own political party.[66] Another minority, though not defined on the basis of language, were the Jews.[67] In Germany, the Jewish minority was recognised as a religious community. It was only as a result of the army's eastern expansion that the German authorities acknowledged that Jews were a minority group displaying peculiar national characteristics.

Whilst Bodenheimer's memorandum was one of the first to directly relate to German foreign policy, the conceptual origins upon which it was based, were not novel. Deconstructing the practical idea of an East European Federation and exposing its conceptual origins, reveals that Bodenheimer, in essence, was challenging the notion that political citizenship and personal nationality needed to align within a polity. In offering a practical solution to the *Ostjudenproblem* and the occupation of West Russia, although not intended as such, Bodenheimer's memorandum also presented a critique of the nation-state principle. It was this conceptual basis of the memorandum, I wish to argue, that was indebted to the lawyer, Austro-Marxist and later Chancellor of the First Republic of Austria, Karl Renner.[68]

The parallels between Bodenheimer and Renner's position on the nationality question merits a brief excursion into Renner's background and his political writings, which I suggest help us to understand the conceptual background to Bodenheimer's memorandum. In a section on the voting system in Bodenheimer's article, he briefly mentioned the 'well-known national economist Renner' who he noted had written extensively on the system of national registries and electoral curia.[69] Yet rather than Renner's position on the voting system, I argue that Bodenheimer was indebted to Renner's notion of the personality principle, which he developed as a theoretical solution to the nationality question in *Staat und Nation. Staatrechtliche Untersuchung über*

---

65   In 1861 the Prussian population included 2,265,042 Poles, 139,428 Lithuanians, 83,443 Wends and 59,850 Czechs. Pflanze, *Bismarck and the Development of Germany, Volume II*, 106.

66   All three parties shared the same fate, after the war as North Schleswig became part of Denmark, Alsace, France, and an independent Polish nation was created, the Danish, Alsace-Lorraine and Polish party all ceased to exist in Germany. McHale, *Political Parties of Europe*, 415–28.

67   Demographics on Masurians and Kashubians are difficult to locate. The number of Jews in the German Reich was 521,153 in 1871 and increased to 615,021 by 1910. However, as a result of apostacy and mixed marriages the percentage of Jews in the population decreased between 1871 and 1914 from 1.25 % to 0.95 %, see Berghahn, *Imperial Germany*, 102–9.

68   Robert Wistrich writes that whilst Karl Renner and Otto Bauer (both Austro-Marxists) favoured a policy of the cultural individuality of nationalities they excluded Jews from this programme. In this section I do not claim that Renner's personality principle was devised with the Jews in mind, but rather that both Bodenheimer and Lucien Wolf applied these ideas to the case of East European Jews. See Robert S. Wistrich, *Socialism and the Jews: The Dilemmas of Assimilation in Germany and Austria-Hungary* (London; East Brunswick, N.J.: Associated University Presses, 1982), 353.

69   Bodmer, 'Ein neuer Staatenbund und das Ostjudenproblem', 22.

die möglichen Principien einer Lösung und die juristischen Voraussetzungen eines Nationali-tätengesetzes written in 1899.[70]

Renner was born in 1870 into an impoverished family of German winegrowers. As a result of his exceptional intelligence, he financed his tuition fees through tutoring and scholarships, graduating, at the age of twenty-six, from the University of Vienna in Law.[71] The same year, Renner joined the Social Democratic Party and commenced work as a research assistant in the library of the Austrian parliament. During this time Renner began to interest himself in politics, in particular the nationality question.

It was under the pseudonym, 'Synopticus' that Renner published his first political work, *Staat und Nation*. Renner tasked himself with answering how multi-ethnic groups could peacefully coexist in the same territory. To this end, he argued for the organisation of groups along supra-territorial, national laws rather than the laws of the state. Regardless of where a citizen resided, they would be bound to the laws of their autonomous national association. What Renner envisioned was that minority populations living within ethnically homogenous geographic areas, would not be constrained by the laws and regulations of the majority group. Rejecting the territorial principle, Renner argued that rather than defining a group by place of residence, a community should instead constitute a legal entity according to its national identity, defined by language and culture.

Renner appreciated the practical advantages of the nation-state. He acknowledged it was a political structure with the least internal friction. However, he concluded that it would not suffice in multi-ethnic territories. Drawing on historical precedent, Renner praised what he termed the 'personality principle' in the Carolingian Empire. The Empire united linguistically diverse tribes under the governance of landed proprietors, allowing each tribe to retain its unique legal code. Rather than language, culture or territory, the question used to determine nationality was, 'Under which law do you live? (*Quo jure visis?*)[72]

For Renner, the problem of the modern state was that the territorial principle had replaced this 'personality principle'. The territorial principle was not an expression of the equality of rights, but dominion, over the minority, by the majority. The paradox, Renner opined, was that 'the territorial principle [...] combines the national concept with patrimonial ideas and thus becomes in many ways anti-national'. From his experience living in a multi-ethnic Empire, Renner recognised that internal migration and economic relations meant that 'no nation can limit itself to specific, narrowly defined

---

70 Synopticus [Karl Renner], *Staat und Nation. Staatsrechtliche Untersuchung über die möglichen Principien einer Lösung und die juristische Voraussetzung eines Nationalitätengesetzes* (Wien: Dietl., 1899).

71 For an overview of Renner's childhood and political career see Jamie Bulloch, *Karl Renner: Austria* (London: Haus Publishing, 2011).

72 Karl Renner, 'State and Nation (1899)', in *National Cultural Autonomy and Its Contemporary Critics*, ed. Ephraim Nimni, trans. Joseph O'Donnell, Routledge Innovations in Political Theory 16 (London; New York: Routledge, 2005), 27.

territories'.[73] He envisioned rescuing the modern state through the nation, concluding that 'the personality rather than the territorial principle should form the basis of
regulation; the nations should be constituted not as territorial entities but as personal
associations, not as states but as peoples, not according to age-old constitutional laws,
but according to living national laws'.[74]

Despite his commitment to the personality principle, Renner accepted why, in the
realm of international affairs, the territorial principle was supported. It clearly demar-
cated relations between states. Dating back to the Treaty of Westphalia, sovereign
integrity was embedded within international affairs. As the First World War broke
up Empires and saw the restructuring of the world order, it is not surprising that the
nation-state model – as the smallest common denominator enabling the smooth conduct of international governance – was adopted. Renner confronted this reality in his
own country, when he signed the Treaty of Saint-Germain on the 10 September 1919
which – much to his dismay – prohibited the creation of German Austria (*Deutsch-
Österreich*) heralding, instead, the First Austrian Republic.

Before continuing to trace the intellectual afterlife of Renner's concept of the personality principle, I will first examine the transfer of ideas into practice, in other words,
how Bodenheimer's memorandum was received in the German Foreign Ministry.

Ideas into practice? Eastern European Jews as mediators of German interests

A week after submitting his proposal, Bodenheimer received a telegram inviting him
to Berlin 'as a matter of urgency' for a consultation with Count Bogdan Franz Servatius von Hutten-Czapsky,[75] Political Director of the General Staff who introduced him
to Baron Diego von Bergen,[76] Head of Polish Affairs.[77] Bodenheimer's memorandum
was unexpectedly well-timed. In the years preceding the outbreak of war, the Franco-
Russian Alliance meant that in the eventuality of war, the German Reich knew that it
would have to fight on two fronts. This inevitability led to the Schlieffen plan, which
aimed for a quick victory over France via Belgium, to then open the war on the Eastern
Front with the Russian Empire.

---

73 Ibid, 28.
74 Ibid, 29.
75 Count Bogdan Franz Servatius von Hutten-Czapsky (1861–1937) was a member of the Prussian Upper
House in Poznan and Head of the Political Department of the German General Staff. In 1918 he became
German Commissar to the Kaiser in the Polish royal government.
76 Baron Diego von Bergen (1872–1944), Prussian and later German Emissary to the Vatican.
77 Szajkowski writes that he was head of the Eastern European Affairs Division. Zosa Szajkowski, 'The
Komitee für den Osten and Zionism', in *Herzl Year Book*, ed. Raphael Patai (New York: Herzl Press, 1971),
206. Bodenheimer writes that he was Head of the Polish Affairs, Bodenheimer, *Max Bodenheimer*, 73.

In the summer of 1914, in the office of Chancellor Theobald von Bethmann-Hollweg, ideas had begun circulating to use the opportunity presented by the outbreak of war to pursue an expansionist geopolitical agenda of *Lebensraum*.[78] The so-called September Programme, outlined large-scale annexations in Western Europe, continued colonisation of Africa and an economic union to stabilise German economic dominance in Europe.[79] If achieved Germany would have secured a position as a hegemonic power.[80]

In the east, the German leadership had not only military but also political objectives in mind. To avoid future Russian aggression, the Germans planned for the construction of a 'Frontier Strip' with national elements, loyal to Germany. The German border would be extended to include Warsaw, and Poles and Jews living in Poznan would be transferred to a new semi-autonomous Polish state under German jurisdiction. Even further east, a buffer zone would secure Germany's new border against Russia. As the army advanced into this territory the policy also detailed plans to secure seaports, develop agricultural areas of Ukraine, whilst protecting the industrial region of Upper Silesia.[81]

For the Reich, the east was seen as a site for settlement and colonisation.[82] It was viewed as a long-term project that the leadership could mould in their image, building a region sympathetic to, and based on, Germany. In this *Kulturpolitik* strategy, the Germans aimed to propel a civilising image of German work in the region and particular emphasis was placed on the administration of cultural activities.[83] The timing of

---

78 *Lebensraum* emerged at the turn of the century from the concept of *Drang nach Osten*, which was cultivated under Bismarck's Chancellorship as he sought to expand German influence after unification. In the years preceding the First World War, there was a growing consensus amongst Germany's political leadership that 'Germany's frontiers were simply too narrow, and in order for the nation to survive they had to be expanded'. Norrell, 'Shattered Communities', 108.

79 Theobald Bethmann-Hollweg, 'Das September-Memorandum', *Bundesarchiv-Lichterfelde*, Reichskanzlei, Grosses Hauptquartier 21, Nr. 24769, September 1914 [https://bit.ly/2xRDMaE, accessed 12/10/2018]. Also translated into English and re-printed in full in Fritz Fischer, *Germany's Aims in the First World War*, 103–4.

80 Historians debate the intentionality of the September Programme. Fischer argued that the Chancellor had a clearly devised war-aim programme and believed in an imminent victory over France. Other historians, such as Wayne C. Thompson argue that the author of the document, Kurt Riezler (Bethmann-Hollweg's assistant) had not previously written about expansionist foreign policy but was responding to changing conditions in the war. See Fritz Fischer, *Germany's Aims in the First World War*, 103 ff.; Wayne C. Thompson, 'The September Program: Reflections on the Evidence', *Central European History* 11, no. 04 (1978): 348–354. For a detailed overview of the historical debate on Germany's aims in the First World War and the role of Bethmann-Hollweg and the September Programme within this, see Gerald D. Feldman, *German Imperialism 1914–1918: The Development of a Historical Debate* (New York: John Wiley & Sons Inc., 1972), 141–95.

81 Fritz Fischer, *Germany's Aims in the First World War*, 113–17.

82 In the 1920s, parliamentary debates on Eastern Europe were framed in colonial language. This framing continued under Hitler during his expansion eastwards. See Jürgen Zimmerer, 'The Birth of the Ostland out of the Spirit of Colonialism: A Postcolonial Perspective on the Nazi Policy of Conquest and Extermination', *Patterns of Prejudice* 39, no. 2 (2005): 201.

83 On this approach see Liulevicius, *War Land on the Eastern Front*, 126–36.

Bodenheimer's memorandum could not have been more ideal as the plan on how to shape the region, was still subject to discussion.

Bodenheimer's memorandum not only offered a blueprint for an extended area of German influence in the east, including a buffer zone with Russia, but, in addition, it proposed Jews as mediators of these interests, a strategy that the German Army quickly realised could work in their favour. As war on the Eastern Front progressed, it quickly became apparent that the Jews were the most receptive population in the region and would become the army's only ally.[84] Years of repression, violence and antisemitism meant that Russian Jews had no loyalty to the Tsar, as predicted by Bodenheimer. As the Russian Chief of General Staff professed in the Russian retreat of 1915, 'the complete hostility of the entire Jewish population towards the Russian army is well established'.[85] General Ludendorff acknowledged that the Jews were crucial for the occupation of Poland and expressed his intention to use them as mediators.[86]

Enmity towards the Russian Empire, as well as language similarities helped the Germans build a relationship with the Jewish population in the east. In preparation for war with Russia, the General Staff had emphasised the study of all derivations of the Russian language, without heeding Yiddish.[87] Yiddish, however, the language spoken by Russian and Polish Jews had German rather than Slavic etymological roots. When the German army began their occupation of the Polish lands and the Pale Settlement, they soon realised that they were able to communicate with the *Ostjuden*. Given their multilingualism, they became essential middlemen.[88] However, perhaps the most compelling reason why Bodenheimer received an invitation to the Foreign Office was because it was in the process of drafting an appeal to Polish Jews.

As a result of his successful consultations in the Foreign Ministry, Bodenheimer contacted his friend Franz Oppenheimer and together they decided to form a committee with a dual objective: to safeguard the national rights of East European Jews and help disseminate pro-German propaganda.[89] In attendance at the meeting on the 17 August, which founded the German Committee for the Liberation of Russian Jews (*Deutsches Comité für die Befreiung der russischen Juden*), were other members of the Zionist Federation (such as Adolf Friedemann, Alfred Klee and Hermann Struck),

---

84 In his seminal account of German Jews in the First World War, Egmont Zechlin emphasised the potential offered by *Ostjuden* in Germany's occupation of Poland. Zechlin, *Die deutsche Politik und die Juden im Ersten Weltkrieg*.

85 Hew Strachan, *The First World War*, 3rd ed. (London: Simon & Schuster, 2014), 144.

86 See Erich Ludendorff, *The General Staff and Its Problems*, trans. F. A. Holt (New York: EP Dutton and Company, 1920), 158.

87 Bodenheimer, *Max Bodenheimer*, 73.

88 Ludendorff, *My War Memories, 1914–1918*, 2nd ed., vol. I & II (London: Hutschinson & Co., 1923), 188.

89 The committee was formed on the 17 August 1914 at the Eden Hotel in Berlin. It was initially called, *Oppenheimer Comité* but the name was quickly changed to *Deutsches Comité für die Befreiung der russischen Juden*. In early November it was changed again to the more neutral, *Comité für den Osten* also often spelt as *Komitee für den Osten*. See Szajkowski, 'The Komitee für den Osten and Zionism', 206.

representatives of the Zionists Inner Actions Committee and the Mannesmann Comité. The latter committee was organised by the prominent German industrialist Reinhart Mannesmann and his partners, for the purpose of using their foreign business contacts, and access to influential German officials, to promote propaganda activities in favour of the Central Powers.[90]

Although the committee was established by Zionists, it was not an official Zionist organisation. When first established it received the support of prominent Zionists, such as Otto Warburg[91] and David Wolffsohn, due to its objective to safeguard the rights of Eastern European Jews. Within three months, however, the Zionist Executive withdrew all support from the committee, aligning with the call by the Zionist Actions Committee for all Zionist institutions and affiliated members to remain neutral for the duration of the war.[92]

Prior to the committee, the German government had only conducted consultations on Jewish affairs with religious leaders and organisations. The committee was the first organisation to consult with the German government on affairs pertaining to Jewish national-cultural rather than civil-religious rights. Not only did the German Foreign Ministry acknowledge the value of collaborating with an organisation with Zionist aims, but for the first time ever, German Jews became key assets in the German army as mediators and interlocutors of occupied lands.

Acting on behalf of the German Foreign Office, the first activity of the Committee for the East was meant to involve the dissemination of propaganda pamphlets to the Jewish population in Congress Poland, the historically Polish lands of the Russian Empire. Shortly following the declaration of war, the Central Powers had begun their advancement into Congress Poland. Under an order from the Austro-Hungarian Empire, the army was instructed to enact a harsh treatment on the Russian population but exclude the Jews with whom they intended to collaborate.[93] In September 1914 leaflets were distributed in Galicia and Poland targeted at the resident Jewish population. To Bodenheimer's dismay, the leaflets that were distributed were militaristic and aggressive in content. They had been written by the Polish noble and close aide to the Kaiser, Count Bogdan Hutten-Czapski and the Head of the East German Information Office Georg Cleinow and approved by the German and Austrian High Command, without prior consultation with Bodenheimer.

Rather than detailing the dire legal status of the Jews in Russia, an issue that Bodenheimer had wanted to include, the leaflets circulated in Galicia called on Jews to 'rise!'

---

90 Ibid, 210.
91 Otto Warburg (1859–1938) was a botanist. From 1911 to 1920, he was the President of the World Zionist Congress.
92 Friedman, *Germany, Turkey, and Zionism*, 235. See also Szajkowski, 'The Komitee für den Osten and Zionism', 210.
93 Norman Stone, *The Eastern Front, 1914–1917* (London: Penguin, 1998), 82.

and 'take up arms!'.[94] The leaflets read, 'we your friends, are approaching' and juxta-posed German occupation to the 'barbaric foreign rule' of Russia, spurring suspicion on the loyalty of Polish Jews to an independent Polish state.[95] Fears amongst German Zionists mounted as the pamphlets elicited accusations of Jewish espionage and pro-vided Russian authorities with a motive for mass Jewish deportations, which became part of official policy the following year.[96]

The intention behind the leaflets was evident, the Foreign Ministry, wanted to use the Jews as a fifth column in the army; the enemy within. This, in spite of the great risk for the resident Jewish population. The incident illustrated the limited influence the Committee for the East yielded over Germany's eastern policy. Rather than building an alliance or collaborating with the Russian Jews, as Bodenheimer had envisioned, the German High Command had instead attempted to instrumentalise the Jewish population for military ends. This would become further evident in late 1916, when the Germans became involved in the creation of a Polish state despite warnings that this would be detrimental for the Polish Jewish population.

Frustrated that he had not been consulted, Bodenheimer submitted another memo-randum to the Foreign Office, once again outlining his plan for a federation and an extended area of German influence.[97] This time, Bodenheimer and Oppenheimer were invited directly to Random, the Head Quarters of the Eastern Command (*Ober-Ost*), where they met with the Commander in the East, Erich Ludendorff, and subsequently dined with Chief of General Staff, Paul von Hindenburg.[98] Ludendorff expressed his appreciation of Bodenheimer's memorandum and encouraged the KfdO to send emis-saries to the occupied territories to discuss the plan with the local Jewish population. On their departure the men were handed a written confirmation from von Hinden-burg certifying his 'benevolent interest' in the efforts of the KfdO and that he was 'ready to advance their aims'[99]

The confirmation reinvigorated the activity of the KfdO. It revived the possibility of an East European Federation recognising Jewish national autonomy. This euphoria did not last long. Just over ten days later, the Russian forces pushed the Central Pow-ers out of the southern territory of Congress Poland.[100] As the Germans were forced into retreat, the promises made to the KfdO lost their relevance. 'Our forward-looking political plan for establishing a national federation from the Baltic to the Black Sea had to be postponed' wrote Bodenheimer.[101] Little did he realise at the time, that on the

---

94 Quoted and trans. in Friedman, *Germany, Turkey, and Zionism*, 232.

95 Anon., 'An die Juden in Polen', *Berliner Tageblatt* 43, no. 442 (1 September 1914): 2.

96 Friedman, *Germany, Turkey, and Zionism*, 235.

97 Ibid, 233.

98 Bodenheimer, *Max Bodenheimer*, 75.

99 Hindenburg to Bodenheimer and Oppenheimer, 15 October 1914. Quoted in ibid, 75.

100 Stone, *The Eastern Front*, 199.

101 Cited in Norrell, *For the Honor of Our Fatherland*, 21.

part of the Germans, the plan for an East European Federation was over. In official correspondence, it was not mentioned again.[102] Over the course of two years, the German Reich's approach to the future of Polish lands would change three-fold.

The retreat of German troops also shifted the goals of the KfdO. As the blueprint for an East European Federation was shelved, the organisation turned its focus to securing cultural autonomy for Galician Jews. And it was this focus, on the cultural autonomous rights of *Ostjuden*, that would come to define the legacy of the Committee for the East.

All noise on the Eastern Front:
Congress Poland and Jewish cultural autonomy

1915 was marked by a series of military successes for the Central Powers on the Eastern Front. By the summer, they had under their control Lithuania, Latvia, Congress Poland and parts of Galicia. In contrast to the first advancement eastwards, where the Central Powers encountered a population of two million Jews, they now occupied an area with around six million Jews. Now, more than ever, the *Ostjuden* became crucial agents in the war effort.[103] With the re-occupation of Congress Poland, the KfdO became politically relevant once again.

When the German Reich entered into negotiations with the Polish national leadership in early 1915 on the subject of the future of Poland, members of the Committee for the East were invited to the table. In attendance was Bodenheimer, who had been invited to lead the negotiations, Oppenheimer, Friedmann and Sobernheim.[104] Following the wishes of the KfdO, during the negotiations, the Germans offered their full support for granting Polish Jews cultural autonomy, announcing that 'the Jew [will have the] full possibility of self-preservation and development of his language and his special culture'.[105]

The meeting concluded that in the eventuality of a 'Greater Poland', the constitution would have to enshrine the right to autonomy for individual nationalities.[106] Echoing the September Programme, the Germans envisioned that was that each of these national groups would 'become part of the German Reich and must become a rich

---

102 Friedman, *Germany, Turkey, and Zionism*, 233.
103 Fritz Fischer, *Germany's Aims in the First World War*, 138–43.
104 Friedman, *Germany, Turkey, and Zionism*, 233. Szajkowski writes that the German government was opposed to separate meetings between the KfdO and the Polish national leaders. On the 1 February 1916 the government authorised that one meeting could be held.'The Komitee Für Den Osten and Zionism', 208–9.
105 AA, *Der Weltkrieg*, no.11 adh. 2 Bd 3.1 Jan.–March 1915. Quoted and trans. in Norrell, 'Shattered Communities', 108.
106 Bodenheimer, *Max Bodenheimer*, 76.

part of the German community'.[107] To safeguard German dominance, 'high German language and culture' would be required in Galicia, but Yiddish, would 'be allowed as a German dialect', thus yielding more than the Polish leaders had conceded to.[108] One of the Polish representatives Wojciech Korfanty,[109] in a prior meeting, had suggested that whilst he was ready to recognise the cultural autonomy of Jews, he refused to accept Yiddish as a language equal in legal status to Polish, even in cities with a majority Jewish population.[110] The recognition of Yiddish by the Germans not only resonated with the aims of the committee but it was also a clear step in the direction of awarding Polish Jews the status of an autonomous cultural community.

By the spring of 1915, in another round of meetings in Poland, the KfdO received the assurance from the Polish Council that Jews would be awarded the equivalent of national rights.[111] They would have educational and linguistic autonomy, and an electoral structure based on a national cadastre.[112] In return, the Polish Council requested that the Committee for the East lobby German officials on the Austro-Polish solution.[113] The origins of this solution dated back to the Congress of Vienna when the Kingdom of Poland was created within the Russian Empire. Shortly after the outbreak of First World War it was proposed once again by the Austrians who wanted Poland to join a Danubian Monarchy under the Kingship of an Austrian Archduke.[114]

Upholding their side of the agreement with the Polish national leadership, the Committee for the East began lobbying German officials. Arguments from Bodenheimer's memorandum were recycled, namely that if Jews were to receive national minority rights in an Austro-Polish solution, the Germans – by working with the Jews – would have indirect control over Poland and Galicia.[115] This alliance, the KfdO stressed, would also weaken Slavic influence in the Austrian Empire, and thus minimise the threat to German dominance.[116] Unbeknownst to the Committee for the East, their interests

---

107 AA, *Der Weltkrieg*, no.11 adh. 2 Bd 3.1 Jan. – March 1915. Quoted and trans. in Norrell, 'Shattered Communities', 108.

108 Ibid, 108.

109 Wojciech Korfanty (1873–1939) was a Polish journalist born in Prussia Silesia. In 1903 he was elected as a to the German Reichstag and in 1904 to the Prussian Landtag representing the Polish Party, when he actively protested against the discrimination of Poles. See Sigmund Karski, *Albert (Wojciech) Korfanty: Eine Biographie* (Dülmen: Laumann-Verlag, 1990).

110 Bodenheimer, *Max Bodenheimer*, 76.

111 Marcos Silber, 'The Development of a Joint Political Program for the Jews of Poland during World War I – Success and Failure', *Jewish History* 19 (2005): 213.

112 According to this system, individuals could register for both population and voter registration by nationality (for example, Jewish). This would ensure the proportional representation of national minorities in parliament.

113 Silber, 'The Development of a Joint Political Program for the Jews of Poland during World War I', 213.

114 Fritz Fischer, *Germany's Aims in the First World War*, 114.

115 Silber, 'The Development of a Joint Political Program for the Jews of Poland during World War I', 213.

116 This line of argument was used in Bodenheimer's 1916 article, which was published shortly after he returned from these negotiations.

were entirely in line with those of the Foreign Office, which not only had already opened negotiations with the Austrians on this solution but was also aware that the KfdO had entered into unauthorised discussions with the Polish Council.[117]

The following year plans regarding the future of Poland changed once again. The Germans now proposed 'a Polish entity with truncated borders and sovereignty, functioning as a German satellite'.[118] In contrast to the successes on the Eastern Front, in 1916, exhausted by the war, the German army experienced a downturn, further precipitated in December when the Empire faced its worst ever food shortages, and famine.[119] To garner manpower for the war effort, General Hans Hartwig von Beseler, Governor of General Government of Warsaw, suggested appealing to Polish volunteers by offering them an independent Polish state. On the 5 November 1916, this plan was put into action with the announcement of the Two Emperor's Manifesto. The manifesto proposed a Polish state with an independent army, which would function as a protectorate of the Central Powers after the war.[120] The intention behind the manifesto quickly became apparent when, shortly after its release an appeal was issued for enlistment in the German army.[121] The plan was a failure. The Poles remained distrustful of the Germans and only twenty Gentile Poles enlisted. The remaining three hundred and fifty Polish volunteers that enlisted were Jewish.[122]

Despite the continued loyalty displayed by Polish Jews, the German army was no longer interested in collaborating with them. The Two Emperor's Manifesto was a blow to the work of the KdfO and disappointed Bodenheimer. Already prior to the Two Emperor's Manifesto, on advice from the Committee for the East, specifically Adolf Friedmann, General Beseler had warned the German Foreign Office of the negative effects that German intervention in Polish independence would have on the local Jewish population. Beseler's letter read, 'the Jews, whose fears are probably correct, believe a German intervention will only compound the differences [between Jews and Poles]

---

117 In August, Stephen von Burian, the Austro-Hungarian Foreign Minister met Chancellor Theobald von Bethamnn Hollweg see Silber, 'The Development of a Joint Political Program for the Jews of Poland during World War I', 217.

118 Ibid, 218.

119 This period in German history is commonly referred to at the *Steckrübenwinter* (Turnip Winter) named after the food available to the German population in the winter of 1916.

120 Piotr S. Wandycz, *The Lands of Partitioned Poland, 1795–1918*, vol. 7, History of East Central Europe (Seattle; London: University of Washington Press, 1974), 350.

121 Ibid, 50–52.

122 Fischer, *Germany's Aims in the First World War*, 245.

by our intervention we are running the risk of injury and massively affecting the [local political] agenda'.[123] This information was, however, disregarded.[124]

As the KfdO was facing increasing detachment and disinterest from the Foreign Office, Bodenheimer resigned in late 1916. The committee turned away from all diplomatic activity and instead concentrated on its philanthropic initiatives. Ludwig Haas, Head of the Jewish Affairs section of the German civil administration of Poland, a once staunch anti-Zionist, felt sympathy for the Zionist cause after the Emperors' Manifesto revealed to him that Polish Jews had no future in Poland, nor could they rely on protection from the German government.[125] For Haas, the Emperors' proclamation was a *gleich Null* in that it undermined all previous efforts to build loyalty amongst Polish Jews towards Germany.[126]

Late 1916 marked the beginning of the end for German-*Ostjuden* relations. The German lower administration authorities began to disregard the original principle of treating all populations equally and antisemitic prejudices became more apparent, evidenced – in part – by a decree issued by the Minister of War to count all the Jews serving on the front lines.[127] By the middle of the following year, the German military authorities handed over control to the local Polish authorities. All initiatives which had granted Jews greater cultural autonomy such as allowing Yiddish and Hebrew to receive equal status in schools to Polish, were halted.[128] Jews began to be discriminated against in social and economic spheres. Polish nationalists, such as Roman Dmowski, saw part of the mission of Polish nationhood as removing the Jewish 'alien'[129] from the economic and social sphere of Poland causing a mass emigration which was hoped to solve the 'Jewish question'.[130] The Central Powers ignored complaints of discrimination against Jews and no longer allocated resources to resolving them.

The Treaty of Brest-Litovsk, signed in February 1918, which granted Germany dominion over the Baltic states and northern Polish territory, ceding the remaining provinces to an independent Ukrainian National Republic, further heightened ethnic tensions.[131] The source of outrage for Poles was that the area of Congress Poland was not

---

123 AA, *Der Weltkrieg*, Nr. 149, K203645–6, Letter from Executive Chief of the General Government of Warsaw to Foreign Ministry, sent 20.11.16, written 25.10.16. Quoted in Norrell, 'Shattered Communities', 166. For the tensions between the Polish Gentiles and Polish Jews in July 1915 see also Prusin, *Nationalizing a Borderland*, 70.

124 Norrell, 'Shattered Communities', 166.

125 Zechlin, *Die deutsche Politik und die Juden im Ersten Weltkrieg*, 200.

126 Norrell, 'Shattered Communities', 168.

127 This decree is the subject of chapter three.

128 Prusin, *Nationalizing a Borderland*, 70–71.

129 Dmowski referred to the notion of *Odzydzenie*, the Polish for *Entjudung*, which in English is often translated as the process of 'de-Jewing'.

130 Prusin, *Nationalizing a Borderland*, 71.

131 Ibid, 71.

mentioned in the treaty.[132] Jews were blamed by the Poles for their pro-Habsburg and German sentiments leading to the eruption of anti-Jewish riots across Polish lands, which had to be contained by Austro-Hungarian forces. Tensions mounted when in October 1918 the newly formed Ukrainian National Council recognised Jews as a distinct nationality, a status the Polish Council had been reluctant to grant.[133] Unlike in 1915, the situation for the *Ostjuden* under the Central Powers was vastly different. The continuously changing plans on the future of West Russian territory, amplified by the Treaty of Brest-Litovsk, only served to sharpen the antagonisms between resident ethnic groups as each struggled to shape their own political future. However, not only did relations deteriorate in Eastern Europe but also in Palestine where another Zionist, Richard Lichtheim, had, as Bodenheimer, lobbied the Foreign Office on German-Jewish collaboration.

Richard Lichtheim and German-Jewish collaboration in the Middle East

During the First World War the Committee for the East under Bodenheimer was focused on recognising Jews as one of several national ethnic minorities within an East European Federation. Nevertheless, the KfdO never abandoned the prospect of a establishing a Jewish state in Palestine. The individual behind the scenes who took on this diplomatic work was another member of the Committee for the East, Richard Lichtheim. In 1913 Lichtheim was posted to Constantinople, in the Ottoman Empire, as a representative of the Zionist Organisation. When the war broke out, Lichtheim remained in Constantinople and built close and valuable relationships with several Foreign Ministry officials who worked to ensure that Zionist activity during the war could continue without obstruction.

The KfdO was not the only Jewish organisation to secure support from the German Foreign Office. The Aid Association of German Jews founded in 1901 by Paul Nathan[134] with the support of James Simon,[135] who was a personal friend of the Kaiser, was far

---

132 On the treaty and its ramifications in post-war international affairs, see Borislav Chernev, 'The Brest-Litovsk Moment: Self-Determination Discourse in Eastern Europe before Wilsonianism', *Diplomacy & Statecraft* 22, no. 3 (2011): 369–87.

133 Prusin, *Nationalizing a Borderland*, 73.

134 Paul Nathan (1857–1927) was a journalist who edited the liberal journal founded by the liberal politician Theodor Barth, *Die Nation*. From 1900 to 1919 Nathan was a member of the Progressive Party in the Berlin city council. During the Weimar Republic he was a member of the German Democratic Party and in 1921, the Social Democratic Party. See his profile online in the *Deutsche Biographie* [https://bit.ly/2XyPsK5, accessed 09/07/19].

135 James Simon (1851–1932) was a textile merchant, philanthropist and art collector. His firm was one of the largest textile companies in Europe, making him one of the wealthiest men in Germany. See his profile online in the *Deutsche Biographie* [https://bit.ly/2YIkyAd, accessed 08/07/19].

more successful in receiving approval for their philanthropic work especially in the area of education. With the support of Under Secretary of State Richthofen the Aid Association established the German School Association for Jews of the Orient (*Der deutsche Schulverein für die Juden des Orients*) in 1898 and in 1912 the Technological College of Haifa. Working to promote German influence, the Aid Association ensured Prussian *Kultur* was encouraged in schools in favour of Hebrew.[136]

With the outbreak of the First World War, in light of the alliance between Germany and the Ottoman Empire, German industry and trade began to take a stronghold in the region. Moreover, the war precipitated a marked increase in the immigration of Russian and Polish Jews to Palestine and these new migrants preferred the German language and to work in German commerce. For years, the international Jewish organisation *Alliance Israélite Universelle*, founded in France, had held a monopoly over Jewish education in the Ottoman Empire.[137] The war offered the Aid Association the opportunity to upset this French dominance over Jewish education. Just as for the Committee for the East, for the Aid Association, Russian Jews could ensure that German surpassed French as the dominant language, culture in the Jewish 'colony'. Whilst the Aid Association was successful in receiving approval for their educational projects and encouraged the German authorities to support Russian Jewish settlement, the following section concentrates on the activities of the Committee for the East which presented the German government with political answers to a practical Jewish Question.

The person promoting the interests of the KfdO in the Middle East was Richard Lichtheim. Lichtheim was born in Berlin in 1885 into a secular Jewish family. At the age of twenty-four, following his father's death, Lichtheim stopped his studies and began working for the Zionist Organisation.[138] In 1913, Lichtheim moved to Constantinople to take over Victor Jacobson's position as representative of the Zionist Organisation.[139] Tasked with overseeing and reporting on the distribution of Jewish funds to Palestine, Lichtheim took it upon himself to restore contact with the German Embassy and establish a working relationship with the German Foreign Office, which the Zionist Inner Actions Committee had struggled to secure.[140]

During his time in Constantinople, Lichtheim engaged in numerous diplomatic meetings with German Foreign Office officials and received several unofficial assurances of support for the Zionist cause in Palestine. One high-ranking official was the

---

136 Friedman, *Germany, Turkey, and Zionism*, 275.

137 On the work of the *Alliance Israélite Universelle* see Lisa Moses Leff, *Sacred Bonds of Solidarity: The Rise of Jewish Internationalism in Nineteenth-Century France* (Stanford, California: Stanford University Press, 2006).

138 George Lichtheim, *Thoughts Among the Ruins: Collected Essays on Europe and Beyond* (New Brunswick, New Jersey: Transaction Publishers, 1973), xiv.

139 Richard Lichtheim, *Ruckkehr: Lebenserinnerungen aus der Frühzeit des deutschen Zionismus* (Stuttgart: Deutsche Verlags-Anstalt, 1970), 260.

140 Ibid, 260.

Ambassador to Constantinople, Hans Freiherr von Wangenheim. Just before the outbreak of the war, Lichtheim had a meeting with Wangenheim who, after revealing his sympathy towards the Zionists, assured Lichtheim that although the German government was not in a position to declare any political commitment to the Zionist cause, Wangenheim was 'unofficially' prepared to offer his support.[141]

Shortly following the outbreak of the First World War, just like Bodenheimer, Lichtheim drafted a memorandum for the German Foreign Office on the benefits of Jewish colonial activity for the economic development of the Ottoman Empire.[142] On the 3 November 1914, before his return to Constantinople, Lichtheim visited the Foreign Office in Berlin where he presented his memorandum to the Director of the Balkans and Orient Section, Baron Friedrich Hans von Rosenberg, who was later appointed Foreign Minister in the Weimar Republic from 1922 to 1923. Aware of Germany's colonial ambitions in the Middle East, Lichtheim advised that the Empire should support Zionist aspirations in the region. Large-scale Jewish colonisation would open up new and valuable economic markets. In the same vein as Bodenheimer's 1902 memorandum, Lichtheim presented the utility of Jews as agents of German interests in Palestine. The proposal was well received. The Director assured Lichtheim that he would contact the German Embassy in Constantinople to report on the meeting. No further promises were offered.[143] When Lichtheim received the official reply to his memorandum it read that 'as far as possible and according to the merit of each case, the Ambassador in Constantinople would take an interest in the Zionist movement'. Based on the international character of Zionism and the mistrust of the Turkish authorities towards the movement, the reply concluded that these factors 'imposed certain limitations' on German actions.[144]

Lichtheim, and Bodenheimer were not alone in their views on the advantages of collaborating with Jews in the Middle East. This position was also held by a cross-section of prominent individuals in German high society. Heinrich Class (leader of the Pan-Germans) and Friedrich von Schwerin (District President in Frankfurt-on-Oder) both expressed a desire for Polish Jews to voluntarily immigrate to Palestine after the war.[145] Werner Sombart in his 1911 lecture series similarly spoke positively about Jewish national regeneration in Palestine.[146] The following year, Professor Martin Hartmann published a series of articles in the *Frankfurter Zeitung* highlighting the importance for

---

141 Lichtheim's report to the Zionist Executive on his meeting with Wangenheim. Quoted and trans. in Friedman, *Germany, Turkey, and Zionism*, 187.
142 Lichtheim, *Ruckkehr*, 261.
143 Ibid.
144 AA, Türkei 195, K 176713–14, memorandum by Lichtheim, 3 November 1914. Quoted and trans. in Friedman, *Germany, Turkey, and Zionism*, 208.
145 'Denkschrift von Heinrich Class betreffend die national-, wirtschafts-, und sozialpolitischen Zeile des deutschen Volkes um gegenwärtigen Kriege' (undated), Beseler Nachlass Papers, 48–50. Cited in ibid, 252.
146 Sombart, *Die Zukunft der Juden*.

German interests of Jewish colonial work in Palestine.[147] That Germany could benefit from Jewish colonisation in its Oriental policy complemented an idea that found expression in a term coined in 1915, *Mitteleuropa*.[148] Semantically versatile, *Mitteleuropa* became associated with the broad idea of controlling the European continent from a dominant German centre.[149] *Mitteleuropa* also, however, became associated with German actions outside of Europe (*Drang nach Osten, Berlin-Bagdad*) and was associated with 'militarism, aggression, Prussianism, conquest, Kaiserism, oppression and annexation'.[150] Friedrich Naumann, a liberal politician, established the parameters to the term *Mitteleuropa* in a book by that title published in October 1915.[151] He described modern war as submitting to contemporary trends of large-scale industrialisation and supra-national organisation. Naumann envisioned that the war would divide the world into several large areas. During the war, as Europe faced the prospect of dividing, Naumann advocated for a *Mitteleuropa* consisting of Austria-Hungary and Germany. After the war he hoped that it would expand to form 'a new community of existence'.[152]

Another prominent advocate of *Mitteleuropa*, who was also part of the Naumann circle, was Paul Rohrbach, Director of the German Foreign Information Service. In 1902 he published a book entitled *Die Bagdadbahn* in which he encouraged building a strong alliance with Turkey in order to strengthen German presence in the Middle East. Rohrbach saw the Middle East as a crucial region for German colonisation.[153] In 1915, Rohrbach delivered the first of a series of lectures to the Prussian parliament on the subject of Zionism and German foreign policy.[154] He argued that only the Zionist movement and the prospect of Palestine could divert the migration of Jewish masses from Europe.[155] He emphasised that the Jewish national body in Palestine was not a

---

147 Friedman, *Germany, Turkey, and Zionism*, 253. On the life and work of the Arabic scholar Martin Hartmann see Martin Kramer, 'Arabistik and Arabism: The Passions of Martin Hartmann', *Middle Eastern Studies* 25, no. 3 (1989): 283–300.

148 Meyer, *Mitteleuropa in German Thought and Action*, 2.

149 Helmut Rumpf, 'Mitteleuropa. Zur Geschichte und Deutung eines politischen Begriffs', *Historische Zeitschrift* 165, no. 1 (1942): 510–27.

150 Meyer, *Mitteleuropa in German Thought and Action*, 4.

151 Friedrich Naumann, *Mitteleuropa*, (Berlin: Druck und Verlag von Georg Reimer, 1916) [https://bit.ly/2KgwuTL, accessed 01 /08/19]. See also Meyer, *Mitteleuropa in German Thought and Action*, 194–215. *Mitteleuropa* was also appropriated by Franz Rosenzweig who published a series of articles countering Naumann's vision. Rosenzweig suggested establishing a political federation extending beyond Central Europe to include, Germany, Austria, the Balkans, Turkey and Egypt. Rosenzweig envisioned a 'New Levante' under German influence. See Jörg Kreienbrock, 'Franz Rosenzweig's Mitteleuropa as a New Levante', in *Personal Narratives, Peripheral Theatres: Essays on the Great War (1914–18)*, ed. Anthony Barker et al. (Cham: Springer International Publishing, 2018), 185–200.

152 Naumann, *Mitteleuropa*, 11–32. Quoted in Meyer, *Mitteleuropa in German Thought and Action*, 199.

153 Meyer, *Mitteleuropa in German Thought and Action*, 97.

154 These lectures were organised by the *Kartell Jüdischer Verbindungen* on behalf of the *Roten Halbmondes*. Anon., 'Deutsche Weltpolitik und türkische Entwicklung', *Jüdische Rundschau* XX, no. 13 (26 März 1915): 105. See also Friedman, *Germany, Turkey, and Zionism*, 253.

155 Ibid, 253.

threat to Germany's colonial ambitions as Jewish and German interests aligned. More-over, the Jews would help promote German *Kultur* and commerce.[156]

Other speakers in the lecture series (*Vortrageszyklus*) to the Prussian parliament in-cluded Martin Buber, a prominent intellectual in the cultural Zionist movement, who lectured on Jewish nationalism. Ernst Jäckh, founder of the German-Turkish Union, concluded that whilst Germans would be unsuitable settlers, Jews and Armenians would be viable candidates for settlement in the Ottoman Empire as 'Jews could repre-sent a permanent link between Orient and Occident'.[157] In the last lecture of the series, Alfons Paquet, a poet and travel writer, spoke on 'experiences in Jewish colonies'. He observed that both Russia and the United Kingdom had tried to exert their influence over Palestine but only German Zionist efforts were of any value. Moreover, the Ger-mans, according to Paquet, were ideally placed to help advance Zionist aims.[158] Accord-ing to a Jewish newspaper report, the lecture cycle was 'one of the most meaningful Zionist events witnessed in Berlin as of late'.[159] The lecture series in the Prussian parlia-ment revealed that there was a clear political interest on how Jewish colonial activity and Zionism could benefit Germany's colonial expansion in the Middle East. The con-tributors to the lecture series stressed the importance of the Zionist movement for Ger-man war aims. Zionist activities aligned with *Mitteleuropa* ideas and could guarantee German dominance, both culturally and linguistically, in the Middle East. A stronger German influence would destabilise the French and English stronghold in the region.[160]

The subject of Zionism and German foreign policy in the Middle East, also be-came a lively public debate through the journal, *Das grössere Deutschland*, co-edited by Rohrbach and Jäckh, which saw contributions from prominent politicians and public figures.[161] The prestigious journal, the Prussian Yearbooks also featured an article on the topic in its autumn 1915 edition, *Der Zionismus: Eine Frage der deutschen Orient-politik* written by the Secretary of the Zionist Federation, Kurt Blumenfeld. The article reached the hands of the Under Secretary of State Arthur Zimmerman, who, although still wary of supporting a Jewish state, was impressed with its argument.[162]

While German officials remained bound by the shackles of *Realpolitik*, protecting their alliance with the Ottoman Empire, they met the constant lobbying by Zionist

---

156 British interests were seen as less aligned to Jewish interests as the British were perceived by Zionists as supporting both the destruction of the Ottoman Empire and Arab national interests.
157 Anon., 'Deutsche Weltpolitik und türkische Entwicklung', 105. On Jäckh's enthusiasm for the Near East see, Meyer, *Mitteleuropa in German Thought and Action*, 95–102.
158 Anon., 'Erlebnisse in jüdischen Kolonien', *Jüdische Rundschau* XX, no. 14 (9 April 1915), 117.
159 Ibid, 117.
160 This was a point stressed by Alfons Paquet. See Anon., 'Erlebnisse in jüdischen Kolonien', 117.
161 Contributors included the leader of the Conservative Party, Count Kuno von Westarp, the Social-Democratic Deputy to the Reichstag, Ludwig Quessel, and the military analyst, Major Karl Endres. See also, Anon., 'Politische Bedeutung des Zionismus', *Das grössere Deutschland* (Jan-June 1915), 290–8.
162 Friedman, *Germany, Turkey, and Zionism*, 255.

individuals and organisations with sympathy. Jewish policy proposals may not have translated into practical actions, but their public prominence testifies to the relevance of Jewish Questions in German political discourse during the war. And although no official assurances were given, during the war the Foreign Ministry worked tirelessly to ensure the activities of Zionists continued unhindered.

During the war, the Foreign Office issued several exemptions of military service to senior members of the World Zionist Organisation and Zionist Federation enabling them to continue their work for the movement.[163] Transit visas and residency permits were also issued to non-German nationals of the Zionist Executive. Victor Jacobson, Head of the Zionist Executive, was given German diplomatic documents to travel freely between Berlin and Constantinople. The motivation for the German government supporting Zionist wartime activity is best encapsulated in one of the exemption letters to the General Headquarters. Written by Foreign Secretary Alfred Zimmermann it read,

> In view of the influence of international Jewry on public opinion and the press in neutral countries, especially in the United States, it would be in Germany's political interest to show, during the war, an accommodating attitude towards Zionism which is the most widespread and best-organised international organisation. It seems, therefore, desirable that the leadership of the Zionist Organisation should centre in Germany, giving thus a greater guarantee that Jewish circles outside Germany are influenced in a pro-German direction.[164]

German support for the Zionist Executive was extended even further when in early 1915 the Foreign Ministry endorsed the establishment of the Zionist Bureau in Copenhagen. This move was favourable to the Germans as it enabled the Zionist Executive in Berlin to 'keep the policies of the national organisations in neutral and Entente countries in line with German and Turkish interests'.[165] As intended, the Bureau was vital in promoting positive attitudes on Germany internationally. Its success even led to Count Brockdorff-Rantzau, then Envoy to Copenhagen, going to great lengths to ensure the continued functioning of this 'essential' Bureau.[166]

---

163 The exemptions had to be renewed every three months. A reason had to be given for each renewal. Zionists who were exempted included Hantke, Lichtheim, Ruppin and Rosenblüth. See Friedman, *Germany, Turkey, and Zionism*, 208. See also AA, Abteilung A, *Die Jüden*, Band 1–2, Internation. Angel. No. 3. (November 1918 – März 1920).

164 AA, Türkei 195, K177743–6, Zimmermann to G.H.Q., 27 June 1916. Quoted and trans. in Friedman, *Germany, Turkey and Zionism*, 270.

165 AA, Türkei 195, K178276–7, Zimmermann to Romberg (Berne), 24 February 1917 (secret). Quoted and trans. in Friedman, *Germany, Turkey and Zionism*, 251.

166 Friedman writes that the German praise of the Bureau was in part due to Germany not being any good at propaganda. See AA, Türkei 195, K177235–42, Brockdorff-Rantzau to AA, 21 August 1915. Quoted and trans. in ibid, 251.

In Constantinople, the German Ambassador Wangenheim interceded a number of times on behalf of the Zionists and in the Jewish interest. Early on in the war, Licht-heim reported that newly settled Russian Jews might be expelled from Turkey should Russia enter the war. Wangenheim responded by guaranteeing the protection of resi-dent Russian Jews.[167] This prediction proved true when in the winter of 1914 the Turk-ish authorities commenced the expulsion of Russian Jews, moving them to Egypt.[168] Lichtheim appealed to the German authorities who intervened. The Germans helped halt the crisis and, in the aftermath, reiterated the promise to safeguard the Jews of Pal-estine.[169] Despite these interventions (of which there were others[170]), and the unofficial support for the Zionist cause, Lichtheim was under no illusion that Germany would 'revoke her alliance with Turkey for our sake' as 'Zionism is not her first priority'.[171]

The Foreign Office's position on Zionism is best surmised in a memorandum writ-ten by the Consul in Jaffa, Heinrich Brode and submitted on 26 August 1915. Brode was requested to present a coherent review of Zionist activities during the First World War and their advantages for Germany, given the competing views on this subject. In the memorandum titled, *Zionismus und Weltkrieg*, Brode made a sharp distinction between German Jews, whom he commended for their patriotism and fulfilling their military obligations, and Russian Zionists, who had been afforded protection in Pales-tine, whose pro-German attitude he distrusted.[172] On this basis, he advised the govern-ment to postpone any commitment to the Zionist cause until after the war. Despite this advice, Brode detailed the overwhelming benefits of Zionism for Germany, fram-ing them in light of the 'Jewish Question'.[173]

Brode's report echoed arguments made by Zionists, Bodenheimer and Lichtheim, on the advantages of Zionism for Germany. He began by outlining the 'tremendous' economic potential of Jewish colonisation for German merchandise. The international character of Zionism meant that the German protection of Jews in Palestine created sympathy amongst international Jewry, especially in America, for Germany. Moreover,

---

167 To read about this event in detail see Andrea Kirchner, 'Ein Vergessenes Kapitel Jüdischer Diplomatie: Richard Lichtheim in Den Botschaften Konstantinopels (1913–1917)', *Naharaim* 9, no. 1–2 (2015): 128–50.
168 Another deportation order for the Jews in Jaffa was issued by Djemal Pasha in 1917. For details on the German intervention in both 1914 and 1917 see Isaiah Friedman, 'German Intervention on Behalf of the Yishuv, 1917', *Jewish Social Studies* 33, no. 1 (1971): 23–43.
169 Important officials in Constantinople that supported Zionist interests were Wangenheim, Mutius, Kühlmann and the First Dragoman, Weber. Another important personality aiding the Jews in Palestine, sometimes in cooperation with the Germans, was the American Ambassador to Constantinople Morgen-thau who early on in the war had been encouraged by U. S. President Wilson to help his 'co-religionists'.
170 See Friedman, *Germany, Turkey, and Zionism*, 241–88.
171 CZA, L 6/45 Lichtheim to Straus, 6 July 1915. Cited and trans. in ibid, 242.
172 This of course is in stark contrast to the actions taken by the Minister of War only a year later to ques-tion the military service of Jews on the front lines. See chapter three.
173 AA, Türkei 195, K177300–46, 'Memorandum über den Zionismus und Weltkrieg' (confidential), 'Ge-heime Bemerkungen zu dem Memorandum', no. 76/1278. Summarised in Friedman, *Germany, Turkey, and Zionism*, 255.

Brode saw in Zionism the potential to ensure that the effects of the war on Russian Jews would not lead to a 'flood to the West' but rather their immigration to Palestine.[174] For Bode, the Zionist movement could make 'a substantial contribution to the solution of the Jewish problem in Germany'.[175]

Whilst praising Zionist activities, one cannot ignore that Brode's support for Zionism was linked to his recognition of the Jews as a foreign element within Germany. Quoting a speech in the Reichstag by General von Herbert who described the Jews as a 'foreign body in the German national entity', Brode concurred that, although 'tactless', the speech was 'to the point'. Brode questioned whether 'our *Volkstum*' was able to integrate 'Jewish characteristics' without 'impairing [Germany's] innate *Wesen*'. He saw Zionism as a way in which to 'preserve our people from the excessive penetration of Oriental blood'. In spite of his appreciation of Jewish military duty he also confessed that the 'very idea that a Jew as a senior officer, or administrative official, might represent the authority of the state is somewhat repellent to our national feeling'.[176]

The German Empire had to carefully balance its approach towards Zionism. As an ally of the Ottoman Empire, it did not want to destabilise the region by supporting the growth of a Jewish majority in Palestine. On the other hand, given the likelihood that the Jewish colonisation of Palestine would continue after the war, which Brode described as 'a justified historical necessity', the German authorities had to ensure they maintained a relationship with leaders of the Zionist movement.[177]

Whilst the war offered the political Zionists renewed hope of a political answer to the Jewish Question events proceeded as they had at the turn of the century. The Zionists received only informal assurances. The German government unofficially encouraged Zionist settlement initiatives, but this was not reflected by any official action or declaration of support. Underlying Germany's limited scope of action was its alliance to the Ottoman Empire, which increased in dependency during the war. In as much as the Zionists were unable to rally the Sultan behind their cause, they had little chance at acquiring any official guarantee from the Kaiser. By the winter of 1916 as relations with the Committee for the East began to worsen, as did those between Lichtheim and the German Embassy in Constantinople. The following year, coinciding with the entry of the United States of America into the war, Lichtheim was accused of conspiring with the Americans and forced to leave Turkey.[178] In Constantinople the Zionists had lost their vital contact.

---

174 It is worth noting that he did acknowledge that it was unlikely German Jews would leave their Fatherland. Like Bodenheimer, he saw Zionism as a means to mitigate the *Ostjudenproblem* in Germany.
175 'Geheime Bemerkungen zu dem Memorandum', no. 76/1278. Summarised in Friedman, *Germany, Turkey and Zionism*, 257.
176 Ibid, 258.
177 Ibid.
178 Vogt, 'The First World War, German Nationalism, and The Transformation of German Zionism', 275.

The final nail in the coffin for the political German Zionists was the announcement of a Jewish homeland in Palestine by the British, rather than the German government. As Zionists, they rejoiced. As German Zionists, the Balfour Declaration marked an inconclusive end to over two decades of diplomatic work. On the 5 January 1918 members of the Zionist Action Committee (Otto Warburg and Arthur Hantke) and the Committee for the East (Franz Oppenheimer and Moritz Sobernheim) received letters from the Under Secretary of the Foreign Ministry Freiherr Axel von dem Bussche-Haddenhaufen.[179] The letter announced German support for 'a flourishing Jewish settlement in Palestine' but did not concede more than had already been granted by the Turkish government.[180] The same German foreign policy towards the Jewish state, dating back to 1898, remained in place.[181] German Zionists were unable to secure a Jewish state under a German protectorate. Nevertheless, the 'huge frequency of communications tens of thousands of dispatches, cables exchanged between Berlin, Jerusalem and Constantinople shows that it was this was no causal aspect of German policy'.[182]

The Committee for the East and the afterlife of its policies

With the defeat of the Central Powers in the First World War, the objectives of the German political Zionists were never put into practice, nor are they well known today. However, the little recognised achievements of these individuals were no small matter. Whilst the Committee for the East did not secure a commitment from the German government on par with the Balfour Declaration, they had two enduring successes: ideational and institutional.

The Committee for the East was never officially recognised by the German government. Nonetheless, it exerted a significant amount of political influence both during the war and after. Early on in the war, in late December 1914, the importance of collaborating with the Jewish population led the Intelligence Bureau of the Foreign Office to employ Nahum Goldmann, who later founded the World Jewish Congress, to investigate Jewish life and activities in Eastern Europe.[183] By the following year, a Jewish Affairs section was opened in the German administration of Warsaw. Ludwig Haas, a non-Zionist liberal Jew and Reichstag Deputy of the Progressive Party, was invited as

---

179 Anon., 'Die Reichsregierung und die Bestrebungen der Zionisten', *Norddeutsche Allgemeine Zeitung* 57, no. 10 (6 Januar 1918).

180 Martin Sicker, *Reshaping Palestine: From Muhammad Ali to the British Mandate, 1831–1922* (Westport, Connecticut: Praeger, 1999), 134.

181 Stefan Vogt, 'The First World War, German Nationalism, and The Transformation of German Zionism', *Leo Baeck Institute Year Book* 57 (11 July 2012): 247.

182 Friedman, *Germany, Turkey, and Zionism*, viii.

183 Raphael Patai, *Nahum Goldmann: His Missions to the Gentiles* (Tuscaloosa: University of Alabama Press, 2003), 45–54.

an expert consultant to oversee the department. In 1917, a similar position was created in the political section of the Eastern Command, headed by Hermann Struck,[184] one of the original fifteen members of the Committee for the East.[185] The representation of Jewish affairs in German administrative divisions continued even after the war when in November 1918, an office for Jewish Affairs was established in the German Foreign Ministry in Berlin. Directing it was Moritz Sobernheim who, like Struck, was one of the original founding members of the KfdO. Officially, the Committee for the East ended all activities with the signing of the Treaty of Versailles in June 1919, and yet its last vestiges continued through the work of Sobernheim.[186]

Turning to Bodenheimer and the KfdO's ideational legacy, whilst the idea of an East European Federation recognising Jewish national rights never materialised during the First World War, the idea was once again adopted by the Anglo-Jewish diplomat, Lucien Wolf in 1917. Building on Renner, Wolf published an article in the *Edinburgh Review* in which he argued in support of Jewish national rights for Eastern European Jewry, despite being an ardent anti-Zionist. Like Renner and Bodenheimer, he envisioned the recognition of Jewish rights in a future Austrian-Hungarian polity following the structure of a federalised state, with a decentralised system of national diets.[187] As the Empire was split into several of ethnically homogenous nation-states and Austria became a Republic, the federalised state system, never found favour.

Nevertheless, the idea espoused by Bodenheimer and the Committee for the East, supporting the recognition of cultural autonomous rights for Jews, endured. The international Zionist movement adopted it as one of the clauses of the Copenhagen manifesto in 1918 and it was campaigned for by the International Worker's Union.[188] Most significantly, the idea became embedded within the concept of minority rights and was enshrined in the Minority Treaty in 1919.[189] In the Paris Peace Conferences, minority rights were removed from an internal concern of states and elevated to the level of international law, under the jurisdiction of the League of Nations.[190] Renner's

---

184   Struck volunteered to serve in the German army. He was sent to the Eastern Front where he worked in the press office of the *Ober-Ost* due to his ability to speak and translate Yiddish. Struck was a political Zionist like Bodenheimer and Oppenheimer, and Orthodox. During the war Struck received the Iron Cross 1st Class and was promoted to the rank of officer.

185   Gilya Gerda Schmidt, *The Art and Artists of the Fifth Zionist Congress, 1901: Heralds of a New Age* (New York: Syracuse University Press, 2003), 109.

186   For a detailed account of Sobernheim's work in the Jewish Affairs department see Nicosia, 'Jewish Affairs and German Foreign Policy during the Weimar Republic'.

187   Mark Levene, 'Nationalism and Its Alternatives in the International Arena: The Jewish Question at Paris, 1919', *Journal of Contemporary History* 28, no. 3 (July 1993): 520.

188   Bodenheimer, *Max Bodenheimer*, 77.

189   The Congress of American Jews came out in support of national rights for Jews where they were guaranteed for other nationalities. Jewish minority rights were campaigned for by representatives in the *Comité des Delegations Juifs'* in Geneva. See ibid, 77.

190   See chapter five for more on this subject.

notion of the personality principle, which I have suggested inspired the idea of cultural autonomy advocated by Bodenheimer, came to form one foundational pillar of the concept of minority rights. Where prior to the war, individuals had been granted equal citizenship on the basis of civil and religious freedom, in the Minority Treaty they were granted the additional right to cultural and/or ethnic distinctions within the state. Renner and Bodenheimer fought for the practical and political recognition of the ethnic, cultural, linguistic distinctions of minority communities within a given territory. And despite the short-lived practical political manifestations of their solution to the nationality question, the conceptual legacy of their ideas lived on.

Social Democratic Member of Parliament, Ludwig Quessel in his article written in April 1918, a few months before the end of the war, perhaps most accurately summarised the union of Renner's and Bodenheimer's ideas in the German occupation of Eastern Europe and the confrontation with a practical Jewish Question. Two facts allowed non-Jewish observers to view the Jewish Question in a new light, began Quessel. The emancipation of the Jews in Eastern Europe, and the Jewish right, 'recognised by nearly the entirety of mankind', to the closed settlement of Palestine.[191] Central to this new conception of the Jewish Question was the understanding that, 'in the east the Jewish Question was always not only a social, but also, a national problem'.[192] This became apparent only as a consequence of the war, which revealed the existence of a new nation (culturally and linguistically unique) of 'six to seven million, living in territory expanding from Riga to Odessa'. On this basis, Quessel stressed the importance, for Eastern European Jews, of the protection of national minority rights through an international treaty. Referencing Renner's concept of the personality principle in the context of minority rights, Quessel remarked that 'like other national minorities in the east, East European Jewry will also have to strive to protect its nationality on the basis of the personality principle' (*Personalitätsprinzips*).[193]

During the occupation of West Russia, as the German army faced a practical Jewish Question, debates that were previously confined to Zionist circles on Jewish nationalism, cultural autonomy and minority rights were propelled into mainstream discourse and became a factor for consideration in German foreign policy decisions. Speaking at his trial, in March 1924, on his involvement in the Munich Putsch, General Erich Ludendorff reflected on how he had made an 'acquaintance during the war' with the 'Jewish question'.[194] Ludendorff was referring to his time as Commander of the East where the Central Powers had encountered a population of approximately six mil-

---

191 Ludwig Quessel, 'Die Judenfrage als nationales Problem', 299.
192 Ibid.
193 Ibid, 300.
194 Anon., 'Ludendorff assails Jews, Pope and Catholic Clergy', *Jewish Telegraphic Agency* (1 March 1924) [https://goo.gl/JScRtR, accessed 12/12/18]. Referenced in Giuseppe Motta, *The Great War against Eastern European Jewry, 1914–1920* (Newcastle upon Tyne: Cambridge Scholars Publishing, 2017), 90.

lion Yiddish-speaking Jews. This encounter raised significant questions pertaining not only to the understanding within Germany of Jewish identity as not just a community of faith but importantly, the German state. Answers initially conceived in response to Jewish questions had a longer legacy within discussions about the modern state in Germany. Jewish questions produced queries and answers that were more widely relevant to a catalogue of problems facing Germany that, as the following chapters will show, emerged throughout the First World War and had ramifications during the Weimar Republic.

III Constitutionalism and secularism in the Jewish census of 1916

'I know parties no longer, I know only Germans' pronounced Kaiser Wilhelm II in his opening speech to parliament on Tuesday 4 August 1914, the day following the German advance into Belgium and the opening of the Western Front.[1] This would mark the end of 'party differences', (*Parteiunterschiede*), of 'differences in ethnicity' (*Stammesunterschiede*) and 'confessional differences' (*Konfessionsunterschiede*) the Kaiser announced. The meaning of the speech was clear. The Kaiser had announced a civic truce (*Burgfrieden*) within the German Empire, intended to unify the citizens of the still young nation to sacrifice their lives, as brothers in arms, for the Fatherland. Just as the rallying cry of the Wars of Liberation united the German states to fight off Napoleon, the First World War offered a similar opportunity to bring together the disparate German-speaking citizens of the Empire, for the first time on a global stage.

Whilst the Kaiser's speech advocated solidarity, it highlighted the disunity within the Empire hinting at the long struggle for unification, which had culminated in an Empire with distinct regional, tribal (*Stammes*) and confessional identities. In the same parliamentary session, the Chancellor Theodor Bethmann-Hollweg similarly addressed the session as the 'people and kinsmen (*Stämme*) of the German Empire'.[2] The common cause presented by the outbreak of the First World War was a unique and opportune moment for the forty-three-year-old Empire, which had not fought a war since unification. Not only did the German leadership embrace this opportunity, stoking up military fervour, but moreover the chance to fight for the German Empire was seized upon by Germany's minority Jewish population.[3]

---

1 'Eröffnungsitzung, 4 August 1914', *Verhandlung Des Reichstag, Band 306, 1916* 1914, 2 [https://bit.ly/2NETflP, accessed 06/12/2019].
2 Ibid.
3 Unlike German Jews, the German population on the whole was less enthusiastic about the war than previously thought. For an account on the myth of the 'spirit of 1914' in Germany see Jeffrey Verhey, *The Spirit of 1914: Militarism, Myth, and Mobilization in Germany* (Cambridge: Cambridge University Press, 2000).

German Jews enthusiastically joined in the in the national impetus afforded by the call to arms. Just under 2 % of the total population of Jews within Germany (which included those unable to serve such as women, children and the elderly) enlisted to volunteer at the start of the war.[4] As the war fired up nationalist sentiments, tellingly Jews (and even Zionists) served in the national armies of which they saw themselves a part, 'for us in this war the Jews fighting alongside us are simply Germans and the Jews in enemy armies are French or English'.[5] The patriotism of German Jews cut across community divides as both liberal Jewish associations and the Zionist Federation, urged Jews to enlist in the army. The organ of the Zionist Federation came out in public support for the war, declaring 'at this hour it is time for us to show again that we, proud Jewish kinsmen [*stammesstolzen Juden*], belong to the best sons of the Fatherland'.[6] Another pamphlet similarly displayed the dedication of Jews to the 'spirit of 1914': *Glaubensstark und voller Weihe ist des Juden Kaisertreue.*[7]

Prior to the outbreak of war in 1914, unbaptised Jews were continually denied promotion to reserve officer status despite their legal right to equality, which was enshrined in the 1871 constitution of the German Empire.[8] For many Jews serving was a matter of honour and dignity *Heerendiest* was *Ehrendienst*.[9] This slight, though one of many grievances suffered by Jews, was repeatedly raised by Jewish politicians and associations who demanded denominational equality. The outbreak of war, which already by the summer of 1914 saw the removal of these discriminations by the military leadership marked an important shift in German-Jewish relations. For the first time, Jewish specialists from the finance sector, education and science were invited by the War Ministry to partake in the war effort. Coupled with the *Burgfrieden,* the moment signalled that the political and civic rights, which had been legally granted to Jews in 1871, would finally be exercised in practice.[10]

The claim that Jews had shirked their wartime duty dealt a serious blow to German Jews. The accusation was propagated by Alfred Roth, writing under a pseudonym Otto Armin, in 1919 when he published a pamphlet on Jews in the army, which was subtitled,

---

4 Jacob Segall, *Die deutschen Juden als Soldaten im Kriege* (Berlin: Philo, 1921) [https://bit.ly/2YAPohf, accessed 07/06/18].

5 Anon., 'Der Weltkrieg und die Judenfrage Rezension', *Im deutschen Reich* 11–12 (November 1916): 282.

6 Anon., *Jüdische Rundschau* 19, no. 32 (7 August 1914): 343 in Reinharz, *Dokumente zur Geschichte des deutschen Zionismus 1882–1933,* 145.

7 Jonas Kreppel, *Der Weltkrieg und die Judenfrage* (Wien: Verlag Redaktion 'Der Tag', 1915).

8 Werner T. Angress, 'Prussia's Army and the Jewish Reserve Officer: Controversy before World War I', *Leo Baeck Institute Year Book* 17, no. 1 (1972): 19.

9 Ibid, 30.

10 The German Diplomat, Graf Bernstorff was quoted to have said that after the war Jewish hatred in Germany would disappear. See Max Simon, *Der Weltkrieg und die Judenfrage* (Leipzig und Berlin: B. G. Teubner, 1916), 12.

'A statistical survey based on official sources'.[11] Roth claimed that only 10 % of the Jewish population served as opposed to 20 % of the German population, based on the supposed official figures collected by the War Ministry in October 1916, which had never been publicly disclosed.[12]

Alfred Roth at the time of writing was known for his antisemitism and membership of the Pan-German League and had intended through his pamphlet to discredit the loyalty of Jews to the German state. The publication unleashed a heated and lengthy debate concerning the exact numbers of Jews that had served in the war. This debate came to be known as the *Statistikstreit*. Beyond this immediate discussion, the legacy of these accusations continued throughout the years of the Weimar Republic where antisemites used the claim that Jews had shirked their war duty to perpetuate the notion that it was the Jews who had stabbed Germany in the back on the home front which had led to Germany's defeat in the First World War.

The statistics used by Alfred Roth in his pamphlet were collected by the War Ministry, ostensibly to dispel antisemitic accusations of Jewish war-shirking, in an event which became known as the Jew census (*Judenzählung*).[13] The census was comparatively short-lived. It was initiated on the 11 October 1916 by a decree authorised by the War Minister, Adolf Wild von Hohenborn.[14] A little over three months later, it was ground to a halt and declared a closed case by Chancellor Theobald von Bethmann-Hollweg. And yet, despite this short time span the event had an enduring legacy.

The *Judenzählung* has received extensive attention in the literature and for this reason, my chapter does not intend to re-examine the census itself, nor the extent to which it affected German Jews and German-Jewish relations.[15] Rather, it will investigate the

---

11 Otto Armin, *Die Juden Im Heere. Eine Statistische Untersuchung Nach Amtlichen Quellen* (München: Deutscher Volks-Verlag, 1919) [https://bit.ly/2Mwo8aj, accessed 06/08/17].
12 Roth attempted to refute a figure given by a Jewish source on the number of Jews that served and used the 'official statistics' from the War Ministry census of October 1916 to prove his argument. Ibid, 18.
13 Rosenthal writes that the *Judenzählung* was a term given retrospectively to the census whereas shortly after the census the term was used in an article in the *Berliner Tagesblatt*, (4 November 1916): 3. See Rosenthal, *Die Ehre des jüdischen Soldaten*, 12.
14 In January 1915 Adolf Wild von Hohenborn replaced General Falkenhayn as War Minister. The Chancellor had objected to Falkenhayn holding both the position as Minister of War and Chief of the General Staff. At the start of the war Hohenborn remained on the frontlines whilst General von Wandel was appointed as acting War Minister. Hohenborn was recalled to Berlin in September 1916.
15 See Michael Geheran, 'Rethinking Jewish Front Experiences', in *Beyond Inclusion and Exclusion: Jewish Experiences of the First World War in Central Europe*, ed. Jason Crouthamel, Tim Grady, and Julia Barbara Köhne (New York; Oxford: Berghahn Books, 2019), 111–43; Hans-Joachim Becker, *Von der konfessionellen Militärstatistik zur "Judenzählung" (1916): eine Neubewertung* (Nordhausen: Verlag Traugott Bautz, 2016); Peter Appelbaum, *Loyal Sons: Jews in the German Army in the Great War* (London & Portland: Valentine Mitchell, 2015); Ulrike Heikaus and Julia Köhne, eds., *Krieg! Juden Zwischen Den Fronten, 1914–1918* (Berlin: Hentich & Hentich Verlag, 2014); David J. Fine, 'Jewish Integration in the German Army in the First World War' (Berlin & Boston: Walter de Gruyter, 2012); Tim Grady, 'Creating Difference: The Racialization of Germany's Jewish Soldiers after the First World War', *Patterns of Prejudice* 46, no. 3–4 (2012): 318–38; Derek Penslar, 'The German-Jewish Soldier: From Participant to Victim', *German History* 29, no. 3 (2011): 423–44;

Judenzählung as an episode which exposed the challenges faced by the young German nation-state as it considered its national homogeneity two years after the Kaiser's civic truce. Advocating in principle equality and toleration through the constitution, and unity (*Einheit*) through the *Burgfrieden,* the singling out of the Jewish population raised questions about the integrity of German institutions and the commitment to upholding these principles.[16]

Gathering statistical data, even based on confession, was not what caused most outrage for many German Jews. Recording confessional status was standard practice in the enlistment questionnaire in Bavaria, for example.[17] Rather it was by the specific targeting of only Jews serving in the military that the War Ministry undermined all claims to inclusivity heralded by the 'spirit of 1914'.[18] The census signalled the desire to exert control over a minority group (consisting of less than 1% of the German population) who, in the final count, served in equal measure to their fellow Gentiles and of whom 10% that served, gave their lives to the Empire.[19]

This chapter will focus on the debate that erupted over the idea of a confessional survey in the Budget Committee meeting in late October and how its continuation in parliament a few weeks later descended into a debate specifically about the War Ministry's decree. It will reveal how Jewish questions became a crystallisation point for controversies about equality before the law, constitutionalism and secularism. The chapter will situate the *Judenzählung* within the turn in Germany towards a bureaucratic state apparatus and the involvement by the Jewish community in statistical data gathering. It will trace the sequence of events which initially led to the authorisation of a decree and subsequently those which led to its closure. Finally, it will turn to the aftermath of the *Judenzählung* and its legacy within antisemitic circles arguing how it was not the act of a census itself that outraged the Jewish community but rather how the event was poorly conducted and subsequently instrumentalised by the far-right to fuel antisemitic propaganda.

Gregory A. Caplan, *Wicked Sons, German Heroes: Jewish Soldiers, Veterans, and Memories of World War I in Germany* (Saarbrücken: VDM Verlag, 2008); Rosenthal, *Die Ehre des jüdischen Soldaten*; Werner T. Angress, 'The German Army's "Judenzählung" of 1916: Genesis – Consequences – Significance', *The Leo Baeck Institute Year Book* 23, no. 1 (1978): 117–38.

16 It is significant that the decree came from the War Ministry, a department that was still answerable to the Reichstag, and that it was not raised in parliament before its authorisation.

17 Fine, 'Jewish Integration in the German Army in the First World War', 16.

18 In a letter to the War Ministry Cassel wrote that he could comprehend a decree to count soldiers serving. He could not understand the specific singling out of Jews. HASt, Oskar Cassel to Hermann von Stein, (29.12.1916), No. 4–11.

19 Using population estimates and the figures of the *Reichsbund* reveals that 17% of the Jewish population served in the war, with 77% serving on the frontlines, compared to 19% of the total German population that served. For these population figures see Berghahn, *Imperial Germany,* 102. Reichsbund Jüdischer Frontsoldaten, *Kriegsbriefe gefallener deutscher Juden* (Stuttgart: Seewald Verlag, 1961), 17.

The significance of the census was that it exposed the disconnect between law and practice in the German Empire. In the course of the debates, the speakers challenged whether Germany would continue to prevail in its past prejudices or support a future embodied by unity, solidarity and (religious) tolerance. The First World War and the Jewish questions that were catalysed by the *Judenzählung* provide a unique lens through which to examine the German Empire at a critical juncture on the path towards becoming a modern state.

Facts behind the figures: the origins of the census

The declaration of war and the call to arms was shortly followed by a surge in antisemitic propaganda, which charged Jews with 'war-shirking'.[20] Already in August 1914 a Pan-German League called the *Reichshammerbund*[21] began to circulate pamphlets requesting an investigation into Jewish participation in the war.[22] The following month, the Central Association sent a letter to the Chancellery highlighting the ubiquity of allegations in newspaper articles and policy reports that Jews were committing unpatriotic crimes, including spying. Right-wing groups and individuals accused Jews of 'not fighting in sufficient numbers and, instead, of profiteering from the nation's war-time struggle'.[23]

In spite of the high volume of antisemitic material received by the War Ministry publications containing offensive allegations were censored.[24] This changed in 1916 when the War Ministry decided to react to complaints of Jews shirking their military duty. On the 11 October, War Minister Adolf Wild von Hohenborn authorised a decree to have all military and red cross units count and record all Jews in service.[25] The introduction to the decree was revealing of the justification given by the Ministry to issue a survey,

---

20 Penslar, 'The German-Jewish Soldier: From Participant to Victim', 432.

21 Founded by Theodor Fritsch in 1912, the organisation coordinated the activities of other smaller antisemitic organisations.

22 Appelbaum, *Loyal Sons*, 241.

23 Grady, 'Creating Difference', 321.

24 Angress, 'The German Army's "Judenzählung" of 1916', 119. For more on military censorship see Anne Lipp, *Meinungslenkung Im Krieg: Kriegserfahrungen Deutscher Soldaten Und Ihre Deutung, 1914–1918* (Göttingen: Vandenhoeck & Ruprecht, 2003), 159; Zechlin, *Die deutsche Politik und die Juden im Ersten Weltkrieg*, 93.

25 In his personal documents Adolf Wild von Hohenborn did not reference the *Judenzählung* once. Nor is it possible to gauge his position on antisemitism. Hohenborn did concede that Falkenhayn was less conservative in his thinking and acted more as a politician than Hohenborn had. This might account for why the census was not authorised under Falkenhayn as War Minister. See Adolf Wild von Hohenborn, *Adolf Wild von Hohenborn: Briefe und Tagebuchaufzeichnungen des preussischen Generals als Kriegsminister und Truppenführer im Ersten Weltkrieg*, ed. Helmut Reichold and Gerhard Granier, Schriften des Bundesarchivs; 34 (Boppard am Rhein: Harald Boldt Verlag, 1986), 11, 209–17.

the War Ministry is continuously receiving complaints from the population that a dispro-
portionate number of eligible members of the Israelite faith are being made exempt or
evading their obligation to serve under every imaginable pretext.[26]

What then marked the shift in attitude and authorisation of a decree? Only a few
months earlier the War Ministry had dismissed a complaint from the General Staff of
the Stettin Army Corps that Jews who were liable for service had been freed from duty.
The Ministry had responded by stressing that 'German Jewish citizens [were] doing
their duty to the same degree as their non-Jewish counterparts'.[27]

Only a month before the census Walther Rathenau had predicted that these accusations were an inevitable consequence of the war. He declared, 'the more Jews fall in this
war, the more enduring their opponents will show that they will have sat behind the
front and profited from the war. The hate will double and treble'.[28] More likely, however, the pandering to accusations of Jewish war-shirking was a result of two changes in
leadership. The first were the appointments in the Supreme Army Command (*Oberste
Heeresleitung*) of General Paul von Hindenburg as Chief of General Staff and Erich
Ludendorff as First Quartermaster General on 29 August. After a series of successive
military failures in the spring of 1916, Hindenburg replaced General Erich von Falkenhayn in an attempt to turn the war in Germany's favour. The second leadership change
occurred on the 27 September when on the request of Hindenburg, Deputy War Minister General Franz Gustav von Wandel stepped down and his superior Lieutenant
General Adolf Wild von Hohenborn resumed command.

Already at the start of the year in January, Chancellor Theobald von Bethmann-
Hollweg and the Chief of General Staff Lieutenant General Erich von Falkenhayn
agreed it was a matter of extreme urgency to end the war before the winter of 1916/17 as
the combined level of raw materials was at its lowest figures.[29] Coupled with this shortage of raw materials, devastating campaigns on the Western Front in Verdun and the
Somme (the failure of Falkenhayn's 'small' offensives strategy) meant that Germany
was also suffering from a critical shortage of manpower. The tipping point came in

---

26 'Fortgesetzt laufen beim Kriegsministerium aus der Bevölkerung Klagen darüber ein, daß eine unver-
hältnismäßig große Anzahl wehrpflichtiger Angehörige des israelitischen Glaubens vom Heeresdienst
befreit sei oder sich von diesem unter allen nur möglichen Vorwänden drücke'. Wild von Hohenborn, 'Erlass', Nr. 247/8. 16. C1b, *Kriegsministerium*, Berlin, W. 66 (11.10.1916), 160 [https://bit.ly/2UnjL5w, accessed
05/03/2019].
27 Appelbaum, *Loyal Sons*, 249.
28 Ibid, 245.
29 'Aufzeichnung Bethmann Hollwegs', AA, *Die Weltkrieg* 18, Band 1. Translated excerpt available online
[https://bit.ly/2SHiG6Y, accessed 14/02/17].

August when Romania entered the war contrary to Falkenhayn's predictions, leading to his replacement.[30]

At this critical moment in the war the Kaiser, under pressure, began devolving his authority as Supreme Warlord to Hindenburg and Ludendorff awarding them with almost complete control over military but also political and economic matters. In this 'first crisis of authority' emanating from a 'military-civilian dualism' General Hindenburg and Ludendorff were posited against the Chancellor Bethmann-Hollweg and the Reichstag. The Empire was straddled between becoming an *Obrigkeitstaat* (authoritarian state) and upholding parliamentary democracy with a total war economy.[31] 'The German's response to the campaigns of 1916 was the total mobilisation of resources, cost what it might'.[32] It was in this spirit that Ludendorff transformed the economy into one of total war through the implementation of the Hindenburg Programme. National service was expanded to include seventeen- to sixty-year-old men and passed as law in December under the Patriotic Auxiliary Service Law (*Hilfsdienstgesetz*).[33] Skilled workers were released from their duty on the front lines and those that had not yet been conscripted were made exempt and sent to work on the production of armaments. The programme had the overall effect of placing a larger strain on the German economy and causing food shortages across the country. Ludendorff's production goals had been unrealistic, and yet after the war, the military leadership shifted the responsibility of Germany's defeat to civilians who had been involved in economic production.[34]

As Hindenburg and Ludendorff assumed control, they reordered the command structures in the War Ministry by forcing Wandel into early retirement and recalling his superior, the Minister of War, Adolf Wild von Hohenborn to Berlin to supervise the Hindenburg Programme.[35] Whilst Wandel's 'default approach' had been to either ignore the far-right's attack on Jews or respond with evasive replies, his successor took a radically different approach.[36] Only a few weeks into this appointment Hohenborn authorised a decree to count the number of German Jews serving in the military.

---

30 Roger Chickering, *Imperial Germany and the Great War, 1914–1918*, 3rd ed. (Cambridge: Cambridge University Press, 2014), 67–72.
31 McElligott, *Rethinking the Weimar Republic: Authority and Authoritarianism*, 4.
32 Chickering, *Imperial Germany and the Great War*, 78.
33 Rüdiger vom Bruch and Björn Hofmeister, eds., *Kaiserreich Und Erster Weltkrieg 1871–1918.*, vol. 8, Deutsche Geschichte in Quellen und Darstellung (Stuttgart: P. Reclam, 2000), 402–4. Excerpt available online [https://bit.ly/2SL9i28, accessed 13 February 2017].
34 William Astore and Dennis Showalter, *Hindenburg: Icon of German Militarism* (Washington, D.C.: Potomac Books, 2005), 41.
35 Gerald D. Feldman, 'The Political and Social Foundations of Germany's Economic Mobilization, 1914–1916', *Armed Forces and Society* 3, no. 1 (1976): 135.
36 Timothy L. Grady, *A Deadly Legacy: German Jews and the Great War* (New Haven & London: Yale University Press, 2017), 139; Rosenthal, *Die Ehre des jüdischen Soldaten*, 16; Angress, 'The German Army's "Judenzählung" of 1916', 122.

Whilst Hohenborn's name appeared on the order, the 'spiritual father' behind the decree was most likely the Director of the General War Department, Colonel Ernst von Wrisberg.[37] Wrisberg was in charge of briefing Hohenborn upon his return and would likely have informed the Deputy about the complaints received by the War Ministry.[38] He was also the officer in charge of handling the details of implementing the census.[39] Moreover, it was Wrisberg who provided Alfred Roth with the classified statistical data which he used in his pamphlet alleging that Jews shirked their war duty. Wrisberg later published these statistical findings in his own memoir.[40] It was also Wrisberg who in June 1916 had to represent Wandel at a high-level staff meeting in order to refute accusations that a large number of Jews were evading their military duty, and thus as Angress writes, 'if one proceeds from the question: *cui bono?*, Wrisberg may well have been the spiritual father of the *Erlass* of 11 October 1916'.[41] After the census was halted and declared closed, a parliamentary session was held on whether the census had been linked to antisemitism. Wrisberg was called forward to refute this connection, indicating that he had been one of the main figures involved.[42]

Whilst Wrisberg was likely involved in the decision to count the number of Jews serving, it was Hohenborn who authored the decree (*Erlass*), issued on the 11 October 1916. The language of the decree was telling and reveals the particular mentalities of Gentile Germans, suggesting a prejudice towards Jews and a growing discontent and disillusionment with the war. Creating a distancing effect between Jews and Gentiles the decree semitised German Jews, apportioning them to the Middle East, as it singled out those, 'belonging to the Israelite faith' (*Angehöriger des israelitischen Glaubens*).[43]

Explaining the purpose behind the census, the decree read that the War Ministry had been receiving complaints that a large number of Jews were evading service and in particular front line duty. In order to 'verify' these complaints and 'if necessary' (*gegebenenfalls*) to counter them, the decree requested that two surveys be carried out by military units and returned within under two months. The first questionnaire demand-

---

37 See Angress, 'The German Army's "Judenzählung" of 1916', 124. Historians remain unsure about the exact origins of the census and more recent works have decided to not focus on this question. See Geheran, 'Rethinking Jewish Front Experiences'; Grady, *A Deadly Legacy*.

38 Angress, 'The German Army's "Judenzählung" of 1916', 123–24; Brian Crim, 'Jew Census (1916)', in *Antisemitism: A Historical Encyclopedia of Prejudice and Persecution*, ed. Richard S. Levy, vol. 1 (Santa Barbara, California: ABC-CLIO, 2005), 371.

39 Crim, 'Jew Census (1916), 371.

40 Ernst von Wrisberg, *Erinnerungen an die Kriegsjahre im königlich-preussischen Kriegsministerium, II: Heer und Heimat, 1914–1918* (Leipzig: Verlag K. F. Koehler, 1921), 93–95. A year following this publication Franz Oppenheimer published a brochure in a series called *Fragen unserer Zeit* on the *Judenzählung* and the antisemitic bias in Wrisberg's memoirs. See Franz Oppenheimer, *Die Judenstatistik des preußischen Kriegsministeriums* (München: Verlag für Kulturpolitik, 1922).

41 Angress, 'The German Army's "Judenzählung" of 1916', 124.

42 Crim, 'Jew Census (1916)', 372.

43 Hohenborn, 'Erlass', 160.

ed statistics on Jews serving on the front line and the second on those in administrative duty. Additional information was also required on the number of Jewish volunteers and officers, and Jews decorated with the Iron Cross.

What the actual intention behind the decree was, is difficult to infer. Certainly, it was far more nuanced than simply being an outright antisemitic act as claimed by several historians.[44] More recent accounts have contextualised the census in a larger transnational history. David Fine argues that the treatment of Jews in the German army was not unique, as segregationist policies were being enforced in the US army with its African American soldiers and officers. He also highlights that, another minority, Alsatians were particularly mistrusted and transferred away from front-line duty whilst German Jews were never segregated from the army.[45] The gathering of statistical data was also increasingly becoming standard practice, both in a bureaucratising German state but also within the Jewish community.[46] Internal correspondence within the War Ministry, reveals that the authorisation of the statistical inquiry was to collect data – 'similar to that of the "Jewish Committee" [the Committee for War Statistics]' – in order to counter complaints that Jews had shirked their war duty. From the start, it was, supposedly, intended to remain an internal matter.[47] Nevertheless, if the decree was issued as part of a wider trend within the German state towards surveillance and centralisation of power by gathering information to gain more control over the population, why were the Jews singled out? As Matthias Erzberger suggested in the Reichstag, why did the War Ministry not decide to conduct a larger census, including a section on confession, on all soldiers in active service?

Do not count on us: the public response to the census

Whilst the idea of authorising a census on the number of Jews in the army was raised and dismissed in the Austrian parliament, this discussion never reached the floor of the

---

44 For a useful overview of the historiography of Judenzählung and which scholars concluded it was driven by antisemitism see Appelbaum, *Loyal Sons*, 297–300.

45 Fine, 'Jewish Integration in the German Army in the First World War', 16. Dreyfus was singled out for his possible dual loyalty as a result of his Alsatian background in the Dreyfus Affair, which proved inconclusive. See Ruth Harris, *The Man on Devil's Island* (London: Allen Lane, 2010), 74–76.

46 Adam Tooze writes about the increasing interest in statistical data gathering and how it formed part of Germany's transformation into a modern state. Nicolas Berg looks at the turn towards statistical data collection within the Jewish community at the turn of the century. See J. Adam Tooze, *Statistics and the German State, 1900–1945: The Making of Modern Economic Knowledge* (Cambridge: Cambridge University Press, 2001). Nicolas Berg, 'Vertrauen in Zahlen: Über Gründung und Selbstverständnis der "Zeitschrift für Demographie und Statistik der Juden" (1905)', in *Kopf oder Zahl: Die Quantifizierung von allem im 19. Jahrhundert*, ed. Matthias Winzen and Wagner (Baden-Baden: Ausstellungskatalog des Museums für Kunst und Technik des 19. Jahrhunderts in Baden-Baden, 2011), 257–75.

47 HASt, Anon., 'Vorgeschichte der Judenstatistik', (20.1.1917), No.33–34.

German parliament.[48] The absence of a parliamentary discussion on whether or not to authorise a decree to count the number of Jews serving in the war was controversial. Unlike the Supreme Command, the War Ministry was an institution partially accountable to the Reichstag.[49] The Reichstag Budget Committee session of the 19 October 1916 revealed how a petition for a census might have been received, had it been discussed in parliament. In this session, Matthias Erzberger, a Catholic Centre politician and later Reich Minister of Finance in the first cabinet of the Weimar Republic, petitioned for a survey, that would be published, on all persons in war agencies listed by sex, age, salary and religious denomination.[50] The reaction to the survey divided parliament. The Catholic Centre, the Conservatives and the National Liberals approved of Erzberger's petition. The Progressives and Social Democrats were outraged. Whilst the petition was never set in motion, it was picked up by the press and unleashed a heated public debate on the intention behind the survey and the focus on religious denomination. Notably, whilst the minutes of the session did not mention any specific confessional group, the dispute pivoted specifically around Jews. The importance of the debate lies in the fact that it went beyond the petition for a survey. It concerned the not yet publicly announced 'Jew census' (*Judenstatistik*). Participants of the debate questioned the necessity and desired outcome of a confessional census. More importantly, the discussion opened up a Jewish Question, which catalysed a debate on unity and the place of religion in the Empire.

Surveying the German press in this period reveals that following the Budget Commission meeting on the 19 October, it was public knowledge that the War Ministry had issued a decree for a Jew census. The reason given: to dispel antisemitic accusations. Yet the authenticity of this intention was viewed with scepticism. In response to an article in the *Deutsche Kurier* defending the National Liberal support for a confessional survey on the grounds that it would help protect their 'fellow Jewish citizens,' the *Berliner Tageblatt* cast doubt on this motivation and hinted at the antisemitic propensities of members of the Reichstag.[51]

---

48 Rosenthal, *Die Ehre des jüdischen Soldaten*, 92–95. A much larger number of Jews fought in the Austro-Hungarian army, approximately 300,000 of which 30,000 died.

49 On the relationship between the General Staff and the (Prussian) War Ministry see Robert T. Foley, 'Prussia: Army 1815–1914', in *Reader's Guide to Military History*, ed. Charles Messenger (London & New York: Routledge, 2013), 477–78; Gerald D. Feldman, *Army, Industry and Labour in Germany, 1914–1918* (London: Bloomsbury Publishing, 1992), 41–45.

50 Historians debate Erzberger's actions. Angress suggests he raised the subject to reveal this knowledge to parliament of the census. Rosenthal argues that Erzberger was antisemitic and says the whole session was prejudiced. In the years preceding the war, the Catholic Centre Party regularly protested the Prussian's army discriminatory laws against denomination, so I believe it is more likely Erzberger was attempting to provoke a response from the War Ministry on the Jew census. See Zechlin, *Die deutsche Politik und die Juden im Ersten Weltkrieg*, 525–27; Angress, 'The German Army's "Judenzählung" of 1916', 125; Rosenthal, *Die Ehre des jüdischen Soldaten*, 55.

51 Anon., 'Eine merkwürdige Statistik', *Berliner Tageblatt*, Morgenblatt (20 Oktober 1916): 3.

An exchange in the *Frankfurter Zeitung* was a telling example of the type of debate that had been set in motion, namely one concerning national unity. The newspaper received a letter from the National Liberal Gustav Stresemann who defended his silent agreement with the petition in the Budget Commission meeting. A respondent to Stresemann's letter declared that the census challenged unity within the Empire asking, 'what does confession have to do with the war?'. Alluding to the civic truce (*Burgfrieden*), the author questioned if uniting under the flag was not part of 'overcoming differences between Protestants, Catholics, Jews and Agnostics?'[52]

One of the most vocal critics of the survey was the Social Democrat Philip Scheidemann. In an article in the organ of the Social Democratic Party, *Vorwärts* he challenged the purpose behind the survey. He suggested its origins could be traced back to 'the thought processes of the gentlemen, to whom the so-called Jewish Question is the alpha and omega [*das A und O*] of genuine German politics'.[53] Scheidemann's statement brought the Jewish Question into the centrefold of the debate. The singling out of Jews, insinuating that they were not loyal citizens to the state and neglecting their patriotic duty, suggested a definitive answer to the question of who was, and who was not, respected and protected as a German citizen. This scathing comment also illuminated how the Jewish Question revealed ideological fault lines amongst the political elite.

The debate on the census did not address the question of German national unity alone. It also touched on the secular foundations of the German Empire, and the role of religion within the state. Scheidemann called the survey 'a monstrous violation of [...] the principles of a denominationally neutral state system' (*konfessionell neutrales Staatswesen*).[54] Needing to reiterate that the Empire upheld religious equality suggested that Jewish questions brought to light the inconsistencies between the constitution and the application of its articles.

Social Democrat Daniel Stücklen[55] similarly appealed to the constitution, using the language of equality and citizenship to protest indirectly against the Jew census. He did this in his speech to parliament on the army's policy to not promote agnostics (*Dissidenten*) to the rank of officer. The implication of Stücklen's speech was clear. The following day in parliament the War Ministry officially admitted to issuing a census to count the number of Jews serving on the front lines.

During his speech, Stücklen reminded the audience of previous debates on religious discrimination in the army in order to appeal to a future where constitutional equality

---

52 Quoted in Rosenthal, *Die Ehre des jüdischen Soldaten*, 55.
53 Anon., 'Die Woche, Berlin den 24. Oktober 1916.' *Allegemeine Zeitung des Judenthums* 43 (27 Oktober 1916): 508.
54 Ibid.
55 Daniel Stücklen (1869–1945), journalist and politician. Representative of the Social Democrats. See the *Bundesarchiv* online files [https://bit.ly/2EJNxe9, accessed 05/03/19].

would be upheld and violations punished. He began by underscoring that the 'the constitution grants religious freedom'[56] further clarifying that it 'does not allow anyone to be treated worse off for their religion than any other citizen'.[57] Stücklen argued that excluding individuals based on their religion and degrading them to the level of 'second-class citizens' was a violation of the constitution. A violation that Stücklen declared 'parliament needs to take a stance against'.[58]

Stücklen was alluding to the fact that Jews who decided to not take to the baptismal front had been continually denied their legal right of promotion to reserve officer, which was enshrined within the Prussian constitution of 1848 and the constitution of the Empire in 1871.[59] For years Jewish parliamentarians had petitioned in Reichstag sessions against the discrimination of religious denomination in the Prussian army. Stücklen called the audience's attention to these past 'intense' (*heftige*) parliamentary debates between Gothein and the Minister of War concerning the appointment of Jews to the rank of officer.

According to Stücklen, these debates involved repeated futile requests by Gothein for statistics from the Ministry on the number of Jews that had been promoted to the rank of officer. What remains unclear was whether or not the statistics had ever been collected by the War Ministry. If they had, it opens another question as to why these statistics had been withheld despite requests from Gothein. One likely reason might have been that the Ministry did not want to reveal that Jews were doing their duty but denied promotion. The Prussian Minister of War Josias von Heeringen confessed as much when he admitted that Jews in principle could become officers but that in practice, the officer corps did not elect Jews to become officers. He conceded that this was a 'violation of the constitution and of the civic principle of equality' but that the Ministry was 'powerless' on the matter.[60]

Appealing to a future German Empire, Stücklen stressed that differences in politics and religious views should not be grounds for exclusion from the army declaring that 'war and religion are concepts that should not be so closely related'.[61] Comparing the years preceding the outbreak of the First World War, where 'only a Christian can be a good soldier' and the years since the outbreak of World War One where 'we are fighting shoulder to shoulder with the Turks whose bravery is recognised in the German army' Stücklen argued that the notion that only Christians can be good soldiers could 'no longer be upheld'. He warned the parliament of not returning to the old military ways of *Kasten- und Klassengeist* that had prevailed before the war.[62]

---

56 '72. Sitzung, 2 November 1916', *Verhandlungen Des Reichstags, Band 308*, 1916, 2009–10.
57 Ibid.
58 Ibid.
59 Angress, 'Prussia's Army and the Jewish Reserve Officer', 19.
60 '72. Sitzung, 2 November 1916', 2009–10.
61 Ibid.
62 Ibid.

For Stücklen, the census had singled out Jews on a denominal basis. He did not mention *Stamm*, race or ethnicity. His argument followed that of previous parliamentary sessions whereby both Jewish and Catholic politicians had protested about the Prussian army's treatment of non-Protestants recruits. It was on this basis that Stücklen equated the 'decree of General Wild von Hohenborn' with being a 'specifically Prussian achievement'. The political response to the Jew census was fundamental, for Stücklen, to ensuring Germany did not return to the ways of the old Empire declaring, 'I have already said that the Reichstag must take a clear stance against this constitutional violation'. In his closing lines, Stücklen made clear that his speech on agnostics in the army had been made in reference to the War Ministry's decree to count Jews serving in the army and demanded from the Ministry a justification for the authorisation of this decree.[63]

The following day, and over three weeks since the census had been commissioned, the Deputy War Minister von Wrisberg responded to Stücklen. He assured Stücklen that the Ministry would review the question of agnostics and take the opportunity to clarify the qualm (*Zweifel*) over the order issued by the War Ministry. What had started as a not wholly uncommon administrative procedure triggered an unprecedented political knock-on effect. The language evoked only days prior in media outlets now reached the floor of the Reichstag.

A constitutional violation? The avowal of the census

In the parliamentary sitting of the 3 November the discussion on agnostics in the army which had taken place in the Budget Committee meeting was scheduled to be discussed again. Speaking on behalf of the Ministry of War was Ernst von Wrisberg. Rather than couching the census in the language of a confessional survey, as other speakers had done, Wrisberg announced that the War Ministry had decreed that 'the number of Jews in the army and their duties' had to be established.[64] He clarified that the purpose of the decree had been to 'collect statistical material' and 'investigate allegations [*Vorwürfe*] made against Jews'. 'Antisemitic intentions' were not behind the decree and he admitted that action had already been taken, before the matter had been put forth for a discussion in parliament.[65]

Several parliamentarians engaged in what one speaker termed, the 'the talk of the day [...] this new *Judenzählung* in the army', moving interchangeably in their speeches from the general (religious discrimination in the army) to the particular (the singling

---

63 Ibid.
64 '73. Sitzung, 3 November 1916', *Verhandlungen Des Reichstags, Band 308*, 1916, 2038.
65 Ibid.

out of the Jews in a census).[66] A theme that emerged in the course of the sitting was reflecting on the census as evidence that past prejudices in Germany and hierarchical forms of citizenship continued to exist, whilst appealing for a reformed, future German Empire guided by unity and national and religious tolerance.[67] Very few of the speakers in the debate protested the authorisation of a census, two speakers even admitted that the actions of the War Ministry might have been well intended, but all complained that it had been poorly executed. They emphasised the consequences of the census for German Jews but more importantly, for the German Empire.

Whilst neither the Progressive politician Ludwig Haas[68] nor the Social Democrat Wolfgang Heine protested the authorisation of a census. Both concurred that the administration of the survey was badly conducted. Heine focused on the effect of the statistic, which he professed would make Jews look like cowards as the figures would not reveal a complete picture of events. In making this argument, however, Heine succumbed to antisemitic stereotypes of Jews as 'suffering bodily damage' from the experience of the ghetto, which made them less capable to serve and thus appear to be shirking front line duty.[69] 'It is not possible that this race on the basis of bodily strength and health can compete with a Pomeranian farmer or Upper Bavarian woodworker' Heine declared. He lamented the prevalence of antisemitism in the army despite efforts by the War Ministry to remove these tendencies. In particular, he emphasised how Jews who served dutifully alongside Gentiles, were often still labelled a 'foreign body' (*Fremdkörper*).[70]

Haas agreed with Heine that the execution of the survey had been 'clumsy' (*ungeschickt*). He complained that the decree had discredited the honour of Jewish soldiers and purposefully intended to 'undermine the authority of Jewish supervisors'. He disagreed, however, that the statistics would reveal Jews to be less represented in front line duty as a result of their physique. Eighty years of emancipation had eradicated these differences, according to Haas. Haas was more concerned with how the data was being collected. He worried that it was focused on military units rather than on the

---

66 Ibid.

67 The debate on religious tolerance and its connection to the Jewish Question dates back much further in Germany to the controversy on Jewish 'civil improvement', which erupted following Christian Wilhelm Dohm's 1781 article on the civil improvement of the Jews. See Purschwitz, 'Von der "bürgerlichen Verbesserung" zur "Judenfrage": Die Formierung eines Begriffs zwischen 1781 und 1843', 23.

68 Ludwig Haas (1875–1930) registered himself, voluntarily, for the army in 1914 and reached the rank of Officer. See the *Bundesarchiv* online files [https://bit.ly/2TFxcAI, accessed 07/03/2019].

69 The discussion of Jewish physiognomy and physical characteristics pre-dates its association with antisemitism. In the eighteenth century it began to be classified as 'objective' scientific analysis. See Klaus Hoedl, 'Physical Characteristics of Jews', *Jewish Studies at the Central European University*, (1999) [https://bit.ly/2TiAMl6, accessed 06/03/2019].

70 '73. Sitzung, 3 November 1916', 2049.

involvement by Jews in the total war effort especially in sectors such as heavy industry, agriculture, the postal service, the transport system and administration.[71]

The Social Democrat Max Quarck similarly highlighted how poorly the census had been administrated. Speaking from personal experience in the XVIII Army Corps, he recounted how Jews were 'periodically removed' from their posts for the period of the census, resulting in a statistically lower number of Jews serving. Moreover, each state command had conducted the census in a different manner. In Bavaria, the census was not even being carried out. In Prussia, the command was torn between statistical and practical duties as it maintained, with a certain antisemitic prejudice, that Jews were best suited to run the finances rather than serve on the front. In Frankfurt, with its large Jewish population, the authorities objected to the premise of the census as they did not wish for Jews in their units to appear as shirkers or suggest that they received preferential treatment in (administrative) duties. In a sarcastic tone, Quarck commented that this was how these 'statistical "truths" materialised' and concluded that the outcome of these 'conflicting facts' resulted in an 'ambivalent attitude towards the statistic'. Neither had the census produced accurate statistics, nor had it identified 'actual shirkers in every confession'.[72]

Aside from the how badly the census had been handled, parliamentarians also criticised the War Ministry for violating the constitution, specifically the article on religious tolerance. For the speakers, this violation tainted Germany's status internationally and necessitated reform. Adolf Neumann-Hofer of the Progressive Party called the decree a 'scandal' that 'without doubt stands in contradiction to the Prussian constitution' citing the law of the 3 July 1869, on religious tolerance.[73] He used the same argument as Stücklen, demonstrating the discrepancy between the constitution and its practice that needed to be overcome in Germany.[74] Using Universalist language Haas appealed to the prospect of the Empire securing its position as a Great Power after the war. Yet, vital for this engagement in world politics, Haas stressed, would be 'national and religious tolerance'. He reminded the audience of the accusation that was frequently assigned to Germans that 'true tolerance cannot be found within the German people'. Asserting that whilst this was unjustified, the decree fell into this aforementioned category.[75]

A letter sent to the War Minister by a member of the Prussia Diet, Felix Waldstein, after the census had officially been closed down used similar language. Waldstein

---

71 Ibid.
72 Ibid, 2053.
73 Ibid, 2037.
74 This disconnect was also highlighted in a letter sent by Oskar Cassel from the VdJ to the War Ministry on the 29 December. Cassel argued that the order went against the constitutional equality of military duty for all confessions. He also quoted Kaiser Wilhelm's *Burgfrieden* speech to evidence how the census went against the civic truce. HASt, Oskar Cassel to Hermann von Stein, (29.12.1916), No. 4–11.
75 '73. Sitzung, 3 November 1916', 2052.

wrote that the census had put 'confessional freedom [...] in danger' and that 'equality has been harmed'. The trust that the military was no longer 'party oriented', Waldstein continued, had disappeared. Highlighting the importance of Jewish relations for German foreign policy, Waldstein noted that the *Judenzählung* was harming German interests abroad in the 'neutral countries' and in particular America.[76]

Heine urged the audience to consider that should no changes be made with regard to the 'poor treatment of Jews and agnostics' Germany's international status would be debased. He implored the audience to look towards France as an ideal model where 'no differences exist between Jews and Christians' where there was 'no discord', only a 'French people' and a 'French will'. He suggested that reform within Germany would require a united concerted effort. One 'cannot assume that this good future will be gifted to us' declared Heine, 'the people must work for this [future]'. Part of this project for unity required the overcoming of intolerance and the 'belief in a future of justice and freedom within Germany'. For Heine, it was bound into the greater German war effort, 'precisely because the Fatherland and its future are sacred to us, we cannot tolerate that through the injustice and inability to learn new things [...] the unanimous German will to victory [will be] destroyed'.[77]

The *Judenzählung* revealed that the German Empire was at a critical juncture. This became a theme that ran throughout the debate. The speakers raised the issue of past prejudices within the Empire including the class-based forms of citizenship and used the war as a framing device to urge for greater unity and not division. Neumann-Hofer termed the decree a 'medieval blunder' (*mittelalterlichen Blunder*) and rhetorically asked if these dispositions (*gesinnungsschnüffelei*) on 'race, class, faith and convictions' could just be 'thrown overboard' as they 'do not belong to our current times'.[78] Heine lamented antisemitism in the army professing that 'it is miserable when one comrade insults another comrade based on his faith or race in a time of the highest exaltation, in a time when the coming together demands all of one's energy, when everyone should only think of unity, of mutual loyalty'. Addressing German Jews, Haas similarly announced that 'the war has not suddenly dispelled age-old prejudices ... the fight against antisemitism will continue to be necessary'.[79]

Heine warned that Germany was already facing a great danger and should not also succumb to internal frictions. 'This feeling of unity' (*Einheitsgefühl*), he stressed was endangered by 'occurrences such as the disregard [...] of Jews'.[80] Like other speakers, Heine spoke to past mistakes in Germany and to a reformed future. He suggested that it was as if Germany had not learnt any lessons from its past. The existence of

---

76 HASt, David Felix Waldstein to Hermann von Stein, (30.08.1917), No. 16–18.
77 '73. Sitzung, 3 November 1916', 2050.
78 Ibid, 2038.
79 Ibid, 2053.
80 Ibid, 2050.

a hierarchical, class-oriented, citizenship meant that whilst everyone might perceive themselves to be on equal standing, some were treated with less rights and less honour than others.

Similar to Heine, Haas invoked the war to bring the house together. He drew on the battle of the Somme to stress that what had been achieved was only possible through a people's army (*Volksheer*) and received an uproarious response from members of the left and right in the sitting. 'This can only be achieved' Haas stated, 'when men stand [together] not as subordinates [...] but as German soldiers and as German citizens'. He emphasised how the decree had caused alienation outside of German Jewish circles at a time when 'inner unity' and 'inner togetherness' (*Geschlossenheit*) was urgently required. He pleaded for unity in the Empire for now and after the war, 'no more agitation, [...] no in-fighting, now above all unity and solidarity in the interest of the Fatherland!'[81]

The speakers concluded the session by imploring the War Ministry to halt the Jew census. Neumann-Hofer appealed to the Minister of War and asked him to ensure that the improper treatment of subordinates would continue to decrease in order to show that 'our army is truly the people in arms and that any supervisor that insults a subordinate is insulting the German people'.[82] Heine asked the 'Gentlemen of the War Ministry' to take action to 'remedy all these evils'. And Quarck advised the Ministry to abandon the whole project rather than utilise figures collected under dubious circumstances. He reassured the War Ministry that the Reichstag fully supported singling out war-shirkers but 'no one can throw, nor wants to throw accusations against a confessional group'.[83]

Whilst the language of the decree issued by the War Ministry, which termed Jews, Israelites (*Israeliten*) racialised their identity, all contributors to the debate focused on the Jews (*Juden*) as a group facing religious discrimination.[84] Neumann-Hofer did not name the Jewish population but rather made reference to a 'religious community' (*Religionsgemeinschaft*). Dressed in his grey Captain's uniform adorned with the Iron Cross First Class, Haas announced that he wished to say a few words on the census because 'I am a Jew'. He described himself as a member of a 'community of faith' (*Glaubensgemeinschaft*).[85] Similarly, Heine protested against religious intolerance to-

---

81 Ibid, 2053.
82 Ibid, 2038.
83 Ibid.
84 The word *Israeliten* suggests national roots and illustrates the complexity of these debates. However, according to Professor Sharon Gillerman, this term was traditionally used in Germany to refer to Jews and had more religious rather than national connotations at the time.
85 This was the same language used by Oskar Cassel in his correspondence with the War Ministry. He did not refer to the Jews as an ethnicity or race but rather as fellow members of a faith (*Glaubengenossen*). The correspondence can be found in the following file, *Hauptstaatsarchiv Stuttgart: Judenstatistik aus dem Jahre 1916*, M 738, Bü 46.

wards a 'state-recognised religious community' (*staatlich anerkannte Religionsgemein-schaft*) and yet he was the only speaker to also refer to the Jews as a race.[86] He argued that less Jews were serving on the front because of their 'bodily differences', which were a result of 'race and history'.[87] Describing the Jews as a race was in contrast to Haas and Quarck who were of Jewish descent and presumably, as liberal Jews, would have wanted to avoid ascribing any additional attributes that could single out Jews as not belonging to the national unifying elements of the Empire.

The debate in the 73 Sitting was the last dedicated discussion to take place on the *Judenzählung*.[88] The absence of a longer follow-up discussion was either the result of pressure from Jewish representatives to stop the census or on a practical level because after the final session of the year on the 12 December the parliament only reconvened on the 22 February 1917 already one month after the census was declared a closed case. As Germany was on the brink of famine, food supplies dominated parliamentary discussions. Similarly, the *Judenzählung* did not feature extensively in the press, such that it had after the Reichstag Budget Committee meeting. Only three short articles mentioned the census. They focused on where it was had been conducted and what had been said in parliament.[89] No further contributions on the subject of the *Judenzählung* appeared in the *Berliner Tageblatt*, not even after the official acknowledgment that the census was a closed case. The reason for this, one may speculate, was due to the wartime censorship promulgated in the spirit of the *Burgfrieden*. Part of the civic truce was ensuring that all news relating to Germany depicted the country as a united front to not enable the enemy to know and seize upon any weaknesses in domestic politics.[90]

The outbreak of the war in 1914 was a caesura in the history of the German Empire, a moment when German citizens took up arms and sacrificed their lives for the Fatherland. Whilst the war heralded unity and solidarity, the *Judenzählung* pulled back this facade and exposed the Empire's past prejudices. The census revealed an Empire at crossroads between its past tainted by constitutional inequality and a future, necessitated by the war, of unity and tolerance. How the Empire would respond was cru-

---

86 '73. Sitzung, 3 November 1916', 2048.

87 Ibid, 2049.

88 The *Judenzählung* was invoked by a minister (Henke) on the 30 November. He used it as an example of previous discriminations and injustices in an argument about increasing worker's rights. See '77. Sitzung, 30 November 1916', *Verhandlungen Des Reichstags, Band 308*, (1916), 2228. The *Judenstatistik* was also very briefly brought up in a discussion on the 12 June 1918 concerning why the highest number of conscripts came from lower classes see '173. Sitzung, 12 Juni 1918', *Verhandlungen Des Reichstags, Band 313*, (1918), 5441.

89 Anon., '*Judenzählung*" beim Roten Kreuz ', *Berliner Tagesblatt*, Morgenblatt, (4 November 1916), 3; Anon., 'Die "konfessioneele Zählung" im Heere und der Reichstag', *Berliner Tagesblatt*, Abendblatt (4 November 1916), 3; Anon., 'Zur Judenstatistik in der Armee', *Berliner Tageblatt*, (5 November 1916), 3.

90 The justification used for censoring *Vorwärts* and the *Berliner Tageblatt* was that they violated the *Burgfrieden* by reporting critically on matters of domestic politics. This discussion is important in that it illustrates how the German nation was negotiating freedom of the press. See '70. Sitzung, 30 October 1916', *Verhandlungen Des Reichstags, Band 308*, (1916), 1913.

cial. Much like the authorisation of the decree itself, the census was declared a closed case with good intentions. However, the ways in which the case was closed was poorly conducted and as a consequence would have fatal repercussions. The aftermath of the parliamentary debate signalled the practical end to a survey on Jewish participation in the army and yet, it marked the beginning of a much longer legacy of the *Judenzählung*.

Not adding up: inconsistencies and the conclusion of the Jewish census

The day after the parliamentary session featuring Wrisberg's official admission of a census, Oscar Cassel, a member of the Progressive Party and representative of the Alliance of German Jews (*Verband der deutschen Juden*, VdJ) visited Colonel Ulrich Hoffmann, Head of the War Ministry Central Department[91] in which he called the decree a 'grave injustice', which had caused sentiments of 'indignation and uneasiness' in the Jewish community.[92] The decree had led to the transferral of Jews away from administrative posts to front line duty, as Quarck had explained in his speech to the Reichstag on the 3 November. Cassel demanded that the War Ministry inform unit commanders that they did not have the right to authorise these transfers simply on the grounds that these servicemen were Jewish. Cassel also requested a formal clarification from the Ministry that the census had been authorised in order to dispel accusations levelled against Jews. In the previous parliamentary debate, Quarck had similarly queried the contradiction between the document received by his army corps, which called the accusations against Jews 'unjustified' and the explanation for the decree given by Wrisberg, which was vague on whether the complaints were baseless.[93]

A week following the meeting, the new War Minister General Hermann von Stein issued a supplementary order to the decree clarifying that it had been issued to collect statistical material for charges against Jews and did not warrant the transferal of soldiers from their current assignments.[94] Hermann von Stein had replaced Adolf Wild von Hohenborn as War Minister on the 29 October, just ten days after the subject of a Jew census first reached the floor of the Reichstag and was hotly contested in the press. The replacement of Hohenborn, a highly respected Lieutenant General, only thirty-two days after his appointment suggests that perhaps the Ministry acknowledged that

---

91 This meeting is referenced by Alfred Roth.
92 Angress, 'The German Army's "Judenzählung" of 1916', 128.
93 '73. Sitzung, 3 November 1916', 2053.
94 Angress, 'The German Army's "Judenzählung" of 1916', 128.

the census had been a blunder and attempted to minimise the damage through internal restructuring.[95]

Acting on his own initiative, the prominent Hamburger banker Max Warburg took on his own defence of Jewish rights. He lobbied at a higher-level of political command than Cassel, the Chancellery. In an essay entitled *Die Judenfrage im Rahmen der deutschen Gesamtpolitik* first written in the summer of 1916, Warburg expressed his disappointment with the false pretences of the 'spirit of 1914'. This spirit, embodied in the civic truce, had not heralded the removal of discriminatory practices against German Jews in the public service nor in the army. When in October, Warburg became aware of the Jew census, he had copies of his essay sent to the War Minister von Stein, Chancellor Bethmann-Hollweg and to the Director of the Chancellery, Under Secretary Arnold Wahnschaffe, with whom he was on good terms.[96] In response to the census, Warburg requested a public declaration, which he would eventually receive, explaining that German Jews had fulfilled their patriotic duty to the same degree as their Christian comrades.[97]

Throughout the winter of 1916 Warburg maintained both a regular correspondence and met frequently with Wahnschaffe to little success. Tensions were high in the winter of 1916 between the Chancellery, the Supreme Army Command and the War Ministry as Germany was confronted with several crucial developments in the war including a shortage of raw materials on the home front, a proposal to open peace negotiations and the question of an independent Poland. Whilst the Chancellery continued to express sympathy for Warburg's cause and the Chancellor was notably embarrassed by the War Ministry's decree, its actions were limited. Moreover, it did not want to cause any further additional friction to the structures of authority.[98]

Once aware of the constraints and unwillingness of the Chancellery to take action, Warburg changed his approach. Going on the offensive, Warburg sent a threatening letter to the Reichsbank official, Oskar Schmiedecke warning him that the census 'might well have unfortunate consequences for the impending sixth war-loan drive because the Jews, and in particular the bankers amongst them who had given very generously in the past, were now bound to be less inclined to exert themselves'.[99] Only a few days prior, the Chief of Police in Frankfurt am Main had sent a letter to Wahnschaffe

---

95 Feldman writes that Hohenborn was removed by Bethmann-Hollweg and Ludendorff because he disagreed with the decisions being made in the Supreme Army Command. He was instead replaced by the more 'tractable' Hermann von Stein. However, Feldman does not explicitly mention whether or not this transfer had anything to do with the *Judenzählung* as it is not the focus of his article. See Feldman, 'The Political and Social Foundations of Germany's Economic Mobilization, 1914–1916', 135–36.

96 Max Waburg, 'Die Judenfrage im Rahmen der deutschen Gesamtpolitik', *Bundesarchiv Koblenz*, No. 110, (1916), 106–110. Cited in Angress, 'The German Army's "Judenzählung" of 1916', 129.

97 Ibid.

98 Ibid, 130.

99 Quoted and trans. in ibid.

reporting that well-known Jews involved in commerce and banking had felt alienated by the census. The Chief of Police had expressed his concern for the impending war-loan drive, which was due the following spring.[100]

Independent of whether or not the letter had a decisive impact on the decision of the War Ministry to stop the census, it certainly had its desired effect. On the 20 January, Cassel received a letter from the War Minister von Stein which reiterated that the census had been conducted to provide evidence that would disprove the allegations that Jews were serving in smaller numbers on the front lines. The letter, however, was not apologetic. The disorganised implementation of the census was blamed on the size of the army. In an army of a 'million men', the letter read that it was 'no wonder' the census had been badly managed. The letter concluded by confirming that the 'the con-duct of Jewish soldiers and fellow citizens during the war has not been the cause that prompted the order of my predecessors, and therefore cannot be associated with it'.[101] The War Minister never made a public statement. The last few lines of the letter were instead made public by Oskar Cassel who published them in the *Allgemeine Zeitung des Judenthums*.[102]

Only four months after the decree had been issued, it was declared a closed case. On the 22 January the War Minister von Stein informed Chancellor Bethmann-Hollweg that no further action regarding the *Judenzählung* would be taken.[103] Whilst officially the census was at an end, unjustified transferals of Jewish soldiers continued to take place in the last years of the war.[104]

The figures collected by the War Ministry were never officially published.[105] The justification given was that they had been collected for internal use only.[106] As the sta-tistics were never published, it left open the possibility for the official figures to be disputed. The exact numbers of Jews that served on the front lines during the war be-came a heated topic shortly after the end of the war. The debate, which took place over several years, was retrospectively called the 'statistical dispute' (*Statistikerstreit*). Rather than serving to counter antisemitic claims, which had been more successfully achieved through the War Ministry's censorship policy, the census commissioned to dispel myths, perpetuated them.

---

100 HASt, Reiss von Scheurnschloss to Wahnschaffe, (16.1.1917), No. 67–68.
101 Ibid, Hermann von Stein to Oskar Cassel, (20.1.1917), No. 38–39.
102 Anon., 'Die Kriegstagung des Centralvereins deutscher Staatsbürger jüdischen Glaubens', *Allgemeine Zeitung des Judentums* 6, (9 Februar 1917), 67.
103 Warburg wasn't satisfied with this response and continued to press for another statement until April 1917. Angress, 'The German Army's "Judenzählung" of 1916', 133.
104 HASt, David Felix Waldstein to Hermann von Stein, (30.08.1917), No. 16–18.
105 Both Alfred Roth and Ernst von Wrisberg published what Wrisberg claimed to be the official results collected by the War Ministry, however, they were not verified by the ministry. See Armin, *Die Juden Im Heere*; Wrisberg, *Erinnerungen*, 93–95.
106 HASt, Anon., 'Vorgeschichte der Judenstatistik', (20.1.1917), No. 33–34. See also Anon., 'Auf Beschwer-den gegen die Judenzählung im Heere', *Im deutschen Reich*, 2 (1917), 69.

1919 and still counting: the legacy of the Judenzählung

Three years after a decree had first been authorised to count Jews in the army, Alfred Roth, writing under the pseudonym Otto Armin published a pamphlet entitled *Die Juden im Heere*. Allegedly using 'official statistical data' the pamphlet demonstrated that Jews had served and died in comparatively smaller numbers to Gentiles during the war.[107] For every Jewish soldier killed, Roth professed that over three hundred Gentiles had died. On this basis, he concluded that Jews had not scarified their lives in equal measure to Gentiles for the Fatherland.[108] As early as March 1916, Alfred Roth and Theodore Fritsch, members of a Pan-German League, the *Reichshammerbund*, had written to the Kaiser, Reichstag delegates and prominent individuals claiming that the Jews were responsible for the 'psychological collapse of the German nation and of German commercial life by the system of Ballin and Rathenau'.[109] They had pleaded the Kaiser to announce an end to the *Burgfrieden* and punish the Jews. Alfred Roth's antisemitic views were well known. His pamphlet on the participation of Jews in the German army was published by the Munich-based antisemitic publishing house *Deutscher Volksverlag*. The intentions behind Roth's pamphlet were clear. He had aimed to discredit the Jewish community by suggesting they were complicit in the defeat of the German army, thus shifting blame away from the faults of the military command. 'The notion of selfless devotion to the people and the Fatherland has no place among them' wrote Roth, 'because they want to be foreigners'.[110]

Antisemitic pamphlets on Jews in the army were not uncommon and yet Roth's pamphlet created a stir.[111] One reason for this was because Roth purposefully disputed statistics published in a pamphlet entitled 'Truth and Justice' by Rabbi Leopold Rosenak. Rosenak had suggested that 20 % of the Jewish population had served in the war (100,000 out of 500,000, according to Rosenak). Secondly, Roth's pamphlet was attacked because it claimed to be using statistics from 'official sources'. The sources that Roth was referring to were confidential and had never been published. According to Roth, the statistics had been leaked to him by the Deputy War Minister, Wrisberg as early as 1917. Using these 'official' statistics, Roth suggested Rosenak's figure, that 100,000 Jews had served in the war, was impossible. According to Roth, this number would have constituted a fifth of the Jewish population.[112] His assessment was, how-

---

107 Armin, *Die Juden im Heere*, 1, 17.
108 Armin, *Die Juden im Heere*, 1, 17; Tim Grady, *The German-Jewish Soldiers of the First World War in History and Memory* (Liverpool: Liverpool University Press, 2011), 59.
109 Appelbaum, *Loyal Sons*, 246.
110 Armin, *Die Juden im Heere*, 7–8. Quoted and trans. in Grady, *The German-Jewish Soldiers of the First World War in History and Memory*, 59.
111 Appelbaum, *Loyal Sons*, 242–246.
112 Armin, *Die Juden im Heere*, 17.

ever, inaccurate as it would have constituted a sixth, of the Jewish population.[113] Instead, Roth listed that 62,515 Jewish soldiers had served in the army of which only half,
he claimed, had served on the more perilous front lines.[114]

That Jewish soldiers had shirked their war duty on the front lines was a central
contention in the Jew census. This idea was perpetuated by a comment by Graf von
Westarp in a parliamentary sitting on the 3 November, when he highlighted that the
accusations against Jews involved the concern that they were overwhelmingly represented in the war corporations (*Kriegsgesellschaft*) on the home front.[115] Only a year
following Roth's pamphlet, another was published by Hans Friedrich, which also al-
leged that Jews had evaded their military duties and cited the same statistics as Roth.[116]

In 1921, the *Statistikerstreit*, which had lain dormant for a year, erupted once again.
The classified statistical data collected by the War Ministry that both Alfred Roth and
Hans Friedrich had cited appeared once again in print, in the memoirs of General Erich von Wrisberg.[117] In response to another publication which suggested that Jews had
not served on the front lines, the sociologist and Chairman of the Committee for War
Statistics (*Ausschuß für Kriegsstatistik*) Jacob Segall published an alternative set of figures on Jewish war-time participation. The committee was founded in the spring of
1915 by several Jewish organisations and coordinated by the director of the Berlin Office for Statistics, Professor Heinrich Silbergleit. It collected data on all Jewish soldiers
that were serving.[118] Using this data, in his pamphlet entitled *Die deutschen Juden als
Soldaten im Kriege*, Segall documented that 100,000 Jews had fought in the war, 80,000
had served on the front lines and 12,000 had died serving.[119] In publishing these figures
Segall hoped to bring the statistical pamphlet war, which had reached its third year, to
an irrefutable end.

The work conducted by the Committee for War Statistics was part of a growing
trend amongst German-Jewish organisations to collect statistical data on the community in order to dispel antisemitic attacks. Some smaller Jewish communities, for
example in Würzburg, even began to collect their own local wartime statistics.[120] The
methodology outlined by the committee was precise. A single formula was used to

---

113 Fine, 'Jewish Integration in the German Army in the First World War', 17.
114 Armin, *Die Juden im Heere*, 17.
115 '73. Sitzung, 3 November 1916', 2058. The war corporations had been set-up by the Raw Materials Section, which had been established in the Prussian Ministry of War under the initiative of Walther Rathenau.
The corporations were responsible for the procurement and distribution of raw materials. See Feldman,
'The Political and Social Foundations of Germany's Economic Mobilization', 124–125.
116 Hans Friedrich, *Die Juden im Heere* (München: Verlag Lehmanns, 1920).
117 Wrisberg, *Erinnerungen*, 93–95.
118 Grady, *The German-Jewish Soldiers of the First World War in History and Memory*, 59. The idea for a
committee to collect statistics first arose in October 1914 see Penslar, 'The German-Jewish Soldier: From
Participant to Victim', 432–33.
119 Segall, *Die deutschen Juden als Soldaten im Kriege*, 9–35, 38.
120 Grady, *The German-Jewish Soldiers of the First World War in History and Memory*, 59.

collect material based on draft status, age, profession, birthplace and it varied according to the size of cities. The compilation of data relied on the collective cooperation of individual researchers who travelled door-to-door as well as on the goodwill of rabbis, teachers and civil servants who sifted through official news reports on wartime statistics.[121] Statistical data collecting was not, however, supported by all German Jewish associations. The Zionist Federation, for instance, thought it was 'ludicrous' to use the same methods as antisemites.[122]

Whilst intending to bring the statistical dispute to a conclusion, Segall's pamphlet did little to deter antisemitic agitation. Shortly following its publication, the *Statistiker-streit* took on a different quality as it descended into a technical debate on statistical analysis, specifically methods of data collection and statistical bias. Supporting Roth, Wrisberg claimed that the War Ministry had withheld the results of the census in order to avoid them being used by antisemites. Wrisberg implied that the figures would have been unfavourable towards Jews and might have spurred antisemitic attacks.[123] Like Segall, Franz Oppenheimer challenged the methodology of the *Judenzählung*, describing it as 'the greatest statistical obscenity perpetrated by any authority'.[124] Oppenheimer who had worked as Wrisberg's subordinate for a number of years in the War Ministry, directly responded to Wrisberg's memoirs in a pamphlet on the *Judenstatistik* published in 1922 where he stressed the bias in Wrisberg's interpretation of the statistics.[125]

The dispute over Jewish participation and the legacy of the *Judenzählung* was not only confined to the *Statistikerstreit* and the written word. The myth of Jewish war shirking was also discussed in a court case in 1921. The case involved Dietrich Eckart, editor of *Auf Gut Deutsch* and founder of the German Worker's Party (*Deutsche Arbei-terpartei*, DAP), and Rabbi Samuel Freund in what came to be known as the 'Eckhart Affair'. Eckart had offered a prize of 1,000 Reichsmarks to anyone that could name one Jewish family whose sons had served on the front lines for longer than three weeks. When Rabbi Freund sent Eckart a list of twenty families, and Eckart refused to pay, he sued him. After providing evidence of a further fifty families who had lost multiple sons in the war, Freud won the court case and was financially compensated.[126] The court case reveals the different legacies of the *Judenzählung*. It shows how Jews fought

---

121 Rosenthal, *Die Ehre des jüdischen Soldaten*, 54.
122 Grady writes, 'as anti-Semites used statistics to attack the Jewish war effort, so German Jews applied the same method in defence'. Grady, *The German-Jewish Soldiers of the First World War in History and Memo-ry*, 59.
123 Appelbaum, *Loyal Sons*, 274.
124 Quoted in Appelbaum, 274.
125 Oppenheimer, *Die Judenstatistik des preußischen Kriegsministeriums*.
126 Appelbaum, *Loyal Sons*, 270.

for their rights in court[127] and how whilst the census was issued to dispel accusations, the aftermath only served to amplify allegations of Jewish war-shirking.

The subject of the *Judenzählung* arose once again in February 1924 in a Reichstag sub-committee meeting, which had been convened in order to examine the reasons for Germany's defeat in the war. In a discussion on shirkers, Albrecht Philipp, minister of the German National People's Party (*Deutschnationale Volkspartei*, DNVP) claimed that the *Judenzählung* had occurred at the command of the Jews and that the results had been kept secret following pressure from pro-Jewish groups. Julius Moses of the Social Democratic Party dismissed his claim citing both the results published by Segall as well as the Freud vs. Eckart court case.[128] The significance of the event lies in the perpetuation of the accusation that Jews did not serve in equal measure in the war and ultimately were responsible for the army's defeat. Whilst the Jews were not explicitly mentioned in General Ludendorff's speech to the new government where he pronounced that the German army had been stabbed-in-the-back,[129] their involvement in the disarming of the 'unconquered' German army became part of the *Dolchstoß-legende*.[130] This claim would continue to flourish within far-right circles throughout the Weimar Republic and into the Third Reich.[131]

In 1932, the Reich Federation of Jewish Front-Line Soldiers (*Reichsbund Jüdischer Frontsoldaten*) published a memorial book listing the names of approximately 10,000 Jewish soldiers that had died during the First World War.[132] The memorial book was published as evidence against continued virulent antisemitic accusations that Jews had not seen battle and was one of several commemorative initiatives by the *Reichsbund*.[133] The federation placed particular importance on front-line service to the extent that members were required to have served in a combat unit and it could not have been

---

127 On the use of law suits by Jews to defend their rights see, for example, Goldberg, *Honor, Politics and the Law in Imperial Germany*.

128 Appelbaum, *Loyal Sons*, 276.

129 For Erich Ludendorff's speech see, 'Speech on the New German Government in February 1919', in *Source Records of the Great War*, ed. Charles F. Horne, Vol. VII, National Alumni, 1923 [https://bit.ly/2JPitMy, accessed 24/06/19].

130 On the *Dolchstoßlegende* see Michael Alme, *Die Entstehung der Dolchstoßlegende nach dem Ersten Weltkrieg im Spiegel von Quellen und Forschung*, 1. (Norderstedt, Germany: GRIN Verlag, 2016); George S. Vascik and Mark R. Sadler, *The Stab-in-the-Back Myth and the Fall of the Weimar Republic: A History in Documents and Visual Sources* (London: Bloomsbury Publishing, 2016).

131 In Hitler's *Mein Kampf* Germany's defeat in the war was blamed on Jews, socialists and communists. Adolf Hitler, *Mein Kampf*, Unabridged ed. (New York: Fredonia Classics, 2003).

132 Reichsbund Jüdischer Frontsoldaten, *Die jüdischen gefallenen des deutschen Heeres, der deutschen Marine und der deutschen Schutztruppen 1914–1918. Ein Gedenkbuch.* (Berlin: Verlag Der Schild, 1932).

133 The Federation was involved in the erection of several permanent war memorials and often planned commemorative events at the local and national level. See Grady, *The German-Jewish Soldiers of the First World War in History and Memory*, 4.

for only a temporary period.[134] The Reich Federation was founded in the first months of 1919 by Reserve Captain Leo Loewenstein when soldiers were returning from the front. It sought to defend the honour of Jewish veterans against antisemitism.[135] By 1926, its membership reached almost 40,000 making it the second largest Jewish association in Germany after the Central Association.[136] The federation published several books including *Kriegsbriefe gefallener deutscher Juden,* which in 1961 was re-printed with a preface written by the West German Defence Minister, Franz Josef Strauß. The legacy of *Judenzälung* was evidenced in the preface where Strauß recognised that,

> 100,000 men of the Jewish faith and Jewish ethnicity wore the grey uniform of the German Empire, more than a third of them were decorated, over 2,000 were officers and 1,200 medics. 12,000 Jewish soldiers fell in struggle and good faith for their Fatherland.[137]

Whilst these figures, mirroring those collected by the Committee for War Statistics and not the classified data leaked by Wrisberg, suggest that the Jewish community had triumphed in the *Statistikerstreit,* the exact numbers will most likely never be known.[138] As the military archives were destroyed in the Allied bombing campaign over Berlin and Potsdam in the Second World War it is impossible to ascertain what the results of the surveys received by the War Ministry revealed. More significant than the exact figures, however, was the persistence with which they continued to be disputed. It demonstrates how the short-lived census had an unprecedented legacy as it was manipulated and instrumentalised to promote a virulent antisemitism.

Historians have tended to focus on the significance of the *Judenzählung* for Jews on the front lines and in the larger narrative of German-Jewish relations, often examining the role that institutional antisemitism played in the events surrounding the census.[139] Although this was not the immediate focus of this chapter, it has contextualised the census within the trend towards statistical data collection in the German state apparatus and the Jewish community. I have shown how assessing whether the census

---

134 Tim Grady, 'Fighting a Lost Battle: The Reichsbund Jüdischer Frontsoldaten and the Rise of National Socialism', *German History* 28, no. 1 (2010): 4.
135 Ulrich Dunker, *Der Reichsbund jüdischer Frontsoldaten, 1919–1938: Geschichte eines jüdischen Abwehrvereins* (Düsseldorf: Droste Verlag, 1977).
136 Grady, 'Fighting a Lost Battle: The Reichsbund Jüdischer Frontsoldaten and the Rise of National Socialism', 3.
137 Reichsbund Jüdischer Frontsoldaten, *Kriegsbriefe gefallener deutscher Juden.* Quoted and trans. in Fine, 'Jewish Integration in the German Army in the First World War', 17.
138 Most historians have accepted Jacob Segall's figures as the most accurate. See Brian E. Crim, *Antisemitism in the German Military Community and the Jewish Response, 1914–1938* (Landham, Maryland: Lexington Books, 2014), 108.
139 Appelbaum and Rosenthal argue that it was a critical milestone in the rise of the National Socialists, whilst Angress and more recent accounts (Fine, Grady) concur that it was not a watershed moment that severed German-Jewish relations. See Appelbaum, *Loyal Sons*; Rosenthal, *Die Ehre des jüdischen Soldaten*; Grady, *A Deadly Legacy*; Fine, 'Jewish Integration in the German Army in the First World War'; Angress, 'The German Army's "Judenzählung" of 1916'.

was governed by antisemitism alone requires a far more nuanced examination than providing a definitive answer. Intentions aside, this chapter has shown how it was the conduct and aftermath of the census that incensed the public and members of parliament. Michael Geheran summarises the consequences of the census accurately when he writes that,

> although allegations of Jewish cowardice and indifference to the Fatherland had been prevalent before the First World War, they were given new life after 1918. The Jew Count gave these accusations a veneer of credibility. It generated ambivalence, uncertainty and reasonable doubt.[140]

The main focus of this chapter, however, was to illustrate how the decree to conduct a statistical survey on the Jewish contribution in the army, crystallised a discourse on equality before the law, religious tolerance and unity in the German Empire. The summer of 1916 was a critical time for the German Empire. Almost complete authority was devolved to the Supreme Army Command under Generals Hindenburg and Ludendorff in a last effort to turn the war in Germany's favour. By the time the Jewish census was issued, the Empire was on the brink between descending into an *Obrigskeitstaat* (authoritarian state) and upholding a semblance of parliamentary democracy as it embraced a total war economy. The *Judenzählung* exposed the Empire at a critical juncture. Jewish questions, as such, provide a lens through which to examine this transitional moment as Germany negotiated its path towards a modern secular state.

---

140 Geheran, 'Rethinking Jewish Front Experiences', 130.

IV 'Article 113 leads into the deepest questions of the concept of nationality': minority rights in the Weimar constitution

1916 was a turning point in the First World War for the Central Powers and for German-Jewish relations. As outlined in chapter two, in October 1916 the War Ministry issued an official decree to count the number of Jews serving on the front lines. Known as the *Judenzählung* the event undermined Kaiser Wilhelm's famous 1914 declaration of a civic truce, *Burgfrieden*. For the first time since the outbreak of war, antisemitic views had found institutional validation in Germany. Framed within parliamentary sessions as a 'Jewish Question' the debate on the census brought forth questions about the future of the post-war modern German state and in particular the place of religion. The final two years of the war for Germany were defined by the misplaced hubris of the German military leadership and a disconnect with sentiments on the home front where an anti-war attitude was gaining momentum. Despite heavy losses in 1916 and the worst winter of the war, which caused a famine across the country, by the following year, the tide turned, albeit briefly, in favour of the Central Powers on the Eastern Front as the Russian Empire collapsed. The Treaty of Brest-Litovsk, signed in March 1918, temporarily boosted moral.[1] In an attempt to end the war before the involvement of the United States of America, the Central Powers rapidly launched the Kaiser's Battle (*Kaiserschlacht*), a series of quick offensives on the Western Front. Crucially, however, Germany lacked the weapons and the manpower. New German recruits were exhausted by the war and revolutionary feelings were rife.

By autumn, the Supreme Army Command confessed to Kaiser Wilhelm and the government that they could no longer hold the lines on the Western Front and that an armistice had to be negotiated immediately. Chancellor Georg von Hertling resigned along with his cabinet. The new Chancellor Prince Max von Baden took on the bitter

---

1 On Germany's experience on the Eastern Front see Liulevicius, *War Land on the Eastern Front*; Stone, *The Eastern Front*.

task of arranging peace negotiations with the President of the United States, Woodrow Wilson.

A series of political and constitutional reforms towards the parliamentarisation of the Empire headed by Max von Baden did little to quell the revolutionary fervour or satisfy Woodrow Wilson's armistice demands.[2] In early November 1918, a major mutiny involving tens of thousands of sailors took place in Kiel. As the civil unrest spread across the country a number of workers and soldiers' councils were formed. By the 7 November the revolution had reached Munich where the Monarch Ludwig III of Bavaria was deposed. On the 8 November, the People's Free State of Bavaria was declared. The next day Kaiser Wilhelm abdicated, and the German Republic was announced.[3] At this critical juncture in Germany's political development another practical Jewish Question arose.

On the 9 November a political vacuum had opened in Germany. At stake were two central questions: what institutions would fill this void and how would these institutions be governed? In an attempt to fill the space and tame the revolution, several bodies sprung up all vying for political power and dominance. By November the newly appointed Chancellor Friedrich Ebert helped establish a provisional government, the Council of People's Representatives,[4] consisting of a coalition between the Social Democrats and Independent Socialists (*Unabhängige Sozialdemokratische Partei Deutschlands*, USPD). The provisional government set in motion the drafting of a new constitution and fixed the date for the election of the new government to January 1919. The German-Jewish lawyer Hugo Preuss was elected to draft the constitution of the Republic, which was ratified on the 11 August 1919. Over the course of only eight months the constitution was drafted, revised and redrafted five times. Within this scope of only a few months, a series of extensive debates took place on the wording of each clause in the constitution. In the discussions on the wording of Article 113, Germany's policy on minority rights, a Jewish Question resurfaced.

The wording of Article 113, Germany's policy on minority rights, as it was debated in the two institutions tasked with drafting the constitution, namely the National Assembly[5] and the Eighth Committee or Constitutional Committee (*Achte Ausschuß*),[6]

---

2 On Max von Baden's constitutional reforms see Lothar Machtan, *Prinz Max von Baden der letzte Kanzler des Kaisers: eine Biographie*, 1. Auflage (Berlin: Suhrkamp, 2013), 405–14.
3 For a recent account on the German revolution see Mark Jones, *Founding Weimar: Violence and the German Revolution of 1918–1919* (Cambridge: Cambridge University Press, 2016).
4 The council included Friedrich Ebert, Philip Scheidemann, Otto Landsberg of the Social Democratic Party and Hugo Haase, Wilhelm Dittmann and Emil Barth of the Independent Socialists. A third of the council were of Jewish descent. The council gave up power on the 13 February 1919.
5 In 1919 the National Assembly had 421 members, of which eight were listed as of the Jewish confession (2 %). This figure excludes any members who did not list their confession or converted.
6 The *Achter Ausschuß* had thirteen members: Benerle, Delbrück, Düringer, Gröber, Hautzmann, Kahl, Katzenstein, Koch, Mausbach, Quarck, Sinzheimer, Spahn and Weitz.

will be the main focus of this chapter.[7] I will demonstrate how debates over how to define minorities, delved into the heart of the so-called 'Jewish Question'. Out of the discussions emerged a Jewish Question. Asked both of Jews with regard to their rights in the constitution and by Jews as they tentatively negotiated questions regarding their social, legal and political status in light of the gradual emergence, and international recognition, of ethnically homogenous nation-states.

Germans of Jewish descent played an active role in post-war political processes and many welcomed the new constitution, which marked the zenith in the struggle for full emancipation.[8] Referring to the continued discriminations against Jews in Germany despite the emancipation act of 1871 one commentator wrote, 'it is only with the establishment of the [Weimar] Republic that in principle these hindrances appear at least to no longer exist'.[9] In the delegation sent to negotiate peace in Versailles two of the six were of Jewish descent, Minister of Justice Otto Landsberg and Chairman of the German Democratic Party, Carl Melchior. Germans Jews were similarly represented in the committee founded to oversee the drafting of the constitution, whereby three of the thirteen members, 23 % were listed as of the Jewish confession.[10] One of the most important figures in these constitutional discussions was the author of the document, Hugo Preuss who was himself Jewish. Of the interlocutors involved in the sittings on minority rights, the majority were listed as Jewish and whilst not all Jews were interested in debating minority rights, as Marcus Kirchhoff writes, 'the particular virulence of these layers of debates, from within and without, lay in the fact that they involved questions of their own collective status and their own political self-understanding'.[11]

Focusing on these constitutional debates reveals that the discussion of Article 113 on minority rights opened up a debate on the Jewish Question, which in turn provoked

---

7 A survey of the minutes of the Council of People's Representatives (14 November 1918 to 8 February 1919) reveals that Jewish questions related to minority rights, citizenship or secularism were not a subject of discussion. Rather the Council was preoccupied with the armistice, the retreat of the army especially from the Eastern Front, the Bolshevist threat and the use of violence by the state. For this reason, whilst the Council was the governing institution that administered the drafting of the constitution it was not the political body that drafted and ratified it, and thus will not be the focus of this chapter. For the translated minutes of the Council see Charles B. Burdick and Ralph H. Lutz, eds., *The Political Institutions of the German Revolution, 1918–1919* (Stanford, New York: Frederick A. Praeger Publishers, 1966), 65–209.

8 On the role of Jews in nation-building in the German Empire and Weimar Republic, especially their involvement in 'constitution-making' see Peter Pulzer, 'Jews and Nation-Building in Germany, 1815–1918', *Leo Baeck Institute Year Book* 41 (1996): 199–214.

9 The document is anonymous however it is probable that Moritz Sobernheim wrote this record as the expert on Jewish Affairs in the Foreign Ministry. See R19605 AA, 'K181838, *Internationale Angelegenheiten Nr. 3: Die Juden, Band 1 (1918–1919)*, März 1919, 1.

10 Of the information available I can infer that three were of Jewish descent (Katzenstein, Quarck and Sinzheimer). See *Verhandlungen der verfassunggebenden deutschen Nationalversammlung*, Band 336, Nr. 391, (Berlin: Julius Sittenfeld, 1920), 1.

11 Markus Kirchhoff, 'Between Weimar and Paris – German Jewry and the Minority Question, 1919' (Draft conference paper for Columbia University, New York, 2012), 2.

more profound enquiries into the concept of national identity and the secular state in this crucial moment in German history. As Oskar Cohn stated in the course of the debates, 'our petition and Article 113 leads into the deepest questions of the concept of nationality'.[12]

The chapter will begin by introducing its protagonists, the drafter of the constitution Hugo Preuss and the only Member of Parliament to challenge his wording on Article 113, the Independent Socialist politician and Zionist, Oskar Cohn. Despite their seminal contributions to German democracy, minority rights and the constitution, both continue to be lesser-known figures in the cannon of Weimar political thinkers.[13] This chapter seeks to rescue these thinkers from obscurity by examining one particular debate in which the policy on minority rights (Article 113) opened a Jewish Question, which, in turn, catalysed a discussion on the foundations of the German nation-state.

The significance of these debates is that they re-opened a nineteenth century debate on ideas of the nation, evoking the language of Moritz Lazarus and Ernest Renan as the French model of the political nation was proposed as an alternative to the German cultural nation. This moment of decisive change opened a window of opportunity to challenge preconceptions on the concept of nationhood and statehood as the German Empire became a Republic. Focusing on the so-called Jewish Question, which wedged open German conceptions of nationhood, statehood, citizenship and secularism offers a unique perspective on how ideas about the modern state were conceptualised, challenged and constructed.

The protagonists: Hugo Preuss and Oskar Cohn

As the drafter of the constitution Hugo Preuss's classification of minority groups as 'foreign-speaking parts of the population' (*fremdsprachliche Volksteile*) cemented the wording of Article 113 within the criteria of language. In Preuss's personal position on Jewry, he maintained that Jews were one of several religious groups in a multi-confessional Germany and saw no need to grant them any minority rights concessions.[14] Nearly all contributors to the debate supported Preuss's wording. Only one representative challenged Preuss's terminology – but stood alone in this assertion. Over the

---

12 '57. Sitzung, 15 Juli 1919', *Verhandlungen Der Verfassunggebenden Deutschen Nationalversammlung, Band 326*, (1920), 1571.

13 In a recent article Caldwell contends that the reception of Weimar political thought in the Anglo-Saxon world is still dominated by Carl Schmidt. See Peter C. Caldwell, 'Hugo Preuss's Concept of the Volk: Critical Confusion or Sophisticated Conception?', *University of Toronto Law Journal 63*, no. 3 (Summer 2013): 1.

14 In private correspondence to his sons, Preuss complained about antisemitism. He commented on how idiotic and irrational it was and how it was taking away his Germanness. Günther Gillessen, *Hugo Preuss: Studien zur Ideen- und Verfassungsgeschichte der Weimarer Republik*, Erstveröffentlichung der Dissertation von 1955, Schriften zur Verfassungsgeschichte, Band 60 (Berlin: Duncker und Humblot, 2000).

course of six months Cohn petitioned several times to alter the wording to 'national minorities' (*nationale Minderheiten*), to no avail. Despite his failure, Cohn brought Jewish questions to the heart of political theoretical discourse on the modern nation-state. Before turning to the debate on Article 113, the following section will start by briefly introducing the two protagonists of this chapter.

On the 14 November 1918 an article appeared in the popular newspaper the *Berliner Tagesblatt* titled *Volksstaat oder verkehrter Obrigkeitsstaat?* Published just under a week after the events of the November revolution and collapse of the Monarchy, the article warned of the challenges facing the new Republic.[15] The day after its publication, the author of the article, Hugo Preuss, was appointed Minister of the Interior by the Chairman of the Council of People's Deputies, and later President of the Republic, Friedrich Ebert who tasked Preuss with drafting a democratic constitution.[16]

Born on 28 October 1860 in the west of Berlin to Jewish parents of the liberal bourgeois milieu, Hugo Preuss studied law and governance at the universities of Berlin and Heidelberg.[17] At the age of twenty-six he stopped work as a legal trainee electing instead an academic career. By twenty-nine his thesis on *Gemeinde, Staat Reich als Gebietskörperschaften* secured him a position as a private tutor at the University of Berlin.[18] Owing to factors unrelated to the quality or output of his academic work (Preuss had become an authority on constitutional law and had an extensive list of publications), not least his left liberal political views and Jewish background, he was never offered a professorship at the University of Berlin.[19] In 1906, aged forty-six, Preuss finally attained a professorship in Public Law at the newly founded private school, the Berlin College of Commerce, a notably less prestigious institution. Hamburger writes that 'Preuss was deeply hurt by the slight, though he rarely talked about it'.[20]

Although Preuss's talents lay in academia, he attempted several times to become politically active combining writing political commentaries in the radical journal *Die*

---

15 Hugo Preuss, 'Volksstaat oder verkehrter Obrigkeitsstaat?' *Berliner Tageblatt* (14 November 1918). Cited in Christoph Schoenberger, 'Hugo Preuss', in *Weimar A Jurisprudence of Crisis*, ed. Arthur J. Jacobson and Bernhard Schlink (Berkeley Los Angeles: University of California Press, 2000), 110.

16 On other lawyers of Jewish descent who were selected to draft the new state constitutions see Ernest Hamburger, 'Hugo Preuß: Scholar and Statesman', *The Leo Baeck Institute Year Book* 20, no. 1 (1975): 179.

17 For years Hugo Preuss's work on democracy and constitutional theory was not recognised alongside that of his contemporaries (Max Weber, Georg Jellinek, Hans Kelsen). This led the German parliament to financially support publishing Preuss's collected works, Hugo Preuss, *Gesammelte Schriften*, ed. Detlef Lehnert and Christopher Müller, 5 vols (Tübingen: Mohr Siebeck, 2007). For a list of the literature on Preuss see, Schoenberger, 'Hugo Preuss', 115.

18 Peter M. R. Stirk, 'Hugo Preuss, German Political Thought and the Weimar Constitution', *History of Political Thought* 23, no. 3 (2002): 498.

19 Hamburger, 'Hugo Preuß: Scholar and Statesman', 182.

20 Ibid. Preuss was not financially disadvantaged by this career hinderance as a result of his book royalties and marriage to Else Liebermann, who came from a wealthy Berlin Jewish family, the same as that of the famous painter Max Liebermann.

Nation (edited by Paul Nathan[21]) with serving in Berlin municipal politics. Preuss's successes in local politics led to his election as honorary member of the magistracy.[22] Peter Stirk writes that it was during this time that Preuss became an advocate of municipal socialism and a critic of the authoritarian state (*Obrigkeitsstaat*), a term he coined. 'Looking back on this he took pride in having been "more anti-capitalist" than the social democrats'.[23]

Officially, however, Preuss was not associated with the socialist party. In local politics Preuss was a representative of the Progressive People's Party (*Fortschrittliche Volkspartei*, FV) and in November 1918 founded, alongside other members of the FV leadership, the German Democratic Party (*Deutsche Demokratische Partei*, DDP). Membership of the German Democrats included notable public figures such as the Protestant pastor Friedrich Naumann, the publicist Theodor Wolff, and Professors Max Weber, Alfred Weber, Albert Einstein and later Foreign Minister, Walther Rathenau. During the Weimar Republic, the German Democratic Party become known for their commitment to maintaining parliamentary democracy whilst upholding individual freedom and social responsibility. Members of the German Democrats were in close contact with the Central Association and as a result of the party's official support for minorities, the German Democratic Party swiftly became the party receiving the highest proportion of Jewish votes. This trend did not go unnoticed by antisemites who termed it the *Judenpartei*. The success of the newly founded German Democrats was such that in the January 1919 elections for the National Assembly they received 18.5 % of the vote which behind the Social Democratic Party and Catholic Centre Party made them the third largest party.[24]

Preuss sat on the left of the German Democrats and had become known as 'the most left leaning scholar of the law of the state in Germany'.[25] That Preuss held liberal-socialist views and applied them to his theories on state law was notable. During the German Empire, a professor of law with social democratic views or affiliations would have struggled to receive an appointment or position of authority.[26] Moreover, in the heat of the revolutionary moment Preuss was 'one of the few informed voices calling for democratisation through legal means'.[27] These qualities did not go unnoticed by Friedrich Ebert. As one contemporary observed, Preuss was appointed to draft the

---

21 Paul Nathan (1857–1927) served as editor until 1907. Nathan was influential in liberal political circles and was notable within the Jewish community for founding the *Hilfsverein der deutschen Juden*. For Nathan's role in the *Hilfsverein* see chapter two.
22 Hamburger, 'Hugo Preuß: Scholar and Statesman', 182–86.
23 Stirk, 'Hugo Preuss, German Political Thought and the Weimar Constitution', 499.
24 Dan Diner, ed., *Enzyklopädie jüdischer Geschichte und Kultur* (Stuttgart, Weimar: Verlag J. B. Metzler, 2015), 143.
25 Schoenberger, 'Hugo Preuss', 110.
26 Ibid.
27 Caldwell, 'Hugo Preuss's Concept of the Volk', 359.

constitution not only because he was a radical democrat with academic credibility but also because he was 'a bridge to the liberal camp in Germany'.[28] Certainly, Preuss's legal expertise combined with his political views made him an ideal candidate to navigate the grievances of the Social Democrats with those of the liberal bourgeois middle class to write a representative, democratic constitution.

However, when the constitution was finally ratified, having undergone eight months of debate and revision, it differed substantially from Preuss's initial draft. Nonetheless, core principles were embedded within the constitution marking Preuss's enduring legacy. He secured that authority in the Republic belonged to the people and that the Republic would be based on the rule of law (*Rechtsstaat*) within an international community.[29] Until his death Preuss was devoted to resolutely defending the Republic and its democratic process.[30] He was particularly distraught by allegations that the constitution was 'un-German' and as a result of his Jewishness was not spared the accompanying antisemitic attacks on his character.[31] Fortunately, Preuss never witnessed the subversion of the constitution he authored as he died in 1925 at the age of sixty-four.

Pitted against Hugo Preuss and his supporters in the debate on Article 113 was Oskar Cohn, the only elected Zionist in the Reichstag. Born on the 15 October 1869 in the town of Guttenberg in Upper Silesia, Cohn died in 1934, having lived through three Germanys – Empire, Republic, and albeit briefly, Dictatorship. Cohn was a member of the Reichstag for six years and during the period of the National Assembly, sat as representative of the Independent Socialists.

It was in this capacity that Cohn was actively involved in the Weimar constitutional debates. Specifically, Cohn petitioned several times to change the wording of Article 113, Germany's policy on minority rights. The issues raised by Cohn in the debate were central to his life work. In addressing them, Cohn ignited a much larger discussion on the foundations of the German nation-state and its future as a Republic. Whilst Cohn's lasting effect on the Weimar constitution was neither visible nor tangible, nonetheless, he left behind a legacy. This was a man who fought throughout his life for the democratic ideals in which he believed: equal rights, representation and toleration.

Oskar Cohn is an elusive figure in Anglophone, but also German scholarship. The single most comprehensive, and often cited, biography on Oskar Cohn remains Ludger Heid's book published in 2002.[32] Scholars have struggled to piece Cohn's life and career together, due to the lack of remaining documentation. Shortly after Cohn fled Germany, in the summer of 1933 Storm Troopers (*Sturmabteilung*, SA) broke into his

---

28 Walter Jellinek, 'Insbesondere: Entstehung und Ausbau der Weimarer Reichsverfassung'. Cited in Stirk, 'Hugo Preuss, German Political Thought and the Weimar Constitution', 500.
29 Caldwell, 'Hugo Preuss's Concept of the Volk', 358.
30 See Hugo Preuss, *Gesammelte Schriften Vierter Band: Politik und Verfassung in der Weimarer Republik*, ed. Detlef Lehnert (Tübingen: Mohr Siebeck, 2008).
31 Hamburger, 'Hugo Preuß: Scholar and Statesman', 202; Schoenberger, 'Hugo Preuss', 110–15.
32 Heid, *Ein Sozialist und Zionist im Kaiserreich und in der Weimarer Republik*.

home destroying his personal documents. Cohn left behind almost no written work. Instead, the sources available are stenographic reports on his prolific speeches.

Although secular himself, Cohn was brought up in a religious household as the youngest of eleven children. After a short dabble in medicine, Cohn graduated in Berlin with a doctorate in law. At the age of thirty, having finished his clerkship, Cohn and his close friend Karl Liebknecht (who later co-founded the Spartacist League with Rosa Luxemburg) opened their own legal practice in Berlin. Alongside the Liebknechts the Cohn family also counted Rosa Luxemburg and Franz Mehring[33] in their social circle, both of whom were close friends of Cohn's wife, Sophie.

Cohn's socialist views were not only reflected in his friendships; he also put his politics to practice. This began in 1909 when, at the age of forty, Cohn started work, similarly to Preuss, as a municipal councillor in Berlin. Only three years later Cohn, representing the Social Democratic Party, won the seat of Nordhausen, in the Prussian province of Saxony (*Sachsen*), and became a member of the parliament, a position he retained until the end of the First World War.[34]

Despite his later fervent anti-militarism, in 1895 Cohn completed his three years of military service and during the First World War served for just over two years as a sentry in various prisoner of war camps mostly in the occupied territories, where like many other German Jewish soldiers, he came into contact with the plight of Eastern European Jews. Cohn was a strong sympathizer of Soviet Russia under the Bolsheviks. Nearing the end of the war he was involved in the revolutionary government, the Council of People's Deputies working as Undersecretary in the Reich Ministry of Justice.[35]

During his time in the National Assembly, Cohn represented the left-wing Independent Socialists and was active in the drafting of the Weimar constitution. Cohn was also a member of the Investigation Committee (*Untersuchungsausschuß*) established in August 1919 to assess the events surrounding the outbreak and prolonging of the war, a position that did him no favours in the eyes of a divided public.[36]

July 1920 marked the end of Cohn's career in national politics. Cohn turned instead to state politics, where he served as a member of the Prussian *Landtag* until 1924. For

---

33 Franz Mehring (1846–1919) was a social democrat, well-known parliamentary reporter and correspondent for a number of newspapers. He was one of the founders, alongside Liebknecht and Luxemburg, of the Spartacus League.

34 Oskar Cohn's parliamentary profile is available online [https://bit.ly/2GHJQrj, accessed 8/08/18].

35 Heid, *Ein Sozialist und Zionist im Kaiserreich und in der Weimarer Republik*, 10.

36 A twenty-eight-member committee established in August 1919. It was tasked to examine the role of the political, economic and military leadership in prolonging the war and what the chances of an earlier peace settlement were. The first Chairman was Fritz Warmuth (German National People's Party) who withdrew from this function just before committee started investigating Hindenburg. Georg Gothein (German Democratic Party) became the new Chairman, but after the Reichstag elections of 1920 declined further cooperation.

reasons unknown, although scholars speculate antisemitism might have played a role, Cohn began his move away from party politics and towards a more active engagement in Jewish community politics, specifically *Poale-Zion*, a radical, left-wing socialist Zionist fraction.[37]

With Germany's descent into dictatorship, as a socialist, member of the League for Human Rights and as a Jew, Cohn knew his days were numbered. The night following the burning of the Reichstag (27 February 1933), Cohn fled Berlin into exile. In the summer of 1934, whilst living in Paris, Cohn began to prepare for settlement in Palestine to join his son, Reinhold who had settled there in 1925. In the same year, he passed away from lung cancer in Geneva where he had travelled to attend the Jewish World Congress.[38]

Cohn was unique because he combined his various identities seamlessly, seeing no contradictions between them, and defying the majority identity of the groups of which he was a part. Of his family background he once stated, 'I come from a strongly emphasised religious family, politically liberal, and for a long time Germanized'.[39] Like his parents, Cohn strongly identified as German, but also fully embraced his Jewish heritage, seeing the latter as 'simultaneous and equal' to his socialism. Not just a socialist, Cohn was also a Zionist because for him, 'Zionism was the most direct route to the rule of socialism in Jewish life.'[40]

Unlike his parents, however, Cohn was secular which led him to resolutely differentiate between the 'Jewish religion' and 'Jewish nationality'. He maintained that 'national movements cannot, should not, be religious. The nation, so to say, takes the place of religion. Religion is a private matter.' Here lay the essence of the Jewish 'dilemma' for Cohn. For Jews, religion was not a private affair but a 'matter for everyone'.[41] Disentangling the political complexity of Jewish identity was part of Cohn's life project as he fought throughout his career for the recognition of Jewish national rights and supported a Jewish state.[42] This devotion was tied to an even greater commitment to halting oppression, representing the voiceless and building a socialist democracy.

It was this set of values, which also saw Cohn becoming involved in the debate on Germany's policy on minority rights. These debates unfolded over the course of six months in the National Assembly and the Constitutional Committee. The central argument in the debate revolved around the criteria for the classification of minority

---

37 *Poale Zion* was founded by Jewish workers in Europe and the Russian Empire in the early twentieth century.

38 Heid, *Ein Sozialist und Zionist im Kaiserreich und in der Weimarer Republik*, 43.

39 Ibid, 3.

40 Ibid, 17.

41 Ibid, 11.

42 Cohn continued to fight for the recognition of national minority rights in Germany. In 1920 he tabled his petition in the Prussian Diet, which was once again rejected. Ibid, 107.

communities in Germany. The article would either recognise minority groups along linguistic, or as Cohn would petition, national lines.

Before turning to the centrality of Jewish questions within this debate I will outline Preuss's reasoning behind Article 113, to illustrate how language triumphed over national criteria in Germany, and the consequences of this for German national self-understanding.

'On a practical level it will always be about language': the wording of Article 113

From the start Preuss did not want a separate bill of rights. As early as 1917, he advised against a catalogue of fundamental basic rights such as those conferred in the 1849 *Paulskirche* constitution.[43] Preuss envisioned that basic rights would be bestowed in the constitution and feared that a separate bill would lead to contestation on the extent and limits of these rights as it had in 1849. He also maintained that the fundamental rights of 1849 had already become embedded within 'the law of the land'.[44] As such, in the first draft of 3 January 1919, Preuss included clauses on fundamental rights within the constitution. Clauses 18 and 19 granted that all Germans were equal before the law and were entitled to freedom of religion and freedom of conscience. The clause on minority rights came under section 21 and afforded 'foreign-speakers' the legal guarantee of the protection of their cultural-traditional (*volkstümlich*) development within the *Reich*, in particular the right to use their mother tongue as a language of instruction and for administrative purposes.[45]

Contrary to Preuss's position on the matter, Friedrich Ebert insisted that he draft a catalogue of fundamental rights to signal the distinctive and new form of governance in Germany.[46] Tasked with having to draft a section on fundamental rights and duties, two factors decisively influenced Preuss's approach to the protection of minorities. Firstly, he saw language as central to national understanding and for this reason of practical importance. Secondly, despite the fact that Article 113 protected minori-

---

43 Hugo Preuss, *Gesammelte Schriften Dritter Band: Das Verfassungswerk von Weimar*, ed. Detlef Lehnert, Christopher Müller, and Dian Schefold (Tübingen: Mohr Siebeck, 2015), 88.
44 Hamburger, 'Hugo Preuß: Scholar and Statesman', 195.
45 [23] Vorentwurf/Entwurf I der WRV: Entwurf des allgemeinen Teils der künftigen Reichsverfassung (3. Januar 1919), Preuss, *Gesammelte Schriften Dritter Band: Das Verfassungswerk von Weimar*, 2015, 535.
46 Hamburger, 'Hugo Preuß: Scholar and Statesman', 195. For more information on why Ebert demanded this catalogue see Susanne Miller and Heinrich Potthoff, eds., *Die Regierung der Volksbeauftragten 1918/19* (Düsseldorf: Droste Verlag, 1969), 240, 247.

ties within Germany, Preuss was more concerned with protecting German minorities abroad, and hoped for an international policy of 'reciprocity'.[47]

In the first draft of the constitution dated 3 January 1919, the clause referring to the rights of minority communities, read as follows,

> The foreign-speaking parts of the population [*fremdsprachige Volksteile*] within the *Reich* may not be hindered in their particular traditional [*volkstümlich*] development, specifically the use of their native language in education as well as in matters of administration and the judiciary system within the confines of their region, through legislation or national administration.[48]

Preuss's definition for minority rights was rooted in a linguistic notion of national understanding, defining the minority as groups whose mother tongue differed from that of the majority. This first draft of the clause resonated word for word from an earlier document Preuss had written in 1917 entitled, *Vorschläge zur Abänderung der Verfassung des Reichs und Preußens*.[49] Notably, Preuss's premise, that the rights of 'foreign-speaking' groups should be legally guaranteed, outlined in 1917 and reiterated in 1919, remained unchanged in the constitution, though not uncontested. A central feature of the debate over how to define the minority in Germany, delved into the historical consciousness of German national development.

Preuss was acutely aware of the history of German national identity based on cultural-linguistic lines as well as the fraught development of German liberalism, having written critically on these subjects in various journals.[50] He defended the centrality of language to German national understanding demonstrating in the course of the debates an awareness that the attempts in the last century to transform Germany from a 'cultural nation' (*Kulturnation*) into a 'state nation' (*Staatsnation*) had fallen short.[51] Scholars debate Preuss's indebtedness to the constitutional law scholar Robert Redslob and author of *Die parlamentarische Regierung in ihrer wahren und in ihrer unechten Form*. The debate questions the extent to which Preuss's constitutional ideas were bound to a pre-1914 German political thought tradition of national unity and authoritarianism.[52] In the case of Article 113 and with respect to his position on minority rights,

---

47 '32. Sitzung, 28 Mai 1919', *Verhandlungen Der Verfassunggebenden Deutschen Nationalversammlung, Band 336*, (1920), 375.

48 'Die fremdsprachlichen Volksteile innerhalb des Reiches dürfen durch die Gesetzgebung und Verwaltung nicht in der ihnen eigenen, volkstümlichen Entwicklung beeinträchtigt werden, insbesondere nicht im Gebrauch ihrer Muttersprache beim Unterrichte sowie bei der inneren Verwaltung und der Rechtspflege innerhalb der von ihnen bewohnten Landesteile.' Hugo Preuss, *Gesammelte Schriften Dritter Band: Das Verfassungswerk von Weimar* (Tübingen: Mohr Siebeck, 2015), 533.

49 Ibid, 89.

50 Ernest Hamburger, 'Hugo Preuß: Scholar and Statesman',182–185.

51 For a comprehensive and accessible account of this national project see Peter Pulzer, *Germany, 1870–1945: Politics, State Formation and War* (Oxford: Oxford University Press, 1997), 3–15.

52 For this debate see, Stirk, 'Hugo Preuss, German Political Thought and the Weimar Constitution', 497 ff.

national unity featured prominently in his wording of the clause. In Article 113 Preuss institutionalised the designation of the majority and minority as rooted in the unifying principles, typical within German tradition: language and culture.[53]

Preuss saw the merit of focusing on language from a practical point of view. In one of the sittings on Article 113, Preuss purported that, 'on a practical level it will always be about language'.[54] This comment echoed an argument made by another speaker who reasoned that language was central to a group's cultural development and identity. Language was also noted for being a more practical criteria for legal, administrative and educational purposes.[55] On the basis of linguistic criteria, Preuss was strongly opposed to the Triple Entente's ban on the incorporation of German-speaking Austrians into Germany. He claimed it violated the principle of self-determination and thus disregarded Woodrow Wilson's fourteen-point programme.[56] In the course of the debates in a rhetorically shrewd attack, one speaker juxtaposed Cohn's focus on national criteria to the practicality of language as he claimed, aside from language 'all else is rather theoretical'.[57]

Alongside the implicit assumption of a language-based conception of national identity and the simple practicality of focusing on language, Preuss's wording of Article 113 also stemmed from the importance he saw in protecting the rights of Germans living abroad. Parallel to drawing up a new constitution, a German delegation was negotiating peace terms in Paris. The specific concern that directly impacted the protection of minorities was the question: what form would Germany's post-war borders take? Tied to this was the question of how many minority groups would still live in German territory and, more pressingly, how many Germans would now reside in foreign territory as minorities.

The second debate on Article 113 held in the special committee illustrates that despite Cohn's second petition, the wording of Article 113 remained firmly rooted in the criteria of language. For Preuss, the developments of the peace negotiations, would in fact give further support to focusing on language. Preuss did not shy away from expressing his opinion on them as he lamented, 'unfortunately, in the future more Germans will live under foreign rule rather than foreign-speakers under German rule'.[58] Ensuring the 'protection of the German-speaking parts of the population' (*deutschsprachige Volksteile*) was thus of central importance to Preuss who empathised openly with the 'fate

---

53 For an overview of this tradition and its legacy in Germany see Kremer, 'Transitions of a Myth? The Idea of a Language-Defined Kulturnation in Germany'.

54 '32. Sitzung, 28 Mai 1919', 375.

55 Ibid.

56 Anon., 'Preuss Denounces Demand of Allies', *The New York Times* (14 September 1919) [https://nyti.ms/2GboC6v, accessed 5/02/19].

57 '32. Sitzung, 28 Mai 1919', 375.

58 Ibid.

of our poor country-men'.[59] Preuss's so-called foreign policy plan, enacted through the provision on minority rights in the constitution, was to lead by example through 'the idea of reciprocity'. Through a policy of reciprocity that was 'noble' and 'wise', Preuss anticipated that, 'if we lead by example and appeal to international public opinion, then other countries will act similarly'.[60] Regaining prestige for Germany on the international stage was at the forefront of Preuss's reasoning on Article 113.

Whilst reciprocity for Preuss was a matter of the respectful treatment and protection of minorities in Germany so that this would be modelled abroad, it was also connected to his desire for the international recognition of minority rights based on language. This is demonstrated in a debate on the 16 June in which Preuss professed that had it not been for Cohn's intervention the draft sent by the German delegation to the Allies would have recognised minorities as 'foreign-speakers' (*Anderssprachige*).[61]

For Preuss, the most prominent minority needing protection were Poles living in eastern Germany and Germans living in the territory of independent Poland, in what he termed the 'Polish Question' (*Polenfrage*).[62] In statistical terms, the Polish minority was the largest minority group in Germany.[63] Preuss's position on German Jews throughout the debates was unfaltering; they were neither a national group nor a community that needed special minority rights protection in Germany. This was exemplified when one of Preuss's supporters, the Catholic Centre politician Adolf Gröber stated, 'also, the Israelites themselves are of divided opinion, the large majority do not want any sort of exceptional status, but rather want to be recognised, and treated, as fully German'.[64] On this basis, merely looking at the final constitution and at Preuss as the main figure in this legislative process, a common trait of the secondary literature on the constitution, would neglect how Jewish questions featured prominently in the German post-war state building process.

Convinced that a *Judenfrage* existed in Germany, Cohn petitioned to change the wording of Article 113. Cohn's counter argument brought Jewish questions to the heart of minority rights protection. In challenging the criteria of who to define as a minority, Cohn made explicit the need to evaluate the national understanding of the majority. Moreover, whilst the developments at the Paris Peace Conference – in the eyes of Preuss and his supporters – gave further credence to their position, Cohn in turn used them to advance his criticism. The international discussion on whether to recognise Jewish national or autonomous rights equipped Cohn with moralistic arguments

---

59 Ibid.

60 Ibid.

61 '40. Sitzung, 16 Juni 1919', *Verhandlungen Der Verfassunggebenden Deutschen Nationalversammlung, Band 336*, 1920, 500.

62 '32. Sitzung, 28 Mai 1919', 375.

63 In the German Empire the Poles were the largest minority, representing around 8 % of the population in 1871. In the same year, Jews made up 1.25 %. Berghahn, *Imperial Germany*, 110–17.

64 '32. Sitzung, 28 Mai 1919', 375.

on the absurd inconsistency should Germany's minority rights policy not align with emerging international principles.

In his first petition to change the wording of Article 113 Cohn challenged the premise of focusing on language by referencing groups within Germany that use German as their mother tongue but nonetheless remain a 'foreign-national part of the population' (*fremdnationaler Volksteil*).[65] Cohn implied that even if a minority group spoke German, they could still remain foreigners in Germany. He pointed out the possibly intractable problem at the core of German national identity. Thus, whilst Preuss's wording illustrated a historical understanding of the German *Kulturnation*, Cohn's counter-response equally exhibited an astute awareness of the exclusiveness of this conception of nationhood and its implications for German-speaking minority groups. Cohn used the example of second or third generation Poles or the Wends. Yet what concerned him the most was, 'the very important question of […] Jewish nationality' (*jüdischen Nationalität*).[66]

Cohn's decision to focus on Jewish minority rights in Germany was not only a result of his Zionist convictions. Rather, he sought to align the Weimar constitution with what he thought, or more accurately hoped, was soon to be internationally recognised: Jewish national rights and a Jewish state. Cohn maintained that Jews constituted a nationality in their own right, thereby rejecting Preuss's fundamental premise that they were part of the German nation, proclaiming, 'in the peace conference, the Jewish people [*jüdisches Volk*] will be recognised as an independent [*selbständige*] Nation.'[67] Arguing that Jewish national rights should similarly be protected in the constitution, Cohn critiqued the idea that Germany had no Jewish Question.

'The Ladies and Gentlemen who maintain that in Germany there is no national "Jewish Question"' Cohn announced, 'would not want to provide national rights for the Jewish population […] but this viewpoint is not uncontested, and I for one, see it as false.'[68] The *Judenfrage* posed in this instance challenged German and Jewish conceptions of national identity. By drawing on it, Cohn reopened the political theoretical discussion on the German nation-state. Namely, what makes a German national? Are Jews a national or religious group and what rights should they be conferred in Germany? Exhibiting his awareness of the significance of the constitutional discussions, Cohn stated, 'our petition and Article 113 leads into the deepest questions of the concept of nationality.'[69]

---

65 '17. Sitzung, 28. Februar 1919', *Verhandlungen Der Verfassunggebenden Deutschen Nationalversammlung, Band 326*, 406.
66 Ibid.
67 Ibid.
68 Ibid.
69 '57. Sitzung, 15 Juli 1919', *Verhandlungen Der Verfassunggebenden Deutschen Nationalversammlung, Band 326*, (1920), 1571.

Cohn pushed the discussion to a profound level of analysis by implying that Germany should rethink its national understanding and compared the German Empire to the Third Republic.[70] Drawing on the French model of the political nation (*Staatsnation*) Cohn illustrated how a country of 'linguistic diversity' could maintain a unique national identity by instead relying on 'whether someone professes to belong to a nation, whether he wants to profess his will' to the nation.[71] Cohn stressed the need to abandon the focus on language in Germany, what he saw as a negative 'Prussian state practice', alluding to the linguistic Germanisation policies under Bismarck during the *Kulturkampf* from the early 1870s to mid-1880s.

Cohn reminded the Assembly of the German draft sent to the League of Nations on minorities where the attendees had been in agreement that 'speaking a foreign language should not be a necessary criterion to constitute a national minority'.[72] Using moralistic language Cohn stressed the dishonesty and detrimental consequences should Germany pursue a different domestic policy to the international community, especially in the need to guarantee a sense of belonging and togetherness to Germans living in new states.[73] Precisely on the strength of the 'will' to remain German, Cohn claimed that Germans living abroad would retain a sense of German national belonging.

By invoking the language of will, namely consenting to be part of the nation, Cohn drew on ideas from the French philosopher and historian Ernest Renan's famous lecture at the Sorbonne in March 1882, entitled 'What is a nation?'. For Renan neither race, language, religious affinity, geography bound a nation together. Rather he described the nation as a 'soul' united by a spiritual principle comprising of memory of the past and the desire to live in the present.[74] Cohn, however, was not the first to apply these ideas to the German context. The Jewish scholar and contemporary of Renan, Moritz Lazarus made an almost identical argument two years prior to Renan's lecture in response to an article by Heinrich von Treitschke which argued that the 'Jews are our misfortune' as they undermined the formation of a unified national culture in Germany. Using the example of Germany as consisting of multiple identities from Polish Germans to Catholic, Protestant, Jewish Germans, Lazarus argued that nation-

---

70 At the turn of the century debates about political reform in the German Empire turned to comparisons with other countries such as the United States and the United Kingdom but in particular the Third Republic. On how thinking about France shaped Wilhelmine political thought see Mark Hewitson, *National Identity and Political Thought in Germany: Wilhelmine Depictions of the French Third Republic, 1890–1914* (Oxford: Clarendon Press, 2000).

71 '57. Sitzung, 15 Juli 1919', 1571.

72 Ibid, 1572. I have been unable to locate the original document and thus cannot verify if Cohn is correct in his statement.

73 Ibid, 1573.

74 Renan, 'What is a nation?' [*Qu'est-ce qu'une Nation?* Paris: Sorbonne, 11 March 1882], in *Becoming National*, 41–55.

ality could be constructed in heterogeneity underpinned by the *will* to belong to the nation.[75]

Already from his opening speech to the assembly Cohn had set the tone of his petition as part of a more profound attempt to renew the concept of the nation in Germany and transform it into a socialist democracy. Aware on a personal level of the sacrifices of Jews during the war and inferring Renan's notion of shared glories and sacrifice, Cohn believed that unity would come through reforming national understanding on the basis of a renewed commitment to belong to the German nation and partake in its future.

For this reason, Cohn appealed to the greater purpose of the constitution as 'an important tool [...] for the renewal of the German nation in its politics and ethics'. He stressed the 'renewal of its soul' (*seelische Erneuerung*), which would take place, according to Cohn, with the 'creation of another state and national ethos' (*Staats- und Volksgesinnung*). Vocalising his political views, Cohn stated that, 'socialism is above all also an ethos in which, everyone sees themselves as part of the whole, as not only entitled but duty bound to their people'. And for Cohn, only when this ethos was not hindered could the constitution truly be the 'product' that the German people had demanded.[76] For Cohn it was of the utmost necessity that Article 113 recognised national minorities as he tied this recognition into his greater plan for the renewal of the German nation as a socialist state.[77] Cohn's political convictions and Zionism were intimately bound to one another.[78]

Yet perhaps by demanding a socialist state, Cohn's arguments did not sway his opponents. Cohn's petition was regarded as Zionist and dismissed for having no place in German politics. The debate on Article 113 became a microcosm of the rifts within the German Jewish community between liberal Jews and a minority faction of Zionists on the subject of German Jewish identity and the post-war future of the diaspora.

In one of the sessions, the speaker, a Catholic Centre politician, Konrad Beyerle, opened the sitting by summarising the previous debates on Article 113. Despite the fact that Cohn had listed a number of national groups that would be affected by the article (Wends, Sorbs, Kashubians, Masurians), the speaker only mentioned the Jews and foregrounded the Zionist movement as being at the heart of the petition. Beyerle announced that it was the Zionist movement that was requiring the Jewish population to heed its national character although it was not a foreign-speaking group.[79]

---

75 The Antisemitism Dispute and Lazarus's ideas are discussed at greater length in chapter one.

76 '17. Sitzung, 28. Februar 1919', 406.

77 This argument resonates from a previous debate in the Reichstag on the *Judenzählung* when speakers appealed to the kind of nation that Germany should aspire to be in the future, namely truly secular and without religious discrimination. For these discussions see chapter three.

78 For Cohn Zionism was the most direct way for the dominance (*Herrschaft*) of socialism in Jewish life. Heid, *Ein Sozialist und Zionist im Kaiserreich und in der Weimarer Republik*, 18.

79 '32. Sitzung, 28 Mai 1919', 375.

Preuss allied with the position of the Catholic Centre Party, specifically that of the parliamentarian Adolf Gröber, and announced that he agreed that he had no intention of showing any consideration to Zionism and would remain committed to the term 'foreign-speaking' (*fremdsprachigen*) and not 'national' (*national*). The position of the Catholic Centre party was to maintain that Judaism was a confession, a position supported by the majority of the liberal German Jewish community. 'Cohn's petition was essentially motivated by Zionism', concluded Preuss.[80] Heid writes that members of *Poale-Zion* encouraged Cohn to submit the petition and thus Cohn did not represent even a majority Zionist position, a point to which I will return.[81]

Defending his position against the criticism that it was a Zionist petition; Cohn reiterated his previous arguments. He outlined that his motion was not novel as the German Empire had adopted this position on minority rights internationally.[82] He explained once again that his petition was not for Zionists but applied to a number of groups within Germany, who would still be considered 'foreign' despite speaking German. Cohn stressed that he had deliberately not focused on the Zionist movement and this should not be grounds for dismissing his petition.[83]

Cohn did highlight the existence, to an increasing degree, of a national movement of German Jews. A movement that, according to Cohn, had been noticed by the League of Nations as well as the German government who had recognised it by 'the well-known declaration on the establishment of a national homeland in Palestine'.[84] Here Cohn was referencing the Balfour Declaration of 2 November 1917, a policy which was officially supported by the German Foreign Ministry in an announcement on the 5 January 1918. Not unsurprisingly Cohn was predicting the international recognition at the Paris Peace Conference of the national status of Jewry, and he believed this same recognition would be vital within Germany.

As Preuss himself had done, Cohn also emphasised the detrimental consequences of not recognising the unique attributes of German-speaking national minorities in Germany. He recognised the significance of theory, or concepts, on practice and political action, stating, 'all these [attributes] will be eliminated by the concept of foreign-speaking *Volksteile*'.[85]

Despite his array of arguments which mounted a critique on the *Kulturnation* and the centrality of language to national understanding, it is telling that all three speakers reduced Cohn to pushing a Zionist agenda. This is particularly interesting given that

---

80 Ibid, 376.
81 Heid, *Ein Sozialist und Zionist im Kaiserreich und in der Weimarer Republik*, 106.
82 In official proclamations the German Empire supported Jewish self-determination in Eastern Europe writes Matthäus. See Jürgen Matthäus, 'Tagesordnung: Judenfrage: A German Debate in the Early Stages of the Weimar Republic', *The Leo Baeck Institute Year Book* 48, no. 1 (2003): 88.
83 '40. Sitzung, 16 Juni 1919', 500.
84 Ibid.
85 Ibid.

for the majority of the debate in Weimar on Article 113 at the Paris Peace Conference discussions were still ongoing on whether to recognise national minority rights or cultural autonomous rights for Jews. Cohn's petition for Germany's policy on minority rights to align with international developments was thus not unfounded. The majority of the constitutional debates on Article 113 took place before autonomous cultural rights for Jews were legally enshrined in the Minority Treaty on the 28 June 1919. On the one hand then, at the core of the debate was what it meant to be Jewish with differing perspectives between Preuss, representing the liberal Jewish camp, and Cohn, representing Zionists. One speaker succinctly captured this difference in a comment directed at Cohn when he stated, 'your feelings cannot be taken away from you, but so long as they are not of a religious nature, I do not know them'.[86]

On the other hand, the debate concerned the future of the German nation-state and its position internationally, which the two men differed on. At the forefront of Preuss's reasoning was the importance of Germany regaining international prestige and protecting the minority rights of Germans abroad. Preuss sought to use the constitution's minority rights policy as a signal to the international community to reciprocate and respect the rights of Germans in the post-war new states. Moreover, as Preuss had hoped, in 1926 Germany took a decisive step towards its international rehabilitation as it was invited to a seat at the League of Nations, in part due to a policy enacted by the Foreign Minister, Gustav Stresemann who championed Germany as a defender of minority rights.[87] In this sense then, 'the situation of German Jews was paradoxically fairly similar to that of other "ethnic" Germans'.[88]

Contrary to Preuss, Cohn was less concerned about prestige and more about the renewal of Germany, its break from the *Kaiserreich* and reforming in line with emerging international principles. Cohn observed the gradual international recognition of (ethnic) national groups as an opportunity to both recognise national rights for Jews and combine this with the renewal and rebirth of the German nation. For Cohn, this entailed reframing the concept of the nation not along cultural-linguistic lines but rather based on the will to remain German. In an era of the collapse of Empires and the rebirth of old countries along new territorial boundaries, Cohn envisioned that national understandings would be redefined and that the choice, desire or will to be part of a nation-state would govern the post-war restructuring of the world map.[89]

Despite Cohn's arguments highlighting the growing national sentiments of the German-Jewish youth, the international recognition of autonomous rights for East

––––––––––

86 Ibid.
87 See Carole Fink, 'Defender of Minorities: Germany in the League of Nations, 1926–1933', *Central European History* 5, no. 4 (1972): 330–57.
88 Mark Mazower, 'Minorities and the League of Nations in Interwar Europe', *Daedalus* 126, no. 2 (1997): 52.
89 Whilst Cohn did not use the language of self-determination his ideas on the concept of the nation align closely with those who advocated for the right to self-determination.

European Jews, and the limited perspective of classifying national identity as based merely on linguistic homogeneity, his petitions received no supporting votes. In the concluding session of the debates, one SPD representative,[90] jibed that should German Zionists embrace Hebrew as their language, then they would qualify for minority rights in Germany as a foreign-speaking group.[91]

Where on the one hand the debate on Article 113 concerned the exact wording of Germany's policy on minority rights, significantly, in reviewing the classification of minority groups in Germany, the negotiations threw into relief considerations as to what defined the national identity of the majority. Moreover, the debate took on a political theoretical dimension as it delved into the depths of the concept of the nation and national identity within Germany. Whilst the article concerned numerous minority groups within Germany including the Poles, Danes and Wends amongst others, as the German borders constricted and former minorities (re)joined their nations, the debates became most consequential for the rights and identity of Jews within Germany.[92]

This is demonstrated in a parallel debate which took place outside of the chamber of the National Assembly involving the liberal German Jewish organisation, the Alliance of German Jews who sought to confirm that German Jews did not wish to be granted national rights in spite of any international discussions regarding the demand for, and possible recognition of, these rights. The episode ensured that within the Foreign Ministry Jewish questions remained a prominent feature of political affairs and further illustrated that minority rights became a concern which most acutely affected the German-Jewish population.

Vying for influence: German-Jewish organisations and Article 113

As the debate on minority rights in parliamentary sessions delved into Jewish questions, German-Jewish organisations felt compelled to respond to ensure their demands would be heard. Whilst the Central Association, representing the largest percentage of the German-Jewish community used their popular organ, *Im deutschen Reich* to reaffirm their position that they were Germans of the Jewish faith, two other associations, the Alliance of German Jews and the Zionist Federation for Germany, deployed a different tactic: political lobbying. In the battle for the support of their position from

---

90 This representative was Simon Katzenstein, an SPD politician who held the portfolio on education. His profile is available online through the database of the German parliament [https://bit.ly/2YCv8If, accessed 30/1/19].

91 '40. Sitzung, 16 Juni 1919', 500.

92 As the Treaty of Versailles did not contain minority obligations towards Jews, and in Germany Jews were not recognised as a minority, during the 1930s the League of Nations could not intervene to halt the Nazis antisemitic persecution and violence. See Mark Mazower, 'The Strange Triumph of Human Rights, 1933–1950', *The Historical Journal* 47, no. 2 (2004): 383.

the German government, despite representing a fraction of all Jews in Germany, the Zionists emerged as a political force to contend with. Zionist representatives, although ultimately unsuccessful in changing the wording of Article 113, consistently lobbied ministers in the highest levels of government and were able to find an audience for their views.

Early on in the debate the Central Association representing approximately 10 % of the German Jewish community, published an official statement distancing the organisation from Cohn's petition. In order to do so, they qualified their position on the concept of nationality within Germany. The article read,

> [for us] Germaness is nation [*Nation*] and people [*Volk*], Judaism is faith [*Glauben*] and kinship [*Stamm*], but [this] faith and kinship does not separate us from the ethnic [*völkisch*] Germans, we are not Jewish-national, but a Jewish religious community and not a Jewish people [*Volk*], least of all in Germany ...[93]

Notably, the Central Association deployed the language of *Stamm*, a discourse that at once enabled a sense of belonging to the many *Stämme* of Germany whilst also remaining sensitive to the unique identity of Jews. Using the language of *Stamm* gained increasing popularity within the German Jewish community in the mid-nineteenth century when the centrality of religion began to decline, and new visions of community were sought out.[94] *Stamm* signalled a shared descent, avoiding the contentious notion of race or ethnicity and suited the German-speaking context, whereby the term was often used to differentiate between regional identities. As the First World War pried the Pandora's box of nationalism open even further, the answer to the question of what constituted Jewish identity was pluralised. For the Central Association, which endeavoured to straddle these various identities the concept of *Stamm* was vague and yet distinct enough to capture these distinctions whilst also legitimate the status of Jews as German national citizens.

Re-affirming the view of the Central Association, on the 3 August 1919 the German Foreign Ministry, the Reich and Prussian Ministry of the Interior all received a letter from the liberal German-Jewish organisation, the Alliance of German Jews. The purpose of the letter was to enquire on the official position within Germany on the rights of national minorities, given, the letter read, 'the recent inclusion of this principle in

---

93 '[...] dass uns das Deutschtum Nation und Volk, das Judentum Glauben und Stamm ist, dass uns die Glaubens- und Stammest aber nicht völkisch von den Deutschen absondert, dass wir nicht jüdisch-national, sondern jüdische Religionsgemeinschaft und kein jüdisches Volk, am allerwenigsten in Deutschland sind ...', *Im deutschen Reich* 4, (April 1919), 188. Quoted in Heid, *Ein Sozialist und Zionist im Kaiserreich und in der Weimarer Republik*, 106.
94 See Rahden, 'Germans of the Jewish Stamm: Visions of Community between Nationalism and Particularism, 1850 to 1933', 30 ff.

the League of Nation's draft treaty', which the letter continued, 'would also include provisions concerning Jews'.[95]

The letter suggests that it was unbeknown to the Alliance that by August 1919 the wording of Article 113 in the constitution would no longer be changed. The constitution awarded minority rights to foreign-speaking groups and the petition to replace the wording with 'national minorities' received no supporting votes. This was a fact which the Zionist Central Bureau was already aware of, having received a letter on the 1 August stating that their petition to change the wording of Article 113 had been rejected.[96]

The letter sent by the Alliance illustrates the complex nature of the debate on minority rights in Germany and abroad and how within the Foreign Ministry it was tied into Jewish affairs. The episode became an epitome of divisions within the German Jewish community between the traditional liberal, and majority, Jewish perspective that Judaism was a confession, and the view, influenced by the experience of Russian Jews that Judaism was a nationality. It was precisely this distinction that the Alliance addressed in their letter to the Foreign Ministry.

The author of the letter argued that it was of no concern to the Alliance if Jews living in 'states outside of Germany' (*ausserdeutsche Ländern*) due to differences in language or culture should be, or want to be, set apart as 'special national groups' (*nationale Sondergruppen*).[97] However, they pleaded that any settlements affecting German Jews would be discussed with their organisation.[98] The letter continued that the Alliance saw it as their 'urgent duty' to ensure the Foreign Ministry was aware that, '<u>German</u> Jews, in their masses, feel <u>only</u> as a special <u>religious</u> community within the heterodox majority of the German population'.[99]

The sentiments expressed by the Alliance went beyond the mere institutional parameters of being classified a citizen of the German nation. They assuredly distanced their position from the possibility of Jews being seen as 'a special national group within the German nation'. Rather they emphasised their belonging to a German people, participants in the social-cultural identity of being German, with the same experience of German 'origin [*Geburt*], language, education, culture and feeling [*Gefühl*]'.[100] Thus, as Cohn had mounted a critique on the principles of the *Kulturnation*, the Alliance evidenced the Jewish belonging to it.

Supporting their position, the letter noted that the Alliance of German Jews along with other Jewish organisations represented the 'majority of the Jewish communities

---

95 R19605 AA, 'K181999', *Internationale Angelegenheiten Nr. 3: Die Juden, Band 1 (1918–1919)*, 3 August 1919.
96 Ibid, 'K181953', 1 August 1919.
97 Ibid, 'K181999', 3 August 1919, 2.
98 Presumably a civil servant from the Foreign Ministry drew a line on the side of the letter to highlight this section.
99 The underling is replicated from the original document. See R19605 AA, 'K181999', 3 August 1919, 2.
100 Ibid.

of Germany of which approximately 200,000 Germans of the Jewish faith are members'.[101] To ensure that there was no misunderstanding on the collective position of German Jewry, the letter also referenced a declaration written in November 1918 signed by several Jewish organisations. Alongside the Alliance of German Jews, represented by 'Privy Councillor Oskar Cassel', representatives of two other major liberal-leaning German Jewish interest groups signed the petition. These included Professor Salomon Kalischer[102] from the Union of German-Jewish Communities[103] (*Deutsch-Israelitischer Gemeindebund*) and 'Privy Councillor Dr Eugen Fuchs' of the Central Association.[104]

The declaration stressed that in contrast to a Zionist 'fraction', the overwhelming majority of German Jews felt themselves to be an 'inseparable, integral part of the German people' (*Volk*). The importance of this majority opinion was emphasised once again as the declaration continued, 'German Jews are a religious community [*Glaubensgemeinschaft*] and not a Jewish people [*Volk*] in Germany'.[105] The use of language, carefully selected, 'integral part' (*Bestandteil*), 'community' (*Gemeinschaft*), and the distancing from the use of the word for 'nation' or 'people' (*Volk*) to refer to their Jewish heritage, as was often done at the time (even before the Zionist movement gained in momentum) was vital to the German Jewish liberal cause, distancing them also semantically from Zionists.

The declaration from November noted the presence of a Zionist fraction in the German-Jewish community. A letter to the Foreign Ministry sent by the Alliance elaborated on this further and qualified that not all Zionists supported Jewish national minority rights. Instead, the letter stressed, this was the position taken by an extreme fraction of Zionists.[106] The Alliance warned, that should the Foreign Ministry concede to this movement, which had always been involved in 'reactionary circles', it would send out the wrong signal, both domestically and internationally.[107]

The Alliance of German Jews saw it as their duty to intervene in the debate on Article 113 to guarantee that Jews would continue to be recognised as a religious com-

---

101 The figure given represents a third of the total Jewish community in the Weimar Republic, which numbered approximately 600,000 not including those that renounced their religion. For more on Jewish demographics in the Weimar Republic see Donald L. Niewyk, 'The Economic and Cultural Role of the Jews in the Weimar Republic', *Leo Baeck Institute Yearbook* 16, no. 1 (1971): 163.

102 Whilst in the declaration Kalischer's first name was not mentioned, it can be assumed that this was Salomon Kalischer one of the board members of the Union. See Eugen Täubler and Selma Stern, *Aufsätze zur Problematik jüdischer Geschichtsschreibung 1908–1950* (Tübingen: Mohr Siebeck, 1977), 1.

103 This organisation was an association of Jewish corporations in Germany, founded on 3 July 1869. It promoted the common interests of German Jews and directed much attention to education and charity initiatives.

104 R19605 AA, 'K182002', November 1918.

105 Ibid.

106 Heid says that not all Zionists demanded the recognition of national rights in Germany as they were aware of how unpopular it was. He argues that Cohn was part of a small group of *Poale Zion* that pushed for them. Heid, *Ein Sozialist und Zionist im Kaiserreich und in der Weimarer Republik*, 106.

107 R19605 AA, 'K181999', 3 August 1919, 3.

munity in a multi-confessional Germany. Like the interlocutors in the parliamentary debate, the Alliance also stressed that the petition was supported by a minority, reactionary fraction of extremist Zionists. The letter sent by the Alliance once again illustrates how the debate on minority rights became a Jewish question that in turn catalysed iterations of German national understanding. In the case of this particular episode, by rejecting the petition for national rights, the Alliance not only outlined the parameters of German Jewish identity, but also had to justify how these fitted into German understandings of national identity. It offers a lens through which to scrutinise the complex nature of these political ideas and how Jews appropriated and contested these concepts in the process of navigating their political identity in a changing political environment.

As illustrated above, according to the Alliance the majority of Zionists did not support Cohn's proposal. Ludger Heid, biographer of Cohn, writes that the Zionists saw the petition as 'futile' and thought it would damage the Zionist cause in Germany rather than supporting it, in spite of Cohn's announcement in the National Assembly that his petition was supported by the Zionist Federation.[108] According to the letter from the Alliance, and Heid, Cohn was prompted to submit his petition by members of *Poale Zion* several of whom were from Eastern Europe where Jewish communities exhibited national tendencies.[109] However, in contrast to Heid, several documents suggest that the Zionist Federation was in fact active in using diplomatic channels to lobby for the recognition of Jewish national rights.

Furthermore, whilst representing a minority within the Jewish community the following events reveal that the Zionists showed themselves to be a force to contend with, as they lobbied with more persistence and in higher levels of government than liberal German Jewish associations. Zionists in Germany were in a minority and yet the decisive and persistent action taken by their representatives to change the wording of Article 113 could have convinced spectators that they were lobbying on behalf of a majority view.[110]

Only a few days before the letter from the Alliance of German Jews the Foreign Ministry received internal correspondence stating that there was no interest in using the proposed changes to Article 113[111] sent in by the Zionists.[112] Written in Weimar, the seat of the National Assembly, the transcript was dated 30 July 1919 and addressed to the

---

108 Heid, *Ein Sozialist und Zionist im Kaiserreich und in der Weimarer Republik*, 106.
109 Ibid.
110 Paying members of the Zionist Federation (6, 200) represented approximately 1 % of the German-Jewish population in 1910. In 1913 membership increased (9, 000) increasing Zionist representation to 1.5 % of the total German-Jewish population. See Lavsky, *Before Catastrophe*, 22–23; Schorsch, *Jewish Reactions to German Anti-Semitism*, 119.
111 In the transcript the article was listed as 112, although it referred to Article 113, Germany's minority rights policy.
112 R19605 AA, 'K181952', 30 July 1919.

Privy Councillor for Legation Otto Göppert[113] and signed by Albert Saunier, the Office Manager to the Legation Council of Hermann Müller, Reich Minister of the Foreign Office during the Gustav Bauer cabinet. Saunier explained that he had presented the Zionist request to change Article 113 in the constitution to the 'Herr Minister' (presumably Hermann Müller) who responded that, 'we have no interest in implementing the wishes of the Zionists'.[114] The transcript continued underscoring that Privy Councillor Nelcken, who worked on 'constitutional questions of section III',[115] responded similarly, because of his conviction that 'the overwhelming majority of German Jews would not approve of the proposal'. As such, Saunier wrote that he had refrained from contacting other ministers on the matter.[116]

The significance of this correspondence amongst ministers in the highest level of political counselling, the Privy Council, is illustrative of the seriousness with which the Zionist proposal was both dealt and decided upon. That no other minister was consulted on the matter following Minister Müller and Nelcken's decision suggests that it was after the 30 July that the final wording of Article 113 was decided upon, and that this decision went beyond the decision-making powers of the drafter of the constitution and the Reichstag alone.

Two days later, on the 1 August a transcript from the office of the Privy Councillor Otto Göppert sent to Victor Jacobson from the Zionist Central Bureau was filed in the Foreign Ministry.[117] The transcript provides an insight into the lobbying of the Zionist Central Bureau on what we can assume was the article in the constitution on minority rights.[118] On the 28 July, after Cohn's final speech in the National Assembly where he referred to a Zionist petition, which argued that language was not criteria enough to define a minority group, Victor Jacobson of the Zionist Central Bureau sent a letter to Göppert. The same evening Göppert forwarded this letter to Weimar where the National Assembly had convened since the elections. According to Göppert, after a more detailed consultation, it was decided that no action on this proposal would be taken

---

113 Otto Göppert's parliamentary profile is available online [https://bit.ly/2Jz6mnZ, accessed 8/11/19].
114 R19605 AA, 'K181952', 30 July 1919.
115 Reviewing all five drafts of the constitution reveals that the article on minority rights was never included in section III. In the first draft it was listed under section I: *Das Reich und die deutschen Freistaaten*. By the second draft it was already listed under section II: *Die Grundrechte des deutschen Volkes* where it remained until the final draft when it came under section II: *Grundrechte und Grundpflichten der Deutschen*, sub-section I: *Die Einzelperson*. See Hugo Preuss, *Gesammelte Schriften Dritter Band*, 533–593. Given this, I am not sure why Nelcken would have been responsible for this subject unless he was working on section II and the transcript was mistyped.
116 R19605 AA, 'K181952', 30 July 1919.
117 Ibid, 'K181953', 1 August 1919.
118 In the transcript, the article is recorded as Article 118. On surveying this article in drafts of the constitution it never relates to minority rights but rather marriage rights. We can thus assume that perhaps this transcript mistyped the article number.

because, reiterating word for word from Saunier's correspondence, the overwhelming majority of German Jews would not agree with the proposed changes.[119]

In the transcript, the Privy Councillor explained that 'due to the imminence of a final decision on the draft constitution, another attempt to win over the dissenting partners to the amendment would have no longer been possible either way'. Whilst the transcript appeared to suggest that any future lobbying on Article 113 would have been ineffective, the Councillor's last comment left more open for interpretation. Directly translated the last sentence read, 'a rejection of the petition by the National Assembly would have drawn the attention of foreign countries onto this issue and made a very unfavourable impression'.[120] It is not entirely certain what Göppert intended to convey. On the 15 July Cohn's petition, backed by the Zionists, had been raised in the National Assembly and rejected due to the fact that it did not receive enough supporting votes. Thus, there are a few reasons he might have written this.

Firstly, it could indicate that Göppert was unaware of the National Assembly session and its outcome. Alternatively, he could have been hinting that, as the constitution was not yet in its final reading, the Zionists should petition once again in the Assembly, and even if the motion were rejected, it would direct international attention onto the Zionist cause. Lastly, he might have been suggesting that the rejection had roused international interest and for this very reason, the Zionist clause still had political clout. Namely, it would imply support for the Zionist cause by a Privy Councillor and thus more support for Cohn's petition than evidenced in the National Assembly, and eighth committee sessions.

These transcripts indicate that German Zionists, despite representing a minority faction, were able to exert a significant influence on constitutional debates. Even after the rejection of Cohn's petition in the National Assembly session of 15 July, the Zionist Central Bureau kept the proposal active, circulating it to ministers with influence in the chain of political decision-making. The Zionists did not have the majority support of the German Jewish community, and yet nevertheless they lobbied far more extensively than the Alliance for German Jews, acting as if they did have it and with relative success. In the battle for recognition, the Zionist Federation championed.[121]

---

119 Whilst it is difficult to infer who was present at this consultation, we can assume the participants were ministers of the Privy Council and not the constitutional committee (*Achter Ausschuß*) whose meeting transcripts do not record any further mention of Article 113 [112] after 28 May 1919.

120 'Eine Ablehnung des Antrags durch die Nationalversammlung würde aber die Aufmerksamkeit des Auslandes besonders auf deisen Punkt gelenkt und einen sehr ungünstigen Eindruck gemacht haben'. R19605 AA, 'K181953', 1 August 1919.

121 On the support for Zionism amongst personnel in the Foreign Ministry see chapter two.

Language triumphs

During the drafting of the Weimar constitution the debate on Article 113, Germany's policy on minority rights delved into the Jewish Question. In the final sitting it was decided that minorities within Germany would be defined on the basis of linguistic criteria rather than national. According to the wording of this policy, German Jews were not recognised as minorities within Germany. Internationally, however, Jews were for the first time recognised as a distinct minority group deserving of cultural autonomous rights. At the Paris Peace Conference, as chapter five will examine, Germany became the only country to sign a peace treaty which did not guarantee minority protections.

The importance of the debates in the National Assembly and constitutional committee on minority rights was that they triggered conceptual discussions on the German state in a two-fold process. On the one hand, Oskar Cohn's petition caused an unintentional conversation on Jewish identity within Germany. The debate clearly pitted the left-liberal Hugo Preuss and his mainly liberal Jewish supporters[122] against the Zionist Cohn revealing larger questions confronting the German Jewish community on their confessional or national status.

On the other hand, the Jewish Question raised by Cohn challenged the concept of German nationhood. The discussion highlighted the rootedness of German national understanding in ideas of culture, language and descent and exposed the challenge that despite speaking German, minority groups would still remain foreigners (*Fremde*) within Germany. Whilst the German national project since the nineteenth century had sought to transform the German *Kulturnation* into a *Staatsnation* the debate on minority rights called into question the effectiveness of this project and the extent to which it had been achieved.

---

122 By 'Preuss's supporters' I mean Katzenstein (SPD), Davidsohn (SPD) and Gröber (Catholic Centre).

V 'Tagesordnung: Judenfrage': a German (Jewish) united front at Paris

On the 26 March Otto Göppert, one of the members of the German Delegation to Paris, and later Chairman of the Peace Delegation, received a telegram inviting him to a meeting at 21 Behrenstrasse in Berlin, the Offices for Peace Negotiations. The agenda of the meeting: the Jewish Question.[1] Convening the meeting was the German Ambassador to the United States of America, Johann Heinrich Graf von Bernstorff[2] who, in his opening speech, clarified the purpose of the meeting,

> Gentlemen, although it is not yet certain whether the Jewish Question will be discussed at the preliminary peace conference, it is still desirable that we express our views on this issue, especially since this is one of the questions where we might be in a position [...] to face our enemies with a positive programme in hand, a programme that will solve the problem in principle, through which we will regain world-wide sympathy, and which will prove that a new spirit is at large in Germany.[3]

Alike to the debate on the *Judenzählung*, which revealed the German Empire at a critical juncture between past and future, the suggestion by Graf von Bernstorff that forming a position on the Jewish Question would show a 'new spirit' in Germany once again revealed the unique function of the Jewish Question as a spotlight on Germany's difficult transition between Empire and Republic, caught between war and peace. Where the previous chapter focused on the Jewish Question in domestic debates on minority rights in the Weimar constitution, this chapter turns to the larger interna-

---

1 Göppert's letter invited him to attend a meeting on *Judenfragen*. The minutes of the meeting described the agenda as the *Judenfrage*. R19605 AA, 'K181842', 26 March 1919.
2 Graf von Bernstorff (1862–1939) served as the German Ambassador to the United States from 1908 to 1917 and Ambassador to the Ottoman Empire for the last year of the war. He was one of the founding members of the German Democratic Party and later became Chairman of the German Pro-Palestine Committee.
3 The conference record has been translated and published in Matthäus, 'Tagesordnung', 91–110.

tional dynamics governing the debate on minority rights, focusing in particular on the German delegations' preparations for the Paris Peace Conference.

In what follows I will firstly trace the German deliberations on minority protections leading up to the Paris Peace Conference which began in March 1919 firstly in the Cabinet, then in the Office for Peace Negotiations (also known as *Pax Konferenz*) and finally in Versailles itself. The events reveal that the German government struggled with how best to define minority protections in light of minorities within Germany but crucially also with German minorities abroad in mind. The differing minority existence for Jews in Germany (who did not want to be considered a nation) and Germans in new states (who did) coupled with the fixation on the notion of reciprocity meant that the authorities struggled to formulate a decisive policy on minority protections for the peace negotiations.

Significantly, in preparation for Paris a meeting was convened on Jewish questions. The Foreign Ministry recognised that this was one of the few issues where Germany could present a 'positive programme' and in doing so, 'regain word-wide sympathy'.[4] By May the German delegation realised that the peace conference would not involve negotiations and that the extensive preparations by the *Pax Konferenz* had been in vain. In Versailles, unlike in Weimar, the minority in focus were Germans in new states. National minority protections were embedded within the Minority Treaty and Jews were awarded cultural autonomous rights. The course of events, unfolding in under a year, from the drafting of the Weimar constitution to the signing of the Treaty of Versailles and the Minority Treaty, reveals how the Jewish Question was not 'solved' as Graf Bernstorff had hoped. Rather in 1919 it became even more inextricably bound to the international system, the structure of modern nation-state and the German Question.[5]

Preparing for Paris: the German delegation and minority protections

On the morning of the 21 March 1919, at 9:30am the Cabinet[6] convened in the Reich Chancellery to discuss a completed draft peace treaty that, the German government had received word, was due to be sent by the Allies. Count Brockdorff-Rantzau remarked that the draft diverged widely from the Wilson programme, which the Germans had initially clung onto during the agreements for armistice. Predicting a harsh

---

4 Opening speech by the Chairman Graf Bernstorff in the meeting on *Judenfragen*. See Matthäus, 91.
5 As Aschheim writes, in Paris, 'Germany's concern for the Jews of the east was made into an issue'. The Germans hoped that the loyalty of Eastern European Jews could help Germany retain its eastern borders. Aschheim, *Brothers and Strangers*, 139–41.
6 The Cabinet was the direct continuation of the Cabinet of the Council of People's Commissars. The first meeting was held on the 11 March 1919. The minutes of this meeting are online as part of the files of the Reich Chancellery of the Weimar Republic [https://goo.gl/inztSS, accessed 11/12/17].

outcome for Germany, should the peace terms be dictated by the European powers, the Germans welcomed the Wilson programme, which had excluded questions on freedom of the seas, the matter of Schleswig in the north and a possible German-Austrian union. However, the draft treaty prepared by the Allies diverged widely from Wilson's initial programme and directly confronted the aforementioned questions.

During the Reich Ministry meeting, in order to prepare for the draft treaty and decide upon Germany's negotiating strategy, the Foreign Minister separated the peace treaty into ten subsections. The protection of minorities was the second point of order, after territorial questions. In the ensuing meeting, out of the four ministers to make a statement on Germany's position, three of these happened to be ministers of Jewish descent.[7] That these ministers, whose portfolios do not suggest any expertise on the subject, spoke on the matter suggests a concern for minority rights amongst Jewish politicians even if not all minority rights issues concerned Jews.

Each minister adopted a slightly different position on what Germany's approach towards minority rights should be in the negotiations, but all largely agreed that it would be vital to secure the rights of German nationals in foreign territory. Reich Minister Georg Gothein suggested that Germany should not stress particular German interests but instead 'advocate protection of national minorities on general principle'.[8] This was a policy also supported by the Zionists, although there is nothing that suggests Gothein was a Zionist.[9] Gothein was more likely advocating that Germany should not fall out of favour in the negotiations on this policy by making specific German demands.

Reich Minister Erzberger[10] believed that minority rights should be limited to inhabitants, not temporary residents, whilst Reich Finance Minister Schiffer pointed at implementing similar guarantees to Austria. These included granting citizenship to Germans resident outside the country, a descent and language-oriented policy that would later be ratified in the constitution. State Under Secretary Lewald noted that the incorporation of 'far-reaching regulations for the protection of national minorities in the constitution' needed to be stressed in the discussions.[11] The fact that he would make this comment when little to no regulations protecting national minorities were being incorporated into the constitution suggests that perhaps the Under Secretary

---

7 These included Schiffer (Finance Minister), Gothein (*Reichsschatzminister*) and Lewald (State Undersecretary).

8 R19605 AA, 'K182002', November 1918.

9 Gothein was Protestant and of Jewish descent. Politically he was always a member of liberal parties, the Progressive Party and later the German Democratic Party. There is no biographical information to suggest he might have been Zionist. His profile can be found online in the *Deutsche Biographie* [https://bit.ly/2KdZtJi, accessed 14/12/17] and Reich Chancellery archives [https://bit.ly/2ZnP8iW, accessed 14/12/17].

10 In the first cabinet under Chancellor Scheidemann, Matthias Erzberger from the Catholic Centre Party did not have an official ministerial portfolio.

11 'Meeting of the Reich Ministry, March 21, 1919, 9:30am in the Reich Chancellery' in Burdick and Lutz, *The Political Institutions of the German Revolution*, 268–274, especially 271.

was misinformed, or that Cohn's petition had a wider support base than that which was represented in the National Assembly and constitutional committee sessions.

Thus, by the 21 March the German government felt that they would soon be confronted with a 'take it or leave it'[12] situation put forth by the Allies. When it came to the position on minority rights, the Cabinet lacked consensus especially given that the policy aimed at minority groups living in Germany might also apply for Germans living abroad.

Just five days later, on the 26 March 1919, Otto Göppert in the Foreign Ministry received a telegram from the Secretariat of the Offices for the Peace Negotiations (*Geschäftsstelle für die Friedensverhandlungen Sekretariat*) inviting him to a meeting on 'Jewish questions'.[13] The Offices for the Peace Negotiations, was the first official organisation founded on the mandate to prepare for future peace negotiations.[14] The necessity of planning for a future peace deal was first realised by Chancellor Hertling who on the 4 December 1917 requested Karl Helfferich[15] to gather information on economic questions, which would have to be negotiated in a future peace treaty with Russia.[16] It was Helfferich who first conceived of the strategy to invite private experts to assist in this preparatory work largely by offering advice and issuing questionnaires to high-level individuals in industry, commerce, banking and agriculture. Yet it was Bernstorff[17] who would, almost a year later in October 1918, put these ideas into practice as head of the organisation *Pax Konferenz*, after being ordered by State Secretary Wilhelm Solf to prepare for an imminent peace deal.[18]

The work of the *Pax Konferenz* consisted of preparing memoranda for the peace conference, as the Germans were convinced that the Allies would invite them to face-to-face negotiations.[19] The organisation consisted of a core of forty civil servants but invited hundreds of experts and government officials to attend meetings to help advise on the specific clauses of each memorandum. Meetings often followed the same structure. Apart from the relevant civil servants and ministers one of two groups of private

---

12 Count Brockdorff-Rantzau used this expression to describe the draft of the Treaty of Versailles. The Germans did not receive the completed draft until the 7 May 1919. Ibid, 269.

13 R19605 AA, 'K181842', 26 March 1919.

14 The second official organisation was the Committee for Peace Negotiations in the National Assembly, founded on 10 April 1919. The only unofficial, yet still influential, body that also started preparations for future peace negotiations was the Association for Policy of Justice, also known as the Heidelberg Association (*Heidlberger Vereinigung*).

15 Karl Helfferich (1871–1924) was a member of the German People's Party. His profile is online in the *Deutsche Biographie* [https://bit.ly/2LWXhrr, accessed 12/05/18].

16 Alma Luckau, *The German Delegation at the Paris Peace Conference*, 2nd ed. (New York: Howard Fertig, 1971), 28.

17 Count Bernstorff was serving in Constantinople at the time but was called back to Berlin to take up this position.

18 Alma Luckau, *The German Delegation at the Paris Peace Conference*, 29.

19 Ibid.

experts would be invited to participate. The first group consisted of thirty-eight experts selected from industry, banking and agriculture. They were called upon to actively participate in drafting memoranda. At the time of the Paris Peace Conference, some of these experts were called upon to advise the German delegation. The second group was unlimited in number and tasked to provide information when necessary.[20]

By March these meetings took place virtually daily as civil servants, experts and government officials assembled to predict which problems could be expected to arise in the upcoming negotiations in Paris. In the few months before the German government was invited to send a delegation to Paris, the *Pax Konferenz* had prepared over fifty-one files on issues they thought might arise in the peace negotiations, which they had inferred from reading Allied newspaper reports.[21] It was against this backdrop of preparation for the Paris Peace Conference that Göppert, one of the members of the German Delegation to Paris, and later Chairman of the Peace Delegation, received a telegram inviting him to a meeting to discuss 'Jewish questions' (*Judenfragen*) in the Offices for Peace Negotiations at 21 Behrenstrasse, Berlin on Monday 31 March 1919.[22]

Convening the 11:30 am meeting at Behrenstrasse was the diplomat Graf von Bernstorff. In attendance were high-ranking Foreign Office ministers, including the future Foreign Minister Walter Simons, civil servants from the Office for Peace Negotiations and an expert commission for Jewish affairs (*Sachverständigenkommission für jüdische Angelegenheiten*).[23] Moritz Sobernheim was in attendance in his capacity as the Jewish Affairs Expert in the Foreign Ministry. Joining him was Eugen Fuchs, Director of the Central Association, Richard Lichtheim, representative of the Zionist Federation, Hermann Struck, who headed the Jewish Affairs section in the *Ober-Ost*, Eduard Bernstein, the Social Democratic politician, James Simon, from the Aid Association of German Jews, Oskar Cohn, Independent Social Democratic politician, and Walther Rathenau, industrialist and future Foreign Minister.[24]

The meeting on Jewish questions was significant for a number of reasons. On the part of Jewish representation, it illustrated that despite political and religious differences within the Jewish community, the attendees were able to organise a united front to present their expectations for the peace negotiations.[25] On the part of the German government the organisation of a meeting on Jewish questions signified that it was in the German interest to respond to Jewish questions which were tied into Germa-

---

20 Ibid.
21 Ibid, 30–31.
22 R19605 AA, 'K181842'.
23 Ibid, 'K181845', 1 April 1919.
24 Matthäus, 'Tagesordnung', 87.
25 The conflict between the Central Association and Zionist Federation had reached its zenith in 1912 and yet at this meeting a cross-section of the Jewish community was represented. On the tensions between Jewish organisations see Lamberti, 'From Coexistence to Conflict'; Jehuda Reinharz, 'Advocacy and History: The Case of the Centralverein and Zionists', *Leo Baeck Institute Year Book* 33, no. 1 (1988): 113–22.

ny's future, internationally. For Graf Bernstorff the *Judenfrage* was Germany's entry ticket back into the international community. Bernstorff hoped that it would help 'regain world-wide sympathy' for Germany and 'prove that a new spirit is at large in Germany'.[26] The language of a 'new spirit' featured prominently in the sitting.

Even before the meeting on the 31 March, the German government unofficially encouraged devising a position on the Jewish Question for the peace negotiations. The Jewish Question was recognised as a topic that would be on the post-war international agenda. On the 30 January 1919 the morning edition of the *Deutsche Allgemeine Zeitung* (DAZ), the unofficial organ of the Foreign Ministry,[27] ran an article entitled, *Die Judenfrage auf der Friedenskonferenz*.[28] The article began by reporting that a Jewish representation would be present at the peace conference and that the United Kingdom had invited Zionists to a seat at the League of Nations table. This information would have piqued the attention of the German delegation who strongly supported the League of Nations project and might have provided the impetus for organising a meeting on *Judenfragen*. The Germans calculated that building closer ties with Jewish representatives would be instrumental to regaining Germany's international prestige. As Graf Bernstorff noted in the meeting on the 31 March, it was one of the few issue areas where Germany was in the position to 'face our enemies with a positive programme in hand'.[29] This was recognised by the author of the article in the DAZ who urged that given Allied recognition of Jewish issues, Jewish demands would need to be taken into account.

When placed next to Jewish demands, German demands did not differ greatly wrote the anonymous author of the article on 'The Jewish Question at the Peace Conference'.[30] The author stressed that Jews would be imperative for post-war German foreign relations, in both a regional context and a colonial one. The article acknowledged the developments in war on the Eastern Front where the German leadership had confronted a practical Jewish Question, as examined in chapter two. To the east, the article stressed, the most important task for German politics would be to encourage national autonomy for the Jews, guaranteeing order in the region. In the Middle East, 'Palestine could solve the difficult Jewish Question'.[31] Given the affinity

---

26 Matthäus, 'Tagesordnung', 91.
27 For the history of the NAZ/DAZ and its rise and fall as an organ of the Foreign Ministry from Bismarck to Hitler see Heinz-Dietrich Fischer, 'The "Deutsche Allgemeine Zeitung" (1861–1945)', *Gazette (Leiden Netherlands)* 13, no. 1 (1967): 35–46. See also Bernard Fulda, *Press and Politics in the Weimar Republic* (Oxford: Oxford University Press, 2009), 22–26.
28 R19605 AA, 'K181762', 30 January 1919.
29 Matthäus, 'Tagesordnung', 91.
30 Whilst it is not clear from this article what these Jewish demands were, one can infer that they were closely related to the demands outlined by the Jewish expert commission in the meeting with the Foreign Office in March.
31 The 'east' the article referred to most likely entailed the area where the *Ober-Ost* command had been stationed. This included modern day Lithuania, Poland, Belarus and Ukraine. Here the army had come into

between Jewish and German language and culture, an East European Jewish presence, the author suggested, would help secure a German gateway for oriental expansion. As chapter two has shown, using the Jews as mediators of German interests was a policy first suggested to the Foreign Ministry by the Committee for the East in August 1914. Whilst these plans were put on hold as a result of the retreat of the Central Powers and their eventual defeat, the article suggests that these ideas were still in circulation within the Foreign Office, even after the war.

The interest amongst the German authorities in Jewish political affairs is also seen in the founding of the German Pro-Palestine Committee (*Deutsches Komitee Pro-Palästina*). The committee was first established in 1918 and re-founded in 1926. It received support from prominent individuals in government and industry, including Matthias Erzberger, Philip Scheidemann, Werner Sombart, Alfred and Max Weber, Hans Delbrück, Gustav Noske and Major Franz Carl Endres.[32] When the first committee was established on the 25 April 1918 a series of articles were published on the benefits of the Jewish Palestine movement for the 'expansion of German culture and economic relations in the Far East'.[33] Winning back the sympathies of Eastern European Jews, which they had lost by the end of the war, in order to advance German interests ran through the Foreign Office's deliberations on preparing for the peace conference. However, as the Germans were not invited to negotiate peace with the Allies, as their borders were reduced and colonies were taken away, the German delegation had no power to dictate the future outcome of international affairs neither beyond German borders nor in the Middle East.

It is undeniable that Jewish questions were on the minds of the German leadership both during as well as at the end of the war. During the war, the German army had confronted a practical Jewish Question on the Eastern Front, and in Palestine. Bodenheimer of the Committee for the East had proposed using Russian Jews as mediators of German interests in return for German protection. After the war, the Foreign Ministry realised once again that supporting Jewish affairs would aid German interests. This time, however, it would involve backing German Jewish demands internationally to, in turn, restore Germany's position in the international community. Of the whole host of issues that the First World War threw into relief it is extraordinary that Jewish questions even featured on the agenda of the German Foreign Ministry. And yet, quite remarkably the German government recognised that the Jewish Question was their key to the door of the international club.

---

contact with East European Jews. With the help of German Jews, they worked closely with Russian Jews due to the linguistic similarities between Yiddish and German. By 1917 the *Ober-Ost* had created a position in their political office to deal specifically with Jewish affairs. It was headed by Hermann Struck.

32 For the first committee in 1918 see Anon., *Judische Rundschau* XVIII, no. 21 (3 Mai 1918):133–34; Zechlin, *Die deutsche Politik und die Juden im Ersten Weltkrieg*, 413–48. For the second committee from 1926 to 1933 see, Walk, 'Das "Deutsche Komitee Pro Palästina"'.

33 Walk, 'Das "Deutsche Komitee Pro Palästina"', 162.

Formulating a position on the Jewish Question for Paris

The minutes of the meeting (*Niederschrift einer Besprechung über Judenfragen*) and a memo recording the Jewish demands (*Aufzeichnung zu den jüdischen Forderungen für die Friedenskonferenz*) are the two remaining documents on the meeting of the 31 March 1919. Of interest are the differences between these two documents. The memo is a summary of the demands with a brief explanation of each and roughly follows Sobernheim's account from the minutes of the meeting although no quotations marks were used, and the document is anonymised.[34] Most likely this memo is a copy of Sobernheim's point by point report to the meeting with slight modifications. The minutes, however, present a wholly different picture of what transpired. They reveal how the discussion of the demands descended into a lively debate. The discussion concerned distrust in the German authorities because of antisemitic policies, the fears of *Ostjuden* immigration, the recognition of Eastern European Jews as a nation or cultural community and the international ramifications of this decision for other (national) minorities.

An underlying theme in the minutes of the meeting was that it was in Germany's interest to support Jewish demands as it would signal the heralding of a truly 'new spirit' in the Weimar Republic. The Germans also hoped that by rekindling the support they had received from Eastern European Jews during the war it would possibly help secure German dominion over their former Eastern borders.[35] And yet, in the course of the meeting, the Jewish representatives continuously reminded the German officials that relations with Eastern Jews had disintegrated and particularly nearing the end of the war Polish Jews had lost complete trust in the German authorities.[36]

The episode brings to light the complexity of the Jewish Question in the post-war context as the DAZ reported, the 'Jewish Question has undergone significant development during the war, and this has given the right to anyone interested, to discuss it'.[37] Moreover, it reveals that the Jewish Question was one significant component in the deliberations on how best to redraw global borders whether by: self-determination, ethnic-national or cultural-national homogeneity or history.[38]

---

34 R19605 AA, 'K181838', March 1919.
35 Aschheim, *Brothers and Strangers*, 139–41.
36 Fuchs explained in the meeting, 'I do not know if you are sufficiently familiar with history to know that in 1914 and 1915 the Polish Jews saw the Germans as liberators, going over to the German camp with drums beating and banners flying high, but that they later said: rather [be] Russian than German-Prussian'. Matthäus, 'Tagesordnung', 98.
37 R19605, AA, 'K181762'.
38 On the use and importance of history at the Paris Peace Conference see Margaret MacMillan and Patrick Quinton-Brown, 'The Uses of History in International Society: From the Paris Peace Conference to the Present', *International Affairs* 95, no. 1 (2019): 181–200.

A total of six demands for the peace negotiations were made by the Jewish expert commission during the meeting on *Judenfragen*. The first two were for equal rights (*Gleichberechtigung*) and equality (*Gleichstellung*) for Jews and Jewry in all countries of the world as well as the abolition of all laws, regulations, and decrees that only discriminated against Jews. Sobernheim began by highlighting the continued gap between law and practice. He explained that 'whilst equal rights for Jews living in the West were anchored in the respective constitutions, in spite of this, until recently, the Jews of Germany were not equal to other citizens and various career paths were closed to them'.[39] In principle, the emancipation act of 1871 had removed all discriminations against German Jews and yet in practice several career paths remained restricted. In public professions in Germany traditional customs prevailed over a meritocratic system of admission. This was particularly evident in the career pathways into the army and higher education, where appointment was still based on personal recommendations and contacts.[40]

Sobernheim emphasised how legal discriminations still prevailed pointing to 'former Russia' (Poland in the recording) and Romania where 'genuine equality for Jews [has] not yet started' but also in Prussia which, during the war, banned Jewish immigration. 'In Prussia' Sobernheim reminded the audience, 'as well as in other countries, such prohibitions [towards Jews] existed either openly or clandestinely during the war'.[41] Sobernheim was referring to the Prussian *Einwanderungsverbot* which came into effect on the 24 April 1918 and was directed only at Jewish workers from Congress Poland.[42] The subject sparked a heated debate at the meeting and dominated the conference proceedings. Whilst it began as a discussion between Sobernheim, Lenz (Prussian Minister of the Interior) and Eugen Fuchs on the decree, it opened up into a larger discussion on Jewish national understandings, the implication of the ban for Germany and on Germany's position on Jewish questions internationally.

Before continuing onto the list of demands made by the Jewish expert commission, a brief detour into this exchange on the *Einwanderungsverbot* offers a wholly unique perspective on a dialogue between liberal, secular, national Jews and German officials on the Jewish Question. It offers a microcosmic study of larger trends within the debate on the Jewish Question. Whereby when arguing against anti-Jewish discriminations, individuals would elevate the issue to a matter concerning humanity. In contrast, the official response from the government instead tried to circumvent the antisemitic implication of the decree and offer logical justifications for why it was enacted.

---

39 R19605, AA, 'K181838', 1. See also, Matthäus, 'Tagesordnung', 92.
40 Whenever a discussion in the Reichstag was raised on military finances, Cohn and Bernstein repeatedly raised the issue that Jews continued to be denied promotion to officer status. For more on the eventual removal of discriminations against Jews in the army see chapter three on the *Judenzählung*.
41 Matthäus, 'Tagesordnung', 92.
42 The Political Archives of the German Foreign Office contains a file with numerous documents on this decree. See, for example, R19605 AA, *Internationale Angelegenheiten Nr. 3: Die Juden, Band 1&2*.

Regarding the April 1918 Prussian decree to ban Jewish immigration, Lenz explained that the order was 'an [unforeseen] consequence of a measure taken by the German administration in Warsaw', which prohibited Jews from working in Germany because it was medically assessed that the Jewish community were the 'inhabitants most likely to increase the danger of typhoid [infection]'. This point was confirmed by his colleague Hering who claimed it was instituted out of 'practical experience'.[43]

On the basis of the decree Fuchs, who described himself as 'representative of the *nationaldeutsche*[44] Jews' throughout, declared that as 'we do not have the necessary trust in how the authorities have acted up to now' it was even more imperative that Point 2[45] was presented at the peace conference.[46] Sobernheim requested that countries wishing to 'prohibit immigration for economic reasons' should have to seek approval from the League of Nations.[47] Markedly, the Jewish experts kept affirming that the immigration of *Ostjuden* was a case of economic migration and an issue affecting not just Jews but also Germans who might be 'forced to emigrate' given the state of the post-war economy.[48] They also noted the economic successes of Jews in America declaring 'there can be no talk of danger when you obtain a work force'.[49]

In response, Hering cautioned against the immigration of *Ostjuden* to Germany 'in the interest of preserving the culture of its own [the German] people' against a people 'who have sunk to a great extent to an extremely low cultural level'.[50] Hering's language epitomised that of an institution locked in its national-cultural tradition in contradistinction to the Jewish representatives who continuously moved between the particular, that the targeting of Jews was antisemitic, and the general that these acts violated 'human rights' and were 'not in keeping with humanity'.[51] The Jewish population was not considered 'unclean' by nature of being Jewish as Lenz had suggested, Bernstein

---

43 Matthäus, 'Tagesordnung', 93.

44 At the time this word was not used to denote party-political affiliation. Rather it was frequently deployed by the Central Association in contradistinction to *jüdisch-national*. For the misinterpretation of this term especially when used by the Central Association see Arnold Paucker, 'Zur Problematik einer jüdischen Abwehrstrategie in der deutschen Gesellschaft', in *Juden in Wilhelminischen Deutschland 1890–1914*, ed. Werner E. Mosse, 2nd ed. (Tübingen: Schriftenreihe wissenschaftlicher Abhandlungen des Leo Baeck Instituts 33, 1998), 526.

45 Point 2 read: 'Abolition and prohibition of all laws, decrees and regulations containing restrictive measures applicable exclusively to Jews, especially bans on immigration and the closing of borders to Jews'. Matthäus, 'Tagesordnung', 91.

46 Ibid, 98.

47 This was, as Sobernheim explained, a demand made at the International Socialist conference. Ibid, 92.

48 Ibid, 95.

49 Ibid, 101.

50 From 1895 to 1905 Prussia wanted to transform into a state of immigration. From 1909 to 1911, on average 8,984 migrants per year were naturalised. See Daniela L. Caglioti, 'Subjects, Citizens, and Aliens in a Time of Upheaval: Naturalizing and Denaturalizing in Europe during the First World War', *The Journal of Modern History* 89, no. 3 (September 2017): 511.

51 Matthäus, 'Tagesordnung', 94.

pointed out. Whilst Fuchs noted that it was unlikely that typhoid would only affect Jewish inhabitants.[52]

The third demand that was made concerned the recognition of national and cultural autonomy in the newly formed states 'to the extent demanded by the majority of Jews', underpinned by the right to self-determination and of concern only for 'states which have yet to be established'. Cohn explained that the demand had been included on the basis that the commission decided that 'the German delegation must somehow take a position on Jewish questions outside of Palestine'.[53] Although directed at the new states, the discussion was also revealing for the future status of German Jews given the possible international recognition of Jewry as a national-cultural community.

Sobernheim elaborated that national autonomy depended upon the 'principle of the right to self-determination', which he accredited not to Woodrow Wilson but rather Karl Renner.[54] Whilst Renner's nationality principle was devised with the Austro-Hungarian Empire in mind, it was quickly picked up by Jewish intellectuals who applied it to the situation of Jews in Eastern Europe. When the German army entered West Russian territory in 1914, Max Bodenheimer presented a blueprint of an East European Federation recognising Jewish nationality, inspired by Renner's writings.[55] From 1914 to 1919 the legacy of this concept can be traced to the peace conference where it was advocated by the British Jewish diplomat, Lucien Wolf who was not a Zionist himself but supported national Jewish rights. As a result of the war liberal Jews became aware of the existence of Jews living in Russia as national, culturally autonomous communities. They began to support national rights but only for these eastern 'national and religious communities', not for all Jews generally.[56]

Written in 1917, Lucien Wolf argued for (Jewish) national rights in Eastern Europe within the framework of a federation of nationalities.[57] His article, 'The Jewish National Movement' was indebted to ideas expressed by Karl Renner in his 'The Struggle of the Austrian Nations for the State' written in 1902. Drawing on Renner, Wolf envisioned a federalised state structure of groups sharing political citizenship but not personal nationality. In other words, Wolf advocated a modernised political structure similar to that of the former Ottoman and Hapsburg Empires.[58] It was this structure, indebted to

---

52 Ibid.
53 Ibid, 107.
54 R19605, AA, 'K181838'; Matthäus, 'Tagesordnung', 101.
55 This is the subject of chapter two where it is explained in greater depth.
56 Term used by Eugen Fuchs to describe Eastern Jews in the *Judenfragen* meeting. Matthäus, 'Tagesordnung', 99.
57 Lucien Wolf, 'The Jewish National Movement', *Edinburgh Review*, 1917. Cited in Mark Levene, 'Nationalism and Its Alternatives in the International Arena: The Jewish Question at Paris, 1919', *Journal of Contemporary History* 28, no. 3 (July 1993): 520.
58 In the peace negotiations Wolf vowed by the 'Renner principle' as a possible system to implement in the new Eastern European states in particular, Ukraine where the Jewish minority was already operating on a semi-autonomous level. See ibid.

Renner but applied to Eastern European Jews that the Jewish expert commission demanded in point three. The paradox of the third demand was that it was in the moment
when the nation-state ideal was taking hold that Jews began to appreciate that their
rights would best be secured under a 'federal, decentralised model'.[59]

Following this strand of thought, advocated by Renner and Wolf, the expert commission requested the recognition of the Jewish minority as a nation in its own right
(*als eigene Nation*). Alike, Sobernheim explained, to the German minorities in Hun-
gary and Bohemia. This meant, he continued, that they would be allowed political
representation,[60] the recognition of their minority language, the right to language interpretation in courts and the appointment of Jewish judges in civil courts. Cultural
autonomy would involve freedom in all cultural domains, especially schools, the de-
duction of cultural tax from state tax and the freedom to observe the Sabbath. The latter was requested to be considered in 'Poland, German-Austria (*Deutsch-Österreich*),
Czechoslovakia and Yugoslavia', four out of the twelve new states that were founded
after the war. The Jewish representatives, however, clearly stressed that this would not
be applied to Jews living in Germany.

On the subject of German Jews, Fuchs intervened to ensure it was made clear that
German Jews were 'German nationals' (*deutschnational*) that they 'belong to the German nation' and 'are part of the German people' (*deutschvölkisch*).[61] Making a theoretical observation, Fuchs used ideas espoused by Lazarus to argue that German Jews
belonged to the German nation, declaring, 'the decisive concept of nationality in my
opinion, is will, putting aside the objective aspects of language, history and baptism of
blood on the battlefields [...] roughly calculated, 500,000 Jews have the will to belong
to Germany [*Deutschtum*] as a people'.[62]

Fuchs clearly differentiated between German Jews and Jews living in Eastern Europe whom he acknowledged had a 'kind of nationality'. Fuchs based this observation on the fact that Eastern European Jews spoke a different language, had a unique,
distinctive culture and lived in a closed 'ghetto-like manner'. These conditions, for
Fuchs, designated that Eastern European Jews could be characterised as a cultural nation. Should 'Polish Jews achieve recognition as a nation according to the law of self-
determination' Fuchs commented, 'I will be happy'.[63] Building on an idea formulated

----

59 Simon Rabinovitch, *Jewish Rights, National Rites: Nationalism and Autonomy in Late Imperial and Revolutionary Russia*, Stanford Studies in Jewish History and Culture (Stanford, California: Stanford University
Press, 2014), 258.
60 'That means they would have their own election register for the legislative authorities and for the local government administration, with the number of seats being in proportion to their percentage in the
population and with representation at all higher administrative authorities on a percentage basis as well'.
Matthäus, 'Tagesordnung', 102.
61 Ibid, 99.
62 Ibid.
63 Ibid, 105.

by Max Bodenheimer in August 1914, Fuchs argued that should Polish Jews become a nation and not succumb to becoming Polonised, they would offer a buffer for the Germans against the Poles.[64]

Deploying a rational, humanitarian argument the representative of the Zionist Federation Richard Lichtheim advised that it would not harm German interests to support this third demand on the grounds of 'general humanitarian principles, on the idea of freedom'. Lichtheim was the only Jewish representative to describe Jews in ethnic terms, as a 'national race [*nationale Rasse*] or religion' but wanted to avoid this discussion of Jewish identity all together. Instead, Lichtheim acknowledged the dangers involved in granting autonomous rights to a smaller national group (*Volksgruppe*). He recognised that it could lead to 'economic exclusion and cultural alienation' but he reminded the attendees of the situation: 'we are confronted by the fact that six million Eastern European Jews demand national or cultural or national-cultural autonomy'.[65]

Contrary to the liberal Jewish position of Fuchs and the Zionist stance of Lichtheim, Walther Rathenau warned of the 'grave international questions' that would arise should the German authorities support this demand. 'At the peace conference we should try to prevent any precedent that could be used against us', advised Rathenau echoing Preuss's position during the constitutional debates. Reciprocity featured centrally in the Foreign Ministry's position on minority protections and Rathenau was of the same opinion,

> At the moment when the government of the German Reich interferes with the self-determination of other nationalities, we have to expect reciprocity as a matter of course. If we advocate that a part of the population in certain states receives autonomy, then we have opened the door to the same claim by minorities on us.[66]

Rathenau also argued that it was important to not 'single out the Jews' but rather advocate for the rights of other minorities. Fuchs's response, however, clearly explained why this demand had been included. Germany 'no longer occupied a dominant position in the east', Fuchs observed, and as such would have little influence over deciding upon minority rights provisions.

Having lost the war, Germany lost all claims to influencing the future of Eastern European affairs. The Germans also lost the support of a valuable ally: Russian Jews who had initially welcomed the German occupation in 1914. Aware of the current state of affairs, the Jewish representatives urged that it was imperative that Germany support the proposals they had listed. Supporting these Jewish demands would signal that the Republic truly embodied the 'new spirt' Graf Bernstorff had alluded to in his opening speech. Moreover, offering this support would not be difficult given that the 'well-

---

64 Ibid, 104.
65 Ibid, 106.
66 Ibid, 105.

understood interests of Germanness [*Deutschtum*] have never excluded the justified claims of the Jews'.[67] As Pick (Head of the Lodz Police Force and Deputy Director of the Press Department) explained,

> What purpose might our conclusions have? They are to show the world that our former policies regarding the Jewish Question, how it has been dealt with in Germany so far, has not been right, and that Germany has learned to mend its ways. We regard it as an essential task for Germany to show the world that the old ways have gone. And they have to go with regard to the Jews as well.[68]

After the war, the treatment of German Jews and the rights of Jews internationally was bound into the heralding of a 'new spirit' in Germany.

The fourth point in the Jewish demands concerned the 'Palestine question'. As the demand for a Jewish commonwealth (*Gemeinwesen*) had already been accepted by the Council for Ten,[69] Sobernheim clarified that the German Jewish addition to this would be that 'no Jew, whichever state he belongs to, is excluded from working, visiting or emigrating to the settlement of Palestine'.[70] The commission clarified that it took a distinctly more neutral and moderate position on Palestine as compared to the Zionist Federation and the Copenhagen Manifesto by not terming it a 'homeland' for the Jewish people but rather a 'commonwealth'.

The penultimate demand requested compensation for victims of pogroms 'by the state concerned'. The wave of violence and pogroms against Jews in the lands of the former Russian Empire including Romania and Ukraine in the spring of 1919 had not gone unnoticed internationally.[71] Reports on these pogroms were often censored to avoid anti-pogrom propaganda affecting the international status of new states.[72] Nonetheless, at the grassroots level, anti-pogrom marches were held in Britain, the Netherlands and America.[73] At the peace negotiations in Paris, the Council of Four was aware of the gravity of the situation. The subject of antisemitism in Poland was raised by both Woodrow Wilson, the President of the United States, and Lloyd George, Prime Minister of the United Kingdom. They agreed that legal and political guarantees would have

---

67 Ibid, 104.
68 Ibid, 100.
69 By March the Council of Ten was reduced to the Council of Four, the latter included the representatives of United Kingdom, United States of America, France and Italy.
70 R19605, AA, 'K181838', 181838; Matthäus, 'Tagesordnung', 108.
71 Levene suggests that the scale and dimension of anti-Jewish pogroms in the Ukraine 'invite comparison with Hitler's 1941 invasion'. Levene, 'Nationalism and Its Alternatives in the International Arena: The Jewish Question at Paris, 1919', July 1993, 526. In December 1918 the *Jüdisch-Politische Nachrichten* reported that ritual murders against Jews were still taking place in the Russian Empire. See R19606, AA, 'K182192'.
72 A telegram was sent to the Foreign Office to report that in Ukraine Jewish massacres were being hushed to avoid bad press. See R19605, AA, 'K181943', 20 Juni 1919. Between November to June 1919 around 197 instances of pogroms in Poland were reported. See ibid, 'K181976', 27 July 1919.
73 Ibid, 'K181948', 28 Juli 1919. See also ibid, 'K182003', 4 August 1919.

to be included in the peace treaty with the new states to control against antisemitism.[74] Ensuring Jewish questions became humanitarian concerns, as the expert commission had done, successfully tied Jewish affairs into the international minorities system.

The sixth and last proposal requested the establishment of an international committee to monitor all outcomes of the Paris Peace Conference concerning Jews. It was envisioned that the committee could aid in protecting Eastern European Jews who would soon reside as minorities in the newly created states. Describing the Jewish Question in universalist language and evoking Woodrow Wilson's fourteen-point programme, as in the penultimate demand, the treatment of Jews was elevated to a level of international, humanitarian proportions. It was described not only as a question for the Jews but as a universal humanitarian concern (*allweltliche Menschheitsfrage*), 'which accordingly has to be solved by all people collectively'.[75] By framing the Jewish Question as above national politics and in humanitarian terms, the Jewish expert commission, was careful to avoid accusations that their proposal meddled with the internal affairs of states.

The session concluded with the indication that further discussions would take place. Graf Bernstorff beseeched the ministry representatives to issue a verbal or oral response on the meeting. Unfortunately, the responses by the ministries, which were not given in the meeting itself are a matter of speculation as no further documents remain on the meeting or its outcome. In all likelihood the records were destroyed or lost. However, it is also possible that further meetings on *Judenfragen* did not take place given that by May the Allies presented the Germans with the terms for peace.

Whilst the meeting did not 'solve the problem in principle' of the Jewish Question as Graf Bernstorff had hoped, it certainly revealed the centrality of Jewish questions in the peace negotiations and the ramifications of these issues internationally. Most importantly, this meeting, which has been buried in obscurity, revealed the 'German's state attitude towards the Jews [and the] general perspective of German-Jewish functionaries regarding a traumatic past and an uncertain future'.[76]

The German delegation and the Treaty of Versailles

All the time and energy spent by the Foreign Office, the *Pax Konferenz* and the Committee for Peace Negotiations in preparing for the Paris Peace Conference unfortunately amounted to little practical use. The one-hundred-and-eighty-person German envoy equipped with thousands of preparatory documents for peace was not even in-

---

74 Paris Peace Conference, *The Deliberations of the Council of Four (March 24 – June 28, 1919): Notes of the Official Interpreter, Paul Mantoux*, Supplementary Volumes to The Papers of Woodrow Wilson (Princeton: Princeton University Press, 1992), 88, 427.
75 R19605, AA, K181838, 4.
76 Matthäus, 'Tagesordnung', 87.

vited to negotiate with the Allies. On the second, and last, formal occasion when the delegation came face-to-face with the Allies, they were handed the draft of the Treaty of Versailles and given a maximum of fifteen days to supply a written commentary on its clauses.[77]

The extent to which the reams of memoranda that had been meticulously prepared were used in practice is debatable.[78] As the German delegation was excluded from negotiations, they were afforded no input on the Jewish Question at Paris. And yet, the Germans had prepared for a discussion on Jewish questions. An orthodox Zionist, Hermann Struck, was selected to join the peace envoy to represent Jewish matters alongside a Catholic and Protestant representative.[79] Within the six-person delegation itself, two of the delegates selected happened to be of Jewish descent (Otto Landsberg and Carl Melchior). Moreover, the German delegation, in one of the few meetings with the Allies, protested the anti-Jewish pogroms by Poles, in order to place doubt on the creation of an independent Poland. Both in the preparation and practical arrangements for Paris, Jewish affairs had been considered by the Germans.

In what follows, I will examine the members of the German delegation, specifically the Zionist representative Hermann Struck, and demonstrate how in Paris the German delegation used Jewish questions strategically. They protested Polish pogroms to in turn demand minority protections for Germans. In Paris, minority rights became first and foremost tied into the German, not Jewish, question. In the final treaty with Germany, the Council of Four decided that Jewish rights was a 'contentious' subject and excluded it from the peace treaty. Aware of the importance of Jewish rights, a special Committee was established and tasked to draft a separate treaty focusing on minority rights. This will be the focus of the final section.

On 18 April 1919, the German Foreign Office received news that they had to send a peace delegation to Paris to 'receive', rather than as they had hoped to negotiate, the treaty. In preparation for this invitation, by late March the National Assembly had already selected six delegates who would represent German interests in the peace negotiations.[80] In a democratic process, each party of the coalition was allowed to put for-

---

77 Prior to this, the only time the plenipotentiaries were officially face-to-face was at the very beginning of the conference when they had to briefly exchange credentials. Apart from this formality they did not meet to discuss the treaty. All diplomacy was conducted in written form. Luckau, *The German Delegation at the Paris Peace Conference*, 62.

78 This is inferred by research conducted by Alma Luckau in the form of testimonies from delegates who were present. Some mentioned seeing the sheets of memoranda lying around, others say they were not used. Ibid, 39.

79 In a meeting of the Executive Committee of the Jewish orthodox organisation based in Frankfurt the organisation praised the selection of Hermann Struck to represent Jewish interests at the peace negotiations. See R19605, AA, 'K181877', 17 April 1919.

80 Luckau writes that on the 22 March the government selected the delegates for Paris. Yet, according to the minutes of the Cabinet meetings, it was only on the 25 March that the Germans received an Allied note that requested six delegates to be sent to Versailles. See Luckau, *The German Delegation at the Paris Peace*

ward a delegate. They were allocated according to the representation of their party in government. For this reason, the Majority Social Democrats put forward a third of the total delegates, Otto Landsberg (Minister of Justice) and Robert Leinert (President of the Prussian Diet). Johann Giesberts (Postmaster General) represented the Catholic Centre Party, and Carl Melchior (Chairman of the DDP) the German Democrats. The final two delegates were selected based on their expertise. This included Walter Schücking (Professor of International Law) and Count Ulrich von Brockdorff-Rantzau (Minister of Foreign Affairs), the latter of whom headed the delegation.[81] This list was formally compiled and sent to the Allies after the 26 April, just a few days before the arrival of the delegation in Paris.[82]

Aiding the six delegates was a staff of experts. These experts were divided into two lists. List A contained the names of twenty-three experts[83] who were invited to accompany the delegation to the negotiations in Paris. Notable Jewish names in the first list included Wilhelm Cuno (Chairman of the Hamburg-America Line), Carl Legien (General Secretary of the Trade Unions), Walther Rathenau (Board Member of the General Electricity Company, AEG) and Max Warburg[84] (a prominent banker). List B was much longer with eighty-three names of experts with relevant areas of expertise in agriculture, transport, unions, industry and banking who would remain in Berlin at the disposal of the peace delegation.[85]

On the 18 March the Cabinet decided to add several additional names to List A on the grounds that these 'men of world renown' could facilitate the 'renewal of international contacts' and whose presence could 'prevent degrading treatment'.[86] The preoccupation with humiliation evidenced in the inclusion of these candidates once again reflected the theme which ran through the *Pax Konferenz* on *Judenfragen*, namely the prioritisation of actions that would enable Germany to regain international prestige. Accordingly, List A was extended to include 'persons of international repute' including

---

Conference, 54; 'Meeting of the Reich Ministry, March 25, 1919, 3:00pm at Weimar Castle' in Burdick and Lutz, *The Political Institutions of the German Revolution*, 279–280, especially 279.

81 See Luckau, *The German Delegation at the Paris Peace Conference*, 54; 'Meeting of the Reich Ministry, Wednesday, March 12, 1919, 4:00pm, in the small committee room of the National Assembly' in Burdick and Lutz, *The Political Institutions of the German Revolution*, 257–259, especially 258.

82 'Meeting of the Reich Ministry, April 25, 1919, 11:00am, at the Reich Chancellery' in Burdick and Lutz, *The Political Institutions of the German Revolution*, 281.

83 For a list of these names see 'Meeting of the Reich Ministry, Tuesday, March 18, 1919, 12:00 noon' in ibid, 264–266, especially 265.

84 Melchior replaced Warburg, who declined, for the peace delegation, ibid, 264. Warburg attended the peace conference as an expert see 'Document 17: Preliminary List of the German Peace Delegation at Versailles, as of May 1, 1919' in Luckau, *The German Delegation at the Paris Peace Conference*, 188–190.

85 'Appendix 3, March 17, 1919 Meeting: List A Experts' in Burdick and Lutz, *The Political Institutions of the German Revolution*, 263–264.

86 Ibid, 264.

amongst others, Professors Max Weber and Moritz Julius Bonn,[87] the Jewish Social Democratic politician who was present at the *Judenfragen* meeting, Edward Bernstein as well as representatives of the Catholic Church, Protestant Church and the Zionist organisation. Of the latter organisation, Alfred Klee was first suggested, before being replaced by Hermann Struck.[88]

What is notable about the lists of representatives sent to negotiate peace both as delegates and as experts is the presence of a significant number of Germans of Jewish descent. Of the six delegates sent to Paris, one third, were of Jewish descent. These were Otto Landsberg and Carl Melchior both of whom were experts in the field of law and finance respectively. Other notable figures included the influential banker Max Warburg, Eduard Bernstein and Walter Rathenau. However, none of these men went to Paris with a portfolio to represent or even discuss (German) Jewish questions, as discussed in the Foreign Office meeting on the 31 March. One individual was designated to accompany the delegation as the 'Expert on the Jewish Question', Hermann Struck.[89]

A lithographer by trade, by the end of the First World War Struck had built a reputation as a spokesman for Jewish affairs. Born in Berlin in 1876, Struck who was training to become a Rabbi elected instead to pursue art.[90] Enrolling in the Berlin Academy of Fine Arts, Struck specialised in etching and engraving and became actively involved in the progressive Berlin *Sezession* movement, which sought to break from conservative art organisations in Germany.[91] Graduating in 1900, aged twenty-four, only three years later, Struck reached acclaim for his art with his etching of Theodor Herzl. Other prominent figures who sat for Struck included Hermann Cohen, Oscar Wilde, Friedrich Nietzsche, Sigmund Freud, Henrik Ibsen and Albert Einstein.[92] Amongst his apprentices Struck counted the famous Jewish artists, Marc Chagall, Max Liebermann, Lesser Ury, Josef Budko and Jakob Steinhardt.[93]

---

87 Moritz Julius Bonn (1873–1965), Professor of the Munich Commercial College was included in the delegation as a financial expert. On the relationship between 'Jewishness and liberalism' in the Weimar Republic in the works of Moritz Julius Bonn, Hermann Heller and Felix Weltsch see, Jens Hacke, 'Jewish Liberalism in the Weimar Republic? Reconsidering a Key Element of Political Culture in the Interwar Era', in *The German-Jewish Experience Reconsidered: Contested Interpretations and Conflicting Perceptions*, ed. Steven E. Aschheim and Vivian Liska (Berlin, New York: De Gruyter, 2015), 155–70.

88 This was decided in a Cabinet sitting held on Tuesday, 18 March 1919. The minutes of this meeting are available in the online files of the Reich Chancellery [https://bit.ly/2DACRhm, accessed 12/02/19].

89 CZA, A124/123, 'An Interview with Hermann Struck', *The Hebrew Standard*, 1920.

90 The only biography on Hermann Struck that I have been able to locate is Jane Rusel, *Hermann Struck (1876–1944): das Leben und das graphische Werk eines jüdischen Künstlers*, Judentum und Umwelt; Band 66 (Frankfurt am Main: Peter Lang, 1997).

91 Schmidt, *The Art and Artists of the Fifth Zionist Congress*, 89.

92 Nathan A. Bernstein, a descendant of Hermann Struck, owns one of the largest private collections of Struck's work [https://bit.ly/2TJZqXW, accessed 12/02/19].

93 Schmidt, *The Art and Artists of the Fifth Zionist Congress*, 90.

Despite not following the path to become a Rabbi, Struck remained devoted to studying the Talmud. When the Zionist Federation was established in Germany, Struck joined with enthusiasm. In 1902 Struck was able to combine his religious views with his political views when he co-founded the Mizrachi movement (*merkaz ruchani* meaning spiritual centre), an extreme orthodox wing of Zionism.[94]

When the First World War broke out, Struck, in an act demonstrative of his patriotism for Germany, voluntarily enlisted in the infantry and following training, was sent to the Eastern Front. Committed to alleviating the plight of East European Jews, Struck was one of the fifteen original members of the Committee for the East.[95] Whilst in the east, Struck completed a study on the language and culture of Jews living in Poland in which he demonstrated the close connections between German and Yiddish. The book became an important document for relations between the German authorities and the local Polish Jewish communities and drew the attention of the German leadership towards Struck's talents.[96]

When in 1915 the Supreme Army Command for the East (*Ober-Ost*) established a press office to control the flow of information in the region, Hermann Struck was brought in as translator of Yiddish. Within two years, Struck had earned an Iron Cross First Class and been promoted to Officer. Based on these merits he was selected by Wilhelm Freiherr von Gayl (Political Director of the *Ober-Ost*) to head the newly created office for Jewish Affairs (*Dezernat für jüdische Angelegenheiten*) in the political division of the *Ober-Ost*.[97] The establishment of Jewish Affairs offices in the *Ober-Ost* began in August 1915 when Ludwig Haas, a Progressive member of the Reichstag, was selected to head the section in Poland. In an interview in 1920, reflecting on this experience Struck framed the appointment as being asked by the 'German Government to take charge of the department dealing with the Jewish question in Oberost'.[98]

With his extensive experience on the affairs of Eastern European Jews, Struck was appointed as the Zionist representative of the German peace delegation. It is particularly noteworthy that the German delegation elected alongside a representative from the Catholic and Protestant Church a representative from the Zionist organisation, rather than a Rabbi or spokesperson of the Central Association, the largest German-Jewish association. There are several reasons why a Zionist was selected; a Zionist rather than Struck specifically as the initial selection had been for Alfred Klee, a German Zionist of the first-generation and close friend of Theodor Herzl.

---

94 After the Fifth Zionist Congress (December 1901) stated that Zionist educational programmes would not be based on religion, the Mizrachi movement was founded. Ibid, 94–96.

95 Nicosia, 'Jewish Affairs and German Foreign Policy during the Weimar Republic', 262.

96 Hermann L. Struck, *Jüdischdeutsche Texte. Lesebuch zur Einführung in Denken, Leben und Sprache der Osteuropäischen Juden* (Leipzig: J. C. Hinrich'sche Buchhandlung, 1917). Cited in Norrell, 'Shattered Communities, 103.

97 Schmidt, *The Art and Artists of the Fifth Zionist Congress*, 109.

98 CZA, A124/123 'An Interview with Hermann Struck'.

Firstly, during the war, German Zionists had proven the strategic importance for the Germans of collaboration with Zionists and Eastern European Jews. Moreover, the success of Zionist activities towards other Great Powers meant that after the war, Zionism emerged as a significant and coherent international movement. As the Germans hoped to reignite German-Russian Jewish wartime collaboration to secure their eastern borders, having a Zionist rather than liberal Jewish representative was more fitting as East European Jews strongly identified as a national-cultural group in line with Zionist attitudes. As Aschheim writes, 'as the war unfolded it became evident that the Eastern Jew increasingly symbolized the greater, more general Jewish question'.[99] Speaking on the subject in an interview, Struck revealed that he had been tasked by the German government with 'questions of minority rights of the Jews in those lands where they live in great masses' in other words, Eastern Europe. He maintained that his position on this had not waivered and that he continued to defend Jewish national rights. Yet asked if his proposals were included in the peace treaty, Struck preferred not to comment.[100]

Whilst the Germans thought they would be invited to discuss the post-war policy on Eastern Europe in actuality, they were not. Of the extensive notes and counterproposals by the German delegation at Versailles there was no mention of Eastern European Jews as the delegation had not been invited to comment on the subject. As the German government ruled that it would not be possible for Struck to meet the Jewish representatives of Allied countries, he did not attend the peace conference, although provisions for his arrival had been made.[101] In spite of the selection of a German Zionist representative for Paris and the meeting on *Judenfragen* in the peace preparations in Berlin, there was no expert on Jewish affairs in Paris to represent German interests in the Jewish organisations, or with the Allies.

National minority rights and the German Question

The reality that unfolded in the Paris Peace Conference differed vastly from the German delegation's expectation of the peace negotiations. For one they were not negotiations. Additionally, in as much as Jewish questions were raised by the German delegation in Paris, Jewish affairs were used strategically, as an instrument to juxtapose the civility of the Germans with the barbarity of the Polish. Then, in turn to demand national minority protections for Germans in an independent Poland. An additional approach pursued by the Germans was to demand protections by assuring the Allies

---

99 Aschheim, *Brothers and Strangers*, 142.
100 CZA, A124/123 'An Interview with Hermann Struck'.
101 The French Government had arranged for kosher meals to be prepared for Struck's arrival in Versailles, ibid.

that these would be reciprocated in Germany. However, whilst a limited number of cultural rights were granted to Germany's minorities, as seen in the Weimar constitutional debates, these did not extend to national groups. Thus, Germany did pursue an inconsistent policy with regard to minority protections, as highlighted by Oskar Cohn. Ultimately, contrary to Weimar where minority rights opened up a Jewish Question, in Paris, minority protections were awarded as a means to answer the German Question.

Simply put, the absence of any extensive discussion on Germany's position on *Judenfragen* was because the draft peace treaty presented by the President of the Conference Clémenceau to the Germans not only demanded a written response in a fortnight but also did not mention minority protections on the list of topics that the Germans were invited to reply to.[102] Only four days earlier on the 3 May, the Council of Four had decided that the question of the protection of minorities, 'so far as it affects the Jews in Poland', was 'so contentious and difficult' that it was decided no conclusions would be reached until after the treaty with Germany was signed.[103]

Around the same time as the meeting on *Judenfragen*, the *Pax Konferenz* compiled a memorandum on 'draft proposals' outlining Germany's position on minority protections under a clause concerning the eventuality of an independent Poland. The document read that care should be taken to ensure 'national and religious minorities be guaranteed an honourable existence within their own borders'.[104] Whilst the German leadership may have had the (religious) Polish Jewish minority in mind when drafting this section, the minority requiring (national) protection that was at the forefront of the Foreign Office's negotiation strategy was Germans. In a follow-up document handed to the German plenipotentiaries of peace, an entire section was dedicated to 'The Protection of National Minorities'.[105] Reminiscent of Hugo Preuss's insistence that Germany pursue a policy of reciprocity with respect to minority protections the document concluded that the Germans would 'try to effect further cultural autonomy based on records in national registry offices.'[106]

In Paris the German delegation was insistent on national minority protection. When, on the 7 May, they were presented with the draft Treaty of Versailles which did not mention minorities protections, the German delegation added it into their

---

102 See 'Document 30: Speech of President Clemenceau on May 7, 1919, at the Trianon Palace Hotel, Versailles' in Luckau, *The German Delegation at the Paris Peace Conference*, 223–224.
103 Oscar Isaiah Janowsky, *The Jews and Minority Rights (1898–1919)* (New York: Columbia University Press, 1933), 344.
104 See 'Document 20: Memorandum: Foreign Office Draft Proposals' in Luckau, *The German Delegation at the Paris Peace Conference*, 195–199, especially 198.
105 In Paris in the Legal Division of the German Peace Delegation the protection of minorities was listed as a point to discuss under the section on International Law. See 'Document 19' in ibid, 193–4.
106 Germany's Jewish population would not have been in the national registry and thus not a 'national minority' according to the Foreign Office. See 'Document 21: Instructions given to the German plenipotentiaries of peace' in ibid, 199–208, especially 202.

counterproposal to the Allies, which they handed over on the 29 May. Listed under part two entitled 'Territorial Questions', sub-section, 'right of self-determination' the delegation demanded cultural autonomy for Germans and guaranteed this autonomy for minorities within Germany.[107] The reciprocal approach advocated by the German delegation, was more tactical than anything else. Most importantly for the Germans minority rights was a territorial question concerning the vast swaths of land to the east that were no longer under German dominion. During the inter-war years the Germans were the largest ethnic minority living within the new states of Eastern Europe including Greece and the Baltic states.[108] The Germans supported the right to self-determination hoping that their scattered national populations would choose to remain German, thus possibly resulting in the acquisition of eastern territory.[109] Not just the German delegation but also German Jews were predominately concerned with the outcome of the war on Germany, in particular Germany's territorial ambitions and the stability of post-war German society.[110] During the Weimar Republic German and Jewish lobby groups worked together closely in the European Congress of Nationalities as they fought for minority guarantees.[111]

Making a case against a large independent Poland (which would include West Prussia and create a corridor in East Prussia), the German delegation interrogated the concept of nationality by attempting to minimise the importance of language and instead stress the significance of descent. The counterproposal to the Allies outlined that in many of the areas being granted to independent Poland the populations were German by nationality, even if the German language was not always the most dominant one. 'The circumstance that, in isolated regions, a non-German language has survived, is in itself of no moment, for, even in the oldest homogenous States, this condition may be observed; the Bretons, Welsh, Basques may be mentioned in this connection'.[112]

Echoing the German delegation's counter-proposal, in the constitutional committee sitting of the 16 June Cohn used the example of France to argue that despite the existence of different language groups in France ('the Basques, Bretons of the North and the Southerners'), the will to be French united these groups and suggested this conception of the nation, not based on language, should be pursued in Germany.[113] Building on unfolding events in Paris, Cohn highlighted how the German delegation

---

107 See 'Document 57: German Counterproposals of May 29, 1919' in ibid, 324.
108 Mazower, 'The Strange Triumph of Human Rights', 383.
109 The German Empire supported self-determination for Jews in the east, presumably on the basis that they might elect to become part of Germany not Poland. Matthäus, 'Tagesordnung', 88.
110 See Sara Panker, 'Between Friends and Enemies: The Dilemma of Jews in the Final Stages of the War', in *Minorities during the First World War. From War to Peace*, ed. Hannah Ewence and Tim Grady (London: Palgrave Macmillan, 2017), 76.
111 Mazower, 'The Strange Triumph of Human Rights, 1933–1950', 383.
112 Quoted and trans. in Janowsky, *The Jews and Minority Rights*, 337.
113 '40 Sitzung, 16 Juni 1919', 499.

supported 'national minority rights' whilst in the constitutional discussions in Weimar these rights were not being recognised.

Abroad then, Germany was driving a policy of national minority rights protection, as announced in the counterproposal to the Allies.[114] In a meeting on the 3 June in the Office for the Peace Negotiations the position of the German authorities with regard to national minorities protection was discussed in the form of two proposals. The first proposal offered a clear definition on what a minority group entailed, 'a minority [...] is a nationally defined group, which is willing and able, based on its size and culture, to lead an independent national existence'.[115] The consensus was that foreign-speaking was an unnecessary criteria for the concept of 'national minority'. The second proposal suggested that in countries where national minorities reside, 'minority communities' would be founded and that this would similarly apply to Jews as long as they demanded a national independent existence.

For Cohn, Germany was being 'dishonest' by pursuing a foreign policy that was not aligned to its domestic policy and yet crucially Cohn's argument rested on the basis that Jews would be recognised internationally as a national minority. Using moralistic language Cohn argued that 'under no circumstances could Germany award their own national minority groups less rights than that which is granted by the Allies in Paris, and eventually the League of Nations'.[116] Yet in Paris, the Jews were not on the forefront of the German delegation's mind. In the twenty-two notes sent by the German delegation to the Allies as well as in the counterproposal, Jews were only mentioned once. Under a section discussing the guarantees to be given to Germany in the ceded eastern districts, the German delegation warned that the Poles had not shown that they could be trusted as 'protectors of the rights of national religious minorities', referring to the anti-Jewish massacres which had broken out on armistice day.[117]

The German delegation used the violence against Jews as an instrument to demand that minority guarantees be enforced in the 'new state' of Poland, thus also ensuring protection for German minority populations. The counter-proposal went as far as to claim that if an independent Poland were to be established without 'guarantees for the minority peoples being accurately established at the same time' (in other words sug-

---

114 Whilst it is clear that the Germans did raise this point in the counterproposal, I did not find it listed under Article 54, which is what Cohn references in his speech. It is possible that the counterproposals were re-drafted before being sent to the German government. This also might also account for the differences in dates such that the counterproposal was given to the Allies on the 29 May, but it was only on the 3 June that Cohn mentions a meeting took place discussing the various articles. See '57. Sitzung, 15 Juli 1919', 1572.
115 Ibid.
116 In the Treaty of Versailles, the League of Nations was established as an international protector of peace. The Covenant of the League, which brought it into existence, was part of the treaty. Germany was only allowed into the League once it could prove that it was a peaceful country. Germany became a member of the League in 1926.
117 See 'Document 57: German Counterproposals of May 29, 1919' in Luckau, *The German Delegation at the Paris Peace Conference*, 306–205, especially 338.

gesting a Minority Treaty, which the Allies had in fact authorised to be drafted on the
1 May) then this would result in the 'advancement of the pogrom limit far towards the
west'.[118] This was not the first time members of the German authority had singled out
the barbarity of the Poles (and Romanians) towards the Jews. It was a recurrent theme
in parliamentary sittings from October 1918 through to August 1919. In the end, despite suggesting a willingness to reciprocate international minority protections within
Germany, the Allies did not include a clause on minority protections in the Treaty
of Versailles, much to the disappointment of the Polish delegate Paderewski.[119] The
absence of an obligation to protect minorities in the peace treaty with Germany would
prove detrimental in the inter-wars. The League was powerless to take action against
the Nazis violent treatment of German Jews.[120]

Setting a double standard? Minority obligations in the Treaty of Versailles

Over the course of four months with an average of approximately two meetings per
day between the Council of Four, only a few brief discussions took place on issues concerning Jews in the peace negotiations.[121] When they did take place, they concerned the
question of (national) minority rights in the 'new states', mostly referring to Poland.
On 1 May, in one of his regular private meetings with Georges Clémenceau and Lloyd
George, Woodrow Wilson first raised the subject of minority rights in the treaty with
Germany.[122]

The urgency Wilson saw in securing minority protection one could assume came
from his observation that, 'one of the things that troubles the peace of the world is the
persecution of the Jews'.[123] Following this statement, Wilson proposed to insert two
clauses into the peace treaty with Germany that would also apply to Poland, 'Bohemia'
as well as other 'new states'. The first clause was to 'grant all racial and national minorities the same treatment in the law [...] to the majority'. The second stated to 'place no
obstacle in the way of the practice of religion'.[124] Yet whilst the manner in which the
conversation initially unfolded suggests that Wilson, through these clauses, had given

---

118 Ibid.
119 Janowsky, *The Jews and Minority Rights*, 356.
120 Mazower, 'The Strange Triumph of Human Rights', 382.
121 See Paris Peace Conference, *The Deliberations of the Council of Four (March 24 – June 28, 1919)*, 439 ff.
122 After the deadlock in the Council of Ten, Wilson decided it was best to proceed with private meetings held in his place of residence in Paris with Lloyd George, Georges Clémenceau and Vittorio Orlando.
Orlando did not regularly attend the meetings apart from those concerning Italy. The first of these meetings
took place on the 25 March. See ibid, xiv.
123 Ibid, 439.
124 Ibid.

implicit support to the Jewish 'nationalist' cause, as he clarified in the meeting, what he most desired was for the inclusion of 'general provisions' in the treaty with Germany on the basis that 'several million' Germans would soon reside in Polish territory.[125]

Wilson was in fact sceptical of using the term 'national minority' to describe European Jewry. He commented, in reference to a draft on the status of Polish citizens, that what he did not like was 'that a sort of autonomy is required for national minorities', to which Lloyd George replied, 'this is a claim of the Jews, who wish to form a kind of state within a state. Nothing could be more dangerous'.[126]

To deal with the specific concern of (Jewish) minority protections, the Allies decided to establish a separate committee to draft a peace treaty. After a brief discussion between Lloyd George and Woodrow Wilson on the loyalty of Polish Jews in the war and the need to 'bring them [Jews] back everywhere under the terms of the law of the land', Wilson proposed to establish a committee of experts to 'settle that question' in Poland.[127] This committee was the Committee on New States and for the Protection of Minorities, which prepared the Minority Treaty that became the template for the peace treaties of the new states.[128] The Council of Four discussion ended inconclusively on the subject of which peace treaty to include minority guarantees in. Wilson thought either the treaty with Germany or Poland, whereas George insisted on the former. The Council also disagreed on the extent of these guarantees, Lloyd George wanted to impose the same 'international obligations [...] as civilised countries', which Wilson thought too expansive.[129]

Only a few days later on the 3 May in a meeting between the Council of Four, attended by experts from the Committee on New States, it was decided to not include a guarantee on the protection of minorities in the Treaty of Versailles. The Council was informed by the experts that the question 'in particular so far as it affects the Jews in Poland is so contentious and difficult'[130] that it could not be resolved in time for the presentation of the draft Treaty of Versailles, which had been scheduled to take place in four days. Instead, it was agreed that the treaty with Germany would include an Annex A, which would state that 'Poland will sign treaties with the Principle Allied Powers to protect ethnic and religious minorities.'[131]

---

125 This supports David Engel's thesis that Woodrow Wilson proposed minority protections, not with the Jews in mind, but rather as a means by which to placate both the Germans and the British who objected to a greater Poland. See Engel, 'Perceptions of Power – Poland and World Jewry'.

126 Paris Peace Conference, *The Deliberations of the Council of Four*, 440.

127 Ibid, 440.

128 The British were represented by James Headlam-Morley, the Americans, David Hunter Miller and the French, Philippe Berthelot. On the 12 May an Italian representative joined, Giacomo de Martino, but showed little interest until the treaty with Serbia.

129 Paris Peace Conference, *The Deliberations of the Council of Four*, 441.

130 Janowsky, *The Jews and Minority Rights*, 344.

131 Paris Peace Conference, *The Deliberations of the Council of Four*, 472. Rather than an Annex, in the final treaty this stipulation was included under articles 86 and 93.

The Treaty of Versailles was unique in not including minority protections. Germany was the only country to not have any clauses on obligations towards its minorities embedded within its peace treaty with the Allies. This would prove detrimental for German Jews during the latter half of inter-war years. In 1933, when the Nazis began to enact increasing violence against the Jewish population, the League of Nations was powerless to take action.[132] No minority protections were included in the peace treaty with Germany because the Allies were more concerned about Germans, the largest post-war ethnic minority, residing in the new states and thus enshrined guarantees in the peace treaties with this minority in mind. Deliberations by the Council of Four revealed that the question of whether or not to include national minority protections in the Treaty of Versailles were conceived with the Germans in mind. In contrast, the Committee on New States, which authored the Minority Treaty, was established with Polish Jews in mind.[133] Historians debate the extent to which the Jewish representations in Paris influenced the formulation of the Minority Treaty and yet, as will be seen below, whilst the Jewish representations ultimately did not command an overwhelming authority on events, they did bring Jewish questions to the international arena and ensured they remained on the agenda.[134]

Jewish rights and the Minority Treaty

This final section of the chapter turns to the specific debates on the wording of minority protections before they were enshrined in the Minority Treaty signed on the 28 June 1919. I pay particular attention to the position held by the different Jewish representations at the Paris Peace Conference. Beginning with the League of Nations Covenant where Wilson first advocated for a legally binding clause on minority rights protections, the section subsequently turns to the views articulated on these protections by the Jewish representations in Paris. I specifically turn my attention to the Jewish anti-nationalists, the American Jewish Congress and the Committee of Jewish Delegations. The final section re-examines the Treaty of Versailles, now from the perspective of the Allies. On the same day the Treaty of Versailles was signed, the Minority Treaty was drafted and signed by the Polish delegation. It was used as a means by which to satisfy

---

132 Mazower, 'The Strange Triumph of Human Rights', 382.
133 Paris Peace Conference, *The Deliberations of the Council of Four*, 440.
134 Janowsky was the first scholar to argue that Jews had a large influence on the Minority Treaty see, Janowsky, *The Jews and Minority Rights*. Mark Levene suggests Lucien Wolff influenced the treaty see Mark Levene, *War, Jews, and the New Europe: The Diplomacy of Lucien Wolf, 1914–1919* (Oxford: G.B. Littman, 2009). Both Engels and Fink have since de-emphasised the Jewish role in these events see Engel, 'Perceptions of Power – Poland and World Jewry'; Fink, 'Defender of Minorities'. For a recent account emphasising Jewish involvement in human rights after the First World War see James Benjamin Loeffler, *Rooted Cosmopolitans: Jews and Human Rights in the Twentieth Century* (New Haven: Yale University Press, 2018).

the German (and British) delegation who otherwise objected to a greater independent Poland. Ultimately, Jews were afforded cultural autonomous rights not national rights in the Minority Treaty, the consequences of which I will examine below. Just as the Jews had been one of the minority groups, along with Armenians, at the 'nodal point' of the emerging system in 1878, when in the Berlin Treaty their protection became a 'constituent element of the international system', once again in the Minority Treaty their fate was bound to the new ordering of states along the 'ideal of state sovereignty rooted in national homogeneity'.[135]

American President Woodrow Wilson first conceived of the idea of a League of Nations in a speech to Congress where he formulated his famous fourteen-point programme envisioning a future world order.[136] The second draft of the League of Nations covenant on the 10 January 1919 that included a distinct article on minorities. It read,

> The League of Nations shall require all new States to bind themselves as a condition precedent to their recognition as independent or autonomous States, to accord to all racial or national minorities within their several jurisdictions exactly the same treatment and security, both in law and in fact, that it accorded the racial or national majority of their people.[137]

Whilst this first clause would not have applied to a country such as Germany, on the 20 January it was re-drafted to extend to all 'recognised sovereignties' when seeking admission to the League of Nations. The new draft also added a line prohibiting religious discrimination.

Following Wilson's fourteen-point programme, the wording on the protection of minorities in the covenant defined minorities as racial or national, rather than religious, foreign-speaking or culturally autonomous. It is curious as to why Wilson included racial equality as one of the cornerstones of the new supra-national organisation dedicated to peace, when this equality was not present in his own country.[138] This double standard, however, became a feature not only of the League of Nations, but of the post-war international system that was created during the Paris Peace Conferences. As Mazower writes,

> Although organisationally the League was a radical departure from the past, in other ways it fitted squarely into an earlier Victorian tradition of Great Power paternalism, a paternalism that coexisted comfortably with both liberal Christianity and racism.[139]

---

135 The principle of national homogeneity was enshrined in the Treaty of Lausanne in 1923, Eric D. Weitz, 'From the Vienna to the Paris System: International Politics and the Entangled Histories of Human Rights, Forced Deportations, and Civilising Missions', *American Historical Review* 113, no. 5 (2008): 1313.
136 On Wilson's world vision see Trygve Throntveit, 'The Fable of the Fourteen Points: Woodrow Wilson and National Self-Determination', *Diplomatic History* 35, no. 3 (2011): 445–481.
137 Janowsky, *The Jews and Minority Rights*, 321.
138 For more on Wilson's racial attitudes and policies and his controversy as a figure see Deborah Yaffe, 'Wilson, Revisited', *Princeton Alumni Weekly,* 3 February 2016 [https://bit.ly/2JNoiHx, accessed 13/12/17].
139 Mazower, 'The Strange Triumph of Human Rights', 382.

The response to including minority protection in the League of Nations Covenant was overwhelming negative. The British thought this clause should be included in the territorial treaties, not the League of Nations. Neither did the French want to 'encumber' the covenant with this. Wilson's advisor David Hunter Miller thought that if a clause were to be included it needed even more specific provisions. When the League of Nations Committee convened on the 3 February, most of the clause had been removed, except for the section on religious liberty. By the 13 February, however, this was also dropped as the Committee was unable to reach consensus. The Japanese delegate had introduced an amendment to include racial equality as well as religious equality and refused to accept the former if the latter was not also guaranteed. The major powers were unwilling to concede to any obligation on racial equality and thus the whole article on minority protections was dropped from the League covenant.[140]

Jewish representatives played a significant role in Paris and advocated on behalf of guarantees for the protection of minorities. The representatives present, however, differed on the criteria for defining the minority. Jewish rights would have been on Wilson's mind when he arrived in Paris for the peace negotiations. Prior to which, he had met with representatives from the American Jewish Congress. As early as mid-February Jewish representatives sent their first formal appeal for Jewish rights.[141]

The first appeals[142] for Jewish rights to be included in the peace treaties came from the 'anti-nationalist camp' of Jewish representatives, namely British and French Jews, represented respectively by the Joint Foreign Committee, Lucien Wolf was secretary and the most active member in Paris, and the *Alliance Israélite Universelle*, whose Chairman was Eugene See. The anti-nationalists, also termed the 'assimilationists' by their critics sought to secure 'civil and political equality' for Jews and purposefully did not mention the word 'national'. Their petition was for the full emancipation of Jews in Eastern Europe following the terms of Western European emancipation acts.[143]

Two petitions were submitted by the Joint Committee and *Alliance Israélite*. One demanded that the peace treaties include clauses ensuring that citizens 'shall enjoy equal political and civil rights without distinction of race, language or religion'. Notably, the petition appealed for more than just minority rights for Jews but was framed in universalist language as a demand for 'religious, cultural and educational autonomy [without] distinction of creed, race or language [on a] footing of perfect equality'.[144]

The other petition made explicit that it concerned Jewish minorities, and specifically Romanian Jewry. The context to this petition dated back to the Treaty of Berlin signed on the 13 July in 1878 which recognised Romania as an independent state. Em-

---

140 Janowsky, *The Jews and Minority Rights*, 322.
141 Ibid, 323.
142 Lucien Wolf sent his appeal on 20 February, whilst the Alliance submitted theirs the following day, ibid.
143 For a global history of Jewish emancipation edicts see Mahler, *Jewish Emancipation*.
144 *Joint Delegation Report*. Quoted in Janowsky, *The Jews and Minority Rights*, 323.

bedded within this was a provision that the Romanian government would refrain from the discrimination of religious minorities and grant full civil and political rights to inhabitants. These clauses were disregarded and when the First World War broke out, Romania and the Russian Empire were the only European states not to have signed emancipation acts.[145] The memory of 1878 and the treatment of the Jewish population featured prominently in the deliberations of the Council of Four in the decision on affording minority protections.[146]

As of January 1919, the Romanian government had declared to the Allies that the 'Jewish Question' had been 'solved' in Romania by a decree of naturalisation. The decree had been issued in December 1918 enabling Jews to enrol in a new process of naturalisation. However, the process was not binding until ratified and essentially Jews still remained exempt from full citizenship, which the petition by the anti-nationalists hastened to illustrate to the Allies.[147]

Alongside the appeal from the anti-nationalists, the American Jewish Congress also attempted to influence the decision on minority rights. The American Jewish Congress was the most influential Jewish representation in Paris, largely because it had a direct line to Wilson through Louis D. Brandeis, a U.S. Supreme Court Judge, close associate of the President and supporter of the Congress. Moreover, as the Congress represented the full spectrum of Jewish opinion from the 'anti-nationalist' through to the 'nationalist' camp it became the mediating body in Paris.

Willing to take an active stance on Jewish affairs at the Paris Peace Conference, in preparation the Congress met in December 1918 and prepared expert reports on all countries with Jewish populations. When Woodrow Wilson returned for a short trip back to the United States (between 24 February to 5 March) the American Jewish Congress seized upon the opportunity to appeal to Wilson for Jewish rights in Eastern Europe and for the recognition of Palestine.

Whilst the Congress employed similar terminology in its communications with Wilson, requesting 'full civil, religious, political and national rights', they carefully outlined the understanding of the latter term. The Congress differentiated between understanding of a nation in Western and Eastern states. In Western states, nation denoted a homogenous political entity. In Eastern states, given the heterogeneous nature of states, nation signified an ethnic unit. Thus, the Congress demanded that national rights be awarded in accordance with the individual case and its context. Whilst Wilson was unwilling to provide any certainty about a clause on 'national' minority rights, according to the Congress representatives, he did reassure them on the recognition of Palestine.[148]

---

145 Mahler, *Jewish Emancipation*, 62.
146 Paris Peace Conference, *The Deliberations of the Council of Four*, 473.
147 Janowsky, *The Jews and Minority Rights*, 323.
148 Ibid, 327.

Despite the initial successes of the Congress, over the course of the Paris Peace Conference it was unable to unite all the Jewish representations into a single delegation. This was due to fundamentally different and unalterable understandings of Jewry as either a singularly religious or also national group. Unable to find a consensus, the American Jewish Congress abandoned its all-inclusive programme. Instead, it formed a united front with the East European Jewish representatives called the Committee of Jewish Delegations, thereby excluding the British and French Jewish representatives.[149]

By April 1919 the Allies were meeting frequently to negotiate on the peace treaties. Since the rejection of Wilson's clause in the League of Nations Committee meeting in February, however, the Allies had not discussed minority protection.[150] In these three months, agitation on the part of Jewish representatives continued and was largely conducted using diplomatic back channels. In April the first public and large-scale petitions for Jewish rights were conducted by the Committee of Jewish Delegations.[151]

The Committee demanded the recognition of national autonomy on the basis that Jewish communities in the emerging new states were already on route to achieving forms of autonomy. These 'bold if brief experiments in Jewish national autonomy' such as the establishment of Jewish national councils were taking place in Ukraine and Lithuania. Jewish nationality was also recognised in the new state of Czechoslovakia.[152] Backing the Committee was the World Zionist Organisation, which sought to guide the multifarious eastern nationalist movements towards a collective goal. Prominent figures of the WZO included Nahum Sokolow and Chaim Weizmann, both of whom later became Presidents of the World Zionist Congress. The goal advanced by the Committee echoed that of the Copenhagen manifesto written by the Zionist World leadership at the end of the war in October 1918. The manifesto called for (1) the full equality of rights for Jews in all countries, (2) national, political and cultural autonomy in countries where the Jewish population demanded it, (3) admission into the League of Nations as a 'Jewish Nation' and (4) the recognition of Palestine as the national home for the Jewish people.[153]

---

149 Whilst Julian Mack was elected as Chairman due to his nationalist sympathies there were other influential figures in the American Jewish Congress. These included Rabbi Stephen S. Wise and Bernard G. Richards. Louis Marshall was in fact shocked to arrive in Paris to find the committee fully formed as he was less sympathetic towards the views of the British and French Jewish representatives. Janowsky, *The Jews and Minority Rights*, 283–307.
150 Paris Peace Conference, *The Deliberations of the Council of Four*.
151 On the organisations in this committee and their demands see Leon Chasanowitsch and Leo Motzkin, 'Die Forderungen Der Jüdischen Delegationen an Die Friedenkonferenz', in *Die Judenfrage Der Gegenwart: Dokumentensammlung* (Stockholm: Bokförlaget Judäa A. B., 1919), 74–81.
152 See David Rechter, 'A Nationalism of Small Things: Jewish Autonomy in Late Habsburg Austria', *The Leo Baeck Institute Year Book* 52, no. 1 (2007): 107. See also Rabinovitch, *Jewish Rights, National Rites*, 248–62.
153 For the Copenhagen manifesto see Chasanowitsch and Motzkin, 'Die Forderungen Der Zionistischen Organisation an Die Friedenskonferenz', 68–69.

The Committee campaigned successfully on the importance of securing rights for Jews, framing it as an issue affecting not only Jews but the larger question of nationality.[154] Two American representatives, Julian Mack and Louis Mashall, attempted to petition the U.S. delegate Lansing to establish a special commission to 'deal with the Jewish question' after they discovered that one had not been set up. However, after consultations, Lansing informed the Committee that their proposal had been decided against.[155] Whilst the Committee also submitted a clause on minority guarantees exactly the day before Wilson raised the subject in the Council of Four meeting, it is difficult to ascertain how much these actions dictated the deliberations and decisions of the Allies. In spite of the polarising views amongst the Jewish representations on Jewish nationalism the majority of Jewish delegates, excluding the French, were able to agree on legally enshrining Jewish autonomy into the peace treaties with new states.[156]

On the 28 June 1919 as members of the German delegation, Müller and Bell, signed the Treaty of Versailles in the hall of mirrors in the Palace of Versailles, Paderewski, the Polish delegate, entered an adjacent room to sign the Minority Treaty. The Minority Treaty went much further than just including articles on the protection of national and religious minorities, as had been discussed for the Treaty of Versailles. Rather, the treaty contained specific protections, which applied only to the Jewish minority in Poland. Precisely because of the complex status of Jewry, as not part of a nation, but neither just a religious group, the members of the Committee of New States decided to mention the Jewish minority in the treaty to ensure it was protected. This was a lesson learned from the Treaty of Berlin in 1878.[157] Memories of Romania disregarding the stipulations concerning the recognition of Jews as citizens, leading to large scale anti-Jewish discrimination and violence, guided the decisions of the Allies in the negotiations.[158] In one meeting on the wording of the Minority Treaty, Headlam-Morley noted that it was preferable to use the word 'inhabitants' over 'citizens' as the use of the latter term had enabled the Romanians to exclude the Jews.[159]

In the meetings preceding the treaty, Jews featured several times in the discussion on the treaty with Poland as the Committee on New States and the Allies balanced an awareness of the danger of antisemitism and the necessity to protect Jews, with the fear of creating separate legal (national) corporate entities within the new states. As such, they uniformly decided to not recognise the Jews as a nation, wanting to avoid encouraging any form of 'aggressive nationalism'. Awarding Jews national rights was perceived

---

154 See, for example, Joseph Tenenbaum, *La Question juive en Polgne* (Paris: Le Comité des Delegations Juives, 1919).
155 Janowsky, '*The Jews and Minority Rights*, 346.
156 Rabinovitch, *Jewish Rights, National Rites*, 262.
157 On the often neglected importance of the Berlin Treaty of 1878 for the decisions on the minority protections system in 1919 see Weitz, 'From the Vienna to the Paris System'.
158 Paris Peace Conference, *The Deliberations of the Council of Four*, 89, 473.
159 Ibid.

as a possible threat to national unity within Poland as Lloyd George commented in one meeting, 'our desire to protect the Jews doesn't have to go so far as to make them into a state within a state'.[160] Balfour, who was also in attendance, similarly opined that 'establishing a Jewish nation within Poland is very dangerous', also remarking 'I greatly fear that the Jewish problem will become one of the most serious in the future'.[161]

In the Minority Treaty, general articles on the guarantee of religious, national freedom were included as well as two articles (10 and 11), which only concerned the Jewish population. Article 2 outlined the 'general provisions' for an independent Poland, namely 'protection of life […] without distinction of birth, nationality, language, race or religion' as well as the 'free exercise […] of any creed, religion or belief'.[162] Article 8 secured the rights of 'racial, religious, or linguistic minorities' to 'establish, manage and control […] charitable, religious and social institutions, schools and other educational establishments'. Article 9 complemented Article 8 and gave linguistic minorities, such as White Russians, Germans and Ruthenians, the freedom and financial support to instruct their children in primary schools in their own language. Whilst the above articles all applied to Jews, specific provisions for them were written into Articles 10 and 11.

Article 10 enabled the Jewish community to appoint representatives to educational committees, and specifically outlined that the share of funds, mentioned in Article 9 would also be allocated proportionally to Jewish schools. Article 11, which had troubled the Allies, compelled the Polish state to not require its Jewish citizens to perform any acts that may violate their holy day on Saturday, the Sabbath, although this did not apply to Jews in military service.[163] The article also guaranteed that in Poland elections would not be held on Saturday. The clause essentially delegated more freedom to the Jewish population than other religious groups in Poland, such as Catholics who would be required to vote on Sunday if necessary.[164]

The Minority Treaty was used as a model for the additional fourteen peace treaties that were signed with the new states. The clauses specifically stipulating provisions for Jews, however, were only repeated in some of the treaties. Articles 10 and 11 were included in the 'Declaration of Lithuania' and the treaty with Greece, with minor modifications.[165] The treaty with Turkey used Article 43 to mirror Article 11 but applied it more broadly to all 'non-Muslim minorities'. The Romanian treaty was carefully presided over to avoid a repetition of the Treaty of Berlin and thus also explicitly men-

---

160 Ibid, 525.
161 Ibid, 527.
162 For the full treaty see 'Document 51' in Mahler, *Jewish Emancipation*, 67–70.
163 Lucien Wolf was one of the more influential figures behind this provision, insisting on its importance. See Paris Peace Conference, *The Deliberations of the Council of Four*, 88. See also Levene, *War, Jews, and the New Europe*.
164 Mahler, *Jewish Emancipation*, 70.
165 Article 11 only applied to districts with a considerable proportion of Jewish inhabitants. The Greek were allowed to hold elections on Saturdays. See ibid, 68.

tioned the Jews, requiring for them *ipso facto* to be recognized as Romanian nationals, 'who do not possess another nationality'.[166] As Jewish populations were accordingly granted cultural autonomous rights, the question of whether the Jews were a nation, state, religion or tribe would continue into the following decade.

The paradox of the new state peace treaties was that precedence was given to the nation-state ideal alongside the endorsement of autonomous Jewish communal rights which threatened to undermine the national homogeneity of new states. The double standards of the Great Powers permeated the treaties as neither the United States, United Kingdom, France, Italy nor Germany were bound by these provisions. Moreover, as the new states sought to unify their states, they simultaneously had to guarantee the cultural, linguistic and educational diversity of their minority populations. By the Treaty of Lausanne in 1923 the principle of national homogeneity was legally enshrined thus providing official legitimation for the forced deportations of peoples, which came to define the inter-war years.[167]

Jewish questions, German questions

Through the particular case of German and Jewish questions this chapter has demonstrated how the constitutions, treaties and principles on minority rights which emerged after the First World War were riddled with inconsistencies and paradoxes. On the international stage, Germany having lost much of its territory in the north to Denmark, the west to France and the east to Poland and Czechoslovakia was confronted with a more homogenous population than before the war. Thus, when it came to minority protections in Paris, at the top of the German's delegation's agenda were the rights of German nationals, resident in the new states of Poland, Czechoslovakia but also the Baltic states and even Greece. In the peace negotiations amongst the Allies this also became a central concern as minority rights became part and parcel of the German Question.

Jewish questions, however, were not entirely absent in Paris. The German delegation, committed to presenting a 'positive programme' to the Allies, and saw in the Jewish Question their key to regaining international prestige and a signal that a 'new spirit' had entered Germany. In preparation, a meeting on Jewish questions was organised by the Office for Peace Negotiations and the Orthodox Zionist Hermann Struck was selected as a German-Jewish representative to accompany the peace envoy. As the German delegation was not invited to negotiations, they were unable to present their position on the rights for Eastern European Jews and Palestine. Jewish affairs were,

---

166 Ibid.
167 On this paradox see Weitz, 'From the Vienna to the Paris System', 1343.

however, raised by the delegation and used strategically as a means to highlight Polish barbarity and stress the necessary inclusion of national minority protections in the peace treaty with Poland.

In the Paris Peace Conference, the Jewish Question, as in the Treaty of Berlin in 1878, once again became a constituent part of the emerging international system. As a distinct minority living over dispersed territories, how to ensure the protection of Jews against discrimination and violence led the Allies to establish a Committee on New States. Jewish representations in Paris petitioned actively for the specific inclusion of provisions for Jews. Whilst they were not decisive in shaping the wording of the Minority Treaty, they successfully ensured Jewish rights remained on the international agenda. In the Minority Treaty, which provided the template for minority guarantees in the peace treaties of the new states, two articles specifically mentioned the Jewish population and awarded them cultural autonomous rights in religious practice and education.

In the aftermath of the Paris Peace Conference, Germany pioneered as a defender of minority rights for all those 'ethnic minorities who felt disadvantaged by the peace treaties and the selective implementation of national self-determination'.[168] German and Jewish lobby groups worked together in the European Congress of Nationalities to ensure the League of Nation was fulfilling its obligations towards protecting minorities.[169] After the war, ensuring the international guarantee of minority rights became a integral component of both Jewish and German questions.

---

168 Panker, 'Between Friends and Enemies', 76.
169 Fink, *Defending the Rights of Others*; Mazower, 'Minorities and the League of Nations in Interwar Europe'; Fink, 'Defender of Minorities'.

Conclusion

Jewish questions exposed a number of critical junctures in the political development of the German Empire. They revealed the prospects and apprehensions on Germany's path from the more monolithic, authoritarian structures of the Wilhelmine Empire to the more liberal, pluralist ones of the Weimar Republic in the liminal period of 1914 to 1919. Jewish questions became debates about the German state, pertaining to rights, religious freedom, equality before the law and national identity. As Peter Pulzer wrote, 'the Jewish Question in Germany was a function of the German concepts of nation and of political rule'.[1] Whilst often viewed as the projection of a myth, I have shown that Jewish questions had distinct practical political ramifications. Rather than merely addressing *the* Jewish Question, I have sought to disentangle the term to reveal that it was multivalent and contingent. In doing so, I have moved beyond the prevalent assumption made within the modern scholarly literature of viewing the Jewish Question as solely an antisemitic phenomenon.

Starting in 1842 when the Jewish Question emerged as a popular catchword in Prussia, chapter one has shown that discussions about the Jewish Question did not follow a continuous narrative but rather erupted at particular moments in time. Both Gentiles and Jews contributed in equal part to these discussions, employing similar vocabulary despite their different political and ideological agendas. Notably, the debates reveal that the Jewish Question was always a reflection on the health of the German state.

Chapter one focused on six publications between 1842 and 1914 concerning the Jewish Question that sparked heated debates on the German state, specifically the separation of the church and state, cultural homogeneity, the relationship between citizenship and nationality, the differences in national versus patriotic allegiance and multiculturalism. These debates revealed that the Jewish Question was symptomatic of an underlying issue in Germany: the need for political and national-cultural reform. A homogenous national culture was not the issue at stake but rather how it was being

---

1 Pulzer, *Jews and the German State*, 30.

conceived in Christian terms, excluding both Jewish contributions to German culture and hindering their integration.

Debates on Jewish questions exposed the challenges faced in the process of modernisation towards a secular, liberal, pluralist state on the one hand, and the desire to maintain a comprehensive, homogenous national identity, on the other. These earlier theoretical debates involving public intellectuals became practically relevant during and after the First World War. As chapters two to four demonstrated, the terminology and ideas invoked in discussions on the Jewish Question were appropriated from these earlier debates.

The outbreak of the First World War presented an opportune moment for German-Jewish collaboration. The desire for unity necessitated by the war brought with it the removal of discriminations against Jews in the army. Kaiser Wilhelm's declaration of a civic truce (*Burgfrieden*) implied that the German Empire had entered a new epoch. He suggested that the German people had become the embodiment of political, religious and ethnic heterogeneity. German Jews took up the call to arms with enthusiasm, seizing the chance to join the army and fulfil their patriotic duty. For the first time ever, unbaptised Jews were promoted to the rank of Officer. Putting their differences aside, both liberal and Zionist organisations encouraged German Jews to volunteer to fight for the Fatherland.

The first years of the war witnessed unprecedented collaboration between the German Foreign Office and German Jewish organisations. Members of the Committee for the East, Max Bodenheimer and Franz Oppenheimer, were invited into meetings with high-ranking diplomats and military Generals, where they participated in discussions on Germany's geopolitical interests and future as a colonial power. Chapter two demonstrated how otherwise theoretical Jewish questions became practically relevant when the Central Powers gained control over West Russia, a territory that extended across the Baltic states, Poland and Belarus. During the occupation, a practical Jewish Question arose when the Central Powers were faced with the jurisdiction over approximately six million Jews.

The encounter with a population of Eastern European Jews raised unparalleled questions about Jewish communal identity and rights but also about the future of the German Empire. As the army was faced, for the first time, with a Jewish population exhibiting national characteristics they were forced to decide on whether or not to support not only religious autonomy for the Jewish population but also cultural rights, such as allowing Polish Jews access to education in Yiddish. These discussions on the Jewish Question, on the subject of cultural national consciousness, had reached maturity in Zionist circles at the turn of the century, as illustrated in chapter one. They revealed an internal dynamic to the Jewish Question; one with Jewish agency and a political answer that with the outbreak of world war, was thought achievable. By 1914 the ideas and vocabulary from Zionist debates about the Jewish Question had entered mainstream discourse on Germany's foreign policy, with practical implications.

The occupation of West Russia not only challenged understandings of Jewish communal identity but also German national belonging. The language affinity between Yiddish-speaking Russian and Polish Jews to German enabled closer collaboration than with other local groups such that Jews were used as translators for the German army. As the Supreme Army Command exerted their authority over the region, establishing schools and administrative departments, the occupation also raised practical questions pertaining to the future of the German polity, both in terms of the structure of Germany's external borders, but also the categorisation of German nationality, based historically on its development as a *Kulturnation*.

When in August 1914 Max Bodenheimer from the Committee for the East submitted a memorandum, which proposed extending Germany's sphere of influence and colonial outreach in Eastern Europe and Palestine by using Jews as mediators of German interests, the moment could not have been more auspicious. Building on Karl Renner's notion of the personality principle, Bodenheimer suggested the creation of an Eastern European Federation (*ein osteuropäischer Staatenbund*) from the Baltic to the Black Sea of autonomous national communities, loyal to Germany. Whilst Bodenheimer's federation was never realised, chapters two and five revealed how his ideas on Jewish cultural autonomy had a longer legacy in the Minority Treaties signed during the Paris Peace Conference. Bodenheimer's success was also institutional. After the war a department for Jewish Affairs was established in the German Foreign Office headed by a former member of the Committee for the East, Moritz Sobernheim. In 1916, however, the war began to take a turn for the worse for the German army. Relations between the Committee for the East and the Supreme Army Command and Foreign Office began to deteriorate and Bodenheimer's blueprint for an extended area of German influence using Jews as mediators was forgotten.

In the summer of 1916, the German Empire found itself in crisis: militarily and politically. With the battle of Verdun at an impasse, on the 1 July the German Army was drawn into the battle of the Somme where they faced stalemate. These battles, some of the longest of the war, raged on until the end of the year.[2] The Central Powers were no more successful on the Eastern Front. Beginning in June, an unexpectedly powerful Russian offensive destroyed the Central Powers' defensive lines forcing them into retreat. The Russian Empire managed to regain almost all the southwest territory it had

---

2 For a collection of essays on the Western Front with a focus on Germany's experience see Roger Chickering and Stig Förster, eds., *Great War, Total War: Combat and Mobilization on the Western Front, 1914–1918* (Cambridge: Cambridge University Press, 2000).

lost during the summer of 1915.[3] Further blows included Italy's defection in April and the Kingdom of Romania's decision to join the war on the side of the Allies in August.[4]

The cumulative military failures began to stir discontent within leadership circles. Intending to turn the tide in Germany's favour, General Paul von Hindenburg took over control of the Supreme Army Command, replacing General Erich von Falkenhayn. Under Generals Hindenburg and Ludendorff, the Supreme Army Command began to challenge the authority of the civilian government by intervening in political and economic affairs. They implemented the Hindenburg Programme, which established a total war economy in Germany. This crisis of authority reached its zenith in July 1917 when a parliamentary majority demanded to open peace negotiations against the decision of the military leadership to secure peace through victory. Parliament lost as Chancellor Theobald von Bethmann-Hollweg was forced into resignation and the Supreme Army Command assumed *de facto* control over the last years of the German war effort.[5]

In October 1916 against the backdrop of military failures and a change in leadership, as chapter two has shown, a practical Jewish Question resurfaced. Once again, whilst focused on the Jewish minority, it concerned the German state more broadly. A Jewish Question arose in parliamentary debates in the context of a decree issued by the War Ministry to count the number of Jews serving on the front lines. The authorisation of a census singling out German Jews stood in stark contrast to the mutually beneficial relationship German-Jewish organisations and the German authorities had shared in the first years of the war. The parliamentary and public debate on the 'Jew census' (*Judenzählung*) which ensued challenged the necessity of the decree but more importantly opened up a discussion on equality before the law, constitutionalism and secularism.

Whilst the war heralded unity and solidarity, the *Judenzählung* pulled down this facade and exposed the Empire's past prejudices. The debate highlighted an Empire caught between a quasi-military dictatorship under the Supreme Army Command and a civilian-parliamentarian government. Gathering statistical data, even based on confession, was not what caused most outrage for many German Jews, it was the specific targeting of Jews that undermined the 'spirit of 1914'. The census signalled the intent to exert control over a minority group that represented less than 1% of the German population. In the final count, Jews were shown to have served on the front lines in equal measure to their fellow Gentile Germans.

---

3 On the German experience on the Eastern Front during World War One see Liulevicius, *War Land on the Eastern Front*; Stone, *The Eastern Front*.

4 On Italy in WWI see John Gooch, *The Italian Army and the First World War* (Cambridge: Cambridge University Press, 2014). For Romania's First World War experience see Glenn E. Torrey, *The Romanian Battlefront in World War I* (Lawrence, Kansas: University Press of Kansas, 2014).

5 See Feldman, 'The Political and Social Foundations of Germany's Economic Mobilization'; Richard Bessel, *Germany After the First World War* (Oxford: Oxford University Press, 1993).

The census highlighted the dualism of Germany's political development. The desire to collect statistical data, on the one hand, was tied into the process of modernisation towards a more bureaucratic state. On the other hand, the targeting of a numerically negligible minority group, raised questions about the integrity of German institutions and the commitment to upholding the principles of equality enshrined in the constitution.

The *Judenzählung* shed an important light on Germany's political culture, specifically the informal powers of parliament against the backdrop of the increasing militarisation of the Empire. In the Reichstag ministers used the Jewish Question to demand redress of the military's constitutional transgressions. Combined with the public outrage over the census and the diplomatic pressure exerted by politically and economically influential German-Jewish representatives, after only three months, the decree was declared closed. In this instance, normative pressures exerted by parliament and German-Jewish representatives had triumphed.

In the last two years of the war, the practical Jewish questions that had surfaced in 1914 and 1916, were no longer on the political agenda as the German Empire was faced with an increasing prospect of defeat and a war-weary population where revolutionary feelings were rife. By autumn 1918, the Supreme Army Command confessed that an armistice had to be negotiated immediately. Chancellor Georg von Hertling and his cabinet resigned, and the new Chancellor Prince Max von Baden took on the bitter task of arranging peace negotiations with the President of the United States Woodrow Wilson. A series of political and constitutional reforms towards the parliamentarisation of the Empire headed by Max von Baden did little to quell the revolutionary fervour or satisfy Woodrow Wilson's armistice demands.[6] Starting with a small revolt, only a few days later a major mutiny involving tens of thousands of sailors took place in Kiel. Disillusioned with the military and political leadership, a number of workers and soldiers' councils were formed across the country as the civil unrest spread. On the 9 November, Kaiser Wilhelm abdicated, and the German Republic was declared.[7]

At this critical juncture in Germany's political development another practical Jewish Question arose during the drafting of a new constitution for the Republic. As chapter four illustrated, discussions on Article 113, Germany's policy on minority rights, concerning how to define the status of minority communities turned specifically to the Jewish Question. The debate was triggered by the Independent Socialist member of parliament, Oskar Cohn, who submitted a petition to change the wording of Article 113 to incorporate rights for national minorities. Cohn resolutely believed that Jews would soon be granted the recognition as a nation during the peace deliberations in Paris and insisted that the constitution reflect these international developments. The debate,

---

6 See Machtan, *Prinz Max von Baden*.
7 For a recent informative account on the German revolution see Mark Jones, *Founding Weimar*.

which took place in the National Assembly and Constitutional Committee, pitted the left-liberal Hugo Preuss, author of the constitution, and his liberal supporters against the Zionist Oskar Cohn.

On the one hand, the discussions brought up larger questions confronting the German-Jewish community on their confessional, cultural or national status, which reached back to earlier Zionist debates discussed in chapter one. During the First World War, as chapter two showed, these ideas had become practically relevant for Germany's geopolitical interests. After the war, in light of the international recognition of ethnically homogenous nation-states at the Paris Peace Conference the subject of Jewish minority rights took on an international and legal dimension, as chapter five illustrated. On the other hand, as the debate centred on how to define the minority it delved into the heart of how to define German nationality.

Comparing the French model of the *Staatsnation* to Germany's historical development as a *Kulturnation*, Cohn criticized the rootedness of German national understanding in ideas of culture, language and descent and exposed the hypocrisy that despite speaking German, minority groups remained foreign (*fremd*) within Germany. The National Assembly resolutely rejected Cohn's petition and the wording of Article 113 recognised only foreign-speaking groups as minorities. According to this criteria, German Jews were not granted any exceptional minority status, satisfying the position of the liberal German Jewish majority. Internationally at the Paris Peace Conference, however, as Cohn had underscored, Jewish minorities living in the new states were granted exceptional minority rights: cultural autonomy. The importance of the short-lived Weimar constitutional debates on Jewish questions was that they pertained to more fundamental questions on how to define nationality. These domestic debates as they related to the Paris Peace Conference expose the piecemeal and inconsistent way in which the post-war minority system developed and was institutionalised.

During the First World War Zionism was recognised as an influential political movement with global reach.[8] For the first time, Jews were internationally recognised as a minority group deserving of exceptional rights. Moreover, the Balfour Declaration reified the Jewish nation by proclaiming a Jewish homeland in Palestine. As a result of these international developments, as chapter five has illustrated, the German Foreign Office saw it as vital that they formulate a position on the Jewish Question in preparation for the peace negotiations with the Allies in Paris. For the diplomat Graf von Bernstorff if the German delegation could present a positive programme on the Jewish Question it would help Germany regain its international prestige. By May 1919, however, the German delegation realised that it would not be invited into negotiations and that the extensive preparations for the peace conference had been in vain. Jewish

---

8 For a formative account on the international recognition of Zionism during the First World War and Germany's relationship with Zionist organisations see Isaiah Friedman, *Germany, Turkey, and Zionism.*

affairs were raised by the German delegation not in a programmatic manner but rather in order to highlight the barbarity of the Poles and stress the inclusion of national minority protections (with German minorities in mind) in the peace treaty with Poland.

Unlike in Weimar, as chapter five revealed, in Versailles minority rights were conceived by the Allies, first and foremost, in light of the German Question, not the Jewish Question. No specific provisions were included in the Treaty of Versailles referring to the protection of minorities within Germany. Instead, Germany became the only country that signed a peace treaty without an obligation to protect its minority communities. This omission had violent repercussions when the League of Nations was powerless against Hitler's anti-Jewish policies after 1933. Having dismissed a universal minority rights regime at Paris, the Nazis' treatment of Jews motivated the writing of the 1948 Universal Declaration of Human Rights.[9]

The protection of religious and ethnic minority rights in a peace treaty with Poland was guaranteed in an appendix included in the Treaty of Versailles. Germans were the largest ethnic minority living dispersed in the new states of Eastern Europe. As such, protecting German minorities abroad became a cornerstone of the Republic's postwar foreign policy. German and Jewish lobby groups worked together in the European Congress of Nationalities and tried to strengthen the League's mandate to protect minorities. Leading this charge was the Foreign Minister Gustav Stresemann who managed, on the basis of this policy, to successfully negotiate Germany's re-entry into the international community. In 1926 the German Republic secured its place at the League of Nations table.[10] Like Zionists at the turn of the century, the German Republic grappled with the similar questions on how to nurture a cohesive national belonging crossing state boundaries, whilst being constrained by the prevalent political structure of the nation-state. During the inter-war years, through the protection of minorities, the German and Jewish Question became further entwined.

In contrast to the Treaty of Versailles, the peace treaty with Poland, known as the Minority Treaty, was drafted with both German and Jewish minorities in mind. Liberal Jewish and Zionist representatives in Paris petitioned actively for the specific inclusion of provisions for Jews. Whilst they may not have been decisive in shaping the wording of the clause, they successfully ensured Jewish rights remained on the political agenda. Jews were explicitly mentioned in the Minority Treaty and specific clauses granted them cultural autonomy. This became the template for all subsequent new state peace

---

9 Mark Mazower argues that the failure of the League of Nations' minority rights system played a significant role in the United Nations' subsequent commitment to human rights. Mazower, 'The Strange Triumph of Human Rights'. See also Samuel Moyn, *The Last Utopia: Human Rights in History* (Cambridge, MA: Harvard University Press, 2010).

10 On Stresemann's minority rights foreign policy see Carole Fink, 'Defender of Minorities: Germany in the League of Nations, 1926–1933', *Central European History* 5, no. 4 (1972): 330–57.

treaties ensuring, for the first time, the international protection of Jews on the basis of their cultural minority status.

In 1919, like in the Berlin Treaty of 1878, the protection of Jews became a constituent element of the newly conceived international system. As a result of the Minority Treaty and their recognition as a culturally autonomous minority, their fate became bound to the new ordering of states according to the nation-state model, coupled with national homogeneity, which was enshrined in the Treaty of Lausanne in 1923. Jewish questions were an important consideration in the drafting of these constitutions and international treaties. As such, they provide a unique vantage point from which to assess the competing ideas behind both the foundations of the nation-state and the post-war international order.

Despite the political strains in the infancy of the new German democracy, the ideals of the Weimar Republic were admirable. In the words of President Friedrich Ebert in his address to the opening session of the assembly on the 7 February 1919, Germans had created 'an Empire [*Reich*] of right and of righteousness, founded on the equality of everything that wears the form of mankind'.[11] The Weimar Republic signified the pinnacle of Jewish emancipation on a legal and societal level. The Republic was a positive expression of all the discontents that Jewish questions in the First World War had thrown into relief. The constitution enshrined the freedom of religious expression, even greater equality was awarded through the institution of universal male and female suffrage. Jews embraced the *Rechtsstaat* and could form a patriotism to the constitution with its liberal democratic values. The formally militaristic state under Prussian hegemony was replaced by a pluralistic, majoritarian-led parliamentary democracy. Significantly, the liberal values of the constitution filtered down to the societal level as well. Discriminations against Jews in the military, politics and academia were removed and Jews began to participate in political life on an unprecedented level.

German Jews were involved in the formation of new political parties. A number of Jews were signatory to the founding of the German Democratic Party including Hugo Preuss, Paul Nathan, Carl Melchior and Albert Einstein. The newly established Communist Party of Germany, which split from the Independent Social Democratic Party whose Chairman was Hugo Haase, the Jewish lawyer, was led by Rosa Luxemburg, a Polish Jew. German Jews were also invited to partake in the peace process. The Minister of Justice Otto Landsberg and Chairman of the German Democratic Party Carl Melchior were selected for the peace delegation sent to Paris. German Jews also helped build the Republic. Hugo Preuss, who had been unable to secure a Professorship at

---

11 Friedrich Ebert, 'Address to the Opening Session of the German Assembly on 7 February 1919', in *Source Records of the Great War*, ed. Charles F. Horne, Vol. VII, National Alumni, 1923 [https://bit.ly/2JPitMy, accessed 12/06/19].

the University of Berlin for being Jewish, was called upon to draft the new German constitution.[12]

A third of the elected members of the first cabinet of the new government headed by Chancellor Philipp Scheidemann were of Jewish descent. This included Otto Landsberg as the Minister of Finance, Eugen Schiffer as Minister of Justice, Georg Gothein as Minister of the Treasury and Eduard David who was a minister without a profile.[13] In 1922, the Jewish industrialist Walther Rathenau became the face of the German Republic internationally when he was appointed to the prestigious position of Foreign Minister. The involvement of Jews in German politics during the Weimar Republic was representative that the grievances expressed through Jewish questions in the previous decades – specifically the equality before the law and institutional discrimination – no longer had to be raised.

The visibility of German Jews in political positions, however, came at a cost. The Weimar Republic witnessed a series of political assassinations, several of which involved antisemitic intent. Proportional to their representation in the German population (under 1%), German Jews were overrepresented in left-wing political movements.[14] This trend was not representative of Jewish political voting behaviour. The majority of Jewish voters favoured the more centrist German Democratic Party. As a result of the collapse of centrist parties, after 1932, Jewish votes were mainly split between the Catholic Centre Party and the Social Democratic Party, which received the majority.[15] Nevertheless, Jews became increasingly subjected to the charge of Judeo-Bolshevism. Over the course of its five chapters, this book focused on the positive bifurcation of the Jewish Question. In doing so, it has filled a gap in the literature which otherwise tends to culminate narratives on the Jewish Question with the Holocaust. After the end of the First World War, the positive bifurcation of the Jewish Question was evident, as aforementioned, in the Weimar Republic's liberal constitution, the removal of political discriminations against Jews and the beginning of a Jewish renaissance in German society.[16] However, there are two sides to every coin, the seeds of the negative bifurcation of the Jewish Question were also sowed in the war.

---

12 On the involvement of Jews in German politics during the Weimar Republic see Pulzer, *Jews and the German State*; Wolfgang Benz, Arnold Paucker, and Peter G. J. Pulzer, eds., *Jüdisches Leben in der Weimarer Republik* (Tübingen: Mohr Siebeck, 1998); Niewyk, *The Jews in Weimar Germany*.
13 The files of the Reich Chancellery of the Weimar Republic are available online [https://bit.ly/2XVvAkF, accessed 24/06/2019].
14 See Sarah Ann Gordon, *Hitler, Germans, and the 'Jewish Question'* (Princeton: Princeton University Press, 1984), 22–24.
15 A smaller percentage of Jewish votes went to the Communist Party and the Socialist Worker's Party. Pulzer also suggests that some strategic votes may have gone to the German National People's Party. See Pulzer, *Jews and the German State*, 287–323.
16 On the Jewish renaissance see Michael Brenner, *The Renaissance of Jewish Culture in Weimar Germany* (New Haven and London: Yale University Press, 1996).

Two of the most prominent allegations that were levelled against Jews during the Weimar Republic originated in the war years: the myth of 'Judeo-Bolshevism' of a fatal 'stab-in-the-back' (*Dolchstoß*) that the German army was dealt by revolutionaries on the home front. The antisemitic trope of Judeo-Bolshevism entered Germany in around 1917 brought over by White Russian troops escaping the Bolshevist revolution in Russia. During parliamentary discussions on the Treaty of Brest-Litovsk, when the Jewish minister Oskar Cohn had to outline the decision taken by the Independent Social Democrats to not accept the treaty, the antisemitic press used the incidence to prove that revolutionary Bolshevism had entered Germany.[17]

The claim of Judeo-Bolshevism gained momentum during the German revolution. In November 1918, the Jewish literary critic and member of the Independent Social Democrats, Kurt Eisner, declared Bavaria a Republic and became its President. A few months later, the Communist Party member Rosa Luxemburg helped organise and lead a general strike against the government. In April, a short-lived Bavarian Soviet Republic was established with the Jewish playwright Ernst Toller as its Chief of Staff. Other German Jews involved in the Soviet Republic included the anarchists Gustav Landauer, Erich Mühsam and Eugen Leviné.[18] With the visibility of Jews in the revolution, the trope of Judeo-Bolshevism became intertwined with the myth of an international Jewish world domination conspiracy which was popularised in Germany through the translation and dissemination of a Russian forgery entitled *Die Geheimnisse der Weisen von Zion*.[19]

During the period of unrest, the mounting fears of a Bolshevist revolution in Germany were used to legitimise antisemitic violence. For Kurt Eisner, as for Gustav Landauer and Rosa Luxemburg, their politics came before their Judaism. Judeo-Bolshevism, however, conflated the two. When Kurt Eisner was assassinated his murderer Count Anton Graf von Arco auf Valley justified his actions on the basis that Eisner was a Jew and that he despised Bolshevism. The irony of the situation was that Eisner was perceived as a Jew whilst Anton Graf a self-declared German nationalist who was Jewish through his mother's line, was not.[20] Whilst Eisner's murderer had acted alone, Rosa Luxemburg and Karl Liebknecht were both summarily executed after the suppression of the Spartacist uprising in January 1919 by the Free Corps (*Freikorps*),

17 On Judeo-Bolshevism in Germany see Brian E. Crim, '"Our Most Serious Enemy": The Specter of Judeo-Bolshevism in the German Military Community, 1914–1923', *Central European History* 44, no. 4 (2011): 624–41.

18 See Grady, *A Deadly Legacy*.

19 It was published in Germany in January 1920. By the end of the year, six editions had been published. See Michael Hagemeister, 'The Protocols of the Elders of Zion: Between History and Fiction', *New German Critique*, no. 103 (2008): 83–95.

20 Sterling Fishman, 'Assassination of Kurt Eisner: A Study of Identity in the German-Jewish Dialogue', in *The German-Jewish Dialogue Reconsidered: A Symposium in Honour of George L. Mosse*, ed. Klaus L. Berghahn (New York: Peter Lang, 1996), 141–54.

a civilian militia that the government used to help contain the revolutionary unrest. Gustav Landauer and Eugen Leviné were also killed by the Free Corps for their involvement in the Soviet Republic.[21]

Alongside Judeo-Bolshevism another antisemitic trope that had its origins in the First World War was the myth that the Germany army had not been defeated. Rather, it had been stabbed-in-the-back by elements on the home front. The *Dolchstoßlegende* was born.[22] The blame was placed on those who had been involved in the revolution and armistice. As the myth gained traction within far-right-wing circles it was directed at Jews and the *Judenrepublik* they had created with the help of socialists and communists. The shared experience of the First World War for German Gentiles and Jews was replaced by myths promulgated by Generals Hindenburg and Ludendorff that Jews had profiteered during the war and shirked their military duty. As chapter three has shown, these claims were able to manifest as a result of the conduct of the *Judenzählung*.

In his speech to the Parliamentary Investigatory Committee on the 18 November 1919 General Hindenburg misquoted the British general Frederick Maurice as saying that the German army had been stabbed-in-the-back. By February, a speech by General Ludendorff on the new government intensified this claim. The new government, according to Ludendorff, had disarmed the 'unconquered' German army to allow for the revolution. The speech made no reference to Jews but was directed at the 'November Criminals' (*Novemberverbrecher*) whom had signed the armistice to end the First World War.[23] The two Generals ignored their own contributions to the demand for an armistice and shifted blame away from the errors of the Supreme Army Command.

As with the spectre of Judeo-Bolshevism, the implications of these myths were realised when words turned into deeds with the assassination of Matthias Erzberger, Reich Minister of Finance, in August 1921 by the ultra-nationalist Organisation Consul. His crime: he was one of the signatories to the Treaty of Versailles and thus a *Novemberverbrecher*. Erzberger's assassination was followed two years later by that of Foreign Minister Walther Rathenau, by members of the same organisation. Organisation Consul was an underground antisemitic organisation consisting of former members of the Marinebrigade Ehrhardt unit, which was attached to the Free Corps. In the same year

---

21 On the violent acts committed by the *Freikorps* during the inter-war years see Brian E. Crim, 'Terror from the Right: Revolutionary Terrorism and the Failure of the Weimar Republic', *Journal of Conflict Studies* 27, no. 2 (2008): 51–63.

22 For further reading on the *Dolchstoßlegende* see Michael Alme, *Die Entstehung der Dolchstoßlegende nach dem Ersten Weltkrieg im Spiegel von Quellen und Forschung*, 1. (Norderstedt: GRIN Verlag, 2016); George S. Vascik and Mark R. Sadler, *The Stab-in-the-Back Myth and the Fall of the Weimar Republic: A History in Documents and Visual Sources* (London: Bloomsbury Publishing, 2016).

23 See Erich Ludendorff's speech, 'Speech on the New German Government in February 1919', in *Source Records of the Great War*, ed. Charles F. Horne, Vol. VII, National Alumni, 1923 [https://bit.ly/2JPitMy, accessed 24/06/19].

as Rathenau's assassination the organisation was also responsible for throwing prussic acid at the Chancellor Philipp Scheidemann, who managed to escape unscathed. These negative bifurcations of the Jewish Question, which emerged out of the war, were factors which contributed to the National Socialist Party's rise to power and the policy to exterminate European Jewry.[24]

Whilst the Jewish Question was appropriated to spread the myths of Judeo-Bolshevism and the *Dolchstoßlegende* and justify antisemitic violence, in this book I have shown the ambivalence of Jewish questions. The inter-war years were not dominated by the negative bifurcation of the Jewish Question but, I suggest, remained ambivalent. The public response to the assassination of Walther Rathenau testifies to this as the subsequent debate erupted into a defence of the Republic. Supporters of the Republic used the assassination to stress the importance of rallying against the threats to the new regime. A number of notable figures came out as *Vernunftrepublikaner* including Thomas Mann, Friedrich Meinecke and Gustav Stresemann. Jewish questions had once again, as this thesis argued, highlighted a significant moment in Germany's political development and the shaky ground upon which the Republic was built. The assassination of Walther Rathenau offers a further avenue of research that would build on this work by identifying another moment when a Jewish Question catalysed a debate on the German nation-state. It would shed light on how political reform in Germany was an ongoing complex process.

This book has shown how Jewish questions brought to the fore issues concerning minority rights, religious freedom, national identity and multiculturalism. Long after the end of the Weimar Republic and the Third Reich, these issues remain salient in the Federal Republic. Questions that the protagonists of this book were asking in the early twentieth century concerning citizenship rights for minority groups, whether cultural homogeneity in the nation-state was important and the role of religion in the state have been given renewed urgency with the rise of populist movements and the reassertion of the nation-state against the backdrop of unprecedented connectivity and increasing globalisation. This research will be of use to scholars interested in the continuities and discontinuities in understandings of the German nation-state, specifically its historical tradition of a *Kulturnation*, and the relationship between the German state and Jewish questions.

---

24 On Organisation Consul and paramilitary violence in the Weimar Republic see Robert Heynen, 'The German Revolution and the Radical Right' in *The German Revolution and Political Theory* eds. Gaard Kets and James Muldoon (Switzerland: Palgrave Macmillan, 2019), 45–68; Arthur D. Brenner, 'Feme Murder: Paramilitary "Self-Justice" in Weimar Germany' in *Death Squads in Global Perspective* ed. Bruce B. Campbell and Arthur D. Brenner (New York: Palgrave Macmillan, 2000), 57–83; Martin Sabrow, *Der Rathenaumord: Rekonstruktion einer Verschwörung gegen die Republik von Weimar,* Schriftenreihe der Vierteljahrhefte für Zeitgeschichte 69 (Munich: Oldenbourg Verlag, 1994); Robert G. L. Waite, *Vanguard of Nazism: The Free Corps Movement in Postwar Germany 1918–1923* (New York: W. W. Norton and Company, 1969); Howard Stern, 'The Organisation Consul', *The Journal of Modern History* 35, no. 1 (1963): 20–32.

Jewish questions continued to be posed in Germany long after the end of the Second World War. On the one hand, after the war, Jewish questions featured in the guise of antisemitism. Overt antisemitism combined with social amnesia of the atrocities committed towards European Jewry in the Second World War, evidenced in the trial of Philip Auerbach, the Restitution Commissioner of Bavaria, permeated German society after the end of the Second World War.[25] A lecture given a few years later by Theodor W. Adorno made explicit the remnants of Nazism in the democratic Federal Republic and the necessity on an ethical-political level for German institutions to work through the past and for Germans as individuals to reflect on their self-understanding in the Federal Republic.[26]

On the other hand, Germans Jews (or 'Jews in Germany' the term used by the Nazis and later appropriated by Jews living in the Federal Republic) played a significant role as mediators of German democracy.[27] Michal Bodemann argues that Jews were vital for West German domestic and foreign policy as they performed the role of 'ideological labourers'.[28] Hannah Arendt similarly studied Jews exercising this role in early capitalist Europe.[29] During the Adenauer era, in domestic policy, Jews became a 'necessary element in German society as an apolitical counterbalance to Nazism'.[30] After the war, German-Jewish organisations expressed a willingness to participate in building democratic structures in Germany and the United States High Commissioner for Germany, John McCloy correlated the development of the German Jewish community with Germany's progress as a democratic state.[31] The role of Jewish public intellectuals in the Federal Republic, especially those within the Frankfurt School also testified to the importance of Jewish voices in shaping the cultural and intellectual life of post-war Germany.[32] In the 1970s, Rainer Werner Fassbinder's 1975 play *Der Müll, die Stadt und der Tod* and the screening of the American mini-series *Holocaust* in 1979, provoked an

---

25 Anon., 'Philip Auerbach Commits Suicide: Act Due to Verdict of German Court', *Jewish Telegraphic Agency* XIX:160 (18 August 1952), 3 [https://bit.ly/2LrE4hw, accessed 17/09/2019].

26 Theodor W. Adorno, 'Was Bedeutet: Aufarbeitung Der Vergangenheit', in *Gesammelte Schriften 10.2, Kulturkritik Und Gesellschaft II: Eingriffe. Stichworte.* (Frankfurt/Main: Suhrkamp, 1977), 555–72.

27 Y. Michal Bodemann, 'The State in the Construction of Ethnicity and Ideological Labor: The Case of German Jewry', *Critical Sociology* 17, no. 3 (1 October 1990): 40. See also Anthony D. Kauders, *Democratization and the Jews: Munich, 1945–1965*, Vidal Sassoon International Center for the Study of Antisemitism (Lincoln, Nebraska: University of Nebraska Press, 2004).

28 Bodemann, 'The State in the Construction of Ethnicity and Ideological Labor'.

29 Ibid, 37. See also Hannah Arendt, *The Origins of Totalitarianism*, 1st ed. (New York: Harcourt, Brace, 1951).

30 Bodemann, 'The State in the Construction of Ethnicity and Ideological Labor', 41.

31 Michael Brenner, 'In the Shadow of the Holocaust: The Changing Image of German Jewry after 1945', *United States Holocaust Memorial Museum*, Ina Levine Annual Lecture, 2010, 4–5 [https://bit.ly/2SuH2CJ, accessed 17/07/19].

32 On the Frankfurt School see Martin Jay, *The Dialectical Imagination: A History of the Frankfurt School and the Institute of Social Research, 1923–1950* (Berkeley: University of California Press, 1996).

unprecedented soul-searching in the Federal Republic about the Nazi past, antisemitism and German national identity.[33]

Jews played an important role not only in Germany's post-war domestic policy but also in its foreign policy. After the war normalising relations with Jews was perceived as important for fostering relations with other West European countries and the United States.[34] When the State of Israel was declared in 1948, maintaining positive relations became a cornerstone of German foreign policy. This attitude echoed that of the German Foreign Office after the First World War when formulating a positive programme on the Jewish Question was envisioned as Germany's ticket back into the international community and a signal that a new democratic spirit had taken hold in Germany. In a recent move, in May 2019, the German parliament ruled that the, Palestinian-led, 'Boycott, Divest and Sanctions' (B. D. S.) movement aimed at Israel is antisemitic.[35] In the wake of the ruling, the Director of the Jewish museum of Berlin, having tweeted an article criticising the resolution, resigned from his post.[36] Worrying trends involving a 20 % rise in antisemitic instances in Germany led, in part, to the anti-B. D. S. resolution. The majority of incidences reported have been committed by the far-right. However, the political party Alternative for Germany (*Alternative für Deutschland*, AfD), known to express far-right views, has instrumentalised this trend to promote Islamophobia. The way in which Jewish questions are embedded within understandings of German nationhood has led to this paradox. Whereby some members of the AfD identify anti-antisemitism as a pillar of Germany's national culture whilst promoting racism towards another minority group.[37]

Jewish questions in Germany also speak to another mechanism, which goes beyond German-Jewish relations. They reveal the dynamics of German nationhood. The notion that the attributes of the *Kulturnation* define German national unity continues to gain traction in the Federal Republic today.[38] When Germany was reunited in 1990, under Article 35 of the Unification Treaty between the Federal Republic of Germany (FRG) and German Democratic Republic (GDR), art and culture were identified as

---

33 Thomas Elsaesser, 'Frankfurt, Germans and Jews: The City, Garbage and Death', in *Fassbinder's Germany: History Identity Subject* (Amsterdam: Amsterdam University Press, 1996), 175–96.
34 Bodemann, 'The State in the Construction of Ethnicity and Ideological Labor', 41.
35 Katrin Bennhold, 'German Parliament Deems B. D. S. Movement Anti-Semitic', *The New York Times*, 17 May 2019 [https://nyti.ms/2LY8d7x, accessed 17/07/19].
36 Melissa Eddy, 'Director of Berlin's Jewish Museum Quits After Spat Over B. D. S.', *The New York Times*, 14 June 2019 [https://nyti.ms/2LsxtDh, accessed 17/07/19].
37 This is not to say that the AfD takes an active anti-antisemitism stance. Quite the opposite. Its members often downplay the importance of the Nazi era and remembrance politics. However, it uses a pro-Israel position strategically to promote Islamophobia. On this phenomenon see Marc Grimm, 'Pro-Israelism and Antisemitism within Germany's Populist Radical Right AfD', *European Journal of Current Legal Issues* 25, no. 1 (2019) [https://bit.ly/30F76xH, accessed 17/07/19].
38 Arndt Kremer, 'Transitions of a Myth?', 54.

the elements which preserved the unity of the German nation.[39] Since 2015, when the Chancellor Angela Merkel announced an open-door policy which welcomed refugees fleeing the civil war in Syria, an earlier debate on *Leitkultur* (guiding culture) was revived.[40] The *Leitkultur* debate centres around the question of what German national culture is, or should be, defined by. As Jewish questions catalysed debates about German national identity in the Wilhelmine era, in the Federal Republic another religious and ethnic minority, Muslims, are at the centre of these discussions.

In the Federal Republic the ongoing *Leitkultur* debate has diverged from the first usage of the term by the political scientist Bassam Tibi who coined it in his 1998 book *Europa ohne Identität*.[41] Tibi argued that Germany's identity should be grounded in European values rather than oriented towards the idea of 'nation' (*Volk*) and 'traditions' (*Gepflogenheiten*).[42] The values upon which this German identity should be based, according to Tibi, should be modelled on those of the liberal-democratic order: democracy, secularism, human rights and pluralism. Tibi saw these values as imperative for a globalised society confronted with immigration from non-European, specifically Muslim, countries. Rather than multiculturalism, Tibi urged for cultural pluralism, which he understood as a society where people from different cultures and religions live together in a community governed by a clear system of values that are respected.[43] Tibi outlined a model not unlike one advocated by the sociologist Werner Sombart in his 1911 lecture on 'The Future of the Jews'. As chapter one revealed, Sombart framed his answer to the Jewish Question as part of a larger claim to a multi-cultural or culturally pluralist German Empire.

The question of multiculturalism remains on the public agenda in Germany today.[44] Arguments made by advocates of a German *Leitkultur* resonate with Heinrich von Treitschke's demand for Jews to assimilate in order to ensure a homogenous Christian national culture in Germany. This debate erupted in 2000 against the backdrop of a discussion regarding revisions to Germany's nationality law. The Christian Democratic Union (CDU) politician Friedrich Merz spoke of a 'liberal German dominant

---

39 Bundesministerium der Justiz und für Verbraucherschutz, 'Vertrag zwischen der Bundesrepublik Deutschland und der Deutschen Demokratischen Republik über die Herstellung der Einheit Deutschlands (Einigungsvertrag) Art 35 Kultur', (31 August 1990) [https://bit.ly/2RUZHad, accessed 04/07/2019].

40 Andrea Dernbach, 'Die Leitkultur stirbt nicht, sie modernisiert sich nur', *Der Tagesspiegel*, 4 September 2015 [https://bit.ly/2FRCEsl, accessed 04/07/2019].

41 Bassam Tibi, *Europa ohne Identität? Die Krise der multikulturellen Gesellschaft* (München: Bertelsmann, 1998).

42 Ibid, xvii.

43 Ibid, 92.

44 The Federal Office of Statistics reported that in 2017, 10.6 million foreign nationals were registered in Germany, which is up 5.8 % from the previous year. See Statistisches Bundesamt, 'Ausländische Bevölkerung wächst im Jahr 2017 um 5,8 %' [https://bit.ly/2RTjiYD, accessed 04/07/2019].

culture' (*Leitkultur*) that needed to extend beyond constitutional patriotism[45] (*Verfassungspatriotismus*) and include liberal European values that migrants would have to be prepared to respect.[46] Since, the debate has become divisive in Germany and is still ongoing.[47] Whilst what a German *Leitkultur* would look like remains unclear,[48] the debate is split between those that believe immigrants should 'assimilate to a set of shared cultural values' and critics who argue that the promotion of a German *Leitkultur* would limit multiculturalism by 'rejecting those who do not succeed in assimilating'.[49]

Until 2000, the German nationality law adopted by the Federal Republic was based on the 1913 citizenship law of the German Empire that provided a unified German citizenship rooted in descent and ethnicity (*ius sanguinis*).[50] This law remained in place throughout the Weimar Republic and was adopted again in the Basic Law of 1949. The nationality law enabled ethnic Germans living within the German borders of 1937 to apply for citizenship. Moreover, West Germany could grant citizenship to East Germans fleeing from the GDR.[51]

Rooted in descent and ethnicity, the nationality law was increasingly scrutinised after unification; in particular the strict naturalisation requirements for children born in Germany to foreign national parents.[52] In 2000, the nationality law was revised to allow for territorial elements (*ius soli*). Children born to foreign parents can acquire German citizenship so long as one parent has been legally residing in Germany for eight years and has the right to remain. Dual nationality, however, is restricted under German law and at the age of eighteen children with dual nationality have to declare if

---

45 The idea of constitutional patriotism is closely associated with the writings of Jürgen Habermas as he used it in order to formulate a collective identity for post-war Germany and for the European Union. See Jürgen Habermas, *Between Facts and Norms: Contribution to a Discourse Theory of Law and Democracy* (Cambridge: MIT Press, 1996); Jürgen Habermas *The Inclusion of the Other* (Cambridge: MIT Press, 1998). More recently, Jan-Werner Müller has built on Habermas and attempted to develop a theory of constitution patriotism. See Jan-Werner Müller, *Constitutional Patriotism* (Princeton: Princeton University Press, 2007). For a useful introduction to constitutional patriotism see Jan-Werner Müller and Kim Lane Scheppele, 'Constitutional Patriotism: An introduction', *International Journal of Constitutional Law* 6, no. 1 (2008): 67–71.
46 Friedrich Merz, 'Einwanderung und Identität', *Die Welt*, 25 October 2000 [https://bit.ly/2pNQZiV, accessed 04/07/2019].
47 For a repository of recent articles on the subject of *Leitkultur* in the *Frankfurter Allgemeine Zeitung* see [https://bit.ly/2NxziB0, accessed 04/07/2019]; *Die Zeit* see [https://bit.ly/2KX5HyJ, accessed 04/07/2019]; *Presse Portal* see [https://bit.ly/2XGbYov, accessed 04/07/2019].
48 Ferda Ataman, 'Ein Leitkultur-Leithammel für die CDU', *Spiegel*, 3 November 2018 [https://bit.ly/3oblflS, accessed 04/07/2019].
49 Anon., 'German Interior Minister speaks out in favor of "Leitkultur" for immigrants', *Deutsche Welle*, 30 April 2017 [https://bit.ly/2LJtcen, accessed 04/07/2019].
50 Deutscher Bundestag, *Basic Law for the Federal Republic of Germany, 23 May 1949*, trans. Christian Tomuschat et al. (Berlin: Deutscher Bundestag, 2018) [https://bit.ly/2uOg2nF, accessed 04/07/2019]. See also Kay Hailbronner, 'EURO Citizenship Observatory. Country Report: Germany', *European University Institute, Florence* (October 2012), 1.
51 Ibid, 2.
52 Ibid, 3–8.

they want to retain their German nationality. Only in exceptional circumstances will dual nationality be awarded.[53]

Since the introduction of *ius soli* criteria to the nationality law, a derogatory distinction has been popularised in Germany to differentiate between German citizens of ethnic German descent, *Biodeutsche,* and ethnically non-German citizens, *Passdeutsche.*[54] The etymology of the term *Biodeutsche* relates to *Leitkultur,* which derives from botany and is used to refer to dominant plant varieties in a biotope.[55] Like the word, *Abstammung,* this vocabulary concerning what constitutes a German national identity continues to originate from biological and descent-based terminology. Whilst the terms *Biodeutsche* and *Passdeutsche* are new and their intention is both exclusionary and derogatory they, nevertheless, reference similar ideas to those raised within Zionist circles in Germany at the turn of the century. As discussed in chapter one, Zionists discussed different types of national consciousness in Germany as derived either from ethnicity or place of birth. Once a central component of the German Jewish Question, in the Federal Republic these questions remain salient in the ongoing German Question.

Jewish questions, discussed in this book, unlocked wider debates on Germany's political system and its national identity. They raised questions and ideas that continue to resonate in contemporary discussions on Germany's nationality law and the place of non-ethnic Germans within the state. More than one hundred years after the Jewish questions discussed in this book, similar questions remain. As I have shown, Jewish questions of the early twentieth century were powerful catalysts for debates about the nature of the German state. As the Berlin Republic faces new questions about immigration, cultural pluralism, minority rights and duties, it would do well to remember these old ones.

---

53 See Federal Ministry of the Interior Building and Community, 'Dual citizenship – multiple nationality' [https://bit.ly/2Xrg1R7, accessed 04/07/2019].
54 Matthias Heine, 'Deutsch ist, wer Rad fährt und im Bioladen kauft', *Welt,* 30 July 2017 [https://bit.ly/2JK36VQ, accessed 17/07/19].
55 Kay-Alexander Scholz, 'What is German "Leitkultur"?' *Deutsche Welle,* 3 May 2017 [https://bit.ly/2YyXlQS, accessed 04/07/2019].

Bibliography

Archival sources

Auswärtiges Amt, R19605. *Internationale Angelegenheiten Nr. 3: Die Juden, Band 1 (1918–1919)*.
- 'K181762'.
- 'K181838'.
- 'K181842'.
- 'K181845'.
- 'K181943'.
- 'K181952'.
- 'K181953'.
- 'K181976'.
- 'K181999'.
- 'K182002'.

Auswärtiges Amt, R19606. *Internationale Angelegenheiten Nr. 3: Die Juden, Band 2 (1920)*.
- 'K182192'.

Central Zionist Archives
- A15/VIII 10/720, Max Bodenheimer, *Zur Lage der Russischen Juden* (undated).
- A124/123, 'An Interview with Hermann Struck', *The Hebrew Standard*, 1920.

Hauptstaatsarchiv Stuttgart M738, Bü 46 (2017). *Judenstatistik aus dem Jahre 1916: Wiedergaben aus den Geheimakten des ehemaligen preußischen Kriegsministeriums.*
- David Felix Waldstein to Hermann von Stein, 30.08.1917, No. 16–18.
- Hermann von Stein to Oskar Cassel, 20.1.1917, No. 38–39.
- Oskar Cassel to Hermann von Stein, 29.12.1916, No. 4–11.
- Reiss von Scheurnschloss to Wahnschaffe, 16.1.1917, No. 67–68.
- 'Vorgeschichte der Judenstatistik', 20.1.1917, No.33–34.

Primary sources

Anonymous, 'An die Juden in Polen', *Berliner Tageblatt* 43, no. 442 (1 September 1914).
- 'Auf Beschwerden gegen die Judenzählung im Heere', *Im deutschen Reich* 2 (1917): 69.
- 'Eine merkwürdige Statistik', *Berliner Tageblatt*, Morgenblatt (20 Oktober 1916): 3.
- 'Der Weltkrieg und die Judenfrage Rezension' *Im deutschen Reich* 11–12 (November 1916): 282.

- 'Deutsche Weltpolitik und türkische Entwicklung', *Jüdische Rundschau* XX, no. 13 (26 März 1915): 105.
- 'Deutschland: Zur Oppeneheimer-Debatte', *Die Welt* XIV, no. 13 (1 April 1910): 287.
- 'Die "konfessioneele Zählung" im Heere und der Reichstag', *Berliner Tagesblatt*, Abendblatt (4 November 1916): 3.
- 'Die Kriegstagung des Centralvereins deutscher Staatsbürger jüdischen Glaubens', *Allgemeine Zeitung des Judentums* 6, (9 Februar 1917): 67.
- 'Die Reichsregierung und die Bestrebungen der Zionisten', *Norddeutsche Allgemeine Zeitung* 57, no. 10 (6 Januar 1918).
- 'Die Woche, Berlin, 24 Juni 1914', *Allegemeine Zeitung des Judentums* 28, no. 26 (26 Juni 1914): 304.
- 'Erlebnisse in jüdischen Kolonien', *Jüdische Rundschau* XX, no. 14 (9 April 1915): 117.
- 'German Interior Minister speaks out in favor of "Leitkultur" for immigrants'. *Deutsche Welle*, 30 April 2017.
- 'Judenzählung" beim Roten Kreuz', *Berliner Tagesblatt*, Morgenblatt, (4 November 1916): 3.
- *Judische Rundschau* XVIII, no. 21 (3 Mai 1918): 133–34.
- 'Letzter Vortrag Professor Sombarts', *Jüdische Rundschau* XVI, no. 50 (15 Dezember 1911): 591.
- 'Ludendorff assails Jews, Pope and Catholic Clergy', *Jewish Telegraphic Agency* (1 March 1924).
- 'Preuss Denounces Demand of Allies'. *The New York Times*. 14 September 1919.
- *Schmeitzner Internationale Monatsschrift: Zeitung für die Allegemeine Vereinigung zur Bekämpfung des Judentums* (Chemnitz und Dresden, 1883): 314–16.
- 'Sein oder nichtsein?' *Jüdische Rundschau* XVI, no. 46 (17 November 1911): 541.
- 'Sombart und wir', *Jüdische Rundschau* XVI, no. 50 (15 Dezember 1911): 589.
- 'Sprechsaal: Aussprache zur Judenfrage', *Der Kunstwart* 25, no. 22 (August 1912): 236–261.
- 'Sprechsaal: Deutschtum und Judentum', *Der Kunstwart* 25, no. 13 (April 1912): 6–15.
- 'Zur Judenstatistik in der Armee', *Berliner Tageblatt* (5 November 1916): 3.
Adorno, Theodor W. 'Was Bedeutet: Aufarbeitung Der Vergangenheit'. In *Gesammelte Schriften 10.2*, 555–72. Kulturkritik Und Gesellschaft II: Eingriffe. Stichworte. Frankfurt/Main: Suhrkamp, 1977.
Armin, Otto. *Die Juden Im Heere. Eine Statistische Untersuchung Nach Amtlichen Quellen*. München: Deutscher Volks-Verlag, 1919.
Ataman, Ferda. 'Ein Leitkultur-Leithammel für die CDU'. *Spiegel*, 3 November 2018.
Auerbach, Elias. 'Deutsche Kultur in Zionismus', *Jüdische Rundschau* VIII, no. 7 (13 Februar 1903): 49–51 in Reinharz, *Dokumente zur Geschichte des deutschen Zionismus 1882–1933*, 68–69.
Avenarius, Ferdinand. 'Aussprachen mit Juden', *Der Kunstwart* 25, no. 22 (August 1912): 225–236.
Bauer, Bruno. *Die Judenfrage*. Braunschweig: Verlag von Friedrich Otto, 1843.
- 'Die Fähigkeit der heutigen Juden und Christen, frei zu werden' in Georg Herwegh (ed.), Ein-undzwanzig Bogen aus der Schweiz, (Zürich und Winterthur, 1843), 56–71.
Bennhold, Katrin. 'German Parliament Deems B. D. S. Movement Anti-Semitic'. *The New York Times*, 17 May 2019.
Bodmer, M. I. 'Ein neuer Staatenbund und das Ostjudenproblem' in ed. Ernst Jäckh. *Der Deutsche Krieg*, Politische Flugschriften, Heft 73. Stuttgart und Berlin: Deutsche Verlags-Anstalt, 1916, 5–36.
Buber, Martin. *Drei Reden über das Judentum*. Frankfurt am Main: Rütten & Loening, 1911.
Bundesministerium der Justiz und für Verbraucherschutz. 'Vertrag zwischen der Bundesrepublik Deutschland und der Deutschen Demokratischen Republik über die Herstellung der Einheit Deutschlands (Einigungsvertrag) Art 35 Kultur'. 31 August 1990.

Burdick, Charles B., and Ralph H. Lutz, eds. *The Political Institutions of the German Revolution, 1918–1919*. Stanford, New York: Frederick A. Praeger Publishers, 1966.

– 'Appendix 3, March 17, 1919 Meeting: List A Experts'. In Burdick and Lutz, 263–264.

– 'Meeting of the Reich Ministry, Wednesday, March 12, 1919, 4:00pm, in the Small Committee Room of the National Assembly'. In Burdick and Lutz, 268–274.

– 'Meeting of the Reich Ministry, Tuesday, March 18, 1919, 12:00 noon'. In Burdick and Lutz, 264–266.

– 'Meeting of the Reich Ministry, March 21, 1919, 9:30am in the Reich Chancellery'. In Burdick and Lutz, 628–274.

– 'Meeting of the Reich Ministry, March 25, 1919, 3:00pm at Weimar Castle'. In Burdick and Lutz, 279–280.

– 'Meeting of the Reich Ministry, April 25, 1919, 11:00am, at the Reich Chancellery'. In Burdick and Lutz, 281.

– 'Minutes of the Council of People's Representatives'. In Burdick and Lutz, 65–209.

Chasanowitsch, Leon, and Leo Motzkin. *Die Judenfrage der Gegenwart: Dokumentensammlung*, 74–81. Stockholm: Bokförlaget Judäa A. B., 1919.

Cohen, Arthur. 'Die Judenfrage – Eine Minoritätenfrage'. *Neue jüdische Monatshefte* 3, no. 7/8 (19 January 1919): 164–68.

Cohen, Helene Hanna. 'Die Judenfrage in Der Internationale'. *Neue jüdische Monatshefte* 2, no. 6 (25 December 1917): 136–39.

Eddy, Melissa. 'Director of Berlin's Jewish Museum Quits After Spat Over B. D. S'. *The New York Times*, 14 June 2019.

Eugen, Dühring. *Die Judenfrage als Racen-, Sitten- und Culturfrage. Mit einer weltgeschichtlichen Antwort*. 1st ed. Karlsruhe und Leipzig: Verlag von H. Reuther, 1881.

Dernbach, Andrea. 'Die Leitkultur stirbt nicht, sie modernisiert sich nur'. *Der Tagesspiegel*, 4 September 2015.

Deutscher Bundestag. *Basic Law for the Federal Republic of Germany, 23 May 1949*. Translated by Christian Tomuschat, David P. Currie, Donald P. Kommers, and Raymond Kerr. Berlin: Deutscher Bundestag, 2018.

Dohm, Christian Wilhelm von. *Über die bürgerliche Verbesserung der Juden*, Berlin, Stettin: Friedrich Nicolai, 1781.

Feuchtwanger, Sigbert. 'Grundsätzliches zur deutschen Judenfrage'. *Neue jüdische Monatshefte* 1, no. 19 (10 Juli 1917): 543–50.

Fuchs, Eugen. 'Die Zukunft der Juden'. *Im eutschen Reich* 6 (Juni 1912).

– *Um Deutschtum und Judentum, Gesammelte Reden und Aufsätze (1894–1919)*. Frankfurt am Main: Verlag von J. Kaufmann, 1919.

Fuld, Ludwig, 'Der Nationaljude als Staatsbürger', *Im deutschen Reich* III (11 November 1897): 531.

Friedrich, Hans. *Die Juden im Heere*. München: Verlag Lehmanns, 1920.

Goldmann-Oppeln, Felix. 'Der Ausklang der "Kunstwartdebatte"!', *Im deutschen Reich* 12 (Dezember 1912): 533–540.

Goldstein, Mortiz. 'Deutsch-Jüdischer Parnaß', *Der Kunstwart* 25, no. 11 (März 1912): 281–294.

Goslar, Hans. 'Werner Sombart über die Zukunft der Juden' *Jüdische Rundschau* XVI, no. 46 (17 November 1911): 543–44.

Green, Emma. 'Paul Nehlen's Fringe Anti-Semitism'. *The Atlantic*, 24 January 2018.

Heine, Matthias. 'Deutsch ist, wer Rad fährt und im Bioladen kauft'. *Welt*, 30 July 2017.

Hertz, Friedrich. *Moderne Rassentheorien*. Wien: C. W. Stern, 1904.

Herzl, Theodor. *The Complete Diaries of Theodor Herzl*. Edited by Raphael Patai. Translated by Harry Zohn. I–V vols. New York & London: Herzl Press and Thomas Yoseloff, 1960.

– *The Jewish State*. London: Penguin Books, 2010.

Herzl, Theodor, and Max Bodenheimer. *Im Anfang der zionistischen Bewegung: Eine Dokumentation auf der Grundlage des Briefwechsels zwischen Theodor Herzl und Max Bodeheimer von 1896 bis 1905*. Edited by Henriette Hannah Bodenheimer. Frankfurt am Main: Europäische Verlagsanstalt, 1965.

Hitler, Adolf. *Mein Kampf*. [Unabridged ed.]. New York: Fredonia Classics, 2003.

Huldschiner, Richard. 'Stammesbewusstsein – Volksbewusstsein', *Die Welt* XIV, no. 9 (4 März 1910): 179.

Kautsky, Karl. 'Are the Jews a Race?', 2nd German edition. London: Jonathon Cape, 1926.

– *Rasse und Judentum*. Berlin und Stuttgart: J. H. W. Dietz, 1914.

Kettle, Martin. 'The political landscapes of Brexit Britain and Weimar Germany are scarily similar'. *The Guardian*, 16 May 2019.

Krieger, Karsten. *Der 'Berliner Antisemitismusstreit,' 1879–1881: eine Kontroverse um die Zugehörigkeit der deutschen Juden zur Nation*. Kommentierte Quellenedition. 2 vols. München: K. G. Saur, 2003.

– Anon., [Moritz Busch], 'Die deutschen Juden in der Gegenwart, und was nun?', *Die Grenzboten* 39 (1880): 177–194. In Krieger, 458–85.

– Herman Cohen, 'Ein Bekenntniß in der Judenfrage' (1880). In Krieger, 337–60.

– 'Interpellation des Abgeordneten Dr Hänel im preußischen Abgeordnetenhause betreffend die Agitation gegen die jüdischen Staatsbürger'. In Krieger, 555–68.

– 'Manifest der Berliner Notablen gegen den Antisemitismus', (12. November 1880). In Krieger, 551–54.

– No author, 'Heinrich von Treitschke über die Judenfrage', *Germania*, Nr. 275, (28.11.1879). In Krieger, 20.

– Theodor Mommsen, *Auch ein Wort über unser Judentum*. Berlin, 1880. In Krieger, 695–709.

– Theodor Mommsen an Emil du Bois-Reymond, [Sonntag, dem 14.11.1880]. In Krieger, 569.

Kreppel, Jonas. *Der Weltkrieg Und Die Judenfrage*. Wien: Verlag Redaktion 'Der Tag', 1915.

Lazarus, Moritz. *Was heißt national? Ein Vortrag von Moritz Lazarus*. Berlin: Dümmlers Verlag, 1880.

– 'What Does National Mean? A Lecture', [2 December 1879] in *The State, the Nation, and the Jews: Liberalism and the Antisemitism Dispute in Bismarck's Germany*, trans. Marcel Stoetzler (Lincoln, Nebraska: University of Nebraska Press, 2008), 317–359.

Lichtheim, Richard. *Ruckkehr: Lebenserinnerungen aus der Frühzeit des deutschen Zionismus*. Stuttgart: Deutsche Verlags-Anstalt, 1970.

Luckau, Alma. *The German Delegation at the Paris Peace Conference*. 2nd edition. New York: Howard Fertig, 1971.

– 'Document 17: Preliminary List of the German Peace Delegation at Versailles, as of May 1, 1919'. In Luckau, 188–190.

– 'Document 20: Memorandum: Foreign Office Draft Proposals'. In Luckau, 195–199.

– 'Document 21: Instructions given to the German plenipotentiaries of peace'. In Luckau, 199–208.

– 'Document 30: Speech of President Clemenceau on May 7, 1919, at the Trianon Palace Hotel, Versailles'. In Luckau, 223–224.

– 'Document 57: German Counterproposals of May 29, 1919'. In Luckau, 306–405.

Ludendorff, Eric. *My War Memories, 1914–1918*. 2nd ed. Vol. I & II. London: Hutschinson & Co., 1923.

– *The General Staff and Its Problems*. Translated by F. A. Holt. New York: EP Dutton and Company, 1920.

– 'Speech on the New German Government in February 1919'. In *Source Records of the Great War* ed. Charles F. Horne, Vol. VII, National Alumni, 1923.

Mahler, Raphael. *Jewish Emancipation: A Selection of Documents*. Pamphlet Series Jews and the Post-War World 1. New York: American Jewish Committee, 1942.

Marx, Karl. 'Zur Judenfrage'. Vol. 1. (Paris: Deutsch-Französische Jahrbücher, 1844) in *Karl Marx / Friedrich Engels Werke*, Band 1 (Berlin: Dietz Verlag, 1976), 347–377.

Marr, Wilhelm. *Der Sieg des Judenthums über das Germanenthum. Vom nicht confessionellen Standpunkt aus betrachtet*. Bern: Rudolph Costenoble, 1879.

Matthäus, Jürgen. 'Tagesordnung: Judenfrage: A German Debate in the Early Stages of the Weimar Republic'. *The Leo Baeck Institute Year Book* 48, no. 1 (2003): 87–110.

Mendelssohn, Moses. *Jerusalem oder über religiöse Macht und Judentum*. Berlin: Friedrich Maurer, 1783.

Merz, Friedrich. 'Einwanderung und Identität'. *Die Welt*, 25 October 2000.

Miller, Susanne, and Heinrich Potthoff, eds. *Die Regierung der Volksbeauftragten 1918/19*. 2 vols. Düsseldorf: Droste Verlag, 1969.

Naumann, Friedrich. *Mitteleuropa*. Berlin: Druck und Verlag von Georg Reimer, 1916.

Oppenheimer, Franz. *Die Judenstatistik des preußischen Kriegsministeriums*. München: Verlag für Kulturpolitik, 1922.

– *Erlebtes, Erstrebtes, Erreichtes: Lebenserinnerungen*. Düsseldorf: Joseph Melzer Verlag, 1964.

– 'Stammesbewusstsein und Volksbewusstsein', *Die Welt* XIV, no. 7 (18 Februar 1910): 139–143.

Paris Peace Conference. *The Deliberations of the Council of Four (March 24 – June 28, 1919): Notes of the Official Interpreter, Paul Mantoux*. Supplementary Volumes to The Papers of Woodrow Wilson. Princeton: Princeton University Press, 1992.

Peters, Dominik. 'Was Weimar für den umgang mit der AfD lehrt'. *Spiegel*, 6 February 2019.

Pinsker, Leon. *Auto-Emancipation: An Appeal to His People by a Russian Jew (1882)*. Masada: Youth Zionist Organisation of America, 1935.

Preuss, Hugo. *Gesammelte Schriften Dritter Band: Das Verfassungswerk von Weimar*. Edited by Detlef Lehnert, Christopher Müller, and Dian Schefold. Tübingen: Mohr Siebeck, 2015.

– *Gesammelte Schriften Dritter Band: Das Verfassungswerk von Weimar*. Tübingen: Mohr Siebeck, 2015.

– *Gesammelte Schriften Vierter Band: Politik und Verfassung in der Weimarer Republik*. Edited by Detlef Lehnert. Tübingen: Mohr Siebeck, 2008.

Quessel, Ludwig. 'Die Judenfrage als nationales Problem'. *Neue jüdische Monatshefte* 2, no. 13 (10 April 1918): 299–306.

R., 'Zionismus ohne Volksbewußtsein', *Frankfurter Israelitisches Familienblattes* 8, no. 10 (11 März 1910): 5.

Rathenau, Walther. *Walther Rathenau, Industrialist, Banker, Intellectual, and Politician: Notes and Diaries, 1907–1922*. Edited by Hilary Pogge von Strandmann and Caroline Pinder-Cracraft. Oxford: Clarendon Press, 1985.

Reichsbund Jüdischer Frontsoldaten. *Die jüdischen defallenen des deutschen Heeres, der deutschen Marine und der deutschen Schutztruppen 1914–1918. Ein Gedenkbuch*. Berlin: Verlag Der Schild, 1932.

– *Kriegsbriefe gefallener deutscher Juden*. Stuttgart: Seewald Verlag, 1961.

Reinharz, Jehuda. ed. *Dokumente zur Geschichte des deutschen Zionismus 1882–1933*. Schriftenreihe wissenschaftlicher Abhandlungen des Leo Baeck Instituts; 37. Tübingen: J. C. B Mohr (Paul Siebeck), 1981.

- Anon., *Jüdische Rundschau* 19, no. 32 (7 August 1914): 343. In Reinharz, 145.
- *Erstes Propaganda-Flugblatt der ZVfD* [Anfang 1898], CZA Z 1/433. In Reinharz, 51–53.
- *Jüdischer Nationalismus und Deutscher Patriotismus*, [Juli/August 1897], CZA W 147/1. In Reinharz, 45–47.

Renan, Ernest. 'What is a nation?' [*Ou'est-Ce Qu'une Nation?*] In *Becoming National: A Reader*, edited and translated by Geoff Eley and Ronald Grigor Suny, 41–55. Oxford and New York: Oxford University Press, 1996.

Renner, Karl [Synopticus]. *Staat und Nation. Staatsrechtliche Untersuchung über die möglichen Principien einer Lösung und die juristische Voraussetzung eines Nationalitätengesetzes*. Wien: Dietl., 1899.

Renner, Karl. 'State and Nation (1899)'. In *National Cultural Autonomy and Its Contemporary Critics*, edited by Ephraim Nimni, translated by Joseph O'Donnell, 15–47. Routledge Innovations in Political Theory 16. London; New York: Routledge, 2005.

Ritter, Gerhard A., and Merith Niehuss. *Wahlgeschichtliches Arbeitsbuch. Materialien Zur Statistik Des Kaiserreich 1871–1918*. München: C. H. Beck, 1980.

Scholz, Kay-Alexander. 'What is German "Leitkultur"?' *Deutsche Welle*, 3 May 2017.

Segall, Jacob. *Die deutschen Juden als Soldaten im Kriege*. Berlin: Philo, 1921.

Simon, Max. *Der Weltkrieg und die Judenfrage*. Leipzig und Berlin: B. G. Teubner, 1916.

Sombart, Werner. *Die Zukunft der Juden*. Leipzig: Verlag von Dunckert & Humblot, 1912.

Stenographische Berichte, *Verhandlungen Des Reichstags*, XIII. Legislaturperiode, II. Session. Band 306. Berlin: Druck und Verlag der Norddeutschen Buchdruckerei und Verlags-Anstalt, 1914.

- 'Eröffnungsitzung, 4 August 1914'.

Stenographische Berichte, *Verhandlungen Des Reichstags*, XIII. Legislaturperiode, II. Session. Band 308. Berlin: Druck und Verlag der Norddeutschen Buchdruckerei und Verlags-Anstalt, 1916.

- '72. Sitzung, 2 November 1916'.
- '73. Sitzung, 3 November 1916'.
- '77. Sitzung, 30 November 1916'.

Stenographische Berichte, *Verhandlungen Des Reichstags*, XIII. Legislaturperiode, II. Session. Band 313. Berlin: Druck und Verlag der Norddeutschen Buchdruckerei und Verlags-Anstalt, 1918.

- '173. Sitzung, 12 Juni 1918'.

Stenographische Berichte, *Verhandlungen Der verfassunggebenden Deutschen Nationalversammlung*, Band 326. Berlin: Druck und Verlag der Norddeutschen Buchdruckerei und Verlags-Anstalt, 1920.

- '17. Sitzung, 28. Februar 1919'.
- '32. Sitzung, 28 Mai 1919'.
- '57. Sitzung, 15 Juli 1919'.

Tenenbaum, Joseph. *La Question juive en Polgne*. Paris: Le Comité des Delegations Juives, 1919.

Treitschke, Heinrich von. 'Unsere Aussichten'. *Preußische Jahrbücher* 44 (15 November 1879): 559–76.

Wild von Hohenborn, Adolf. *Adolf Wild von Hohenborn: Briefe und Tagebuchaufzeichnungen des preussischen Generals als Kriegsminister und Truppenführer im Ersten Weltkrieg*. Edited by Helmut Reichold and Gerhard Granier. Schriften des Bundesarchivs; 34. Boppard am Rhein: Harald Boldt Verlag, 1986.

– 'Erlass' Nr. 247/8. 16. C1b, *Kriegsministerium*, Berlin W. 66 (11.10.1916).

Winz, Leo. 'Die Judenfrage im künftigen Europa, I: Anschwellen die judenfeindlichen Strömungen'. *Ost Und West: Illustrierte Monatsschrift für das gesamte Judentum* XIX, no. 7/8 (Juli 1919): 162–66.

Wrisberg, Ernst von. *Erinnerungen an die Kriegsjahre im königlich-preussischen Kriegsministerium, II: Heer und Heimat, 1914–1918*. Leipzig: Verlag K. F. Koehler, 1921.

Secondary sources

Alme, Michael. *Die Entstehung der Dolchstoßlegende nach dem Ersten Weltkrieg im Spiegel von Quellen und Forschung*, 1. Norderstedt: GRIN Verlag, 2016.

Almog, Shmuel. 'What's in a Hyphen?'. *SICSA Report:* Newsletter of the Vidal Sassoon International Center for the Study of Antisemitism 2 (1989): 1–2.

Arendt, Hannah. *The Origins of Totalitarianism*. 1st ed. New York: Harcourt Brace, 1951.

Angress, Werner T. 'Prussia's Army and the Jewish Reserve Officer: Controversy before World War I'. *Leo Baeck Institute Year Book* 17, no. 1 (1972): 19–42.

– 'The German Army's "Judenzählung" of 1916: Genesis – Consequences – Significance'. *The Leo Baeck Institute Year Book* 23, no. 1 (1978): 117–38.

Appelbaum, Peter. *Loyal Sons: Jews in the German Army in the Great War*. London and Portland: Valentine Mitchell, 2015.

Aschheim, Steven E. '1912 The Publication of Mortiz Goldstein's "The German-Jewish Parnassus"'. In *Yale Companion to Jewish Writing and Thought in German Culture, 1096–1996*, 299–305. New Haven; London: Yale University Press, 1997.

– *Brothers and Strangers: The East European Jew in German and German Jewish Consciousness, 1800–1923*. Madison, Wisconsin, University of Wisconsin Press, 1982.

Aschheim, Steven E., and Vivian Liska, eds. *The German-Jewish Experience Revisited*. Perspectives on Jewish Texts and Contexts. Berlin, Boston: De Gruyter, 2015.

Astore, William, and Dennis Showalter. *Hindenburg: Icon of German Militarism*. Washington, D. C.: Potomac Books, Inc., 2005.

Becker, Hans-Joachim. *Von der konfessionellen Militärstatistik zur "Judenzählung" (1916): Eine Neubewertung*. Nordhausen: Verlag Traugott Bautz, 2016.

Bein, Alex. *The Jewish Question: Biography of a World Problem*. Translated by Harry Zohn. Rutherford, N. J.: Fairleigh Dickinson University Press, 1990.

Benz, Wolfgang, Arnold Paucker, and Peter G. J. Pulzer, eds. *Jüdisches Leben in der Weimarer Republik*. Tübingen: Mohr Siebeck, 1998.

Berek, Mathias. 'Neglected German-Jewish Visions for a Pluralistic Society: Moritz Lazarus'. *The Leo Baeck Institute Year Book* 60 (2015): 45–59.

Berg, Nicolas. 'Vertrauen in Zahlen: Über Gründung Und Selbstverständnis Der "Zeitschrift Für Demographie Und Statistik Der Juden" (1905)'. In *Kopf oder Zahl: Die Quantifizierung von allem im 19. Jahrhundert*, edited by Matthias Winzen and Wagner, 257–75. Baden-Baden: Ausstellungskatalog des Museums für Kunst und Technik des 19. Jahrhunderts in Baden-Baden, 2011.

Berghahn, Volker R. *Imperial Germany, 1871–1914: Economy, Society, Culture and Politics*. Providence, RI and Oxford: Berghahn Books, 1994.

Bessel, Richard. *Germany After the First World War*. Oxford: Oxford University Press, 1993.

Birnbaum, Pierre, and Ira Katznelson. *Paths of Emancipation: Jews, States, and Citizenship*. Princeton, New Jersey: Princeton University Press, 2014.

Blackbourn, David, and Geoff Eley. *The Peculiarities of German History: Bourgeois Society and Politics in Nineteenth-Century Germany*. Oxford: Oxford University Press, 1984.

Böckenförde, Wolfgang Ernst. 'Der deutsche Typ der konstitutionellen Monarchie im 19. Jahrhundert'. In *Recht, Staat, Freiheit*, 112–45. Frankfurt am Main: Suhrkamp, 1986.

Bodemann, Y. Michal. 'The State in the Construction of Ethnicity and Ideological Labor: The Case of German Jewry'. *Critical Sociology* 17, no. 3 (1990): 35–46.

Bodenheimer, Henriette Hannah. *Max Bodenheimer 1865–1940: Political Genius for Zionism*. Translated by David Bourke. Edinburgh: The Pentland Press, 1990.

– ed. *Prelude to Israel: The Memoirs of M. I. Bodenheimer*. Translated by Israel Cohen. New York; London: Thomas Yoseloff, 1963.

Boehlich, Walter. *Der Berliner Antisemitismusstreit*. Sammlung Insel, 6. Frankfurt am Main: Insel-Verlag, 1965.

Boer, Roland. 'Friends, Radical and Estranged: Bruno Bauer and Karl Marx'. *Religion and Theology* 17, no. 3–4 (2010): 358–401.

Brenner, Arthur D. 'Feme Murder: Paramilitary "Self-Justice" in Weimar Germany'. In *Death Squads in Global Perspective* edited by Bruce B. Campbell and Arthur D. Brenner. New York: Palgrave Macmillan, 2000, 57–83.

Brenner, Michael. *The Renaissance of Jewish Culture in Weimar Germany*. New Haven and London: Yale University Press, 1996.

– 'In the Shadow of the Holocaust: The Changing Image of German Jewry after 1945'. *United States Holocaust Memorial Museum*, Ina Levine Annual Lecture, 2010, 1–22.

Brömsel, Sven, Patrick Küppers, and Clemens Reichhold. *Walther Rathenau im Netzwerk der Moderne*. Oldenbourg: Walter de Gruyter GmbH & Co KG, 2014.

Bruch, Rüdiger vom, and Björn Hofmeister, eds. *Kaiserreich Und Erster Weltkrieg 1871–1918*. Deutsche Geschichte in Quellen und Darstellung, Band 8. Stuttgart: P. Reclam, 2000.

Brustein, William I., and Ryan D. King. 'Anti-Semitism in Europe before the Holocaust'. *International Political Science Review* 25, no. 1 (2004): 35–53.

Bulloch, Jamie. *Karl Renner: Austria*. London: Haus Publishing, 2011.

Caglioti, Daniela L. 'Subjects, Citizens, and Aliens in a Time of Upheaval: Naturalizing and Denaturalizing in Europe during the First World War'. *The Journal of Modern History* 89, no. 3 (September 2017): 495–530.

Caldwell, Peter C. 'Hugo Preuss's Concept of the Volk: Critical Confusion or Sophisticated Conception?' *University of Toronto Law Journal* 63, no. 3 (Summer 2013): 347–84.

Caplan, Gregory A. *Wicked Sons, German Heroes: Jewish Soldiers, Veterans, and Memories of World War I in Germany*. Saarbrücken: VDM Verlag, 2008.

Case, Holly. *The Age of Questions*. Princeton: Princeton University Press, 2018.

– 'The "Social Question," 1820–1920'. *Modern Intellectual History* 13, no. 3 (2016): 747–75.

Chernev, Borislav. 'The Brest-Litovsk Moment: Self-Determination Discourse in Eastern Europe before Wilsonianism'. *Diplomacy & Statecraft* 22, no. 3 (2011): 369–87.

Chickering, Roger. *Imperial Germany and the Great War, 1914–1918*. 3rd edition. Cambridge: Cambridge University Press, 2014.

Chickering, Roger, and Stig Förster, eds. *Great War, Total War: Combat and Mobilization on the Western Front, 1914–1918*. Cambridge: Cambridge University Press, 2000.

Christian, Dietrich. 'Eine deutsch-jüdische Symbiose? Das zionistische Interesse für Fichte und Sombart, Moritz Goldsteins Überlegungen zur deutsch-jüdischen Kultur und die Schwierigkeiten mit dem Bindestrich'. In *Das Kulturerbe deutschsprachiger Juden: Eine Spurensuche in den Ursprungs-, Transit- und Emigrationsländern*, edited by Elke-Vera Kotowski, 43–55. Berlin/München/Boston: Walter de Gruyter GmbH, 2015.

Clark, Christopher M. *The Sleepwalkers: How Europe Went to War in 1914*. 1st U.S. edition. New York: Harper, 2013.

Craig, David M. '"High Politics" and the "New Political History"'. *The Historical Journal* 53, no. 2 (2010): 453–75.

Crim, Brian. 'Jew Census (1916)'. In *Antisemitism: A Historical Encyclopedia of Prejudice and Persecution*, edited by Richard S. Levy. Santa Barbara, California: ABC-CLIO, 2005, 371–72.

Crim, Brian E. *Antisemitism in the German Military Community and the Jewish Response, 1914–1938*. Landham, Maryland: Lexington Books, 2014.

– '"Our Most Serious Enemy": The Specter of Judeo-Bolshevism in the German Military Community, 1914–1923'. *Central European History* 44, no. 4 (2011): 624–41.

– 'Terror from the Right: Revolutionary Terrorism and the Failure of the Weimar Republic'. *Journal of Conflict Studies* 27, no. 2 (2008): 51–63.

Davis, Christian. *Colonialism, Antisemitism, and Germans of Jewish Descent in Imperial Germany*. Michigan: University of Michigan Press, 2012.

Diner, Dan, ed. *Enzyklopädie Jüdischer Geschichte Und Kultur*. 6 vols. Stuttgart und Weimar: Verlag J. B. Metzler, 2015.

– 'Negative Symbiose: Deutsche und Juden nach Auschwitz'. *Babylon* 1 (1986): 9–20.

Dinnerstein, Leonard. *Antisemitism in America*. Oxford University Press, 1995.

– *The Leo Franks case*, revised edition. Athens, Georgia: University of Georgia Press, 2008.

Drescher, Seymour, and Allan Sharlin, eds. *Political Symbolism in Modern Europe: Essays in Honor of George L. Mosse*. New Brunswick, London: Transaction Books, 1982.

Dunker, Ulrich. *Der Reichsbund jüdischer Frontsoldaten, 1919–1938: Geschichte eines jüdischen Abwehrvereins*. Düsseldorf: Droste Verlag, 1977.

Eley Geoff. 'Bismarckian Germany' in *Modern Germany Reconsidered, 1870–1945*, ed. Gordon Mantel. London: Routledge, 1992, 1–32.

Elon, Amos. *The Pity of It All: A Portrait of Jews in Germany 1743–1933*. New York: Picador, 2002.

Eloni, Yehuda. 'The Zionist Movement and the German Social Democratic Party, 1897–1918'. *Studies in Zionism* 5, no. 2 (1984): 181–199.

Elsaesser, Thomas. 'Frankfurt, Germans and Jews: The City, Garbage and Death'. In *Fassbinder's Germany: History Identity Subject*, 175–96. Amsterdam: Amsterdam University Press, 1996.

Elton, Geoffrey R. *Political History: Principles and Practice*. London: Allen Lane, 1970.

Engel, David. 'Perceptions of Power – Poland and World Jewry'. In *Simon Dubnow Institute Yearbook*, 1st ed. Stuttgart und München: Deutsche Verlags-Anstalt, 2002, 17–29.

Evans, Richard J. *Society and Politics in Wilhelmine Germany*. London and New York: Croom Helm; Barnes & Noble, 1978.

Feldman, Gerald D. *German Imperialism 1914–1918: The Development of a Historical Debate*. New York: John Wiley & Sons Inc., 1972.

– 'The Political and Social Foundations of Germany's Economic Mobilization, 1914–1916'. *Armed Forces and Society* 3, no. 1 (1976): 121–45.

Fine, David J. 'Jewish Integration in the German Army in the First World War'. Berlin and Boston: Walter de Gruyter, 2012.

Fine, Robert, and Philip Spencer. 'Marx's Defence of Jewish Emancipation and Critique of the Jewish Question'. In *Antisemitism and the Left*. Manchester: Manchester University Press, 2018, 30–43.

Fink, Carole. 'Defender of Minorities: Germany in the League of Nations, 1926–1933'. *Central European History* 5, no. 4 (1972): 330–57.

– *Defending the Rights of Others: The Great Powers, the Jews, and International Minority Protection, 1878–1938*. Cambridge: Cambridge University Press, 2004.

Fischer, Fritz. *Germany's Aims in the First World War*. New York: W. W. Norton & Co., 1967.

Fischer, Heinz-Dietrich. 'The "Deutsche Allgemeine Zeitung" (1861–1945)'. *Gazette (Leiden Netherlands)* 13, no. 1 (1967): 35–46.

Fischer, Lars. 'The Non-Jewish Question and Other "Jewish Questions" in Modern Germany (and Austria)'. *The Journal of Modern History* 82, no. 4 (2010): 876–901.

Fishman, Sterling. 'Assassination of Kurt Eisner: A Study of Identity in the German-Jewish Dialogue'. In *The German-Jewish Dialogue Reconsidered: A Symposium in Honour of George L. Mosse*, edited by Klaus L. Berghahn. New York: Peter Lang, 1996, 141–54.

Foley, Robert T. 'Prussia: Army 1815–1914'. In *Reader's Guide to Military History*, edited by Charles Messenger. London & New York: Routledge, 2013, 477–78.

Formisano, Ronald P. 'The Concept of Political Culture'. *The Journal of Interdisciplinary History* 31, no. 3 (2001): 393–426.

Frauendienst, Werner. 'Demokratisierung Des Deutschen Konstitutionalismus in Der Zeit Wilhelms II'. *Zeitschrift Für Die Gesamte Staatswissenschaft* 113, no. 4 (1957): 721–24.

Friedman, Isaiah. 'German Intervention on Behalf of the Yishuv, 1917'. *Jewish Social Studies* 33, no. 1 (1971): 23–43.

– *Germany, Turkey, and Zionism 1897–1918*. Oxford: Oxford University Press, 1977.

Fulda, Bernard. *Press and Politics in the Weimar Republic*. Oxford: Oxford University Press, 2009.

Gay, Peter. *Freud, Jews and Other Germans. Masters and Victims in Modernist Culture*. New York: Oxford University Press, 1978.

– *Weimar Culture: The Outsider as Insider*. 1st ed. New York: Harper & Row, 1968.

Geheran, Michael. 'Rethinking Jewish Front Experiences'. In *Beyond Inclusion and Exclusion: Jewish Experiences of the First World War in Central Europe*, edited by Jason Crouthamel, Tim Grady, and Julia Barbara Köhne. New York; Oxford: Berghahn Books, 2019, 111–43.

Geller, Jay. *The Other Jewish Question: Identifying the Jew and Making Sense of Modernity*. Fordham University Press, 2011.

Gestrich, Andreas, and H. Pogge von Strandmann. *Bid for World Power? New Research on the Outbreak of the First World War*. Studies of the German Historical Institute London. Oxford: University Press, 2017.

Gillessen, Günther. *Hugo Preuss: Studien zur Ideen- und Verfassungsgeschichte der Weimarer Republik*, Erstveröffentlichung der Dissertation von 1955, Schriften zur Verfassungsgeschichte, Band 60 (Berlin: Duncker und Humblot, 2000).

Goldberg, Ann. *Honor, Politics and the Law in Imperial Germany, 1871–1914*. Cambridge: Cambridge University Press, 2010.

Goldstein, Moritz. 'German Jewry's Dilemma'. *The Leo Baeck Institute Year Book* 2, no. 1 (1957): 236–54.

Gooch, John. *The Italian Army and the First World War*. Cambridge: Cambridge University Press, 2014.

Gordon, Peter Eli, and John P. McCormick. *Weimar Thought: A Contested Legacy*. Princeton: University Press, 2013.

Gordon, Sarah Ann. *Hitler, Germans, and the 'Jewish Question'*. Princeton: Princeton University Press, 1984.

Grady, Tim. 'Creating Difference: The Racialization of Germany's Jewish Soldiers after the First World War'. *Patterns of Prejudice* 46, no. 3–4 (2012): 318–38.

– 'Fighting a Lost Battle: The Reichsbund Jüdischer Frontsoldaten and the Rise of National Socialism'. *German History* 28, no. 1 (2010): 1–20.

– *The German-Jewish Soldiers of the First World War in History and Memory*. Liverpool: Liverpool University Press, 2011.

Grady, Timothy L. *A Deadly Legacy: German Jews and the Great War*. New Haven and London: Yale University Press, 2017.

Gräfe, Thomas. 'Der Hegemonieverlust des Liberalismus. Die "Judenfrage" im Spiegel der Intellektuellenbefragungen 1885–1912'. In *Jahrbuch für Antisemitismusforschung 25*, edited by Stefanie Schüler-Springorum. Berlin: Metropol Verlag, 2016, 74–100.

– 'Deutsch-Jüdischer Parnaß (Artikel von Moritz Goldstein, 1912)'. In *Handbuch Des Antisemitismus. Judenfeindschaft in Geschichte Und Gegenwart*, edited by Wolfgang Benz, 7. Berlin: De Gruyter, 2015, 68–70.

Grimm, Marc. 'Pro-Israelism and Antisemitism within Germany's Populist Radical Right AfD'. *European Journal of Current Legal Issues* 25, no. 1 (2019).

Habermas, Jürgen. *Between Facts and Norms: Contribution to a Discourse Theory of Law and Democracy*. Cambridge: MIT Press, 1996.

– *The Inclusion of the Other*. Cambridge: MIT Press, 1998.

Hacke, Jens. 'Jewish Liberalism in the Weimar Republic? Reconsidering a Key Element of Political Culture in the Interwar Era'. In *The German-Jewish Experience Reconsidered: Contested Interpretations and Conflicting Perceptions*, edited by Steven E. Aschheim and Vivian Liska, 155–70. Berlin and New York: De Gruyter, 2015.

Hagemeister, Michael. 'The Protocols of the Elders of Zion: Between History and Fiction'. *New German Critique*, no. 103 (2008): 83–95.

Hailbronner, Kay. 'EURO Citizenship Observatory. Country Report: Germany'. *European University Institute, Florence*, October 2012, 1–34.

Hamburger, Ernest. 'Hugo Preuß: Scholar and Statesman'. *The Leo Baeck Institute Year Book* 20, no. 1 (1975): 179–206.

– 'Hugo Preuß: Scholar and Statesman'. *The Leo Baeck Institute Year Book* 20, no. 1 (1975): 179–206.

– *Juden im öffentlichen Leben Deutschlands: Regierungsmitglieder, Beamte und Parlamentarier in der monarchischen Zeit, 1848–1918*. Schriftenreihe wissenschaftlicher Abhandlungen des Leo Baeck Instituts 19. Tübingen: JCB Mohr Paul Siebeck, 1968.

Harris, Ruth. *The Man on Devil's Island*. London: Allen Lane, 2010.

Hart, Mitchell Bryan. *Jews and Race: Writings on Identity and Difference, 1880–1940*. The Brandeis Library of Modern Jewish Thought. Waltham, Massachusetts: Brandeis University Press, 2011.

Hartston, Barnet P. *Sensationalizing the Jewish Question: Anti-Semitic Trials and the Press in the Early German Empire*. Studies in Central European Histories, vol. 39. Leiden: Brill, 2005.

Heid, Ludger. *Ein Sozialist und Zionist im Kaiserreich und in der Weimarer Republik*. Frankfurt am Main: Campus Judaica, 2002.

Heikaus, Ulrike, and Julia Köhne, eds. *Krieg! Juden Zwischen Den Fronten, 1914–1918*. Berlin: Hentich & Hentich Verlag, 2014.

Hewitson, Mark. *Germany and the Modern World, 1880–1914*. Cambridge: Cambridge University Press, 2018.

– *National Identity and Political Thought in Germany: Wilhelmine Depictions of the French Third Republic, 1890–1914*. Oxford: Clarendon Press, 2000.

Heynen, Robert. 'The German Revolution and the Radical Right'. In *The German Revolution and Political Theory*, edited by Gaard Kets and James Muldoon. Switzerland: Palgrave Macmillan, 2019, 45–68.

James, Pierre. *The Murderous Paradise: German Nationalism and the Holocaust*. Westport, Connecticut: Greenwood Publishing Group, 2001.

Janowsky, Oscar Isaiah. *The Jews and Minority Rights (1898–1919)*. New York: Columbia University Press, 1933.

Jay, Martin. *The Dialectical Imagination: A History of the Frankfurt School and the Institute of Social Research, 1923–1950*. Berkeley: University of California Press, 1996.

Jones, Mark. *Founding Weimar: Violence and the German Revolution of 1918–1919*. Cambridge: Cambridge University Press, 2016.

Kampe, Norbert. *Studenten und 'Judenfrage' im Deutschen Kaiserreich*. Göttingen: Vandenhoeck & Ruprecht, 1988.

Kauders, Anthony D. *Democratization and the Jews: Munich, 1945–1965*. Vidal Sassoon International Center for the Study of Antisemitism. Lincoln, Nebraska: University of Nebraska Press, 2004.

– 'Weimar Jewry'. In *Weimar Germany*, edited by Anthony McElligot, Short Oxford History of Germany. Oxford: Oxford University Press, 2009, 234–59.

Kaplan, Marion A. *The Making of the Jewish Middle Class: Women, Family, and Identity in Imperial Germany*. Oxford University Press, 1991.

Karski, Jan. *The Great Powers and Poland: From Versailles to Yalta*. Landham, Maryland: Rowman & Littlefield, 2014.

Karski, Sigmund. *Albert (Wojciech) Korfanty: Eine Biographie*. Dülmen: Laumann-Verlag, 1990.

Kirchner, Andrea. 'Ein Vergessenes Kapitel Jüdischer Diplomatie: Richard Lichtheim in Den Botschaften Konstantinopels (1913–1917)'. *Naharaim* 9, no. 1–2 (2015): 128–50.

Klier, John Doyle. *Russia Gathers Her Jews: The Origins of the 'Jewish Question' in Russia, 1772–1825*. Dekalb, Illinois: Northern Illinois University Press, 1986.

Kocka, Jurgen. 'German History before Hitler: The Debate about the German Sonderweg'. *Journal of Contemporary History* 23, no. 1 (1988): 3–16.

Kramer, Martin. 'Arabistik and Arabism: The Passions of Martin Hartmann'. *Middle Eastern Studies* 25, no. 3 (1989): 283–300.

Kreienbrock, Jörg. 'Franz Rosenzweig's Mitteleuropa as a New Levante'. In *Personal Narratives, Peripheral Theatres: Essays on the Great War (1914–18)*, edited by Anthony Barker, Maria Eugénia Pereira, Maria Teresa Cortez, Paulo Alexandre Pereira, and Otília Martins. Cham: Springer International Publishing, 2018, 185–200.

Kremer, Arndt. 'Transitions of a Myth? The Idea of a Language-Defined Kulturnation in Germany'. *New German Review: A Journal of Germanic Studies* 27, no. 1 (2016): 53–75.

Kreuzer, Marcus. 'Parliamentarization and the Question of German Exceptionalism: 1867–1918'. *Central European History* 36, no. 3 (2003): 327–57.

Kritzman, Lawrence D., ed. *Auschwitz and After: Race, Culture and 'the Jewish Question' in France*. Oxford and New York: Routledge, 1995.

Lamberti, Marjorie. 'From Coexistence to Conflict – Zionism and the Jewish Community in Germany, 1897–1914'. *Leo Baeck Institute Year Book* 27 (1982): 53–86.

– 'The Attempt to Form a Jewish Bloc: Jewish Notables and Politics in Wilhelmian Germany'. *Central European History* 3, no. 1–2 (1970): 73–93.

Lavsky, Hagit. *Before Catastrophe: The Distinctive Path of German Zionism*. Detroit, Jerusalem: Wayne State University Press; Magnes Press, 1996.

Leff, Lisa Moses. *Sacred Bonds of Solidarity: The Rise of Jewish Internationalism in Nineteenth-Century France*. Stanford, California: Stanford University Press, 2006.

Lenger, Friedrich. *Werner Sombart, 1863–1941: eine Biographie*. München: Beck, 1994.

Leopold, David. 'The Hegelian Antisemitism of Bruno Bauer'. *History of European Ideas* 25, no. 4 (1999): 179–206.

Levene, Mark. 'Nationalism and Its Alternatives in the International Arena: The Jewish Question at Paris, 1919'. *Journal of Contemporary History* 28, no. 3 (1993): 511–31.

– 'Nationalism and Its Alternatives in the International Arena: The Jewish Question at Paris, 1919'. *Journal of Contemporary History* 28, no. 3 (1993): 511–31.

– *War, Jews, and the New Europe: The Diplomacy of Lucien Wolf, 1914–1919*. Oxford: G. B. Littman, 2009.

Levenson, Alan. 'German Zionism and Radical Assimilation before 1914'. *Studies in Zionism* 13, no. 1 (1992): 21–41.

Levinson, David. *Jewish Germany: An Enduring Presence from the Fourth to the Twenty-First Century*. Portland, Oregon: Vallentine Mitchell, 2018.

Levy, Richard S. *The Downfall of the Anti-Semitic Political Parties in Imperial Germany*. New Haven and London: Yale University Press, 1975.

Lichtheim, George. *Thoughts Among the Ruins: Collected Essays on Europe and Beyond*. New Brunswick, New Jersey: Transaction Publishers, 1973.

Lipp, Anne. *Meinungslenkung im Krieg: Kriegserfahrungen deutscher soldaten und ihre Deutung, 1914–1918*. Göttingen: Vandenhoeck & Ruprecht, 2003.

Liulevicius, Vejas Gabriel. *War Land on the Eastern Front: Culture, National Identity, and German Occupation in World War I*. Cambridge: Cambridge University Press, 2000.

Loeffler, James Benjamin. *Rooted Cosmopolitans: Jews and Human Rights in the Twentieth Century*. New Haven: Yale University Press, 2018.

Machtan, Lothar. *Prinz Max von Baden der letzte Kanzler des Kaisers: eine Biographie*, 1. Auflage. Berlin: Suhrkamp, 2013.

Mack, Michael. *German Idealism and the Jew: The Inner Anti-Semitism of Philosophy and German Jewish Responses*. Chicago: University of Chicago Press, 2003.

MacMillan, Margaret. *The War That Ended Peace: The Road to 1914*. New York: Random House Trade Paperbacks, 2014.

MacMillan, Margaret, Anand Menon, and Patrick Quinton-Brown. 'Introduction: World Politics 100 Years after the Paris Peace Conference'. *International Affairs* 95, no. 1 (1 January 2019): 1–5.

MacMillan, Margaret, and Patrick Quinton-Brown. 'The Uses of History in International Society: From the Paris Peace Conference to the Present'. *International Affairs* 95, no. 1 (2019): 181–200.

Mazower, Mark. 'Minorities and the League of Nations in Interwar Europe'. *Daedalus* 126, no. 2 (1997): 47–63.

– 'The Strange Triumph of Human Rights, 1933–1950'. *The Historical Journal* 47, no. 2 (2004): 379–98.

Mazura, Uwe. *Zentrumspartei und Judenfrage, 1870/1933: Verfassungsstaat und Minderheitenschutz*. Mainz: Mathias Grünewald Verlag, 1994.

McElligott, Anthony. *Rethinking the Weimar Republic: Authority and Authoritarianism, 1916–1936*. London: Bloomsbury, 2014.

McHale, Vincent E., ed. *Political Parties of Europe*. Vol. 1. Westport, Connecticut: Greenwood Press, 1983.

McMeekin, Sean. *The Berlin-Baghdad Express*. Cambridge, Massachusetts: Harvard University Press, 2010.

Mendes-Flohr, Paul and Jehuda Reinharz. *The Jew in the Modern World, A Documentary History*. 2nd edition. Oxford and New York: Oxford University Press, 1995.

Meyer, Henry Cord. *Mitteleuropa in German Thought and Action, 1815–1945*. The Hague: Martinus Nijhoff, 1955.

Meyer, Michael A. 'Great Debate on Antisemitism – Jewish Reaction to New Hostility in Germany 1879–1881'. *Leo Baeck Institute Year Book* 11, no. 1 (1966): 137–70.

– 'Heinrich Graetz and Heinrich Von Treitschke: A Comparison of Their Historical Images of the Modern Jew'. *Modern Judaism* 6, no. 1 (1986): 1–11.

Moeller, Robert. 'The Kaiserreich Recast? Continuity and Change in Modern German Historiography'. *Journal of Social History* 17, no. 4 (1984): 655.

Mosse, George. *German Jews beyond Judaism*. Illinois: Hebrew Union College Press, 1985.

Mosse, George L. and Klaus L. Berghahn, *The German-Jewish Dialogue Reconsidered: A Symposium in Honor of George L. Mosse*. Vol. 20, German Life and Civilization; New York: Peter Lang, 1996.

Motta, Giuseppe. *The Great War against Eastern European Jewry, 1914–1920*. Newcastle upon Tyne: Cambridge Scholars Publishing, 2017.

Moyn, Samuel. *The Last Utopia: Human Rights in History*. Cambridge, MA: Harvard University Press, 2010.

Müller, Jan-Werner. *Constitutional Patriotism*. Princeton: Princeton University Press, 2007.

Müller, Jan-Werner and Kim Lane Scheppele, 'Constitutional Patriotism: An introduction', *International Journal of Constitutional Law* 6, no. 1 (2008): 67–71.

Nicosia, Francis. R. 'Jewish Affairs and German Foreign Policy during the Weimar Republic: Moritz Sobernheim and the Referat für jüdische Angelegenheiten'. *The Leo Baeck Institute Year Book* 33, no. 1 (1988): 261–283.

Niewyk, Donald L. *The Jews in Weimar Germany*. Manchester: Manchester University Press, 1980.

– 'The Economic and Cultural Role of the Jews in the Weimar Republic'. *Leo Baeck Institute Year Book* 16, no. 1 (1971): 163–73.

Nipperdey, Thomas. *Deutsche Geschichte 1866–1918*. Vol. II. Machstaat vor der Demokratie. Munich: Verlag C. H. Beck, 1992.

Nirenberg, David. *Anti-Judaism: The Western Tradition*. 1st ed. New York: W. W. Norton & Co., 2013.

Norrell, Tracey Hayes. *For the Honor of Our Fatherland: German Jews on the Eastern Front during the Great War*. Landham, Maryland: Lexington Books, 2017.

Panker, Sara. 'Between Friends and Enemies: The Dilemma of Jews in the Final Stages of the War'. In *Minorities during the First World War. From War to Peace*, edited by Hannah Ewence and Tim Grady. London: Palgrave Macmillan, 2017, 63–87.

Patai, Raphael. *Nahum Goldmann: His Missions to the Gentiles*. Tuscaloosa: University of Alabama Press, 2003.

Paucker, Arnold. 'Zur Problematik Einer Jüdischen Abwehrstrategie in Der Deutschen Gesellschaft'. In *Juden in Wilhelminischen Deutschland 1890–1914*, edited by Werner E. Mosse, 2nd ed. Tübingen: Schriftenreihe wissenschaftlicher Abhandlungen des Leo Baeck Instituts 33, 1998, 479–548.

Peled, Yoav. 'From Theology to Sociology: Bruno Bauer and Karl Marx on the Question of Jewish Emancipation'. *History of Political Thought* 13, no. 3 (1992): 463–85.

Penslar, Derek. 'The German-Jewish Soldier: From Participant to Victim'. *German History* 29, no. 3 (2011): 423–44.

Perry, Marvin, and Frederick M. Schweitzer. *Antisemitism: Myth and Hate from Antiquity to the Present*. New York: Palgrave, 2002.

Pflanze, Otto. *Bismarck and the Development of Germany, Volume II: The Period of Consolidation, 1871–1880*. Princeton, New Jersey: Princeton University Press, 2014.

Polkehn, Klaus. 'Zionism and Kaiser Wilhelm'. *Journal of Palestine Studies* 4, no. 2 (1975): 76–90.

Prusin, Alexander Victor. *Nationalizing a Borderland: War, Ethnicity, and Anti-Jewish Violence in East Galicia, 1914–1920*. Tuscaloosa, Alabama: University of Alabama Press, 2005.

Pulzer, Peter. *Germany, 1870–1945. Politics, State Formation and War*. Oxford: Oxford University Press, 1997.

– 'Jews and Nation-Building in Germany, 1815–1918'. *Leo Baeck Institute Year Book* 41 (1996): 199–214.

– *Jews and the German State: The Political History of a Minority, 1848–1933*. Detroit, Michigan: Wayne State University Press, 2003.

Purschwitz, Anne. 'Von der "bürgerlichen Verbesserung" zur "Judenfrage": Die Formierung eines Begriffs zwischen 1781 Und 1843'. In *Die 'Judenfrage': Ein Europäisches Phänomen?* Berlin: Metropol Verlag, 2013, 23–53.

Rabinovitch, Simon. *Jewish Rights, National Rites: Nationalism and Autonomy in Late Imperial and Revolutionary Russia*. Stanford Studies in Jewish History and Culture. Stanford, California: Stanford University Press, 2014.

Rahden, Till van. 'Germans of the Jewish Stamm: Visions of Community between Nationalism and Particularism, 1850 to 1933'. In *German History from the Margins*, edited by Neil Gregor, Nils H. Roemer, and Mark Roseman. Bloomington: Indiana University Press, 2006, 27–40.

Rauh, Manfred. *Die Parlamentarisierung des Deutschen Reiches*. Beiträge zur Geschichte des Parlamentarismus und der politischen Parteien, Band 60. Düsseldorf: Droste, 1977.

– *Föderalismus und Parlamentarismus im Wilhelminischen Reich*. Beiträge zur Geschichte des Parlamentarismus und der politischen Parteien, Band 47. Düsseldorf: Droste, 1973.

Rechter, David. 'A Nationalism of Small Things: Jewish Autonomy in Late Habsburg Austria'. *The Leo Baeck Institute Year Book* 52, no. 1 (2007): 87–109.

Reinharz, Jehuda. 'Advocacy and History: The Case of the Centralverein and Zionists'. *Leo Baeck Institute Year Book* 33, no. 1 (1988): 113–22.

– *Fatherland or Promised Land: The Dilemma of the German Jew, 1893–1914*. Ann Arbor: University of Michigan Press, 1975.

– 'Ideology and Structure in German Zionism, 1882–1933'. *Jewish Social Studies*, Articles Devoted to Zionism and Israel, 42, no. 2 (1980): 119–46.

Rogger, Hans. *Jewish Policies and Right-Wing Politics in Imperial Russia*. Berkeley Los Angeles: University of California Press, 1986.

Rose, Paul Lawrence. *German Question / Jewish Question: Revolutionary Antisemitism in Germany from Kant to Wagner*. Princeton, New Jersey: Princeton University Press, 1990.

Rosenthal, Jacob. *Die Ehre des jüdischen Soldaten: Die Judenzählung im Ersten Weltkrieg und ihre Folgen*. Frankfurt am Main: Campus, 2007.

Rotenstreich, Nathan. 'For and against Emancipation: The Bruno Bauer Controversy'. *The Leo Baeck Institute Year Book* 4, no. 1 (1959): 3–36.

Roudinesco, Élisabeth. *Revisiting the Jewish Question*. Translated by Andrew Brown. Cambridge: Polity, 2013.

Rowland, Richard H. 'Geographical Patterns of the Jewish Population in the Pale of Settlement in Late Nineteenth Century Russia'. *Jewish Social Studies* 48, no. 3 (1986): 207–234.

Rumpf, Helmut. 'Mitteleuropa. Zur Geschichte und Deutung eines politischen Begriffs'. *Historische Zeitschrift* 165, no. 1 (1942): 510–27.

Rürup, Reinhard. 'Emancipation and Crisis: The "Jewish Question" in Germany, 1850–1890'. *Leo Baeck Institute Year Book* 20 (1975): 13–25.

– *Emanzipation und Antisemitismus: Studien zur 'Judenfrage' der bürgerlichen Gesellschaft*. Göttingen: Vandenhoeck & Ruprecht, 1975.

Rusel, Jane. *Hermann Struck (1876–1944): das Leben und das graphische Werk eines jüdischen Künstlers*. Judentum und Umwelt, Band 66. Frankfurt am Main: Peter Lang, 1997.

Gilya Gerda Schmidt, *The Art and Artists of the Fifth Zionist Congress, 1901: Heralds of a New Age*. New York: Syracuse University Press, 2003.

Sabrow, Martin. *Der Rathenaumord: Rekonstruktion einer Verschwörung gegen die Republik von Weimar*, Schriftenreihe der Vierteljahrhefte für Zeitgeschichte 69. Munich: Oldenbourg Verlag, 1994.

Schoenbaum, David. *Zabern 1913: Consensus Politics in Imperial Germany*, 1st edition. London: Harper Collins, 1982.

Schoenberger, Christoph. 'Hugo Preuss'. In *Weimar: A Jurisprudence of Crisis*, edited by Arthur J. Jacobson and Bernhard Schlink. Berkeley Los Angeles: University of California Press, 2000, 110–27.

Scholem, Gershom. 'Wider den Mythos vom deutsch-jüdische Gespräch'. In *Auf Gespaltenem Pfad: Für Margarete Susman*, edited by Manfred Schlösser. Darmstadt: Erato-Presse Verlag, 1964, 229–33.

Schönwälder, Karen. 'The Constitutional Protection of Minorities in Germany: Weimar Revisited'. *The Slavonic and East European Review* 74, no. 1 (1996): 38–65.

Schorsch, Ismar. *Jewish Reactions to German Anti-Semitism, 1870–1914*. New York & London: Columbia University Press, 1972.

Sicker, Martin. *Reshaping Palestine: From Muhammad Ali to the British Mandate, 1831–1922*. Westport, Connecticut: Praeger, 1999.

Silber, Marcos. 'The Development of a Joint Political Program for the Jews of Poland during World War I – Success and Failure'. *Jewish History* 19 (2005): 211–26.

Smith, Helmut W. *The Continuities of German History: Nation, Religion, and Race across the Long Nineteenth Century*. Cambridge: Cambridge University Press, 2008.

Sniderman, Stephen L. 'Bibliography of Works about Heinrich Graetz'. *Studies in Bibliography and Booklore* 14 (1982): 41–49.

Spencer, Philip, and Robert Fine. *Antisemitism and the Left: On the Return of the Jewish Question*. Manchester: Manchester University Press, 2017.

Stern, Howard. 'The Organisation Consul', *The Journal of Modern History* 35, no. 1 (1963): 20–32.

Stirk, Peter M. R. 'Hugo Preuss, German Political Thought and the Weimar Constitution'. *History of Political Thought* 23, no. 3 (2002): 497–516.

Stoetzler, Marcel. *The State, the Nation, and the Jews: Liberalism and the Antisemitism Dispute in Bismarck's Germany*. Lincoln, Nebraska: University of Nebraska Press, 2008.

Stone, Norman. *The Eastern Front, 1914–1917*. London: Penguin, 1998.

Strachan, Hew. *The First World War*. 3rd ed. London: Simon & Schuster, 2014.

Szajkowski, Zosa. 'The Komitee für den Osten and Zionism'. In *Herzl Year Book*, edited by Raphael Patai, 199–240. New York: Herzl Press, 1971.

Täubler, Eugen, and Selma Stern. *Aufsätze zur Problematik jüdischer Geschichtsschreibung 1908–1950*. Mohr Siebeck, 1977.

Thompson, Wayne C. 'The September Program: Reflections on the Evidence'. *Central European History* 11, no. 4 (1978): 348–54.

Throntveit, Trygve. 'The Fable of the Fourteen Points: Woodrow Wilson and National Self-Determination', *Diplomatic History* 35, no. 3 (2011): 445–481.

Tibi, Bassam. *Europa ohe Identität? Die Krise der multikulturellen Gesellschaft*. München: Bertelsmann, 1998.

Ticker, Jay. 'Max I. Bodenheimer: Advocate of Pro-German Zionism at the Beginning of World War I'. *Jewish Social Studies* 43, no. 1 (1981): 11–30.

Tooze, J. Adam. *Statistics and the German State, 1900–1945: The Making of Modern Economic Knowledge*. Cambridge: Cambridge University Press, 2001.

Torrey, Glenn E. *The Romanian Battlefront in World War I*. Lawrence, Kansas: University Press of Kansas, 2014.

Tourlamain, Guy. *Völkisch Writers and National Socialism, a Study of Right-Wing Political Culture in Germany, 1890–1960*. Cultural History and Literary Imagination. Oxford; Bern: Peter Lang, 2014.

Toury, Jacob. 'Organizational Problems of German Jewry: Steps towards the Establishment of a Central Organization (1893–1920)'. *The Leo Baeck Institute Year Book* 13, no. 1 (1968): 57–90.

– *Die politischen Orientierungen der Juden in Deutschland: von Jena bis Weimar*. Schriftenreihe wissenschaftlicher Abhandlungen des Leo Baeck Instituts 15. Tübingen: Mohr Siebeck, 1966.

– '"The Jewish Question" A Semantic Approach'. *The Leo Baeck Institute Year Book* 11, no. 1 (1966): 85–106.

Traverso, Enzo. *The Jewish Question: History of a Marxist Debate*. Translated by Bernard Gibbons. Historical Materialism Book Series, 178. Leiden; Boston: Brill, 2019.

Vascik, George S., and Mark R. Sadler. *The Stab-in-the-Back Myth and the Fall of the Weimar Republic: A History in Documents and Visual Sources*. London: Bloomsbury Publishing, 2016.

Verhey, Jeffrey. *The Spirit of 1914: Militarism, Myth, and Mobilization in Germany*. Cambridge: Cambridge University Press, 2000.

Viefhaus, Erwin. *Die Minderheitenfrage und die Entstehung der Minderheitenschutzverträge auf der Pariser Friedenskonferenz 1919: eine Studie zur Geschichte des Nationalitätenproblems im 19. und 20. Jahrhundert*. Würzburg: Holzner Verlag, 1960.

Vogt, Stefan. *Subalterne Positionierungen: Der deutsche Zionismus im Feld des Nationalismus in Deutschland, 1890–1933*. 1st edition. Wallstein Verlag, 2016.

– 'The First World War, German Nationalism, and the Transformation of German Zionism'. *Leo Baeck Institute Year Book* 57 (11 July 2012): 267–91.

Volkov, Shulamit. *Walther Rathenau: Weimar's Fallen Statesman*. New Haven: Yale University Press, 2012.

Waite, Robert G. L. *Vanguard of Nazism: The Free Corps Movement in Postwar Germany 1918–1923*. New York: W. W. Norton and Company, 1969.

Walk, Josef. 'Das "Deutsche Komitee Pro Palästina" 1926–1933'. *Bulletin des Leo Baecks Instituts* 15, no. 52 (1976): 162–93.

Wandycz, Piotr S. *The Lands of Partitioned Poland, 1795–1918*. Vol. 7. History of East Central Europe. Seattle and London: University of Washington Press, 1974.

Weber, Max. *Economy and Society*. 2 vols edited by Guenther Roth and Claus Wittich. California: University of California Press, 1978.

Weber, Peter C. 'The Paradoxical Modernity of Civil Society: The Weimar Republic, Democracy and Social Homogeneity', *Voluntas*, 26 (2015), 629–648.

Wehler, Hans-Ulrich. *Das deutsche Kaiserreich, 1871–1918*. Göttingen: Vandenhoeck & Ruprecht, 1973.

– *The German Empire 1871–1918*. Translated by Kim Traynor. Leamington Spa: Berg, 1985.

Weiss, Yfaat. '"Wir Westjuden haben jüdisches Stammesbewußtsein, die Ostjuden jüdisches Volksbewußtsein". Der Deutsch-Jüdische Blick auf das polnische Judentum in den beiden ersten Jahrzehnten des 20. Jahrhunderts'. *Archiv Für Socialgeschichte* 37 (1997): 157–78.

Weitz, Eric D. 'From the Vienna to the Paris System: International Politics and the Entangled Histories of Human Rights, Forced Deportations, and Civilising Missions'. *American Historical Review* 113, no. 5 (2008): 1313–43.

Wistrich, Robert S. *Socialism and the Jews: The Dilemmas of Assimilation in Germany and Austria-Hungary*. London and East Brunswick, N. J.: Associated University Presses, 1982.

Zechlin, Egmont. *Die deutsche Politik und die Juden im Ersten Weltkrieg*. Göttingen: Vandenhoeck & Ruprecht, 1969.

Zimmerer, Jürgen. 'The Birth of the Ostland out of the Spirit of Colonialism: A Postcolonial Perspective on the Nazi Policy of Conquest and Extermination'. *Patterns of Prejudice* 39, no. 2 (2005): 197–219.

Zipes, Jack. 'The Negative German-Jewish Symbiosis'. In *Insiders and Outsider: Jewish and Gentile Culture in Germany and Austria*, edited by Lorenz Dagmar and Gabriele Weinberger. New York: Palgrave, 2002, 31–45.

Unpublished secondary sources

Hoedl, Klaus. 'Physical Characteristics of Jews', *Jewish Studies at the Central European University*, (1999).

Kirchhoff, Markus. 'Between Weimar and Paris – German Jewry and the Minority Question, 1919'. Draft conference paper for Columbia University, New York, 2012.

Norrell, Tracey Hayes. 'Shattered Communities: Soldiers, Rabbis, and the Ostjuden under German Occupation: 1915–1918'. University of Tennessee, Unpublished Doctoral Dissertation, October 2010.

WEIMARER SCHRIFTEN ZUR REPUBLIK

Herausgegeben von Michael Dreyer und Andreas Braune

Franz Steiner Verlag   ISSN 2510-3822

1. Michael Dreyer / Andreas Braune (Hg.)
    Weimar als Herausforderung
    Die Weimarer Republik und die
    Demokratie im 21. Jahrhundert
    2016. XIV, 310 S., 10 Abb., 11 Fotos, 3 Tab.,
    kt.
    ISBN 978-3-515-11591-9
2. Andreas Braune / Michael Dreyer (Hg.)
    Republikanischer Alltag
    Die Weimarer Demokratie und die Suche
    nach Normalität
    2017. XVIII, 353 S., 4 Abb., 4 Fotos, 3 Tab.,
    kt.
    ISBN 978-3-515-11952-8
3. Andreas Braune / Mario Hesselbarth /
    Stefan Müller (Hg.)
    **Die USPD zwischen Sozialdemo-
    kratie und Kommunismus 1917–1922**
    Neue Wege zu Frieden, Demokratie und
    Sozialismus?
    2018. XXXII, 262S., 3 Abb., 7 Fotos, kt.
    ISBN 978-3-515-12142-2
4. Michael Dreyer
    Hugo Preuß
    Biografie eines Demokraten
    2018. XXV, 513 S., 2 Tab., kt.
    ISBN 978-3-515-12168-2
5. Albert Dikovich / Alexander Wierzock
    (Hg.)
    **Von der Revolution zum Neuen
    Menschen**
    Das politische Imaginäre in Mitteleuropa
    1918/19: Philosophie, Humanwissen-
    schaften und Literatur
    2018. 347 S.
    ISBN 978-3-515-12129-3
6. Andreas Braune / Michael Dreyer (Hg.)
    **Zusammenbruch, Aufbruch,
    Abbruch?**
    Die Novemberrevolution als Ereignis und
    Erinnerungsort
    2019. XXVI, 326 S., 3 Abb., kt.
    ISBN 978-3-515-12219-1

7. Patrick Rössler / Klaus Kamps /
    Gerhard Vowe
    **Weimar 1924: Wie Bauhauskünstler
    die Massenmedien sahen / How
    Bauhaus artists looked at mass
    media**
    Die Meistermappe zum Geburtstag von
    Walter Gropius / The Bauhaus masters' gift
    portfolio for Walter Gropius
    2019. 208 S., mit zahl. Abb., geb.
    ISBN 978-3-515-12281-8
8. Sebastian Schäfer
    **Rudolf Olden – Journalist und
    Pazifist**
    Vom Unpolitischen zum Pan-Europäer.
    Moralische Erneuerung im Zeichen
    moderner Kulturkritik
    2019. 438 S., kt.
    ISBN 978-3-515-12393-8
9. Sebastian Elsbach / Ronny Noak /
    Andreas Braune
    Konsens und Konflikt
    Demokratische Transformation in der
    Weimarer und Bonner Republik
    2019. XXIII, 354 S., 9 Abb., 4 Tab., kt.
    ISBN 978-3-515-12448-5
10. Sebastian Elsbach
    **Das Reichsbanner Schwarz-Rot-
    Gold**
    Republikschutz und politische Gewalt in
    der Weimarer Republik
    2019. 731 S., 3 Abb., 15 Tab., geb.
    ISBN 978-3-515-12467-6
11. Andreas Braune / Michael Dreyer (Hg.)
    **Weimar und die Neuordnung
    der Welt**
    Politik, Wirtschaft, Völkerrecht nach 1918
    2020. XIII, 326 S., 8 Abb., kt.
    ISBN 978-3-515-12676-2

12. Daniel Führer
    Alltagssorgen und Gemeinschafts-
    sehnsüchte
    Tagebücher der Weimarer Republik
    (1913–1934)
    2020. 378 S., 12 Abb., kt.
    ISBN 978-3-515-12583-3

13. Sebastian Elsbach / Marcel Böhles /
    Andreas Braune (Hg.)
    Demokratische Persönlichkeiten
    in der Weimarer Republik
    2020. XIX, 241 S., 7 Abb., kt.
    ISBN 978-3-515-12799-8

14. Elias Angele
    „Schützt die Revolution!"
    Die Stadtwehr Bremen 1919–1921:
    Geschichte und Quellen
    2021. 260 S., 13 Abb., 5 Tab., kt.
    ISBN 978-3-515-13009-7